D1108502

A SOURCE BOOK
OF
SCOTTISH HISTORY

VOLUME THREE
1567 to 1707

Edited by

William Croft Dickinson D.Lit., LL.D.

Gordon Donaldson D.Litt.

THOMAS NELSON AND SONS LTD
LONDON EDINBURGH PARIS MELBOURNE JOHANNESBURG
TORONTO AND NEW YORK

THOMAS NELSON AND SONS LTD
Parkside Works Edinburgh 9
36 Park Street London W1
312 Flinders Street Melbourne C1

302–304 Barclays Bank Building
Commissioner and Kruis Streets
Johannesburg

THOMAS NELSON AND SONS (CANADA) LTD
91–93 Wellington Street West   Toronto 1

THOMAS NELSON AND SONS
19 East 47th Street New York 17

SOCIÉTÉ FRANÇAISE D'ÉDITIONS NELSON
97 rue Monge Paris 5

———

First published October 1954
Second edition (revised and enlarged) 1961

PREFACE

THIS third volume of *A Source Book of Scottish History* begins with the deposition of Mary, Queen of Scots, and ends with the Treaty of Union. The material for this eventful period is more copious than that for the two preceding periods, and neither documents nor commentary could have been reduced to smaller compass if an accurate and balanced account of many complex movements were to be given.

It has been our aim in the first part of the book, which consists of a consecutive account of ' Church and State,' to present a fresh and objective treatment of the Presbyterian-Episcopalian controversy and the Covenanting movement. Here a thorough and comprehensive commentary was necessary, for brevity and simplicity might have led to misrepresentation ; moreover, the texts are here given of many documents which, though often cited, are too rarely available for the general reader. Yet the Scottish people were by no means wholly absorbed in ecclesiastical politics, and the second part of the book deals with foreign relations and with the constitutional, economic, social and educational history of the country

We have to record with regret that we have lost the collaboration of Miss I. A. Milne, who was responsible with us for the first two volumes. Because of her marriage and departure for Australia Miss Milne (now Mrs Durack) was able to take part only in the initial stages of the preparation of the volume and was unable to share in the writing of the commentaries and the later editorial work.

Accordingly she felt that this third volume should not bear her name.

In the preparation of this volume we have to record our grateful thanks to Mrs M. Macintyre for her help in the onerous task of checking the transcripts of all the documents.

Finally, while it was at first our intention to include in this volume a general index to all three volumes, their clear-cut chronological divisions seemed on second thoughts to render such an index inappropriate. This volume therefore contains only an index to its own contents ; when Volumes I and II are reissued each will contain its own index.

W. Croft Dickinson
Gordon Donaldson

Edinburgh
1954

PREFACE TO THE SECOND EDITION

We have taken the opportunity of a second edition to correct some minor errors and to provide a few additional documents at the end of the volume.

W. C. D.
G. D.

Edinburgh
1961

CONTENTS

SECTION II

CONTENTS

ABBREVIATIONS

A.P.S.	Acts of the Parliaments of Scotland
B.U.K.	*Booke of the Universall Kirk of Scotland*, Acts and Proceedings of the General Assemblies of the Church of Scotland (Maitland Club)
Calderwood	David Calderwood, *History of the Kirk of Scotland* (Wodrow Society)
R.M.S.	Registrum Magni Sigilli Regum Scotorum
R.P.C.	Register of the Privy Council of Scotland
S.H.R.	*Scottish Historical Review*
Spottiswoode	John Spottiswoode, *History of the Church of Scotland* (Spottiswoode Society)
Wodrow	Robert Wodrow : *History of the Sufferings of the Church of Scotland* (1721)

SECTION I

CHAPTER ONE

THE REIGN OF JAMES VI, 1567-1625

THE REVOLUTION OF 1567

The deposition of Mary, Queen of Scots, in 1567, put an end to a political situation in which the position of the reformed church had been precarious. The legislation which had been passed in its favour in 1560,[1] but which had all along been of questionable validity, was re-enacted, the coronation oath now prescribed for the infant sovereign and his successors committed them to the support of the reformed church, and the administration was from this time in the hands of a succession of protestant regents.

In consequence of the failure of the parliament of 1560 to deal with polity and endowment, and of the adoption subsequently of the compromise represented in the ' Assumption of Thirds ',[2] the entire fabric of the old regime still remained intact. While, on the one hand, superintendents, commissioners,[3] ministers, exhorters and readers carried on the work of the reformed church, on the other hand all bishops, dignitaries, parsons and vicars continued in possession of their benefices (less, of course, the third). Not only so, but the bishops still had their places in parliament and council, still from time to time exercised judicial functions and were still the instruments by which admission to lesser benefices was normally obtained.[4] There were thus, from 1560 onwards, two distinct ecclesiastical structures, with no link between them except the purely personal and fortuitous one that a considerable number of beneficed clergy (including three bishops) served in the reformed church and so were within both structures.

It is somewhat remarkable that ir. the hour of victory in 1567 no

---

[1] Vol. ii, 2nd edn., 185-7   [2] Vol. ii, 2nd edn., 191-4

[3] Superintendents (who were full-time organisers and administrators) were appointed for only five districts ; elsewhere their functions were carried out by ' commissioners,' i.e. ministers who combined supervisory duties with their parochial work.

[4] Much of the abundant evidence for this is contained in the *Register of the Privy Seal*, vol. v.

serious attempt was made to revert to the programme of the Book of Discipline. There was, indeed, some talk of ' dissolving the prelacies ' by separating from abbeys, and perhaps also from bishoprics, the parish churches which formed their spirituality,[1] but every step actually taken represented a very different policy, aimed at preserving the existing benefices and securing them to the clergy of the reformed church. It was ordained, by one of the statutes printed below, that patrons should in future present ' qualified persons ' for examination and admission by superintendents or commissioners. This meant that the reformers would ultimately obtain possession of the benefices and that the two structures which had been distinct since 1560 would merge or coalesce. Two further proposals were made,[2] which would have had the effect of dispossessing existing holders who were not sympathetic to the reformed faith, but these were not put into effect,[3] and all men appointed before 1567 remained in possession.

For the time being, therefore, and for years to come, many benefices would be held by persons not taking part in the work of the reformed church, while, on the other hand, many ministers would be without benefices. Thus, pending a comprehensive settlement which, in one way or another, would put the reformed church in possession of ' its proper patrimony, which is the teinds,' the device of ' the Thirds ' had to continue. By a statute printed below, collection of the thirds was now to be by the church, whose claims were to have priority, while the crown's rights were restricted to the ' superplus ' remaining after stipends had been paid.

1567. *The Coronation Oath*

Because that the incres of vertew, and suppressing of idolatrie cravis, that the Prince and the peple be of ane perfyte religioun, quhilk of Goddis mercie is now presentlie professit within this Realme Thairfoir it is statute and ordanit . . . that all Kingis and Princes, or magistratis quhatsumever halding thair place, quhilkis heirefter in ony tyme sall happin to regne and beir reule over this Realme,

---

[1] *A.P.S.*, iii, 37, c. 6 ; *B.U.K.*, i, 151   [2] *A.P.S.*, iii, 37, cc. 2, 5
[3] The first of them was put into effect in 1573 (see *infra*, p. 15) ; in the meantime an act expressly declared valid all Mary's appointments to benefices since 1560 (*A.P.S.*, iii, 31, c. 26).

at the tyme of thair coronatioun, and ressait of thair princely
authoritie, mak thair faithfull promise, be aith, in presence
of the eternall God, that induring the haill cours of their
lyfe thay sall serve the samin eternall God to the uttermaist
of thair power, according as he hes requyrit in his maist
haly word, revelit and contenit in the new and auld
Testamentis. And according to the samin word, sall
mantene the trew Religioun of Jesus Christ, the preicheing
of his haly word, and dew and rycht ministratioun of the
Sacramentis now ressaifit and preichit within this Realme.
And sall abolische and gainstand all fals Religioun contrare
to the samin. And sall reule the pepill committit to thair
charge according to the will and command of God, revelit
in his foirsaid word, and according to the lovabill Lawis
and constitutiounis ressaifit in this Realme, nawyse repugnant to the said word of the eternall God. And sall procure
to the uttermaist of thair power, to the Kirk of God, and
haill cristiane pepill, trew and perfyte peice in all tyme
cuming. The rychtis and rentis, with all just privilegeis of
the Crowne of Scotland to preserve and keip inviolatit,
nouther sal thay transfer nor alienat the samin.[1] Thay sal
forbid and repres, in all Estatis and degreis, reif, oppressioun,
and all kynde of wrang. In all Jugementis thay sall command and procure that Justice and equitie be keipit to all
creaturis, without exceptioun, as the Lord and father of all
mercyis be mercifull to thame. And out of thair landis and
Empyre thay salbe cairfull to ruite out all Heretykis and
enemeis to the trew worschip of God, that salbe convict be
the trew Kirk of God of the foirsaidis crymis. And that
thay sall faithfullie affirme the thingis abone writtin be thair
solempnit aith.

A.P.S., iii, 23, c. 8.

1567. *Act securing to the reformed church the succession to the
benefices*

It is statute and ordanit . . . that the examination and
admissioun of ministeris within this realme be onlie in

---

[1] See vols. i, 2nd edn., 184, and ii, 2nd edn., 17

power of the kirk now oppinlie and publictlie professit
within the samin ; the presentatioun of lawit patronageis
alwayis reservit to the just and ancient patronis, and the
patroun presentand ane qualifyit persoun (within sex
monethis efter it may cum to thair knawlege of the deceis
of him quha bruikit the benefice of befoir) to the superintendent of thay partis quhair the benefice lyis or utheris
havand comissioun of the kirk to that effect, utherwayis the
kirk to have power to dispone the samin to ane qualifyit
persoun for that tyme. [*In the event of the refusal of the
superintendent or commissioner to give collation to the presentee,
appeal lies to the superintendent in his diocesan council, and beyond
that to the general assembly.*]

A.P.S., iii, 23, c. 7

1567. *Act anent the Thirds of Benefices*

Our soverane lord, with avise of my lord regent, and thre
estatis of this present parliament, hes statute and ordanit
that the haill thriddis of the haill benefices of this realme
sall now instantlie, and in all tymes to cum, first be payit
to the ministeris of the evangell of Jesus Christ and thair
successouris ; and ordanis the lordis of the sessioun to grant
and gif letteris chargeing all and sindrie intromettouris or
that beis addettit in payment of the samin to answer and
obey to the saidis ministeris and thair collectouris (to be
nominat be the saidis ministeris, with avise of my lord
regent) . . . ; ay and quhill the kirk cum to the full
possessioun of thair propir patrimonie, quhilk is the teindis ;
provyding alwayis that the collectouris of the saidis ministeris
mak yeirlie compt in the chakker of thair intromissioun ;
swa that the ministeris may be first answerit of thair
stipendis, appertening to everie ane of thame, and the rest
and superplus to be applyit to our soverane lordis use.

A.P.S., iii, 24, c. 10

6

The Settlement of 1572–3

The administration of the regents, although clearly in the interests of the reformed church, was far from being universally acceptable. Within a year of Mary's deposition (24 July 1567), she escaped from Lochleven (2 May 1568) and, although she was defeated at Langside (12 May) and fled to England, a ' Queen's Party ' remained in being, in opposition to the ' King's Party.' The Marian faction was not wholly or even mainly Roman Catholic, but comprised a variety of elements. Divergence among the confederate lords who had brought about Mary's fall had appeared quite soon after Carberry, for there were those who felt that Mary's guilt, grave though it was, did not justify deposition, and that an abdication extorted by force was not binding. Again, while the Hamiltons, for dynastic reasons, objected to the coronation of a king who represented the rival family of Lennox,[1] and considered that their own head had the best claim to the regency, there were many other nobles who, from personal, family or religious motives, would not submit to the rule of Moray and his successors. The attitude of Queen Elizabeth did nothing to secure stability in Scotland. An examination, in England, of the charges against the captive Mary was inconclusive,[2] and in 1569 Elizabeth made proposals for her restoration, at least as joint-sovereign with her son ; at one point (May 1570) an English force did indeed cross the Border and harry the Hamilton lands,[3] but Elizabeth continued to withhold the effective support which would have cut short the civil war.

It was by a Hamilton that Moray was murdered (23 January 1570), and the Hamiltons held Dumbarton Castle for Mary until April 1571. From that time fighting centred on Edinburgh Castle, the last Marian stronghold. Kirkcaldy of Grange, in command of that fortress, attempted a coup against a convention of the King's Party at Stirling which led to the death of the second regent, Lennox (4 September 1571). Only after yet another short regency, that of Mar, and the assumption of power by the earl of Morton (24 November 1572), was Edinburgh Castle captured,

---

[1] While the Hamiltons were the heirs of Mary, it was not at all clear that they were the heirs of James. By the normal rules of inheritance the right of succession would pass, through his father, to the Lennoxes.

[2] See *infra*, p. 427   [3] See *infra*, p. 430

with English assistance (28 May 1573), and the civil war brought to an end.[1] The strong and effective rule of Morton continued, with only one brief intermission (in 1578), until 1580.

The church settlement of 1567, while it was clear as to the general practice that ministers should succeed to benefices, had made no specific provision for the greater benefices, including the bishoprics, and their destination had remained an open question. The problem was raised in an acute form when, on the fall of Dumbarton Castle, Archbishop Hamilton of St. Andrews was captured and hanged (April 1571). The government proceeded, in September 1571, to nominate ministers as archbishops of St. Andrews and of Glasgow,[2] but did so simply by letters patent and apparently without consulting the church. This high-handed action met with severe criticism, expressed in a letter written by John Erskine of Dun, superintendent of Angus, to the Regent Mar, in November. In this letter, extracts from which follow, Erskine states emphatically that the office of bishop or superintendent is founded upon the Word of God and is a spiritual office ; therefore, he insists, it is the duty of the kirk to reject bishops who have been appointed merely by secular authority.

1571. *Erskine of Dun to the Regent Mar*

. . . So by the kirk spiritual offices are distributed, and men admitted and receaved thereto. And the administratioun of the power is committed by the kirk to bishops or superintendents. Wherefore, to the bishops and superintendents perteaneth the examinatioun and admissioun of men to offices and benefices of spiritual cure, whatsoever benefice it be, als weill bishopricks, abbaceis and pryoreis, as the inferior benefices. That this perteaneth, by the Scriptures of God, to bishops and superintendents is manifest. . . . We have expressed plainlie by Scriptures that to the office of a bishop perteaneth examinatioun and admissioun to spiritual cure and office, and also to oversee them who are admitted, that they walke uprightlie and exerce their office faithfullie and purelie. To tak this

---

[1] See *infra*, p. 431
[2] Archbishop James Betoun had been an absentee in France since 1560.

power from the bishop or superintendent is to tak away the office of a bishop, that no bishop be in the kirk ; which were to alter and abolishe the order which God hath appointed in his kirk. . . . A greater offence or contempt of God and his kirk can no prince doe, than to sett up by his authoritie men in spiritual offices, as to creat bishops and pastors of the kirk ; for so to doe is to conclude no kirk of God to be ; for the kirk can not be, without it have the owne proper jurisdictioun and libertie, with the ministratioun of suche offices as God hath appointed. In speaking [of] this tuiching the libertie of the kirk, I meane not the hurt of the king or others in their patronages, but that they have their privileges of presentatioun according to the lawes ; providing alwise that the examinatioun and admissioun perteane onlie to the kirk, of all benefices having cure of soules. . . .

As to the questioun, if it be expedient a superintendent to be where a qualified bishop is, I understand a bishop or superintendent to be but one office ; and where the one is the other is. But having some respect to the cace whereupon the question is moved, I answere, the superintendents that are placed ought to continue in their offices, notwithstanding anie others that intruse themselves, or are placed by suche as have no power in suche offices. . . . And, therefore, the superintendents which are called, and placed orderlie by the kirk, have the office and jurisdictioun ; and the other bishops, so called, have no office nor jurisdictioun in the kirk of God ; for they enter not by the doore, but by another way, and therefore are not pastors, sayeth Christ, but theeves and robbers.

Calderwood, iii, 156–62.

With regard to the revenues of the bishoprics, Erskine contended that the ideal solution lay in the distribution of their spirituality among the parish churches from which it was derived ; this, as he admitted, might be impracticable, and in that event the kirk would be prepared for a bargain : provided that admission to the bishoprics is controlled by the church, no objection will meantime

9

be raised to the diversion to the crown of such proportion of the episcopal revenues as is not required for stipend. ' The kirk,' he concluded, ' contendeth not for worldly profit.'

No doubt as a result of representations by Erskine and others, an extraordinary General Assembly, styled a ' convention ', met at Leith in January 1571/2. It appointed commissioners to treat with the government, and gave its approval to arrangements which have been called the ' Concordat of Leith.' This was an agreed settlement, superseding the unilateral action initially taken by the government in the previous September. While the nomination of archbishops and bishops (the equivalent of the patron's right to present) was to remain with the crown [1], examination and admission were to be in the hands of reformed chapters, composed of ministers, and the new bishops were to be subject to the general assembly *in spiritualibus*. The English *formulae* for nomination, licence to elect, mandate to consecrate and admission to temporality were adopted, with unimportant changes [2] ; the English and Scottish styles of the oath of supremacy are printed below, and show that the only significant alterations are the introduction of the language of the Scots Confession of Faith of 1560, which had attributed to princes ' the conservation and purgation of religion,' and the insertion later of the phrase ' under God.'

1572. *Arrangements for the bishoprics*

It is thocht, in consideratioun of the present state, that the names and titillis of archebischoppis and bischoppis are not to be alterit or innovat, nor yit the boundes of the dioceis confoundit ; bot to stand and continew in tyme cuming as thay did befoir the reformatioun of religioun : at leist to the kingis majesties majoritie, or consent of parliament.

That personis promovit to archebischoprikkis and bischoprikkis be, safar as may be, indewed with the qualiteis specifeit in the Epistlis of Paule to Timothe and Tytus.

That thair be a certane assembly or cheptoure of learnit ministeris annext to every metropolitan or cathedrall seatt.

---

[1] It should be recalled that the appointment of superintendents had initially been by the Lords of Council (Knox, ii, 293).

[2] Calderwood, iii, 181-5 ; cf. Prothero, *Statutes and Documents*, 242-5.

To all archebischoprikkis and bischoprikkis vacand, or that sall happin to vaik heirefter, personis qualifeit to be nominat within the space of yeir and day eftir the vacance ; and the personis nominat to be xxx yeirs of age at the leist.

The deane, or, failyeing the deane, the nixt in dignitie of the cheptoure, during the tyme of the vacance salbe vicar generall and use the jurisdictioun *in spiritualibus* as the bischop mycht have usit.

All bischoppis and archebischoppis to be admittit heirefter sall exerce na farther jurisdictioun in spirituall functioun nor the superintendentis hes and presently exerces, quhill the same be agreit upoun.

And that all archebischoppes and bischoppis be subject to the kirk and generall assembly thairof *in spiritualibus* as thay ar to the king *in temporalibus*, and haif the advise of the best learnit of the cheptoure, to the nowmer of sex at the leist, in the admissioun of sic as sall have spirituall functioun in the kirk. As alsua, that it be lauchfull to als mony utheris of the cheptoure as plesis to be present at the said admissioun and to voit thairanent.

B.U.K., i, 209

1572. *The Oath of Supremacy*

Scottish version

I, *A.B.*, now elected bishop of *C.*, utterlie testifie and declare in my conscience that your Majestie is the onlie lawfull and supreme governour of this realme, als weill in *things temporall as in the conservatioun and purgatioun of religioun* ; and that no forraine prince, prelat, state or potentate, hath or ought to have anie jurisdictioun, power, superioritie, pre-eminencie, or authoritie ecclesiasticall or spirituall, within this realme ; and therefore I utterlie renounce and forsake all forraine jurisdictiouns, powers, superioriteis and authoriteis, and promise that from this furth I sall and will bear faith and true allegiance to your Majestie, your heyres and lawfull successours ; and to my power sall assist and defend all jurisdictiouns, priviledges, pre-eminencies, and authoriteis granted and belonging to your Highness, your heyres and lawfull successours, or united and annexed to your royall crowne. And further, I acknowledge and confesse, to have and hold the said bishoprick and possessiouns of the same, *under God*, only of your Majestie and crowne royall of this your realme ; and for the saids possessiouns I do my homage presentlie unto your Majestie, and unto the same your heyres and lawfull successours sall be faithfull and true.

Calderwood, iii, 184-5 ; *B.U.K.*, i, 220

1572. *The Oath of Supremacy*

English version

I, *A.B.*, now elect bishop of *C.*, do utterly testify and declare in my conscience that the Queen's Highness is the only supreme governor of this realm, and of all other her Highness' dominions and countries, as well in all *spiritual and ecclesiastical things or causes as temporal* ; and that no foreign prince, person, prelate, state or potentate hath or ought to have any jurisdiction, power, superiority, pre-eminence or authority ecclesiastical or spiritual, within this realm ; and therefore I do utterly renounce and forsake all foreign jurisdictions, powers, superiorities and authorities, and do promise that from henceforth I shall bear faith and true allegiance to the Queen's Highness, her heirs and lawful successors ; and to my power shall assist and defend all jurisdictions, pre-eminences, privileges and authorities granted or belonging to the Queen's Highness, her heirs and successors, or united or annexed to the imperial crown of this realm. And further, I acknowledge and confess to have and to hold the said bishopric of *C.* and the possessions of the same, *entirely, as well the spiritualities as the temporalities*, only of your Majesty and crown royal of this your realm ; and for the said possessions I do mine homage presently unto your Highness, and to the same your heirs and lawful successors shall be faithful and true.

Prothero, *Statutes and Documents*, 7 (see also 243)

It can be readily observed that the arrangements now made represented no serious innovation. As the new bishops had only the powers of superintendents, and were subject to the General Assembly, the existing system of government was unchanged—the church was still ruled by superintendents, bishops and commissioners, under the Assembly, as it had been since 1560. The appointment now of ministers to greater, as well as lesser, benefices, was a logical development of the practice pursued since 1567. A financial compromise, whereby bishops would be the means of diverting a proportion of the episcopal revenues to the crown or its nominees, had been plainly suggested by Erskine of Dun,[1] but was in any case no novelty, for such arrangements had been common in Scotland for a generation and were conspicuous in contemporary England also.[2]

Plainly, however critical the church had been of the initial action by the government in September 1571, there was little ground for grave objection to the settlement finally reached. There was, indeed, criticism of the choice of the aged and infirm John Douglas for St. Andrews,[3] there was a certain amount of uneasiness about the retention of so many titles—dean, chapter and so forth —which seemed to ' savour of popery ', and there was complaint about the reversion to the old diocesan boundaries ; but clerical opinion generally, when not actively favourable, was at least acquiescent. Knox, who had been bitterly hostile to the government's initial action and to the appointment of Douglas to St. Andrews, finally gave the new arrangements an emphatic blessing in a letter written to the General Assembly in August 1572, urging ' that all bishoprics vacant may be presented, and qualified persons nominated thereunto, within a year after the vaiking thereof, according to the order taken in Leith in the month of January last.' [4]

A further important step towards the absorption of the benefices into the reformed church came by the following act, providing for the deprivation of clergy who would not accept the reformed Confession of Faith and acknowledge the King. It was a belated

[1] See *supra*, p. 9.
[2] See references in *English Historical Review*, lx, 361n.
[3] Not only was Douglas aged and infirm, but he was not relieved of his Rectorship of the University of St Andrews (cf. James Melville, *Diary* [Wodrow Soc.], 31, and Bannatyne, *Memorials*, 228).
[4] *B.U.K.*, i, 248-9

fulfilment of a proposal made in 1567,[1] and formed part of the agreement made at Leith in January 1572,[2] but did not become law until 1573. This statute, coinciding with the conclusion of the civil war, demonstrates the attainment by the reformed church of full ' establishment '.

1573. *Act of Conformity and Supremacy*

Forsamekle as the conservatioun and purgatioun of the religioun cheifly pertenis to the Christane and godly kingis, princes, rewlaris and magistratis,[3] and that it is maist requisite that the kirk within this realme be servit be godly persounis of sound religioun obedient to the authoritie of the kingis majestie our soverane lord, it is thairfoir concludit, statute and ordanit . . . that every persoun quha sall pretend to be ane minister of Goddis word and sacramentis or quha presently dois or sall pretend to have and bruke ony benefice, use of the frutes, stipend, pensioun or portioun furth of benefice and ar not alreddy under the discipline of the trew kirk and participatis not with the sacramentis thairof sall in presence of the archebischop, bischop, super-intendent or commissionar of the diocie or province quhair he has or sall have the ecclesiasticall leving gif his assent and subscrive the articklis of religioun contenit in the actis of our soverane lordis parliament and gif his aith for acknawledgeing and recognoscing of our soverane lord and his authoritie and sall bring ane testimoniall in wryting thairupon : and oppinly on sum Sonday in tyme of sermone or publict prayeris . . . reid baith the testimoniall and confessioun . . . under the pane that everie persoun that sall not do as is abone appointit salbe *ipso facto* depryvit.

A.P.S., iii, 72, c. 3

Many recusant clergy were deprived under the terms of this act, but it did not wholly eliminate ' unqualified ' persons from the benefices. Besides, although the Concordat of Leith had proposed

---

[1] See *supra*, p. 4.   [2] *B.U.K.*, i, 212
[3] This is the phraseology of the Confession of Faith of 1560 (cf. *supra*, p. 10).

to find a place for the abbacies within the framework of the reformed church, the existing holders of abbeys—whatever their character or status—remained in possession of vast revenues, still including the teinds of appropriated churches. The only means by which the reformed church could tap the revenues of benefices not held by ministers was through the ' Thirds ', which therefore continued to be levied. Collection by the church, authorised in 1567, had proved a failure, and in 1573 the government resumed collection. Stipends remained a first charge, and under Morton their payment became much more efficient than before.

THE RISE OF MELVILLIAN PRESBYTERIANISM

The prospects of stability opened up by the settlement of 1572–3 did not endure. In 1574 Andrew Melville returned to Scotland after an academic career at Geneva, and at home he attained an influential position as Principal of Glasgow (1574) and then of St. Andrews (1580).[1] His views on church government included the inviolable parity of pastors and the consequent ' unlawfulness ' of episcopal government.

The two extracts printed below recount the beginning of the controversy which was to continue within the Scottish Church until 1690. The writer of the first of them, an archbishop, had no reason to love the presbyterian leader, but Melville's own nephew and close associate, James, the diarist, acknowledges that on Melville's arrival in Scotland there was general acquiescence in the existing system of church government, and that he was instrumental in forming a party, mainly of younger men, opposed to it.[2]

1575. *The opening of the presbyterian-episcopalian controversy*

In the Church this year began the innovations to break forth that to this day have kept it in a continual unquietness. Mr. Andrew Melvill, who was lately come from Geneva, a man learned (chiefly in the tongues), but hot and eager upon any thing he went about, labouring with a burning

[1] For Melville's educational work, see *infra*, pp. 409 *et seq.*

[2] James Melville, *Diary* (Wodrow Soc.), 32, 48, 52. See also McCrie, *Life of Andrew Melville* (edn. 1899), 64.

desire to bring into this Church the presbyterial discipline
of Geneva ; and having insinuated himself into the favour
of divers preachers, he stirred up John Dury, one of the
ministers of Edinburgh, in an Assembly which was then
convened, to propound a question touching the lawfulness
of the episcopal function, and the authority of chapters in
their election.

Spottiswoode, ii, 200

Anent the question proponit by certaine brether of the
assemblie of the haill kirk whither if the bischops, as they
are now in the Kirk of Scotland, hes thair function of the
Word of God or not, or if the chapiter appointit for creating
of them aucht to be tollerated in this reformed kirk : For
better resolution heirof, the generall assemblie of the kirk
appoints thair lovit brether, Mr. Johne Craig [minister of
Aberdeen], Mr. James Lowsone [minister of Edinburgh]
and Mr. Andrew Melvill, Principall of the Colledge of
Glasgow, on that ane part ; George Hay [Commissioner
of Caithness], David Lindsey [minister of Leith], Johne Row
[minister of Perth], on that uther part, to conveine, reason
and conferre upon the said questioun and to report thair
judgement and opinioun therupon to the assemblie befor
the dissolving therof, if they be resolvit betuixt and the
same.

[They reported their judgment in writing, as follows :]

They thinke it not expedient presentlie to answer directlie
to the first questioun ; bot if any bischop be chosen who
hes not sick qualities as the Word of God requyres, let
him be tryit be the Generall Assemblie *de novo*, and so
deposit. . . .

The name of bischop is common to all them that hes a
particular flock, over the quhilk he hes a peculiar charge.
. . . Attour, out of this number may be chosen some to
have power to oversie and visite sick reasonable bounds
besydes his awin flocke, as the generall kirk sall appoint ;

and in these bounds to appoint ministers, with the consent of the ministers of that province and the consent of the flock to quhom they salbe appointit . . . ; and to suspend ministers for reasonable causes, with consent of the ministers forsaids.

B.U.K., i, 340, 342–3

This report, which was confirmed by the Assembly of April 1576, pointed the way to a possible compromise—that bishops might be commissioned by the Assembly as ' visitors ' of their dioceses, provided that, like other ' commissioners ', they would accept the charge of ' particular congregations ' in addition.[1] There was, however, all too little disposition to compromise on either side,[2] and the campaign against episcopacy proceeded to the logical conclusion that the essential functions of admission and supervision of ministers were to be exercised not, as hitherto, by individuals—bishops or superintendents—but by courts or committees of ministers—especially the presbytery, a new body which was to operate within an area smaller than the diocese. The outcome of prolonged discussion on every aspect of ecclesiastical polity and jurisdiction was the second Book of Discipline, which was approved by the Assembly in April 1578. That book did not mention the presbytery as a body intermediate between the diocesan synod and the kirk session, but the position was clearly defined in a resolution by the Assembly of October 1578 that bishops were not to usurp the powers of presbyteries.[3]

The Melvillian movement raised other, and wider, issues, including that of the relations between church and state. The reformers, confronted by a queen who could be neither supreme head nor supreme governor of their church, had placed authority in the hands of a General Assembly. So far from representing ' The Church ' as against ' The State ', the Assembly had been initially a version of the three estates of the realm—barons, burgh commissioners and clergy—and looks like a device to assign to a constitutional organ the ecclesiastical supremacy which could not be exercised by a Roman Catholic queen. With the advent of James VI and his protestant regents, and more particularly with

[1] *B.U.K.*, i, 352–3
[2] For the views of the archbishops, see Calderwood, iii, 429 ; iv, 53–4, 499–501.   [3] *B.U.K.*, ii, 425

the strong rule of Morton, the question was raised whether the
Assembly should not give place to the supreme governorship of a
' godly prince '.[1] Melville's answer was that as church and state
were distinct and separate—' Two Kingdoms '—and the crown had
no ecclesiastical authority, therefore the Assembly must continue,
now as an ecclesiastical body composed primarily of ministers and
elders representing the lesser courts in the presbyterian hierarchy ;
and this assembly, or indeed any minister, was entitled to ' teach '
the magistrate how to exercise his civil jurisdiction ' according to
the Word '. On the other hand, the Regent Morton, and James
VI after him, saw clearly that crown supremacy could most
readily be exercised through the bishops ; thus crown supremacy
and episcopal government stood on one side, against parity, the
General Assembly and ecclesiastical independence (which might
mean domination) on the other.

On the question of endowment, Melville proposed to return to a
policy in some respects even more radical than that of the first
Book of Discipline, and completely at variance with developments
since 1567. Benefices and patronage alike were to go, and a
comprehensive claim was made to all ecclesiastical property,
which was to be administered by deacons. Here a strong motive
arose from the progressive dilapidation and secularisation of church
property. Benefices were still held by ' unqualified ' persons, the
abbeys were as far as ever from the grasp of the reformed church,
and the wealth of the bishoprics, too, was now being diverted to
lay pockets through lavish grants of feus of lands and tacks of
teinds. Here was a further ground for controversy, as it was
plainly not in the interests of the crown and the nobility to further
Melville's financial policy.

In the main, the course of the controversy between Melville
and his opponents can be followed only in the formal records of
the General Assemblies ; but a letter written by the Lord Chancellor of Scotland to Theodore Beza, Calvin's successor at Geneva,
probably in 1576, gives glimpses of the reasoned arguments which
were being put forward with reference to the three main subjects
at issue.

---

[1] It was at least arguable that such a development accorded with the
conception embodied in the Confession of 1560, the phraseology of
which had been used in the oath of supremacy in 1572 (*supra*, p. 12).

1576. *Letter of Lord Chancellor Glamis to Theodore Beza*

[Parity]

Since a pastor and minister is appointed in each congregation, and since the power of all ministers in the church of Christ seems to be equal and identical, it is asked whether it be necessary in the church to have the office of bishops, who will be responsible for summoning the ministers to synods when circumstances demand it, for admitting to the ministry and for removing from office for just causes ; or whether all ministers, enjoying equal power and not subject to the authority of any bishop as superior, ought, with the consent of the patron (having the right of presentation) and of the people themselves, to choose men suitable in religion, to discipline them and to remove them from office. Two considerations can move us to the retention of bishops : one is the character and unruliness of the people, who can only with difficulty, if indeed at all, be retained in their duty unless constrained by the authority of bishops, who visit and inspect all the churches ; the other is the laws of the realm, . . . which provide that whenever there is deliberation in the public assemblies of the kingdom about matters concerning the safety of the state nothing can be settled without the bishops, since they form one of the three orders and estates of the realm, to alter or wholly uproot which would be most perilous to the commonwealth.

[The Assembly and Crown Supremacy]

After the Reformation it became the accepted custom that the bishops and as many of the ministers, pastors and elders as the bishops commanded should assemble in one place with the notable barons and nobles professing the true religion, to investigate matters of both faith and morals. Now, however, when the sovereign is careful of the true religion, it is asked whether assemblies of this kind can be summoned without his order or consent, or whether it is permissible for the ministers alone to assemble as often as they wish, or, finally, whether it is lawful and expedient for nobles and others given to devotion, and the elders who are chosen among us yearly from the people and also from the nobility, to come to such assemblies without the king's command. A gathering of nobles and laity seems to some to be unnecessary under a godly prince, because it was accepted a few years ago, by custom alone and not by any particular law, under a sovereign hostile to the faith . . . ; and, moreover, there may seem a danger that the nobles, gathering so often and in such large numbers without the king's consent, should sometimes deliberate on matters other than those concerning religion. Others again think that they [sc. assemblies] should not be rejected . . . ; otherwise it will come about, if a prince not attached to the faith should ascend the throne in the future, that the ministers may not be able to assemble in safety or have their decisions enforced without the consent and help of the nobles.

[The Patrimony]

Since in earlier times great riches, under the name of alms, have been granted by the kings and many others to bishops, monasteries and such like, and since such wealth seems rather a hindrance than an advantage to bishops, while monasteries are useless in the state and in the church, it is asked what should be done with such goods, which once were dedicated to the church. For, as bishops and ministers have enough from the teinds on which to live comfortably and honourably, it is asked whether the sovereign, with consent of the estates of the realm, can appropriate the remainder so that he be free to convert it into his own or the public use, especially as such goods do not consist only of teinds but also of lands in the country or the towns.

Translated in *Scot. Hist. Soc., Miscellany*, viii, 101, 105, 110–1

1578. *The second book of discipline*

[The Two Kingdoms]

I. 2.   The kirke . . . hes a certane power grantit be God, according to the quhilk it uses a proper jurisdiction and governement, exerciseit to the confort of the haill kirk. This power ecclesiasticall is an authoritie granted be God the Father, throw the Mediator Jesus Christ, unto his kirk gatherit, and having the ground in the Word of God ; to be put in execution be them, unto quhom the spirituall government of the kirk be lawfull calling is committit.

I. 3.   The policie of the kirk flowing from this power is an order or forme of spirituall government, quhilk is exercisit be the members appoyntit thereto be the Word of God ; and therefore is gevin immediatly to the office-beararis, be whom it is exercisit to the weile of the haill bodie. . . .

I. 4.   This power and policie ecclesiasticall is different and distinct in the awin nature from that power and policie quhilk is callit the civill power, and appertenis to the civill government of the commonwelth ; albeit they be both of God, and tend to one end, if they be rightlie usit, to wit, to advance the glorie of God and to have godlie and gud subjectis.

I. 5.   For this power ecclesiasticall flowes immediatlie from God, and the Mediator Jesus Christ, and is spirituall, not having a temporall heid on earth, bot onlie Christ, the onlie spirituall King and Governour of his kirk.

I. 7.   Therefore this power and policie of the kirk sould leane upon the Word immediatlie, as the onlie ground thereof, and sould be tane from the pure fountaines of the Scriptures, the kirk hearing the voyce of Christ, the onlie spirituall King, and being rewlit be his lawes.

I. 8.   It is proper to kings, princes and magistrates, to be callit lordis, and dominators over their subjectis, whom they govern civilly ; bot it is proper to Christ onlie to be callit Lord and Master in the spirituall government of the kirk :

and all uthers that bearis office therein aucht not to usurp dominion therein, nor be callit lordis, bot onlie ministeris, disciples and servantis. For it is Christis proper office to command and rewll his kirk universall, and every particular kirk, throw his Spirit and Word, be the ministrie of men.

I. 9. Notwithstanding, as the ministeris and uthers of the ecclesiasticall estait ar subject to the magistrat civill, so aught the person of the magistrat be subject to the kirk spiritually and in ecclesiasticall government. And the exercise of both these jurisdictiones cannot stand in one person ordinarlie. The civill power is callit the Power of the Sword, and the uther the Power of the Keyes.

I. 10. The civill power sould command the spiritual to exercise and doe their office according to the Word of God : the spiritual rewlaris sould requyre the Christian magistrate to minister justice and punish vyce, and to maintaine the libertie and quietness of the kirk within their boundis.

I. 14. . . . The ministeris exerce not the civill jurisdictioun, bot teich the magistrat how it sould be exercit according to the Word.

I. 15. . . . Finally, as ministeris are subject to the judgement and punishment of the magistrat in externall things, if they offend ; so aucht the magistratis to submit themselfis to the discipline of the kirk gif they transgresse in matteris of conscience and religioun.

[Offices in the Church]

II. 6. . . . There be three extraordinar functiones [in the kirk] : the office of the apostle, of the evangelist, and of the prophet, quhilkis ar not perpetuall, and now have ceisit in the kirk of God, except quhen He pleasit extraordinarly for a tyme to steir sum of them up againe. There are foure ordinarie functiones or offices in the kirk of God : the office of the pastor, minister or bishop ; the doctor ; the presbyter or eldar ; and the deacon.

II. 8. Therefore, all the ambitious titles inventit in the kingdome of Antichrist, and in his usurpit hierarchie,

23

quhilkis ar not of ane of these foure sorts, togither with the offices depending thereupon, in ane word, aucht all utterlie to be rejectit.

III. 5. In the order of election it is to be eschewit that na person be intrusit in ony of the offices of the kirk contrar to the will of the congregation to whom they ar appointed, or without the voce of the elderschip. . . .

IV. 1. Pastors, bischops or ministers ar they wha ar appointit to particular congregationes, quhilk they rewll be the Word of God and over the quhilk they watch. In respect whairof sumetymes they ar callit pastors, becaus they feid their congregation ; sumetymes *episcopi*, or bischops, because they watch over their flock ; sumetymes ministers, be reason of their service and office ; and sumetymes also *presbyteri*, or seniors, for the gravity in manners quhilk they aucht to have in taking cure of the spirituall government, quhilk aucht to be most deir unto them.

VI. 5. As the pastors and doctors sould be diligent in teiching and sawing the seed of the Word, so the elders sould be cairfull in seiking the fruit of the same in the people.

[Church Courts]

VII. 2. Assemblies ar of four sortis. For aither ar they of particular kirks and congregations, ane or ma, or of a province, or of ane haill nation, or of all and divers nations professing one Jesus Christ.

VII. 3. All the ecclesiasticall assemblies have power to convene lawfully togidder for treating of things concerning the kirk, and perteining to thair charge. They have power to appoynt tymes and places to that effect ; and at ane meiting to appoynt the dyet, time and place for anuther.

VII. 10. . . . When we speik of the elders of the particular congregations, we mein not that every particular parish kirk can or may have their awin particular elderschips, specially to landwart ; bot we think thrie or four, mae or fewar, particular kirks, may have ane common elderschip to them all, to judge thair ecclesiasticall causes.

VII. 25. There is . . . an uther mair generall kynde of assemblie, quhilk is of all nations and estaits of persons within the kirk, representing the universall kirk of Christ ; quhilk may be callit properlie the Generall Assemblie or Generall Councell of the haill Kirk of God.

[Deacons]

VIII. 3. [Of deacons.] Thair office and power is to receave and to distribute the haill ecclesiasticall gudes unto them to whom they ar appoyntit. This they aucht to do according to the judgement and appoyntment of the presbyteries or elderschips (of the quhilk the deacons ar not), that the patrimonie of the kirk and puir be not convertit to privat men's usis, nor wrangfullie distributit.

[The Patrimony of the Kirk]

IX. 1. Be the patrimonie of the kirk we mein whatsumever thing hath bene at ony time before, or shall be in tymes coming, gevin, or be consent or universall custome of countries professing the Christian religion applyit to the publique use and utilitie of the kirk. Swa that under this patrimonie we comprehend all things gevin, or to be gevin, to the kirk and service of God, as lands, biggings, possessions, annual-rents, and all sic lyke, wherewith the kirk is dotit, aither be donations, foundations, mortifications, or ony uther lawfull titles, of kings, princes or ony persons inferiour to them ; togither with the continuall oblations of the faithfull. We comprehend also all sic things as be lawis, or custome, or use of countries, hes bene applyit to the use and utilitie of the kirk ; of the quhilk sort ar teinds, manses, gleibs, and sic lyke, quhilks, be commoun and municipall lawis and universall custome, ar possessit be the kirk.

IX. 2. To tak ony of this patrimonie be unlawfull meinis, and convert it to the particular and profane use of ony person, we hald it ane detestable sacriledge befoir God.

IX. 3. The gudes ecclesiasticall aucht to be collectit and

distributit be the deacons, as the Word of God appoynts, that they who beir office in the kirk be providit for without cair or solicitude. . . .

IX. 4. The same canons mak mention of ane fourfald distribution of the patrimonie of the kirk, quhairof ane part was applyit to the pastor or bischop for his sustentation and hospitalitie ; anuther to the elders and deacons, and all the clergie ; the third to the puir, sick persons, and strangers ; the fourth to the uphald and uther affaires of the kirk, speciallie extraordinar : We adde hereunto the schules and schuile maisters also, quhilk aucht and may be weill susteinit of the same gudes, and ar comprehended under the clergie. To wham we joyn also clerks of assemblies, als weill particular as generall ; syndicks or procu[ra]tors of the kirk affaires, takers up of psalmes, and siclyke uther ordinar officers of the kirk, sa far as they ar necessar.

[The Duty of the Christian Magistrate]

X. 2. It perteinis to the office of a Christian magistrat to assist and fortifie the godly proceidings of the kirk in all behalfes ; and namely, to sie that the publique estait and ministrie thereof be manteinit and susteinit as it apperteins, according to Godis Word. . . . [4] To assist and manteine the discipline of the kirk, and punish them civilly that will not obey the censure of the same ; without confounding alwayis the ane jurisdiction with the uther. [5] To sie that sufficient provision be made for the ministrie, the schules and the puir. . . . [7] To mak lawis and constitutions agreeable to God's Word, for advancement of the kirk and policie thereof. . . .

[Abuses]

XI. 2. . . . The admission of men to Papisticall titles of benefices, sic as serve not, nor have na function in the Reformit Kirk of Christ, as abbottis, commendatoris, prioris, prioressis, and uther titles of abbyis, quhais places are now

for the most pairt, be the just judgement of God, demolishit
and purgit of idolatrie, is plaine abusion. . . .

XI. 3. Siclyke that they that of auld wer callit the chapiters
and convents of abbayis, cathedrall kirks, and the lyke
places, serve for nathing now, bot to set fewes and tacks, if
onything be left of the kirk lands and teinds, in hurt and
prejudice thairof, as daily experience teiches, and thairfoir
aucht to be utterly abrogat and abolishit. Of the lyke
nature ar the deanes, archdeanes, chantors, subchantors,
thesaurers, chancellars, and uthers having the lyke titles
flowing from the Pape and canon law onlie, wha heve na
place in the reformit kirk.

XI. 5. Neither aucht sic abusers of the kirk's patrimony
to have vote in parliament, nor sit in councell under the
name of the kirk and kirk-men, to the hurt and prejudice
of the libertie thairof, and lawes of the realm made in
favouris of the reformit kirk.

XI. 7. And albeit it was thocht gude, for avoyding of
greater inconvenientis, that the auld possessors of sic benefices quha had imbracit the trew religion suld injoy be
permission the twa pairt of the rentis quhilks they possesst
of befoir induring thair lyftyme, yit it is not tolerabil to
continew in the lyke abuse and geve these places and uthers
benefices of new to als unmeit men or rather unmeitar, quha
ar not myndit to serve in the kirk, bot leife an idle lyfe, as
uthers did quha bruikit them in the tyme of blindnes.

XI. 8. And in sa farr as in the order takin at Leith, in the
yeir of our Lord 1571, it appeires that sic may be admittit,
being found qualifiet ; either that pretendit order is agains
all gude ordor, or else it must be understood not of them
that be qualifiet in worldly affaires, or to serve in court ;
bot of sic as are qualifiet to teich Godis Word, having their
lawfull admission of the kirk.

[Bishops]

XI. 9. As to bischops, if the name ἐπίσκοπος be properly
takin, they ar all ane with the ministers, as befoir was

declairit. For it is not a name of superioritie and lordschip, bot of office and watching. Yit, because in the corruption of the kirk, this name (as uthers) hes bene abusit, and yit is lykelie to be, we cannot allow the fashion of thir new chosin bischops, neither of the chapiters that ar electors of them to sic offices as they ar chosen to.

XI. 10. Trew bischops sould addict themselves to ane particular flock, quhilk sindry of them refuses ; neither sould they usurpe lordship over their brethren and over the inheritance of Christ, as these men doe.

XI. 13. It agries not with the Word of God that bischops sould be pastors of pastors, pastors of monie flocks, and yit without anie certaine flock, and without ordinar teiching. . . .

XI. 16. And be act of parliament it is provydit that the Papisticall kirk and jurisdiction sould have na place within [this realm], and na bischop nor uther prelate in tymes cuming sould use ony jurisdiction flowing from his authoritie. And, again, that na uther ecclesiasticall jurisdiction sould be acknawledged within this realm, bot that quhilk is and shall be in the reformit kirk, and flowing therefra. Sa we esteim halding of chapiters in Papisticall manner, aither in cathedrall kirks, abbayis, colledges, or uther conventuall places, usurping the name and authoritie of the kirk, to hurt the patrimonie thairof, or use ony uther act to the prejudice of the same, sen the yeir of our Lord 1560, to be abusion and corruption, contrar to the libertie of the trew kirk and lawis of the realme ; and thairfoir aucht to be annullit, reducit, and in all tyme cumming all utterlie dischargit.

[General Assemblies]

XII. 8. The nationall assemblies of this countrey, callit commonlie the Generall Assemblies, aucht alwayes to be reteinit in their awin libertie, and have their awin place ; with power to the kirk to appoynt tymes and places convenient for the same : and all men, als weill magistrats as inferiours, to be subject to the judgement of the same in ecclesiasticall causes, without any reclamation or appellation to ony judge, civill or ecclesiasticall, within the realm.

[Distribution of Revenues]

XII. 12. As for the kirk rents in generall, we desyre the order to be admittit and mentainit amangis us that may stand with the sinceritie of God's Word and practise of the purity of the kirk of Christ ; to wit, that as was before spoken, the haill rent and patrimonie of the kirk, exceptand the small patronages before mentionat, may be dividit in four portions : Ane thereof to be assignit to the pastor for his intertainment and hospitalitie : An uther to the eldars, deacons, and uther officers of the kirk, sic as clerks of assemblies, takers up of the psalmes, beadels and keipers of the kirk, sa far as is necessar ; joyning therewith also the doctors of schules, to help the ancient foundations where neid requires : The third portion to be bestowit upon the puir members of the faithfull, and on hospitals : The fourth, for reparation of the kirks, and uther extraordinar charges as ar profitable for the kirk ; and also for the common weil, if neid requyre.

[Advantages of the Programme]

XIII. 1. Seing the end of this spirituall government and policie, quhairof we speik, is that God may be glorifiet, the kingdom of Jesus Christ advancit, and all who are of his mysticall bodie may live peaceable in conscience ; therefore we dar bauldlie affirme that all these who have trew respect to thir ends will even for conscience caus gladlie agrie and conforme themselfis to this order and advance the same as far as in them lyes ; that their conscience being set at rest they may be replenishit with spirituall gladnes in giving full obedience to that quhilk Godis Word, and the testimonie of their awin conscience does crave, and in refusing all corruption contrar to the same.

XIII. 2. Nixt, we sall becum an example and paterne of

gude and godly order to uther nations, countries and kirks, professing the same religion with us ; that as they have glorified God in our continueing in the sinceritie of the Word hitherto, without any errours (praise be to His name) ; so they may have the lyke occasion in our conversation, when as we conform ourselfis to that discipline, pollicie and gude order quhilk the same Word and purity of reformatioun craveth at our hands : utherwise, that fearfull sentence may be justly said to us, ' The servant knawing the will of his Maister, and not doing it, etc.'

XIII. 3. Mairover, gif we have any pity or respect to the puir members of Jesus Christ, who so greatly increase and multiplie amanges us, we will not suffer them to be langer defraudit of that part of the patrimonie of the kirk quhilk justly belangs unto them : And by this order, if it be deuly put to execution, the burden of them sall be taken of us to our great confort, the streits sall be cleansed of thair cryings and murmurings ; swa as we sall na mair be an skandall to uther nations, as we have hitherto bene, for not taking order with the puir amanges us, and causing the Word quhilk we profess to be evill spokin of, giving occasion of sclander to the enemies and offending the consciences of the sempil and godly.

XIII. 4. Besydes this, it sall be a great ease and com-moditie to the haill common people, in relieving them of the beilding and uphalding of thair kirks, in bigging of brigges, and uther lyke publick warks. It sall be a relief to the labourers of the ground in payment of their teinds ; and schortlie, in all these things, whereinto they have bene hitherto rigorously handlit be them that were falslie callit kirkemen, thair tacksmen, factours, chalmerlanes and extortionars.

Finally, to the king's Majestie and common weill of the countrey this profite shall redound : that the uther affaires of the kirk beand sufficientlie provydit according to the distribution of the quhilk hes bene spokin ; the superplus beand collectit in the treasurie of the kirk, may be profitablie imployit and liberallie bestowit upon the extraordinar support of the effaires of the prince and commoun weill, and speciallie of that part quhilk is appoyntit for reparation of kirks.

Sa, to conclude, all beand willing to apply themselfis to this order, the people suffering themselfis to be rewlit according thereto : the princes and magistrates not beand exemit, and these that ar placit in the ecclesiasticall estait richtlie rewling and governing, God sall be glorifiet, the kirk edifiet and the bounds thereof inlargit ; Christ Jesus and his kingdome set up, Satan and his kingdome subvertit ; and God sall dwell in the middis of us, to our comfort, through Jesus Christ, who, togither with the Father and the Holy Ghost, abydes blessit in all eternity.   Amen.

Calderwood, iii, 529 *et seq.*[1] ;   *B.U.K.*, ii, 488 *et seq.*

THE FIRST PRESBYTERIAN EXPERIMENT

The Melvillian programme, with its logical and comprehensive answers to outstanding problems and its apparent advantages on grounds of expediency, made a strong appeal to ecclesiastical opinion which sufficiently explains its adoption by the General Assembly.   Yet its first opportunity to become effective arose from a politico-religious crisis which was not of its own making.

Esmé Stuart, Lord d'Aubigny, who had arrived in Scotland in the autumn of 1579, had at once gained the affection of the young James VI and a considerable influence over him.   But d'Aubigny, as was then suspected, and as it would now appear, had been entrusted with a mission to secure the overthrow of Morton (with his Anglophile policy) and to work for the restoration of Mary and the religion of Rome.

At first everything favoured d'Aubigny, whom the king created Earl of Lennox in March 1580.   The castles of Dumbarton and Edinburgh were held by him ; he was made High Chamberlain,

---

[1] The extracts are here printed in the simpler orthography of Calderwood. The *Book of the Universal Kirk of Scotland* is not an official register, but a compilation of items selected from the original registers (which were destroyed by fire in 1834). It is, however, important to note that the second Book of Discipline was officially recorded in the Books of the General Assembly.

with command of the king's bodyguard ; and Morton, accused by one of Lennox's friends, Captain James Stewart, of complicity in the murder of Darnley, was warded in Edinburgh Castle (January 1581) and later removed to Dumbarton.

But despite his public abjuration of the Roman faith (July 1580), the ministers of the church remained suspicious of Lennox and his friends. Amid much tangled intrigue, Elizabeth wrote to James warning him of Catholic conspiracies (and particularly of Lennox's true intent) and demanding a fair trial for Morton, while rumours spread abroad of Jesuit priests in the country, and of a plot to kidnap James and to carry him from Dumbarton to France.

Amid these excursions and alarms, James, possibly prompted by Lennox himself, caused a Second Confession of Faith to be drawn up which he, Lennox, James Stewart, and others of his courtiers and household subscribed on 28 January 1581, and which on 2 March 1581 was ordered to be publicly subscribed throughout the kingdom.

This Second Confession, known as ' The King's Confession ' or ' The Negative Confession ' (because of its denial of ' all contrary religion and doctrine, but chiefly, all kind of Papistry ') was later to form the basis of the National Covenant of 1638.

1581. *The ' King's Confession '*

Ane shorte and generall confessione of the true Christiane fayth and religion according to Godis worde and actis of our perliamentis subcryved by the kingis majestie and his houshold with sindrie otheris to the glorie of God and good example of all men, at Edinburght the 28 day of Januare 1580 [1581] and 14 yeare of his Majesties Reigne.

We all and everie one of us underwritten protest, that after long and dew examination of our owne consciences in matteris of true and false religioun, are now throughly resolved in the trueth by the worde and sprit of God, and therefore we beleve with our heartis, confesse with our mouthes, subscryve with our handis, and constantly affirme before God and the whole world, that this onely is the true Christiane fayth and religion pleasing God and bringing salvation to man, quhilk is now by the mercy of God reveled to the World by the preaching of the blessed evangell, and is receaved, beleved and defended by manie and sindrie notable kyrkis and realmes, but chiefly by the kyrk of Scotland, the kingis majestie, and three estatis of this realme, as Godis eternall trueth and onely ground of our salvation, as more perticulerly is expressed in the confession of our fayth stablished and publictly confirmed by sindrie actis of perlamentis, and now of a long tyme had bene openly professed by the kingis Majestie and whole body of this realme both in brught and land : To the quhilk confession and forme of religion we willingly aggree in our conscience in all poyntis as unto Godis undoubted trueth and veritie grounded onely upon his written worde. And therefore we abhorre and detest all contrarie religion and doctrine, but cheifly all kynd of papistrie in generall and perticular headis even as they are now damned and confuted by the worde of God and kyrk of Scotland ; but in speciale we detest and refuse the usurped authoritie of that Romane Antichrist upon the scriptures of God, upon the kyrk, the civill magistrate and conscience of men : All his tyrannous lawes made upon indifferent thinges, agaynst our christiane libertie ; his erroneous doctrine agaynst the sufficiencie of the written worde, the perfection of the lawe, the office of Christ, and his blessed ewangell ; his corrupted doctrine concernyng originall synne, our naturall inabilitie and rebellion to godlines,[1] our justification by fayth onely, our imperfect sanctification, and obedience to the law ; the nature, number and use of the holie sacramentis ; his fyve bastard sacramentis, with all his ritis, ceremoneis, and false doctrine added to the ministration of the true sacramentis without the worde of God : his cruell judgement agaynst infantis deperting without the sacrament, his absolute necessitie of baptisme, his blasphemous opinion of trans-substantiation, or reall presence of Christis body in the elementis, and receaving of the same by the wicked, or bodeis of men ; his dispensationeis with solemnet othes,

[1] God's Law, 1638

33

perjuries, and degrees of mariage forbidden in the worde, his crueltie agaynst the innocent devorced ; his divilishe mes, his blasphemous preisthead, his prophane sacrifice for the synnes of the dead and the quyck, his canonization of men, calling upon angelis, or sainctis deperted, worshiping of imagrie and croces,[1] dedicating of kyrkis, altaris, dayis, vowes to creatures, his purgatorie, prayeris for the dead, praying or speaking in a strange language, with his processioneis and blasphemous letanie, and multitude of advocattis or mediatoreis ; his manyfold ordoures, auricular confession, his despered and uncertayne repentance, his generall and doubtsome fayth, satisfactioneis of men for theyr synnes ; his justification by workes, his opus operatum, workes of supererogation, meritis, perdones, peregrinationes, and stationeis ; his holy water, baptisyng of bellis, cungering of spritis, crocing, saning, anoynting, conjuring, hallowing of Godis good creatures with the superstitious opinion joyned therewith ; his worldlie monarchie and wicked hierarchie, his three solemnit vowes with all his shavelingis of syndrie sortes ; his erroneous and bloodie decretes made at Trent, with all the subcryveris and approveris of that cruell and bloodie band conjured agaynst the kyrk of God ; and fynally we detest all his vane allegories, ritis, signes and traditioneis broght in the kyrk without or agaynst the worde of God and doctrine of this true reformed kyrk, to the quhilk we joyne our selves willingly in doctrine, fayth, religion, discipline, and use of the holie sacramentis, as lyvely memberis of the same in Christ our head, promising and swearing by the great name of the Lord our God that we shall continue in the obedience of the doctrine and discipline of this kyrk and shal defend the same according to our vocation and power all the dayes of our lyves, under the panes conteyned in the law, and danger both of body and saule in the day of Godis fearfull judgement. And seing that manie are styrred up by Satan and that Romane Antichrist to promise, sweare, subcryve, and for a tyme use the holie sacramentis in the kirk deceatfully agaynst there

[1] Imagery, relics and crosses, 1638

34

owne conscience, mynding hereby fyrst, under the externall clok of the religion to corrupt and subvert secretly Godis true religion within the kirk, and afterward, when tyme may serve, to become open ennemeis and persecutoris of the same, under vane hope of the papis dispensation, divised agaynst the worde of God to his greater confusion and theyr dowble condemnation in the day of the Lord Jesus, we therefore, willing to tak away all susspition of hypocrisie and of syk dowble dealing with God and his kirk, protest and call the searcher of all heartis for witnes, that our myndis and heartis do fullely aggree with this our confession, promise, othe, and subscription ; so that we are not moved for any worldly respect, but are perswaded onely in our conscience throught the knawledge and love of Godis true religion prented in oure heartis by the holie sprit, as we shall answer to him in the day when the secretis of all heartis shalbe disclosed.   And because we perceave that the quietnes and stabilitie of our religion and kirk doth depend upon the savetie and good behaviour of the kyngis majestie as upon ane confortable instrument of Godis mercy graunted to this countrey for the mainteining of his [1] kyrk and ministration of justice amongis us, we protest and promise solemnetly with our heartis under the same othe, hand writ, and panes, that we shall defend his persone and authoritie with our geyr,[2] bodyes, and lyves in the defence of Christis evangell, libertie of our countrey, ministration of justice, and punishment of iniquitie, agaynst all enemeis within this realme or without, as we desyre our God to be a strong and mercyfull defender to us in the day of our death and cuming of our Lord Jesus Christ, to whome with the Father and the Holie Sprit be all honour and glorie eternally.   Amen.   *Nat. MSS. Scot.*, iii, No. LXX

If the Negative Confession did anything to allay alarm, new grounds for tension soon arose. Morton was tried and executed (June 1581) ; Lennox (created Duke) and Captain James Stewart (created Earl of Arran) had complete ascendancy over the king.

[1] This, 1638   [2] Goods, 1638

The ministers were soon aware of the presence of Roman Catholic agents ; plots and conspiracies multiplied, in which England, France and Spain were all involved.

The ultra-protestant opinions expressed in the Confession had no direct bearing on the presbyterian-episcopalian controversy, but it is plain that at this point the ministerial aversion to prelacy was intensified by fears of Rome. In July 1580 the General Assembly had pronounced a comprehensive denunciation of episcopal government, a decision clarified in April 1581. The complementary step of planning a scheme of presbyterian government was taken at the same time. But presbytery could not be effectively substituted for episcopacy without parliamentary action ; and the civil power, so far from countenancing the presbyterian project, not only adhered to the existing forms of church government but accepted the Assembly's challenge by making a fresh appointment to the archbishopric of Glasgow (with substantial financial advantages to Lennox).

The General Assembly's condemnation of Episcopal Government

July 1580.

Forsameikle as the office of a bischop, as it is now usit and commouuly takin within this realme, hes no sure warrand, auctoritie nor good ground out of the [Book and] Scriptures of God, but is brocht in by the folie and corruptions of [men's] invention, to the great overthrow of the kirk of God : the haill assemblie of the kirk, in ane voyce, after libertie givin to all men to reason in the matter, none opponing themselves in defending the said pretendit office, finds and declares the samein pretendit office, usit and termit as is above said, unlaufull in the selfe, as haveand neither fundament, ground nor warrant within the Word of God ; and ordaines that all sick persons as bruiks, or sall bruik heirafter, the said office, sal be chargeit *simpliciter* to demitt, quyt and leave of the samein, as ane office quherunto they are not callit be God : and siclyke, to desist and cease from all preaching, ministration of the sacraments, or using any way the office of pastors, quhill they receive, *de novo*, admission from the generall assemblie.

B.U.K., ii, 453

April 1581.

Anent the act made in the assemblie [holden] at Dundie, against bischops, beand [*sc.* because] some difficultie appeirit to some brethren to arise be the word Office, conteinit in the said act, quhat sould be meanit therby, the assemblie present, for the most part of them that was present and voted in [the assemblie at] Dundie, to take away the said difficultie and resolve men of the true meaning and understanding of the said act, declares that they meanit haillelie to condemne the [whole] estate of bischops, as they are now in Scotland, and that the same was the determinatioun and conclusion of the kirk at that tyme.

B.U.K., ii, 474-5

A scheme for Presbyteries

April 1581.

[*The General Assembly laid down that of the 924 churches in the country only 600 should have ministers.*] Thir sax hundreth kirks to be divydit in fiftie presbyteries, twelve to every presbytrie or therabout. Thrie of thir presbyteries, or moe or fewer as the countrey lyis, to make ane diocie, according to ane forme after following, to be considderit of. Of thir number, certaine of presbyteries salbe the synodall assemblie ; and ilk synodall assemblie sall appoint the place within that province for thair nixt synodall. Of persons direct from the synodall assemblies sall the general assemblie consist. [*There follows* ' A forme of the presbyteries and diocies,' *a complete scheme for the whole country.*]

B.U.K., ii, 480-82

It must have been plain even to the Assembly that the ecclesiastical government of the country could not be changed overnight at its mere *fiat*. A more practical step was taken in the following

4

provision for the organisation of thirteen model presbyteries at places in the Lowlands.

April 1581.

Tuiching the report of the brethrein appointed to consider the placing of the kirks givin in to them in rolls, and to report their judgment what they thinke meet to be reformed therein, a great part of the saids rolls being reproduced, with their judgment, which they could presentlie resolve upon, in suche shortnesse of time, whill they be further resolved, with advice of their countreis, the whole assemblie thought meet, that a beginning be had of the presbytereis instantlie, in the places after following, to be exemplars to the rest which may be established heerafter, viz. Edinburgh, Sanct Andrewes, Dundie, Perth, Stirline, Glasgow, Air, Irwing, Hadinton, Dumbar, Chirnside, Linlithquo, Dumfermline. To some of thir presbytereis were assigned twelve, to some sixteene, to some twentie, to some foure and twentie kirks, as the brethrein deputed to join them thought meetest till better advice be had.

Calderwood, iii, 523 ; cf. *B.U.K.*, ii, 482–7

In Lennox's suspected association with Roman Catholic powers, in fears of plans for the restoration of Mary, and in apprehension about the absolutist tendencies of the government, there were ample grounds for organised opposition, in which a leading part was taken by certain of the nobility. Amid plot and counter-plot [1], in which Mar and Gowrie were prominent on one side, and Lennox and Arran on the other, Mar and Gowrie seized James when he was hunting in Atholl and carried him to Ruthven Castle (August 1582), where, shortly afterwards, they were able to seize Arran also. James was compelled to order Lennox to leave Scotland (which, after lingering for a while at Dumbarton, he did, in December 1582).

The Kirk had excellent reasons for welcoming the new *régime*, which at once issued a proclamation affirming the right of ministers

[1] See *Collected Essays and Reviews of Thomas Graves Law* (ed. P. Hume Brown), 217–43

to 'general, synodal and particular assemblies.'[1] The General Assembly of October 1582 gave its full approval to the seizure of the king, which it called 'the late action of the Reformation '[2]— an approval which James never forgave ; it sought to turn the political change to account by petitioning that presentations should in future be directed to presbyteries and that these organs should be given certain powers hitherto exercised by bishops and superintendents.[3] In practice, while the Assembly pushed on busily with plans for presbyteries,[4] and quite a number of presbyteries were organised, no steps were taken to legalise their operations, and official recognition continued to be given to bishops.

The ' Black Acts '

The success of the ' Ruthven Raiders ' was short-lived, partly because Queen Elizabeth hesitated to give them full support. After a ten months' ' captivity,' James escaped (June 1583), and Arran was at once in the ascendant again. The leaders of the ' Raid ' were dispersed or fled, and Andrew Melville took refuge south of the Border. Later a new plot to seize the king and ' remove ' Arran failed ; Gowrie was executed ; Mar, with the leading presbyterian ministers, fled to England ; and Arran was stronger than ever.[5]

Forthwith the Church was brought to book for its support of the ' Raid.' The so-called ' Black Acts,' of May 1584, asserted the authority of king, parliament and council over all estates, spiritual and temporal ; and they reaffirmed that authority over the lower clergy, and Church government generally, must rest with bishops and commissioners—responsible now to the king and not, as previously, to the General Assembly. Convocations of ministers were forbidden except with the king's express consent ; kirk sessions were excepted,[6] and it was explained that the act was aimed especially at ' that form lately invented in this land, called the presbytery,'[7] but in practice the General Assembly did not meet while Arran's rule lasted. Finally, Buchanan's *History* and

---

[1] Calderwood, iii, 650–51   [2] *B.U.K.*, ii, 594   [3] Ibid., 601
[4] Ibid., 586–7   [5] See *infra*, p. 437
[6] *Reg. of the Kirk Session of St Andrews*, ii, 529
[7] Calderwood, iv, 260

his *De Jure Regni apud Scotos* (which had asserted that kings rule with the consent of their people), were to be purged.

1584.

c. 2. . . . Our soverane lord and his thrie estatis assemblit in this present Parliament ratefeis and apprevis and perpetuallie confirmis the royall power and auctoritie over all statis alsweill spirituall as temporall within this realme in the persoun of the kingis majestie our soverane lord his airis and successouris. And als statutis and ordinis that his hienes, his said airis and successouris, be thame selffis and thair counsellis, are and in tyme to cum salbe juges competent to all personis his hienes subjectis of quhatsumevir estate degrie functioun or conditioun that ever they be of, spirituall or temporall, in all materis quhairin they or ony of thame salbe apprehendit summound or chargeit to ansuer to sic thingis as salbe inquirit of thame be our said soverane lord and his counsell. . . .

c. 3. . . . It is statute and ordinit be our said soverane lord and his thrie estatis assemblit in this present parliament that nane of his liegeis and subjectis presume or tak upoun hand to impugne the dignitie and authoritie of the saidis thrie estatis. Or to seik or procure the innovatioun or diminutioun of the power and auctoritie of the same thrie estatis or ony of thame in tyme cumming under the pane of treasoun.

c. 4. Forsamekle as in the trublous tymis during thir xxiiij yeris bypast syndrie formis of jugementis and jurisdictionis alsweill in spirituall as temporall causis ar enterit in the practis and custome quhairby the kingis majesties subjectis ar oftymis convocat and assemblit togidder . . . na sic ordour as yit being allowit of and approvit be his majestie and his thrie estatis in Parliament. . . . And speciallie his hienes and his estatis considering that in the saidis assembleis certane his subjectis have takin upoun thame to justifie and auctorize the fact perpetrate aganis his hienes persoun and

40

estate at Ruthven and prosecutit thairefter, quhill his
majestie at Goddis pleasour recoverit his libertie, having in
thair pretendit maner maid actis thairupoun, kepis the
same in register, and as yit semis to allow the said attemptat,
althocht now publictlie condampnit be his hienes and estatis
as treasounable. . . . Oure soverane lord and his thrie
estatis assemblit in this present parliament dischargeis all
jugementis and jurisdictionis spirituall or temporall accus-
tomat to be usit and execute upoun ony of his hienes
subjectis quhilkis ar not approvit be his hienes and his saidis
thrie estatis convenit in Parliament : and decernis the same
to ceis in tyme cumming quhill the ordour thairof be first
sene and considerit be his [hienes and his saidis thrie] estatis
[convenit] in Parliament and be allowit and ratefeit be
thame. . . . And als it is statute and ordinit . . . that
nane of his hienes subjectis of quhatsumever qualitie estate
or functioun they be of, spirituall or temporall, presume or
tak upoun hand to convocat convene or assemble thame
selffis togidder for halding of counsellis conventionis or
assembleis to creat consult and determinat in ony mater of
estate, civill or ecclesiasticall (except in the ordinare jugementis), without his majesties speciall commandement,
expres licence had and obtenit to that effect under the panis
ordinit be the lawis and actis of Parliament aganis sic as
unlawfullie convocatis the kingis liegeis.

c. 5. Oure soverane lord and his thrie estatis assemblit in
this present parliament willing that the word of God salbe
prechit and sacramentis administrat in puritie and synceritie,
And that the rentis quhairon the ministeris aucht to be
sustenit sall not be possest be unworthie personis . . . : It
is thairfoir statute and ordinit be his hienes with avise of
the saidis thrie estatis, That all personis ministeris or
reiddaris or utheris providit to benefices sen his hienes
coronatioun (not having vote in his hienes parliament)
suspectit culpable of heresie, papistrie, fals and erroneous
doctrine, commoun blasphemie, fornicatioun, commoun
drunkinnes, non residence, pluralitie of benefices having

cure quhairunto they ar providit sen the said coronatioun, symonie and dilapidatioun of the rentis of benefices contrare the lait act of parliament, being lawfullie and ordourlie callit, tryit and adjugeit culpable in the vices and causis abonewrittin, or ony of thame, be the ordinare bishop of the diocie or utheris the kingis majesties commissionaris to be constitute in ecclesiasticall causis, Salbe deprivit alsweill fra thair functioun in the ministrie as fra thair benefices. . . .

c. 8. . . . It is statute and ordinit . . . That nane of his subjectis . . . sall presume or tak upoun hand privatlie or publictlie in sermonis, declamationis or familiar conferencis, to utter ony fals, untrew or slanderous spechis to the disdane, reproche, and contempt of his majestie, his counsell and procedingis, or to the dishonour, hurt or prejudice of his hienes, his parentis and progenitouris, or to midle in the effairis of his hienes and his estate, present bygane and in tyme cumming, under the panis contenit in the actis of Parliament aganis makaris and tellaris of lesingis . . . : Attour becaus it is understand unto his hienes and to his thrie estatis that the buikis of the *Cronicle* and *De jure regni apud Scotos* maid be umquhill Mr George Buchannan and imprentit sensyne contenis syndrie offensive materis worthie to be delete, It is thairfoir statute and ordinit that the havaris of the saidis tua volummis in thair handis inbring and deliver the same to my lord secretare or his deputis within fourtie dayis efter the publicatioun heirof, To the effect that the saidis tua volumis may be perusit and purgit of the offensive and extraordinare materis specifiit thairin not meit to remane as accordis of treuth to the posteritie . . .

c. 20. Oure soverane lord and his thrie estatis of Parliament statutis and ordinis That Patrik, Archiebischop of Sanctandrois, and utheris the bishopis within this realme useand and exerceand the functioun and auctoritie of bishoppis, with sic utheris as salbe constitute the kingis majesties Commissionaris in Ecclesiasticall causis, Sall and may direct and put ordour to all materis and causis

ecclesiasticall within thair dioceisis, viset the kirkis and
state of the ministrie within the same, Reforme the collegeis
thairin, Resave his hienes presentationis to benefices, And
gif collationis thairupoun as they sall find the personis
presentit qualefeit and worthie, And mak report of sic as
they find insufficient in dew tyme, And that na presentationis to benefices be directit in tyme cumming to ony
utheris . . .

A.P.S., iii, 292–303

TRANSITION TO PRESBYTERIAN GOVERNMENT

The exiled lords returned from England in November 1585 and
by a demonstration before Stirling brought about the dismissal of
Arran.[1] Andrew Melville and most of the other presbyterian
leaders hastened home, and in February 1586 a conference of
councillors and ministers, at Holyrood, agreed on the following
compromise between episcopal and presbyterian government.

1586. *Compromise on Church government*

It is condescended to in reasouning that the name of a
bishop hath a speciall charge and function annexed to it
by the Word ; his electioun to be, by a presentatioun to be
directed by his Majestie to the Generall Assemblie, of whom
he sall receave his admissioun.

That he sall be appointed to a speciall kirk, where he sall
keepe residence, and there serve the cure as a minister. . . .

That the Generall Assemblie sall choose out a senat or
presbyterie of the most learned and godlie ministers within
his bounds, to be limited to him, to have the oversight of in
visitatioun, which sall be onlie used by advice of the
presbyterie.

By the senat's advice he sall receave all presentatiouns of
ministers within his said bounds, and by their advice proceed to their triell and collatioun. . . .

If he be slanderous in his life or doctrine, he sall be
answerable to the Generall Assemblie. . . .

[1] See *S.H.R.*, xx, 181–6.

If he admit or deprive without the consent of the most part of his senat, the deid to be null. . . .

Calderwood, iv, 491–2.

The General Assembly met in the following May, and, after long discussion and with considerable hesitation, accepted the foregoing compromise.[1] It also drew up a complete scheme of presbyteries, each to have its constant moderator, who would in some cases be a bishop or a commissioner.[2] In practice the Assembly and the presbyteries showed little disposition to accept a *modus vivendi* with the bishops, and it soon seemed likely that episcopal government would become a mere façade.

Action of another kind came in the Act of Annexation of 1587, a measure which the king was later to regret.[3] On the ground that the Crown's financial needs could be met, without recourse to taxation, by the resumption of that part of its patrimony which had of old been alienated to the Church, Parliament annexed to the Crown the ecclesiastical temporalities, with the following exceptions : (1) properties already ' erected ' into temporal lordships, and a few special cases ; (2) the castles and ' yards ' of bishoprics and other great benefices ; (3) the manses and glebes of parochial benefices ; and (4) properties devoted to educational purposes. The express exclusion of all teinds from the annexation no doubt implied a recognition of the long-standing claim that they formed the especial patrimony of the Church ; but, although in succeeding years it was a common practice to ' disjoin ' a parsonage from a bishopric or abbey to which it had been appropriated, and unite it to the vicarage in order to provide a living for a minister, there was no attempt at any *general* extrication of the teinds.

1587. *The Act of Annexation*

Oure soverane lord and his thrie estaitis of parliament perfitelie understanding the greitest pairt of his proper rent to haif bene gevin and disponit of auld to abbayis, monasteries and utheris personis of clergy quhairby the crown hes bene sa greitly hurte that thairefter his maist noble progenitouris had not sufficient meanis to beir furth the honour of thair estait as thai had befoir, quhilk hes bred sindrie

[1] *B.U.K.*, ii, 652-4   [2] Ibid., 667 *et seq.*   [3] See *infra*, p. 51.

inconvenientis within this realme, and seeing the causes of
the dissolutioun of the patrimonie of the crown to the kirk
efter the trewth knawin ar fund nathir necessar nor proffitable and that be mony occasionis throw a lang process of
tyme the derth hes sa gritlie increscit not onlie in this realme
bot in all cuntries that the princes chairges ar not able to
be uphaldin be that part of the patrimonie quhilk now
restis in his handis ; and his hienes for the grite luif and
favour quhilk he beiris to his subjectis being nawayes myndit
to greve thame with importable taxationis specialie for his
royall supporte, it is fund maist meit and expedient that he
sal have recours to his awin patrimonie disponit of befoir
. . . as ane help maist honourable in respect of himself
and leist grevous to his people and subjectis.

And thairfoir oure said soverane lord and his saidis thrie
estaitis of parliament be the force of this present act haif
unit, annexit and incorporat and unitis, annexis and
incorporatis to the crown of this realme to remane tharwith
as annext and as it wer propirtie thairof in all tyme cuming
. . ., all and sindrie landis, lordschippis, baronies, castellis,
touris, fortalices, mansionis, maner places, milnis, multuris,
woddis, schawes, parkis, fischeingis, townis, villages,
burrowis in regalitie and baronie, annuelrentis, tenementis,
reversionis, custumes greit and small, fewfermes, tennentis,
tennendries and service of frie tennentis and all and sindrie
utheris commoditeis, proffittis and emolumentis quhatsumevir alsweill to burgh as to land, quhilkis at the day and
dait of thir presentis, viz. [29 July 1587] pertenis to quhatsumevir archibischope, bischop, abbot, prior, prioresse,
quhatsumevir uther prelate, uther ecclesiasticall or beneficit
persoun of quhatsumevir estait, degrie hie or law, and at
the day and dait of thir presentis pertenis to quhatsumevir
abbay, convent, closter, quhatsumevir ordour of freris or
nunis, monkis or channonis howsoevir thai be namit, and
to quhatsumevir college kirk foundit for chantorie and
singing or to quhatsumevir prebendarie or chaiplanrie
quhairevir they ly or be situate . . ., and siclike all and
sindrie commoun landis bruikit be chaptouris of cathedrall

kirkis and chantorie colleges as commoun . . ., to be in all
tymes heireftir takin, haldin and reput as it wer the propertie
and patrimonie of the croun, to remane thairwith in all
tyme cuming efter the forme . . . of the act of annexatioun
maid in the tyme of . . . King James the secund. . . .

The landis, lordschippis and baroneis underwrittin erectit
be his hienes in temporall lordschippis and baronies befoir
the dait of this present act quhilk is [29 July 1587] ar not
nor sall not be comprehendit in the said annexatioun . . .,
thay ar to say the landis and lordschip of Torphichen, the
erldome of Gowrie, the lordschip and leving of Deir now
callit the lordschip of Altrie, the landis and baronies of
Newbotle . . ., the baronies of Brochtoun and Kers, the
burgh of the Cannogait and ane pairt of the toun of Leyth,
the baronie of Alhammer als callit Quhytkirk, quhilkis of
befoir pertenit to the abbacie of Halyruidhous, the lands
and lordschip of Mussilburgh quhilkis of befoir pertenit to
the abbay of Dumfermling . . . and als exceptit the haill
remanent landis of the abbay of Dumfermling declairit as
yit to abyd with the said abbay [*and Paisley, Pluscarden and
Arbroath*].

It is alwayes understand . . . that under the said annexatioun or ony claus heirin specifiet the teyndscheves and
utheris teyndis of quhatsumever landis within this realme
pertening to ony persounage or vicarage ar not nor sall not
be comprehendit except quhair the teynd and stok is sett
togidder as is heirefter declairit, bot that the samin sall
remane with the present possessouris . . . notwithstanding
the said annexatioun. . . .

Reservand alwayes and exceptand to all archibischoppis,
bischoppis, abbottis, priouris, priorisses, commendatairis
and utheris possessouris of greit benefices of the estait of
prelattis and quhilkis befoir had or hes voit in parliament
thair principall castles, fortalices, houssis and mansionis
with the biggingis and yairdis thairof . . . quhilkis sall
remane . . . for thair residence and habitatioun. . . .

Exceptand alsua furth of the said annexatioun all and
quhatsumever mansionis of persounages and vicarages

annext to parroche kirkis with four aikeris of the gleib maist ewest [1] to the kirk and commodious for the minister serving the cuir thairof for his better residence. . . .

Exceptand in lyk maner all and sindrie landis, profittis, tenementis, annuelrentis, teyndscheves and utheris emolumentis and proffittis quhatsumever gevin, grantit and disponit for intertenement of maisteris and studentis in colleges erectit for the exercise of lerning and for grammer scuillis and for sustentatioun of ministeris makand thair residence in burrowis quhair thair is na uther stipend appointit to thame. . . .

A.P.S., iii, 431

The failure of the compromise of 1586, followed by the Act of Annexation, inevitably led to the temporary eclipse of episcopacy. The development of an effective presbyterian government during succeeding years, though not associated with any fresh enactment, was in practice very marked. Examination of the records of crown presentations to benefices shows a steady increase in the proportion directed to presbyteries—the fraction is about a quarter in 1588, a third in 1589 and a half in 1590. By 1592, it is clear, presbyteries were operating in nearly every part of the country, and presentations directed to bishops had become extremely rare.

This development of presbyteries had its logical result in the parliamentary recognition of presbyterian government in 1592. It was not, however, the only feature in the background of that enactment. The exploits of Francis Stewart, Earl of Bothwell, who with impunity defied the proceedings taken against him and seriously threatened the king's person, revealed the weakness of James's government. The mild measures taken against the Roman Catholic earls of Huntly and Errol, and the failure to punish the former after his murder of the earl of Moray, were held to reveal not only weakness, but sympathy with the Roman cause. Confronted with a general outcry, James, on the advice of his Chancellor, Maitland of Thirlestane (who saw an opportunity to establish his power and gain popularity with one section of the community), decided on the enactment which follows. This statute approved the presbyterian hierarchy of courts and annulled the

[1] Nearest

statute of 1584 in favour of the bishops, but it affirmed—though with qualifications—the act of 1584 in favour of royal control over the Church and gave the king certain rights in the calling of assemblies. Meantime, the ministers, realising that the Act of Annexation had brought them no tangible gains, had been pressing afresh for a solution of the problem of the patrimony. The act of 1592 represented a concession which might give them some satisfaction but which yet made no real innovation, caused no dislocation, and cost nothing.

1592. *Act establishing Presbyterian Government*

Oure soverane lord and estaittis of this present parliament, following the lovable and gude example of thair predicessouris, hes ratifiet and apprevit and be the tennour of this present act ratifies and apprevis all liberties, privileges, immunities and freedomes quhatsumevir gevin and grantit be his hienes, his regentis in his name or ony of his predicessouris, to the trew and haly kirk presentlie establishit within this realme. . . .

And siclyk ratifies and apprevis the general assemblies appoyntit be the said kirk, and declairis that it salbe lauchfull to the kirk and ministrie everilk yeir at the leist and ofter *pro re nata* as occasioun and necessitie sall require to hald and keip generall assemblies providing that the kingis majestie or his commissioner with thame to be appoyntit be his hienes be present at ilk generall assemblie befoir the dissolving thairof nominat and appoint tyme and place quhen and quhair the nixt general assemblie salbe haldin. And in cais nather his majestie nor his said commissioner beis present for the tyme in that toun quhair the said generall assemblie beis haldin, than and in that cais it salbe lesum to the said generall assemblie be thame selffis to nominat and appoynt tyme and place quhair the nixt generall assemblie of the kirk salbe keipit and haldin as they haif bene in use to do thir tymes bypast.

And als ratifies and apprevis the sinodall and provinciall assemblies to be haldin be the said kirk and ministrie twyis ilk yeir as thay haif bene and as presentlie in use to do

48

within every province of this realme. And ratifeis and apprevis the presbiteries and particulare sessionis appointit be the said kirk with the haill jurisdictioun and discipline of the same kirk aggreit upoun be his majestie in conference had be his hienes with certain of the ministrie convenit to that effect. . . .

And becaus thair ar divers actis of parliament maid in favouris of the papisticall kirk . . . not abrogat nor annullit : thairfoir his hienes and estaittis foirsaidis hes abrogat, cassit and annullit etc. all actis of parliament maid be ony of his hienes predecessouris for mantenance of superstitioun and idolatrie with all and quhatsumevir actis, lawes and statutes maid at ony tyme befoir the day and dait heirof aganis the libertie of the trew kirk, jurisdictioun and discipline thairof as the samyn is usit and exerceisit within this realm. . . .

Item the kingis majestie and estaittis foirsaidis declairis that the secund act of the parliament haldin at Edinburgh the xxii day of May, the yeir of God [1584] sall na wayes be prejudiciall nor dirogat any thing to the privilege that God hes gevin to the spirituall office beraris in the kirk concerning headis of religioun, materis of heresie, excommunicatioun, collatioun or deprivatioun of ministeris or ony sic essentiall censouris speciall groundit and havand warrand of the Word of God. Item . . . annullis the xx act of the same parliament [at Edinburgh 1584] granting commissioun to bishoppis and utheris juges constitute in ecclesiastical caussis to ressave his hienes presentatioun to benefices, to give collatioun thairupoun and to put ordour in all caussis ecclesiasticall . . . and thairfoir ordanis all presentationis to benefices to be direct to the particular presbiteries in all tyme cuming, with full power to thame to giff collationis thairupoun and to put ordour to all materis and caussis ecclesiasticall within thair boundis. . . .

A.P.S., iii, 541–2

The Restoration of Episcopal Government

The legislation of 1592 left many problems unsolved. One was the ultimate fate of the lands taken from the bishops in 1587 ; another was the matter of increased provision for the parish ministers, which could be attained only if some means were devised of extracting the teinds which had been appropriated to abbeys and which were now being drawn by commendators and lords of erection. There were also the questions of the destination of the episcopal titles and remanent properties, the cathedral and diocesan dignities (for which there was no place in a presbyterian system), and, not least, the clerical estate in Parliament. As bishoprics fell into abeyance, the spiritual estate so-called would consist only of the commendators, who were laymen, leaving the Kirk unrepresented. Could some reform be effected so that the spiritual estate would really represent the Kirk, and if so, how ?

To these problems the king offered his solution—the restoration of episcopal government. Despite his concession of the ' Golden Act ' of 1592, James remained firmly opposed to the presbyterian system of church government and the independence of the ministers. He saw in episcopacy his only hope of royal control over the Church—perhaps even over the State as well. He set forth his views with great frankness in the *Basilikon Doron*, in which he propounded his theories and programme for the benefit of his son, Prince Henry. The work was probably written in 1598 and first printed (for private circulation) shortly thereafter, but no doubt it represents conclusions which James had reached much earlier.

Extracts from the Basilikon Doron *relating to ecclesiastical affairs*

The reformation of religion in Scotland being made by a popular tumult and rebellion . . . and not proceeding from the Prince's order (as it did in England), some of our fiery ministers got such a guiding of the people at that time of confusion, as finding the gust [taste] of government sweet, they began to fantasy to themselves a democratic form of government ; . . . and after usurping the liberty of the

time in my long minority, settled themselves so fast upon
that imagined democracy, as they felt themselves with that
hope to become *tribuni plebis*. . . . And because there was
ever some learned and honest men of the ministry that were
ashamed of the presumption of these seditious people, there
could no way be found out so meet for maintaining their
plots as parity in the church, whereby the ignorants were
emboldened . . . to cry the learned, godly and modest
out of it : parity, the mother of confusion and enemy to
unity, which is the mother of order ; by the example
whereof in the ecclesiastical government, they think (with
time) to draw the politic and civil government to the
like. . . .

For preservative against their poison, entertain and
advance the godly, learned and modest men of the ministry,
whom of (God be praised) there lacketh not a reasonable
number : and by their preferment to bishoprics and
benefices (annulling that vile Act of Annexation, if ye find
it not done to your hand) ye shall not only banish their
parity (which I can not agree with a monarchy) but ye
shall also re-establish the old institution of three estates in
parliament, which can no otherwise be done. . . .

Cherish no man more than a good pastor ; hate no man
more than a proud puritan ; thinking it one of your fairest
styles to be called a loving nurse-father to the church, seeing
all the churches within your dominions planted with good
pastors, the doctrine and discipline maintained in purity
according to God's word, a sufficient provision for their
sustentation, a comely order in their policy, pride punished,
humility advanced : and they so to reverence their
superiors, and their flocks them, as the flourishing of your
church in piety, peace and learning may be one of the chief
points of your earthly glory ; being ever alike at war with
both the extremities, as well as ye repress the vain puritans,
so not to suffer proud papal bishops.

. . . .

What is betwixt the pride of a glorious Nebuchadnezzar
and the preposterous humility of our puritan ministers,

51

claiming to their parity, and crying, ' We are all but vile worms ' ; and yet will judge and give law to their king, but will be judged nor controlled by none. Surely there is more pride under such a one's black bonnet nor under great Alexander's diadem.

The king's opportunity to put his theories into practice arose from a series of events which demonstrated the bold claims of the ministers and the conflict between them and James's conception of his authority, but which led at the end of 1596 to a crisis which the king was able to turn to his own advantage.

James's decision to recall the exiled Roman Catholic earls had been criticised in the General Assembly in March (when very plain words had been used of him) ; and in the following September Melville had plucked him by the sleeve, addressed him as ' God's sillie vassal ', and told him that there were ' two kings and two kingdoms in Scotland.' Then, in November, David Black, minister in St. Andrews, charged by the King and Council to answer for certain ' unreverent, reproachful and infamous ' passages in a recent sermon, declined the jurisdiction of the Council in a matter that was spiritual, and was supported by the standing Commissioners of the General Assembly. James's answer to the declinator was an Act of the Privy Council discharging the meetings of the Commissioners with, later, a command to Black to enter in ward north of the Forth. From the messages passing between the king and the Commissioners of the General Assembly it is clear that James was determined to put some limit not only to the freedom of speech of the ministers but also to the powers of the General Assembly.

A sudden tumult in Edinburgh at this juncture (17 December 1596), of which the causes are not easily discernible, but one in which some thought the king in danger and some the ministers, gave James the opportunity to weaken the position both of the Church and of its stronghold, Edinburgh. Leaving the town, he proclaimed that Edinburgh was no longer the capital of the kingdom (a proclamation which, though later recalled, made the burgesses of Edinburgh more circumspect lest they should again lose their privileges).

' Parliamentary Bishops '

One of the problems outstanding since 1592 had been clerical representation in Parliament, and it was this which opened the way to the king's next expedient—that of ' parliamentary bishops.' The problem of the ecclesiastical estate had exercised men's minds intermittently since 1581,[1] and it grew more acute as the probable extinction of the bishoprics became imminent in the 1590s. At this time the General Assembly was not by any means averse to representation in Parliament, but there were differences between it and the king as to whether the representatives should be nominated by the presbyteries or by the crown, whether they should be styled ' bishops ' or ' commissioners ' and whether their commissions should be for life or for only a year at a time. To secure compliance with his wishes, James took advantage of the clause in the act of 1592 which entitled him to name the place of meeting of each General Assembly, and summoned meetings at towns like Dundee, Perth and Montrose, where opinion was much less radical than in the south, and where the atmosphere was likely to be less perfervid. His first step was to persuade the Assembly of May 1597 to appoint commissioners ' to give advice to his majesty in all affairs concerning the welfare of the Kirk ' ; these commissioners were referred to by Calderwood as ' the king's led horse.' When, in December 1597, these commissioners presented a petition that ministers should have a seat and vote in Parliament, James's answer was the following act—the first definite move in his insinuation of an episcopal form of government into the presbyterian constitution recognised in 1592.

1597.

c. 2. Oure soverane lord and his hienes estaitis in parliament haveand speciall consideratioun and regard of the great privelegis and immuniteis grantit be his hienes predicessoris of maist worthie memorie to the halie kirk within this realme, And to the speciall personis exercing the officis titillis and digniteis of prelaceis within the samin, quhilkis personis hes evir representit ane of the estaitis of this realme in all conventionis of the saidis estaitis, And that the saidis privelegis and fredomis hes bene frome tyme to [tyme]

[1] Melville, *Diary*, 118 ; Calderwood, iv, 261, v, 431 ; *B.U.K.*, ii, 787

renewit and confermit in the same integritie and conditioun quharin they war at ony time of befoir Sua that his majestie now agknawlegeing the samin to be fallin and becumin under his majesties favorable protectioun, Thairfoir his majestie of his great zeall and singular affectioun quhilk he alwayis hes to the advancement of the trew religioun presentlie professit within this realme with advyis and consent of the saidis estaitis statutis decernis and declaris that . . . sik pasturis and ministeris within the samin as at ony tyme his majestie sall pleis to provyid to the office place title and dignitie of ane bischoip abbott or uther prelat sall at all tyme heirefter haif voitt in parliament siclyk and als frelie as ony uther ecclesiasticall prelat had at ony tyme bigane, And als declaris that all and quhatsumevir bishopreis presentlie vacand in his hienes handis quhilkis as yit ar undisponit to ony persone or quhilkis salhappin at ony tyme heirefter to waik [1] salbe onlie disponit be his majestie to actuell prechearis and ministeris in the kirk or to sik utheris personis as salbe fundin apt and qualifeit to use and exerceis the office and functioun of ane minister or precheour and quha in thair provisionis to the saidis bishoprikis sall accept in and upoun thame to be actuell pasturis and ministeris And according tharto sall practeis and exerce the samin thairefter.

A.P.S., iv, 130

After further negotiations between the king and later assemblies, this act became effective in 1600, when ministers were appointed to the sees of Ross, Aberdeen and Caithness with power to vote in Parliament but with no ecclesiastical functions as bishops.[2]

Before James proceeded to further measures towards the restoration of episcopal government, he had succeeded in curbing the General Assemblies. Again he took advantage of the clause in the act of 1592 (p. 48) which provided that the king or commissioner, at the end of each Assembly, should name time and place for the

[1] Fall vacant
[2] For their express exclusion from episcopal functions, see B.U.K., iii, 955–6.

next meeting (the Assembly being free to do so only if both king and
commissioner were absent), but which was silent as to procedure
if the commissioner, though present, did not appoint the next
meeting. At the Assembly of November 1602 it had been arranged
that the next meeting should be at Aberdeen in July 1604. James's
announcement that it was to be postponed was accepted, though
there was a protest from three representatives of the presbytery
of St. Andrews, on the ground that ' the warrant of keeping was
greater than the warrant of continuation.' In July 1605, when the
deferred meeting was expected to take place, the Privy Council
forbade attendance on pain of outlawry. This time a number of
ministers did meet, formally constituted a General Assembly, and
fixed a date for a further meeting. They were summoned before
the Council to answer for their action, and on their refusal to
acknowledge the Council's jurisdiction in spiritual matters were
tried for high treason. Six of them were found guilty (January
1606) and ultimately banished. Later in 1606 James summoned
eight of the leading ministers to London, where they were illegally
detained. Six were later allowed to return home, but Andrew
and James Melville had to remain in exile. These high-handed
actions formed a suitable atmosphere for James's further proceedings, which, designed to give the bishops some ecclesiastical
standing, reverted to the ' constant moderators ' which had been
proposed in the compromise of 1586 (*supra*, p. 44).

' Constant Moderators '

In December 1606 a convention of clergy at Linlithgow—which
James insisted on regarding as a General Assembly—approved a
scheme for constant moderators of presbyteries. The king's letter
instructing the Council to enforce this act follows.

1607.

Quhairas it may fall furth that sum of the prisbitereis,
being too muche addicted to this anarchie and confusioun
in the estaite of the Churche of that oure kingdome, will
refuise to admit and ressave suche ane Constant Moderatour
as hes bene concludit upoun [in] the Generall Assemblie
laitlie haldin in that oure kingdome, as in lyke maner
perhappis some of those moderatouris that ar choisin

(pretending thair conscientious zeale to all paritie and rather wishing a continewing volubilitie than any setled and constant forme of governament in the Churche) will mak a schaw of refuise of any supremacie above thair bretherine ; bot, becaus heirby the hole proceidingis of that Assemblie may turne ineffectuall gif the refuise ather of the one or uther wer ony way tollerate, it is thairfoir oure pleasour and will that ye direct chairgeis aganis any suche prisbitereis or moderatouris that sall mak any suche refuise, commanding thame, under the pane of horning, to conforme thameselffis to the will of the said Assemblie.

R.P.C., vii, 299–300

James now proceeded to the assumption that the approval of the Linlithgow convention extended to moderators of synods as well as of presbyteries, and to the acceptance of bishops as constant moderators of synods. The following document is the charge by the Council to the Synod of Fife to accept the Archbishop of St. Andrews as constant moderator.

1607.

Forsamekle as, at the Assemblie of the Kirk keipit and haldin at the burgh of Linlithqu in the moneth of [December] last bypast, and assisted with a verie frequent number of the Nobilitie, Counsale, and Estaittis of this kingdome, it wes ordanit that the moderatour of every synode sould be nominat and chosin out of the Moderatouris of the prisbitereis quhair[of] the synode consisted, and gif thair be a Bischop within the synode that the Bischop salbe Moderatour of the synode, as in ane Act of the said Assemblie maid to this effect at lenth is contenit : and seing the Synode of Fyff is appointed to be haldin at the burgh of Dysart upoun the nynt day of Junii instant, necessar it is that the Archibischop of Sanctandrois, who is ane of the number of that Synode, be nominat, electit, and chosin Moderatour of the said Synode, conforme to the said Act of Linlithqu : Thairfore the Lordis of Secrite Counsale ordanis letters to be

direct chairgeing the bretherine of the ministerie of the said
Synode to ressave and admit the said Archibischop of
St. Androis as Moderatour of the said Synode within three
houris nixt efter the chairge, undir the pane of rebellioun,
etc. ; as alsua chairgeing the said Archibischop to accept
that chairge upoun him. . . .

R.P.C., vii, 380

The next step was to give the bishops adequate endowment. This
was achieved by the Act for the Restitution of the Estate of Bishops
(1606), which, being primarily designed to remove the episcopal
temporalities from the scope of the Act of Annexation of 1587,[1]
was purely civil and financial in its effects.   In 1609 their ancient
consistorial jurisdiction was restored to the bishops by act of parliament, and in 1610 the episcopal regime was fortified against its
critics by the establishment of the Courts of High Commission.
For the time being, Parliament could hardly do more, but the
year 1610 saw two other significant developments—the acceptance
by the General Assembly of the bishops' powers in excommunication
and in the admission, deposition and supervision of ministers ;
and a ceremony of consecration at Westminster whereby English
bishops transmitted the 'Apostolic Succession' to their Scottish
brethren.

1606.   *Restitution of the estate of bishops*

Oure soverane lord, now in his absens furth of his kingdome
of Scotland, ernestlie desyring sa to provyde for the just
and politique government of that estait as his faithfull
subjectis thairof may perfytlie knaw that absens breidis nocht
in his royall mind oblivioun of thair gude bot that he is
daylie mair and mair cairfull of sic thingis as may tend
maist to the honour, proffitt and perpetuall stabilitie and
quietnes of the said kingdome, quhairin understanding
religioun and justice to be sa necessar fundamentis and

---

[1] The complement to this measure was the process of ' erecting ' the
temporal lands of abbacies into secular lordships, a process which went
ahead rapidly at this point, to the advantage of the nobility, who thus
secured hereditary possession of that which they had previously held
only as commendators.

pillaris as by thame the authoritie of the princes and quietnes
of the peopill in all tymes bypast hes cheiflie bene establischit
and mantenit quhill of lait in his majesteis young yeiris and
unsetlit estaitt the ancient and fundamentall policie consisting in the mantenance of the thrie estaittis of parliament
hes bene greatumlie imparit and almost subvertit, specialie
by the indirect abolischeing of the estait of bischoppis by
the Act of Annexatioun of the temporalitie of benefices to
the crowne maid in his hienes parliament haldin at Edinburgh in the moneth of Julii 1587, quhairby albeit it wes
nather menit by his majestie nor by his estaittis that the
said estait of bischoppis consisting of benefices of cure and
being ane necessar estait of the parliament suld onywayes
be suppressit, yit his majestie by experience of the subsequent
tyme hes cleirlie sene that the dismembering and abstracting
frome thame of thair levingis hes brocht thame in sic
contempt and povertie that they ar nocht hable to furneis
necessaris to thair privat familie, mekill less to beir the
charges of thair wonted rank in parliament and generall
counsaillis . . . : Thairfoir his majestie with express advyse
and consent of the saidis haill estaittis of parliament, being
cairfull to repone, restoir and redintegrat the said estait of
bischoppis to thair ancient and accustomed honour, digniteis, prerogatives, privilegis, livingis, landis, teyndis, rentis,
thriddis and estaitt, as the samyn wes in the reformit kirk
maist ample and frie at ony tyme befoir the act of annexatioun foirsaid, be the tennour heirof retreittis, rescindis,
reduces, cassis, abrogattis and annullis the foirsaid act of
annexatioun of the temporalitie of benefices to the crowne
maid in the yeir of God 1587.

A.P.S., iv, 281-2

1609. *Restoration of the bishops' consistorial jurisdiction*

Oure soverane lord, undirstanding that in all weill governed
republictis the jurisdictioun civill and ecclesiastik ar severall,
distinct and divers jurisdictiounes, whiche ocht to be
administrat by the persones to quhome the samin propirlie

belongis, and according to his highnes most loving and princelie affectioun borne alwayes to the Christiane reformed church within this realme being maist willing that the said churche sould brook and jois their liberteis, privileges, fredome and jurisdictioun granted unto them by his majestie (frome whom onlie thair temporall jurisdictioun doth flow) and in that regaird belonging to them as being ane of the estaitis of parliament most necessar to be mantenit for geving of thair advyse, counsaill and assistance in all his majesties great and weichtie affairis, hes with express advyse and consent of the estaitis restored and redintegrate the archibischoppis and bischoppis of this realme to thair former authoritie, dignitie, prerogative, privileges and jurisdictiounes lauchfullie pertening and shall be knawin to pertene to thame (always flowing from his majestie alsweill as ony uther ordinar jurisdictioun doth) and speciallie to the jurisdictioun of commissariatis and administratioun of justice by thair commissioneris and deputeis in all spirituall and ecclesiasticall causes controvertit betwene ony persones dwelling within the boundis and dioceses of thair prelaceis and bischopricks.

A.P.S., iv, 430

1610. *The Courts of High Commission*

In 1610 two Courts of High Commission were established, one for the province of St Andrews, the other for that of Glasgow. Each had a very large membership—bishops, peers, lairds and ministers —but a quorum of only five, of whom the archbishop was to be one. Their function was mainly to fortify the normal operation of ecclesiastical discipline as conducted by ministers and kirk sessions, with power to fine and imprison offenders, and they in their turn were to be supported by the Privy Council and the Court of Session ; but they were also to deal with ministers who made public speeches against ' the established order of the kirk or against any of the conclusions of the bypast general assemblies ' (Calderwood, vii, 57–62).

In 1615 a single court was substituted for the existing two, the presence of one or other of the archbishops being necessary in the

quorum of five. The Commission now referred not only to
' offenders in life and religion ' but to Jesuits and other recusants ;
and the clause relating to malcontents among the ministers was
altered to read ' the present established order of the kirk or estate,
against any of the conclusions of the bypast general assembly
holden at Glasgow, acts of parliament and specially the act of
parliament holden at Edinburgh in October 1612 ' [1] (Calderwood,
vii. 204–10).

1610. *Acts of the Glasgow Assembly*

Item, it is thought expedient that the Bischops salbe
Moderatours in every Diocesian Synod, and the Synods
salbe haldin twyse in the yeir of the kirks of every Dyocie,
viz. in Apryle and October. . . .

Item, that no sentence of excommunicatioun, or absolu-
tioun therfra, be pronouncit against or in favours of any
person without the knowledge and approbation of the
Bischop of the Dyocie, quho must be ansuerable to his
Majestie for all formall and unpartial proceidings therin. . . .

Item, that all presentatiouns be direct heirafter to the
Bischop ; and upon any presentatioun givin, or utherwayes
sute made be any to be admittit to the Ministrie, the
Bischop is to requyre the Ministers of these bounds quher
he is to serve, to certifie by thair testificat unto him of the
partie suter his conversatioun past, and abilitie, and qualificatioun for the functioun : and upon the returne of thair
testificat, the Bischop is to take farther tryall ; and finding
him qualified, and being assisted be such of the Ministrie
of the bounds quher he is to serve, as he will assume to
himselfe, he is then to perfyte the haill act of ordinatioun.

Item, in depositioun of Ministers, the Bischop associating
to himselfe the Ministrie of these bounds quher the delin-
quent served, he is then to take tryall of his fault, and, upon
just cause found, to depryve him.

Item, the visitatioun of ilk dyocie is to be done be the
Bischop himselfe . . . And quhatever Minister, without
just cause and laufull excuse made, sall absent himselfe from

---

[1] i.e. the act ratifying episcopal government

the visitation of the Diocesan Assembly, he salbe suspendit from his office and benefice, and, if he amend not, he salbe deprivit.

Item, the Bischops salbe subject, in all things concerning thair lyfe, conversatioun, office, and benefice, to the censures of the Generall Assemblie ; and being found culpable, with his Majesties advyce and consent, to be deprivit.

B.U.K., iii, 1096-7

The acts of the Assembly of 1610 were ratified by Parliament in 1612 (*A.P.S.*, iv, 469-70), and in 1617 cathedral chapters were formally restored to their duties and revenues (ibid., iv, 529). With these measures, which were James VI's final contribution to ecclesiastical polity, it had come about that all those parts of the structure of the Church which had formerly belonged to the secular clergy passed into the possession of the ministers. The abbey property, at least for the most part, was still outwith their grasp, and the recovery of the monastic spirituality for the Reformed Church was to be the work of Charles I.

JAMES VI's LITURGICAL POLICY

Initially the Scottish reformers had made use of the second Prayer Book of Edward VI, but a rival to it soon appeared in the Book of Common Order. That book, previously used by Knox when he ministered to the congregation of English exiles which had assembled at Geneva in Mary Tudor's reign, was commended in the first Book of Discipline, and, after being reprinted in Scotland, was prescribed by the General Assembly—in 1562 for the sacraments and two years later for the ' common prayers ' as well. While less distinctly liturgical than the Book of Common Prayer, the Book of Common Order was no mere directory, and it was constantly affirmed that the ' *reading* of common prayers ' was a part of public worship. (For an examination of the whole of this subject, see vol. ii, 2nd edn., 210.)

The Book of Common Order maintained its official position for eighty years. Yet, on the one hand, it did not wholly displace the Prayer Book, which, as time went on, found increasing favour with some of the episcopalian party and, after 1603, with many of the Scots who formed close contacts with England ; on the other hand, the presbyterians tended to fall under the sway of English puritan thought, which was rigidly opposed to the Prayer Book and later rejected much that the Scottish reformers had preserved. There was a good deal of unofficial experiment, in deviation from the Book of Common Order.

A movement for revision of the Book of Common Order had been active since at least 1601 (when the General Assembly raised the question), if indeed it cannot be dated from 1584, when there had been talk of ' a uniform order in common prayer.' The king's serious consideration of liturgical matters was deferred until after his completion of his reform of church government in 1612. From that point two series of measures can be traced. One was concerned with the restoration of practices which had been universal before the Reformation and which had been retained by some other protestant churches, but which had been laid aside in Scotland. The king's first concern (in 1614) was for the observance of Easter, later for that of some other holy days in the Christian year—a matter which did not encounter serious opposition, for no part of the reformers' programme had been less effective than their attempt to suppress the observance of the festivals. Equally, his proposal for recognition of private administration of Baptism and Holy Communion was in accord with practice already existing in some places. He gave his attention also to provision for the examination and blessing of children by bishops on their visitations—the equivalent of Confirmation. By far his most controversial proposal was that communicants should kneel when they received the Sacrament, and when all his requirements took shape in the Five Articles of Perth it was this last one which aroused most hostility. An assembly of clergy at St. Andrews at the end of 1617 rejected his proposals, and they were forced through the Perth assembly in the following year only with difficulty.

Concurrently, the question of a revised liturgy had been under consideration. In 1616 a new draft of a Sunday morning service had been compiled by a committee appointed by the General Assembly, and in 1618 there was a second draft, now of an entire Prayer Book. This liturgy was a compromise between the Book of Common Order and the Book of Common Prayer, and in more favourable conditions might have been well received. As it was, the storm raised by the Five Articles made consideration of any new service book on its merits quite impossible.

For the sake of his Five Articles, James sacrificed the project of liturgical revision. It seems that in 1621, when the Five Articles came before Parliament, he gave an undertaking that if they were accepted he would make no further innovations, and he kept his word. A licence to print the new liturgy had been issued, but the book remained unprinted. As James, who, as he said, 'knew the stomach of that people,' had retreated, and as the bishops generally did not press the Five Articles, the indications were that the Church would settle down under a moderate regime, and the close of the reign saw the Church substantially at peace.

1618. *The Five Articles of Perth*

[*On 21 October 1618 the Acts of the General Assembly held at Perth in the preceding August were ratified by the Privy Council, and on 26 October the ratification was proclaimed at the Market Cross of Edinburgh.*]

James, by the grace of God, etc.

Forsameikle as in the Generall Assemblie of the Kirk, holden latelie at our burgh of Perth, in the moneth of August last bypast, which was countenanced by the presence and assistance of certane commissioners for us, and of diverse noblemen, barons, and commissioners from the cheefe and principall burrowes of this our kingdome, there were certane godlie and good acts made and sett doun, concerning the glorie of God and governement of his church, agreeable to that decent and comelie order which was observed in the primitive kirk, when the same was in the greatest puritie and perfection ; as namelie,

An act ordaining, that everie minister sall have the commemoration of the inestimable benefites received from God by and through our Lord and Saviour Jesus Christ his Birth, Passion, Resurrection, Ascension, and sending doun of the Holie Ghost, upon the days appointed for that use ; and that they sall make choice of severall and pertinent texts of Scripture, and frame their doctrine and exhortation

63

thereto, and rebuke all superstitious observation and licentious profanation of the said dayes :

An act anent the administration of baptisme in privat houses, when the necessitie sall require :

An act anent the catechizing of young children of eight yeers of age, and presenting them to the bishop to lay hands upon them, and blesse them, with prayer for increase of their knowledge, and continuance of God's heavenlie graces with them :

An act anent the administration and giving of the Holie Communion in private houses to sicke and infirme persons :

An act, that the blessed sacrament of the Holie Communion of the bodie and blood of our Lord and Saviour Jesus Christ be celebrate to the people humblie and reverentlie kneeling upon their knees :

[*And other acts cited*]

Which acts being seene and considered by us, and we finding that the same has beene verie wiselie, gravelie, and with good deliberation, made and sett doun for the weill of the kirk : Therefore we, out of our true respect to the honour of God, and to have him honoured by all our people, has by our authoritie royall, with the advice of the Lords of our Privie Counsell, ratified, allowed, approven, and confirmed, and by the tenor of this our present act ratifies, allowes, approves, and confirmes the acts particularlie above writtin, in all and sundrie points, clauses, heads, articles, and conditions therof ; and ordains the same to have the force and strength of lawes in all time coming, and to have effect and execution in all places of this our kingdome. And in speciall, that there sall be a cessation and abstinence from all kinde of labour and handie-worke upon the five dayes above written, which are appointed to be dedicate to God's service, to the effect our subjects may the better attend the holie exercises which are to be keeped in the kirks at these times. . . . Certefying [*that all those who do not observe the acts and who do not abstain from labour upon the five days mentioned*] sall be repute, holden, and esteemed as seditious, factious, and unquyett persons, disturbers of the peace and quyet of the kirk, contemners of our just and royall commandement, and sall be punished therefor in their persons and goods with all rigour and extremitie to the terrour of others, at the arbitrement of the Lords of our Privie Counsel. . . .

Given under our signet, at Halyrudhouse, the 21st day of October, and of our raigne the 16 and 52 yeers, 1618.

Calderwood, vii, 337–9 ; *A.P.S.*, iv, 596–7

CHAPTER TWO

THE POLICY OF CHARLES I AND THE
FIRST COVENANTING PERIOD

THE ACT OF REVOCATION AND THE SETTLEMENT
OF THE TEINDS

There were three statesmanlike reasons for entering on a settlement of the problems of ecclesiastical organisation and endowment bequeathed to Charles I by his father : (i) There were the needs of crown finance, reflected in the constant and increasing taxation.[1] (ii) The one source from which ministers' stipends could be augmented was the spirituality of the abbeys, now held by the lords of erection and other ' titulars ' and increasingly confused with land rent. (iii) An arrangement which would substitute a fixed proportional payment, in money or in kind, for the actual exaction by the titulars or their agents of a tenth of the produce would be in the interests of the heritors or farmers, at present prejudiced by the need to leave crops on the ground until teinding had taken place. Such an arrangement had been craved by the compilers of the first Book of Discipline, who held that every man should have his own teinds, and the same words were now used by the king : ' His Majestie desyris that the grite disordouris and incommodities ariseing about teyndis may be redressed by procureing (als far as his Majestie can laughfullie doe) that everie man may haif his awne teyndis upoun reasounable conditionis . . . that the saidis teyndis may no longer be (as they haif bene heirtofore) the cause of bloode, oppressionis, enmities and of enforced dependencies, and manie tymes by untymelie teynding a meanis to ruine the stock, to the grite damage of the whole kingdome.' [2] Behind and above these motives of expediency lay what were guiding principles with Charles—the wellbeing and dignity of the Church, and a conception of the sanctity of property originally devoted to its maintenance which had been paralleled only in the sweeping claims of the second Book of Discipline.

[1] See *infra*, pp. 290 *et seq.*   [2] *R.P.C.*, 2nd. ser., i, 228-9

A revocation according to the usual practice [1] was issued by the king first in July 1625, and, in a fuller form, in the following October.[2] In January 1626 the king intimated that his policy was directed towards the settlement of the teinds and the avoidance of taxation,[3] and on 11 July 1626 there came from him the following communication, expressly restricting the scope of the revocation and inviting voluntary surrenders of the properties affected.

1626.

Howsoever we haif maid our revocatioun after the maner that our praedicessouris had formarlie done, we doe certifie and declair by these praesentis that we doe intend to mak no benefite thairof by extending it ony further then onlie aganis the erectionis and other dispositionis whatsomevir of landis, teyndis, patronageis, benefices, formarlie belonging to the Churche and since annexed to the Crowne, and of other landis and patronages whiche onywayes sould justlie belong to the Churche or Crowne, and aganis dispositionis of lands and benefices mortified and divoted to pious uses, and of regalities and heretable offices, and aganis the change of holdingis since the yeir of God [1540] from the ancient tenour of warde and releiff to blenshe and taxt warde. As for other particularis, though we might in law mak advantage of thame, yitt it is noway oure purpois, bot rather we will confirme the formar rightis of suche as sall stand in neid thairof ; and it is more for the publict goode then for our awne benefite that we ar moved to seik the annulling of all suche grantis abone named whiche ar derogatorie to oure crowne and pracrogative royall. And though we might laughfullie doe this without ony respect at all to the harme that may arrise thairby to the praesent possessouris who haif unjustlie acquired the same, yit, being loathe that ony of our good subjectis who will within the tyme praefixt accept of reasoun sould haif caus by our meanis to suffer or complayne, and to the effect that all suche as will voluntarlie

---

[1] See vol. ii, 2nd. edn., 34   [2] *R.P.C.*, 2nd. ser., i, 81–2, 193
[3] Ibid., 228–9

surrender ony right they haif of the nature foirsaid betuix
and the first day of Januar nixt ensueing the date heirof
may haif some reasounable compositioun for the samine,
we haif appoyntit commissionaris to treate with thame
thairupoun, who hathe power from us bothe to treate and
aggree with thame, and to dispose of suche teyndis as ar
recovered for our use (the churches being planted and
schooles and the poore provydit for) to the heretouris of
the ground from whence the teyndis ar drawne at such a
rate as thay sall think expedient, as by the commissioun
gevin for that purpois may appeare.

R.P.C., 2nd ser., i, 352

After a month, during which no surrenders were reported, the
king proceeded to raise an action of reduction, whereby the
existing charters of kirk lands would be annulled at the
instance of the king, as ' having good and undoubted right to all
kirk lands within this kingdom by act of annexation, as being
universal patron of all abbacies, priories and all other ecclesiastical
benefices by the right of our crown, and being obliged by our oath
to be given by us at our coronation . . . to maintain the hail lands
and rents pertaining to the crown and kirk within the said kingdom.' [1]

This threat of legal action had the effect of producing a petition
for a fresh commission to receive surrenders, and on 3 February
1627 there was issued such a commission, extracts from which
follow.

Proclamation of commission for surrenders

CHARLES [*etc.*] Forsamekle as we being of late humbly
petitioned by a great number of our nobilitie and gentrie
of this our ancient kingdome of Scotland desiring a competent number of commissioners to bee appoynted to conveene
and treate of all that may concerne our profite and patrimonie within our said kingdome, whereby such lawfull
meanes may be advised as may give all reasonable satisfaction to our just desires and supplie to our patrimonie

[1] R.P.C., 2nd. ser., i, 398n

and affaires extraordinarlie important in these difficult
times, as the said petition at more length proports ; and
wee being willing to take a faire course with all such of our
loving subjects of our said kingdome as shall before the
expiration of this our commission (which wee do hereby
speciallie appoynt to begin to sit upon the first daye of
March next ensewing . . .) voluntarilie treate with our
commissioners after-mentioned concerning the erections and
temporalities of benefices, superiorities, few dueties, or other
certaine rent of silver or victuall of the said temporalities,
teynds, and patronages of the said benefices, mortified
landes and rents, heritable offices and regalities, changed
tenours or holdings, and taxt wardes, propertie and casualities of our crowne or principalitie, unlawfullie acquired or
possessed by any of them, and yet fitting to bee secured
unto the present possessours thereof upon reasonable conditions, and concerning what compositions shall be given by
the said possessours unto us for new rights of the said
patrimonie or propertie : Therefore wee, for freeing of our
said subjects from their preposterous feares causleslie conceived upon our late revocation, and from the unnecessarie
charges which they might perhaps sustaine either by repairing unto our person or by our persueing of our right and
title to the premises by due course of law, have nominat
and appoynted . . . the persons after-mentioned . . . with
full power to them . . . or any twelve of them . . . provyding that there bee three of the said number of twelve of
the nobilitie, three of the bishops, three of the gentrie, and
three of the burgesses, to treate, deale, compone, transact,
and aggrie with such person or persons as shall at any time
heereafter before the expiration of this our commission bee
contented to treate, aggrie and modifie suche reasonable
satisfaction for the said erections and temporalities of
benefices [etc.] unlawfullie acquired or possessed by any of
them and yet fitting to be secured unto the present possessours of the said propertie upon reasonable conditions,
as said is ; and concerning what composition shall be given
by the said proprietars and possessours unto us for securing

6

their titles of such of the premisses as are fitte for them to hold in all time coming ; . . . and with power to our saide commissionars . . . to make sufficient provision for those churches whereof the teynds shall be resigned or disponed as aforesaid, if the saide churches bee not already sufficiently provided, and for provyding of their ministers with sufficient locall stipendes and fies, and to treat, conclude and aggree upon such pious use, and for establishing of such schooles in the remote places of our said kingdome as shall bee by them . . . thought expedient. And also with power and authoritie to our saids commissioners, or any twelve of them as said is, to call and convene before them the immediat heritours, tackesmen, and possessours of all such lands out of which the teynds so to bee treated for by the parties are led or otherwise payed, and to advise for them such new lawfull rights and securities of the said teynds as they shall thinke fit, and for such compositions and yeerely dueties to bee reserved to us as our said commissioners . . . and the said parties shall aggree upon. . . .

And, to the effect that all parties interest in any of the premisses may take notice of our gracious disposition and intention towards them, and that they may have due warning to prepare and provyde themselves for the better buying of their owne teynds and for settling of the securities of thair lands, Our Will is . . . that . . . yee passe and in our name and authoritie make publicatioun and intimatioun hereof . . . that thereby notice may be given to all our said subjects who pretend any right to any of the particulares above-mentioned that wee have appointed the said commissioners . . . ; with further certification that, incace the proprietares or tacksmen or rentallers of lands [doe] not come in and aggree with our said commissioners before the expiration of this our commission for their owne teynds to bee secured unto them, that then and in that cace wee shall further secure the same unto the parties now having titles thereto for suche a reasonable yeerely rent to our crowne as our said commissioners shall appoint or thinke expedient . . . ; and with further intimation that

it is not our intention or pleasure to quarrell or annull any
of the confirmed fewes or other lawfull rights of any of the
lands of the temporalities of benefices formally set by the
ancient titulars thereof without diminution of the rentalls,
or fewes granted by our dearest lord and father of worthie
memorie unto any of the Lords of Erections before their
erections without diminutioun of the rentall, nor fewes
formarly *bona fide* bought by any of the Lords of Erections
or by any others from them before our late revocation from
any heritour thereof without diminution of the rentall, nor
yet to quarrell or annull any of the fewes set by the said
Lord[s] of Erections before the dait of our late Revocation
. . . unto any of their owne vassels without diminution of
the rentall ; provyding alwayes that the immediate superioritie and few dueties of the same may bee lawfully divolved
and established upon us and our successors by resignation
or otherwise as shall be thought most meet.   As also that
it is our expres pleasure and intention that the mansion
places, circuits, orchards and gardens of all the said
abbacies, priories, nunries, colledges, hospitalls and etc.
shall be fewed unto such of the Lords of Erection as now
are in present and actuall possession thereof, without any
other composition then a very small few duety, to be a
testimony that the same are holden of us immediatly.

R.P.C., 2nd ser., i, 509-14

Shortly afterwards (11 April and 29 May 1627), intimation was
made of the readiness of the Crown to facilitate the settlement of
the teinds by buying them from the titulars and disposing them to
the heritors, and of the decision that the Crown should receive a
specified annuity from most of the teinds except those drawn by
bishops and ministers.[1]   The submissions which came in to the
commission were in 1628 reduced to the form of four documents in
each of which a group of persons undertook to accept the king's
decision as to the properties affected by the revocation : (1) By the
lords of erection, titulars, tacksmen and gentry, heritors of lands,
agreeing to accept terms for the feu-duties of their superiorities

[1] *R.P.C.*, 2nd. ser., i, Intro. cxc, cxcii

and for the teinds which they drew from other men's lands ; (2) By the bishops and clergy, agreeing to accept composition for the teinds due to them from heritors ; (3) By the burghs, agreeing to accept composition for teinds due to them from heritors ; and (4) By certain tacksmen and others having right to teinds, accepting the king's decision as to a means of denuding themselves of their teinds in favour of the heritors.[1] The king's decisions on the submissions thus made to him, contained in decreets arbitral dated 2 September 1629,[2] were in 1633 incorporated in acts of parliament, extracts from which follow.

1633. *The Kings General Revocatione*

Forsomuch as oure soverane lord the kings Majestie, . . . following the laudable custome used befor by his Majesties predicessors in making of thair revocationes, did upon the twelf day of October 1625 mak and give furth his generall revocatione under his privie seale, as the same in the selff at more lenth beares :

And his Majestie being now present in his royall persone within this kingdome and having by Gods grace, favour and blessing and with the generall acclamatione, joy and comfort of his subjects, accepted the crowne thairof, quhairin he is gloriouslie inaugurate, and now holding the first parliament of his whole estates of the said kingdome, with quhome his Majestie haith advysed and resolved anent the said revocatioun :

Thairfor his Majestie, with consent of the thrie estates and whole bodie of this present parliament, haith statuite, enacted and ordanit and by these presents statuites, enactes and ordaines in maner following :—

[*After revoking grants made from the Principality of Scotland and from the lordship of Dunfermline, grants made contrary to Acts of Annexation, and other grants in prejudice of the Crown ;*] his Majestie with consent of the estates revokes, casses, annulls, retreats and rescinds all grants and infeftments of erectiones of quhatsumevir abbacie or uther prelacie in whole or in pairt, temporalitie or spiritualitie thairof, maid and grantit

---

[1] *A.P.S.*, v, 189 *et seq.*   [2] Ibid., 198 *et seq.*

or consented unto by his Majestie at any tyme preceeding the dait heirof to and in favours of quhatsumevir persone or persones and declares the same null and of nane availl by way of actione, exceptione or reply ; and als his Majestie and estates revoke all infeftments of erectiones maid and grantit by . . . any his Majesties predicessors kings or queines of Scotland of quhatsumever abbacie, priorie, nunrie, preceptorie or any uther erected benefice quhatsum-ever of quhatsumever nature qualitie or conditione quhairof the presentatione sould pertein to his Majestie if the same wer not erected in a temporall baronie, lordschip or leving, or of any pairt or pendicle thairof ather spiritualitie or temporalitie of the same to and in favours of quhatsumevir persone or persones and that in soe far as the same is or may be verrified to be grantit against the generall lawes and acts of parliament of the kingdome.

A.P.S., v, 23–6

Anent Annexatione of his Majesties Propertie

. . . Attoure his Majestie with consent forsaid declares the richt and title of superioritie of all and sundrie lands, baronies, mylnes, wodes, fishings, towers, fortalices, manour places and whole pertinents thairof perteining to quhat-sumever abbacies, pryories, pryoressis, preceptories and quhatsumever uther benefices of quhatsumever estate degrie title name or designatione the same be of, erected in temporall lordschipes, baronies or livings befor or eftir the generall act of annexatione of kirklands maid in the moneth of Julii 1587 yeirs, togither with the whole few maills, few fermes and other rents and dewties of the saids superiorities, to be annexed and to remaine with the crowne for ever ; reserving to such lords and titulars of erectiones and each one of thame who have subscryved the generall surrander the few maills and few fermes of thair said superiorities ay and quhyle they receave payment and satisfactione of the soume of ane thousand merkes usuall money of Scotland for each chalder of few ferme victuall overhead and for

each hundreth merks of few maills and for each hundreth
marks worth of all uther constant rent of the saids superiorities not consisting in victuall or money and not being
naked service of vassalles, according to the tennor of his
Majesties generall determinatione and according to the
conditiones thairin exprest ; and reserving to thame and
to all uthers titulars of erectione thair propertie and propper
lands, to be holdin of his Majestie and his successors in few
ferme for payment of the few ferme dewties and other
dewties contenit in the old infeftments maid to thame, thair
predicessors and authors befor the said act of annexatione. . . .

A.P.S., v, 27

Anent his Majesties Annuitie of Teinds

Oure soverane Lord and estates of parliament ratifies and
approves the act of the generall commissioun of teinds and
surranders of the dait at Holyrudhous [29 May 1627]
whairby it is fund and ordanit that his Majestie and his
successors sall have the constant rent and dewtie following
payed out of the teind bolles of victuall and out of the bodie
of the rest of the teinds of the kingdome redacted in money,
except the teind bolles and silver payit to the bischops being
the rent perteining to thame in the estait quhairin the same
is presentlie payit or presentlie payable to thame and except
the teind bolles and silver payit to ministers in name of
stipend for serving the cure, and to the colledges, hospitalls
and other pious uses : that is to say of everie teind boll of
the best quheat ten schillings of everie boll, of the best teind
bear aucht schillings, and of everie boll of the best teind
oates, meale, peise and ry sax schillings ; and quhair oates
ar of that nature that they will not rander abone half meale
the rent to be thrie schillings ; and quhair the bolles of
victuall ar of inferiour goodnes worth and pryce nor the
best, that his Majesties annuitie furth thairof sall be modifiet
proportionallie ; and quhair the rent doeth not consist in
victuall bot in money, that his Majestie and his successors

sall have of everie hundreth merkes of parsonage and
viccarage teind not consisting in victuall rent the soume of
sax markes money. . . .

A.P.S., v, 32

Anent the Rate and Pryce of Teinds

His Majestie with consent of the thrie estates by these
presents statuites, ordaincs and declares that thair sall be
no teind scheaves or other teinds personage or viccarage
led and drawin within the kingdome bot that each heretor
and lyfrentar of lands sall have the leiding and drawing of
thair awin teind, the same being first trewlie and lawfullie
valued, and they paying thairfor the pryce eftir specifiet in
caice they be willing to buy the same, or otherwayes paying
thairfor the rate of teind eftirspecifiet :

Lyk as his Majestie and estates find and declair that the
just and trew rate of teinds is and sall be the fyft pairt of
the constant rent which each land payeth in stock and teind
quhair the same ar valued jointlie, and quhair the teinds
ar valued a pairt and severallie that the just rate thairof is
and sall be such as the same is alreadie or sall be heireftir
valued and proved befor the saids commissioners or sub-
commissioners, deduicing the fyft pairt thairof for the ease
of the heretors ; . . .

: And also his Majestie with consent of the thrie estates
finds and declares that the pryce of all teinds which may
be sold and annalied, consisting ather in money, victuall or
other bodies of goodes, is and sall be rewled and estimat
according to nyne years purchase . . . and . . . that each
heretor in the kingdome being willing to buy his awin teind
frome the titulars having power to sell the same sall be
obliged to buy the teinds of his awin lands except soe much
as sall be locallie assigned to the minister serving the curc
of the kirk for his maintenance, and to pay the pryces
forsaids [*within two years after valuation by the Commissioners on
Teinds, after the expiry of which time the titulars are not compelled
to sell*].

A.P.S., v, 34–5

75

Commissione for Valuatione of Teinds

. . . His Majestie and estates forsaids have ratified the act of commissione of surranders and teinds of the dait at Holyrudhous the twentie saxt day of June 1627 yeirs, whairby it is fund meit and expedient that the lowest proportione for maintenance of ministers sall be aucht chalder of victuall or aucht hundreth markes proportionallie except such particular kirks occure whairin thair sall be a just, reassonable and expedient caus to goe beneath the forsaid quantitie . . . [*and reciting the foregoing act on the valuation and sale of teinds*] . . . and forasmuch as it is necessarie for determinatione of the particulars forsaids and of all such other pointes which ar fitt and expedient for the finisching and full perfectione of the said glorious worke anent the teinds, maintenance of ministers and others forsaids . . . Thairfor his Majestie . . . haith grantit . . . commissione to the persones eftir following . . . to prosecute and fallow furth the valuatione of quhatsumever teinds . . . which ar as yett unvalued . . . ; to appoint, modifie and sett downe a constant and locall stipend and maintenance to ilk minister to be payit out of the teinds of ilk parochine . . . ; to divide ample and spatious parochines . . . or to unite divers kirks in whole or in pairt to others . . . ; to appoint and provyde for such other pious uses in each parochin as the estate thairof may bear ; and siclyk with power to the saids commissioners as said is to tak order that everie heretor and lyfrentar of lands sall have the leiding of thair awin teinds parsonages and viccarages thairof, they paying the pryce contenit in the act abonespecifiet in caice they be willing to buy the same frome the titular having power to sell or otherwayes paying the rate of teind exprest in the forsaid act . . . ; to discusse and determine all questiones which may arise betuixt the titulars and heretors anent the pryce of teinds . . . ; and generallie with power to the saids commissioners to decide and determine in all other pointes which may concerne the leiding and drawing of teinds, the selling and buying of the same, or payment of

the rate thairof contenit in the actes of parliament abonespecifiet or sett downe in his Majesties generall determinatione. . . .

A.P.S., v, 35–8

THE GRIEVANCES OF THE NOBLES

Charles had provided machinery whereby the teinds could be
made available for stipend, and had regularised the whole position
of the ecclesiastical property. But he did it at great cost. A
revocation was no novelty, but the uncommonly comprehensive
scope of this measure of Charles made it affect almost every land-
holder in the country, while the secrecy which at first surrounded
the king's proceedings was the opportunity for exaggerated
rumours. On 17 November 1625 the Privy Council protested to
the king that ' nothing hes at ony tyme heirtofore occurrit whilk
hes so far disquyeted the myndis of your goode subjectis and
possest thame with apprehensionis and feares of the consequences
thairof, as if all thair formair securiteis grantit be your majestie
and your royall progenitouris were thairby intendit to be annullit.'[1]
Later, the threatened action of reduction aroused alarm, and,
while the nobles did not in practice lose their lands, the initial
fears about the king's intentions, far from being allayed, remained
acute. As the settlement finally took shape, the nobles were
denuded of their teinds and were to be deprived of their feu-duties
if the crown chose to redeem them ; compensation was to be given,
but they stood to lose the power and influence over heritors and
ministers which they had formerly possessed. The king, in a later
apologia for his proceedings, remarked of the nobles that ' They
fretted for being robbed, as they conceived, of the clientele and
dependence of the clergy and laity, and of that power, command
and superiority over them which by that tie of tithes they had
enjoyed.'[2]

The king's policy in Council and Parliament was a further source
of grievance and apprehension, centred in part around the emi-
nence accorded to the bishops. In the list of members of the new
Privy Council in 1626, Archbishop Spottiswoode's name took
precedence even of the chancellor's, and in 1635 Spottiswoode was
himself advanced to the office of chancellor—a position which had

---

[1] *R.P.C.*, 2nd. ser., i, 193   [2] *Large Declaration* (1639), 9

been in lay hands since the Reformation and which meant the
virtual premiership of Scotland. Again, while the king had made
an attempt to recall the old hereditary peers to the Privy Council,
they had not responded, and in this reign the bishops began to play
a more conspicuous part as councillors than they had done
for some time past.

Disquiet over the Crown policy in Parliament emerged in an
acute form in 1633, when the king forbade separate meetings of
the estates for informal discussion of the legislative programme
and personally noted the speeches and votes of members. There
was objection to the royal control, through the bishops, of the
composition of the Committee of Articles, to the exclusive powers
of that body in directing legislation and to the lack of opportunity
to consider acts before they were put to the vote.[1] A 'Supplication' incorporating these complaints was directed specially against
an act referring the apparel of churchmen to the royal prerogative,
and clearly anticipated the combination of constitutional and
ecclesiastical grievances which was later to be conspicuous in the
National Covenant. The 'Supplication' was never received by
the king, but it resulted in the trial of Lord Balmerino, one of the
'Supplicants'—an episode which suggested that the king would
disregard any attempt by an opposition to state its case. By 1636
the country was swept by extravagant rumours as to the king's
intentions, and the inflammable state of opinion is reflected in the
account of Scotland written by Sir William Brereton, an English
visitor. The concern of the Scottish nobles was for their property
and their constitutional rights.

1633. *Anent his Majesties royall prerogative and apparell of
Kirkmen*

Our soverane Lord, with advyse, consent and assent of the
whole estaites acknowledging his Majesties soveraigne
authoritie, princelie power, royall prerogative and priviledge of his crowne over all estaites, persones and causes
quhatsumevir within this kingdome, ratifies and approves
the act of parliament maid in the yeir 1606 anent the kings
royall prerogative, and perpetuallie confirmes the same for
his hienes, his airs and successors, als amplie, absolutelie

[1] See *infra*, pp. 234-5

and frielie in all respectis as ever any of his Majesties royall
progenitors did possess and exercise the same ; and withall
remembring that in the act of parliament maid in the yeir
1609 anent the apparell of judges, magistrats and kirkmen
it was agried that quhat order soever his Majesties father
of blissed memorie sould prescryve for the apparell of
kirkmen and sent in writte to his clerke of register sould be
a sufficient warrand for inserting the samen in the bookes
of parliament to have the strength of ane act thairof, have
all consented that the same power sall remaine with the
persone of oure soverane lord and his successors that now
is. . . .

A.P.S., v, 20–1

[For the use made by the king of the powers given to him by this
Act, see infra, p. 87.]

1634. *Supplication relating to the King's Proceedings*

To the king's most excellent majesty, the humble
supplication of a great number of the nobility and
other commissioners in the late parliament,

Humbly sheweth, That the notes which your majesty put
upon the names of a number of your supplicants in voting
about these acts which did imply a secret power to innovate
the order and government long continued in the Reformed
Church of Scotland, and your majesty's refusing to receive
from some of your supplicants their reasons for dissenting
from the said acts, before your majesty and in your hearing
in parliament, to [sc. does] breed a fear of our becoming
obnoxious unto your majesty's dislike if your highness
should still remain unacquainted with the reasons of our
opinions delivered concerning the said acts : seeing your
supplicants are confident . . . that no want of affection to
your majesty's service, but a careful endeavour to conserve
unto your majesty the hearty affections of a great many of
your good subjects that are tender in these points of
novation covertly thrust upon this church, did induce our

79

wishes and voices to appear in opposition to the said
acts ; . . .

First, we humbly beseech your majesty to consider that
though these acts as they are conceived and may concern
your majesty's prerogatives and the liberties of the church
had never been moved or concluded (as they are), your
majesty would have suffered no prejudice in your benefit,
honour nor power ; . . . that in deliberation about matters
of importance, either in councils or parliaments, opinions
do often differ, and they that have been of contrary mind
to a resolution carried by the plurality of votes have never
hitherto been censured by a prince of so much justice and
goodness as your majesty.

We do also most humbly beseech your majesty to believe
that all your supplicants do, in most submissive manner,
acknowledge your royal prerogative in as ample manner as
is contained in the Article 1606 made thereanent, and withal
do consider that the long experience and incomparable
knowledge your royal father had in matters of government,
as well in church as in commonwealth, is the very cause
expressed in the act 1609 for giving power to his majesty
to prescribe apparel to kirk-men, with their own consent.
And since in all the time of his life and government for the
space of 16 years thereafter he did forbear to make any
change upon their former habits, we are bold to presume
that in his great wisdom he thought fit that the apparel used
in time of divine service ever since the Reformation of
religion till his death, and to this day, should be continued,
as decent in the church and most agreeable to the minds
of his good subjects in this nation.

We do also beseech your majesty to consider, That under
the act intitled, ' A ratification of the liberty of the church ',
the acts ratifying the assembly of Perth in parliament 1621
were declared to be comprehended ; that most part of us
being then in parliament did oppose the same ; that
experience hath shewed how much these articles of Perth
have troubled the peace of this church and occasioned
innumerable evils and distractions in it ; that there is now

a general fear of some novations intended in essential points of religion ; and that this apprehension is much increased by the reports of allowance given in England for printing books of popery and Arminianism, and the restraint of answers made to them ; and by preaching Arminianism in this country without censure. . . .

That the minds of most of your good people being in this perplexity, your supplicants have great reason to suspect a snare in the subtle junction of the act 1609, concerning apparel, with that of 1606, anent your royal prerogative ; which by a sophistical artifice should oblige us either to vote undutifully in the sacred point of prerogative or unconscionably in church novations, which blessed King James would never have confounded. . . .

We do therefore dis-assent from the foresaid acts, as importing a servitude upon this church unpractised before, and giving ground for introduction of other new indefinite devices.

We do further offer unto your majesty's consideration, That albeit our just and heavy grievances allowed of in the late convention of estates 1625, and 1630, to have been represented to your majesty, in hopes of refreshment to the country's sufferings, have been altogether slighted in this your first parliament ; albeit your majesty denying your nobility their freedom by authority to meet with the Lords of the Articles, may seem against the constitution of a free parliament . . . which before the parliament held in anno 1609 did always elect and chuse the Lords of the Articles from among them of their own rank and quality ; there having been no parliamentary bishops from the reformation of religion till then, nor were they such as now do cull and single out such noblemen either popishly affected in religion or of little experience in our laws, as having had their breeding abroad, and so none of the ablest to be upon our Articles, but fittest only for the clergy's mystical ends ; whereas the former practice was such as seemeth most agreeable to reason, and what every estate should do, that so they may communicate their minds with the rest of their

81

body ; . . . albeit the meeting of the gentry, and happily [1] of the burrows too, in a joint purpose to have represented . . . things worthy your majesty's consideration, were in your majesty's name interrupted ; . . . yet have we all as one man consented to all your majesty's demands, and more, even to have taxations multiplied. . . .

Therefore we are confident that your majesty finding such a harmony in our affections to your service in preserving our religion and liberties, will be unwilling . . . to introduce upon the doctrine or discipline of this your Mother-Church anything not compatible with your majesty's honour, your good people's consciences, or that hath been rejected by acts and public practice of this Reformed Church.

Cobbett, *State Trials*, iii, 603–7 ; also, with variants, in Row, *History of the Kirk of Scotland* (Wodrow Soc.), 376–81

1636. *The state of opinion in Scotland*

In this kingdom the clergy of late extend their authority and revenues. [The archbishop] of St. Andrews is Lord Chancellor of Scotland and Regent here. And, as I was informed by some intelligent gentleman, it is here thought and conceived that they will recover so much of that land and revenues belonging formerly to the Abbeys as that they will in a short time possess themselves of the third part of the kingdom. The Duke of Lennox and Marquis Hamilton are possessed of the largest proportion of Church-land ; it is expected that they should resign and deliver up their interests and rights therein to the Church, whose example it is thought will induce the rest of the nobility to do the like. And to the end that they may carry some sway in Parliament, it is now endeavoured . . . to restore abbots, and to invest them in the revenues and seats of abbeys ; hereof they say there are forty-eight which are intended to be established, who are all to sit and carry voices in Parliament ; which, if it can be effected, then there will be

[1] i.e. haply

always in the parliament-house so strong a party for the king, considering those officers that have an immediate dependence upon him and the bishops and abbots, as that they will be able to sway the whole house.

Sir William Brereton, in Hume Brown, *Early Travellers in Scotland*, 137–8

CHARLES I's FINANCIAL POLICY, ESPECIALLY AS AFFECTING EDINBURGH

Not only was taxation becoming more regular, but the practice of taxing annual rents, initiated in 1621 and repeated in 1625, 1630 and 1633 (on the last occasion at a higher rate) affected a much larger proportion of the population than earlier taxes had done, more especially in the burghs.[1] The composition of £40,000 paid by Edinburgh for taxations voted in each of the years 1621, 1625 and 1630 was more than double the amount payable under the old method of taxation. In 1633 the composition was £60,000.

By that time Edinburgh was finding that other features of the king's policy were imposing a heavy burden on the city's finances. The idea that the Crown should itself bear the expense of buildings for the use of the Parliament and the central law courts had not yet emerged, and in 1632 Charles ordered Edinburgh to build a new Parliament House to accommodate parliaments, the Court of Session and other courts. A new tolbooth had been built as recently as Mary's reign, but it incorporated part of the church of St. Giles, for which the king had other designs, and it was no longer adequate for parliaments, the attendance at which, with the introduction of shire commissioners, fuller burgh representation and the creation of new peerages, had grown from about 67 in 1587 to about 170 in 1617. The site chosen for the new building was the ground which then sloped down from the church of St. Giles to the Cowgate and which was occupied partly by a graveyard and partly by three manses and their ' yards.' In order to provide a hall on the level of the present Parliament Square, there had to be elaborate and costly under-building (part of which, the ' Laich Parliament House,' may still be seen) ; and the manses

[1] See *infra*, pp. 293–4

had to be replaced. The total cost, from 1633 to 1640, was in the region of £127,000.

In 1633 came the king's visit, for which the burgh raised £40,000, and which so strained its finances that the £12,000 solemnly presented to the king on a silver basin at his state entry was borrowed money. Immediately afterwards Charles founded his new bishopric of Edinburgh, by a charter which also made Edinburgh a city and gave it formal recognition as the capital of the kingdom, besides ordaining that the kirk of St. Giles should become a cathedral. The preparation of the church as a fitting cathedral involved the demolition of the partitions which, since the Reformation, had divided it into three, the pulling down of the goldsmiths' shops which had been set up between the buttresses, and the provision of new accommodation for the congregations ousted from the old church. Two new kirks were projected, one of them at the Castlehill, but only that at the Tron was completed, at a cost, between 1636 and 1640, of over £14,000.

The period saw also the provision of increased stipends for the city ministers, by means of a new assessment on house rentals to the extent of 10,000 merks annually.

Between 1603 and 1625 burghal expenditure only once exceeded £51,000 ; after 1625 it was only once as low as that and in 1635-6 it reached nearly £150,000. Only twice between 1625 and 1636 was there a credit balance, and the deficit ran into five figures on three occasions. The city's debt in 1638 was £151,000.

When the revolt against Charles had succeeded, the abolition of episcopacy opened the way to supply the capital's financial needs, for Edinburgh received gifts of the revenues of the bishoprics of Orkney and Edinburgh. The former was intended to assist with ministers' stipends ; the latter was given for the ' Town's College,' or University, but on the ground of the expense incurred by the city in erecting a ' very costly ' Parliament House and in founding churches for divine worship, as well as in ' amplifying the academy of King James.'

See R. K. Hannay, ' The Building of the Parliament House,' in *Book of the Old Edinburgh Club*, xiii ; and *Extracts from the Records of the Burgh of Edinburgh*, 1626-41.

1633.   *Abstract of Charles I's charter founding the Bishopric of Edinburgh*

Charles [I] etc. Being determined out of kingly solicitude to advance the church within the realm of Scotland, and having received a petition from John, Archbishop of St. Andrews, that his diocese is wide and extensive and cut by the Firth of Forth which is often disturbed by tempest, storms and contrary winds, and that therefore he would crave to be relieved of the charge and burden of the churches to the south of the Forth ; and we calling to mind that our burgh of Edinburgh is the most prominent and the capital of all the burghs of our kingdom, and is in the diocese of St. Andrews and also on the south side of the Forth : THEREFORE we have decided to separate and disjoin the churches to the south of the Forth from the archbishopric of St. Andrews and from its jurisdiction, and to erect a new bishopric, diocese and jurisdiction ; and we do so separate and disjoin the whole churches and parishes within the sheriffdom of Edinburgh principal, the constabulary of Haddington, the sheriffdoms of Linlithgow, Stirling, and Berwick, and the bailiary of Lauderdale (but reserving all temporalities, all churches and teinds of parsonage and vicarage, and all rights of patronage to the Archbishop of St. Andrews and his successors), the which we erect into one whole bishopric, with all liberties and privileges and with full commissary jurisdiction (but reserving during their lifetime the offices and fees of the present commissaries of Edinburgh). And reflecting that Edinburgh should be the chief city of the newly erected bishopric : THEREFORE we erect Edinburgh into a CITY (without any prejudice to, or diminution of all its rights and liberties as a burgh) to be the principal and capital city of our realm and of the newly erected bishopric ; and we erect the Church of St. Giles into a Cathedral Church to be the Cathedral of the new Bishopric of Edinburgh ; the bishop of Edinburgh to enjoy all the honours and privileges of a diocesan bishop, to be suffragan to St. Andrews, and to have precedence immediately after the archbishops of St. Andrews and Glasgow and before any other of the bishops of Scotland. The chapter of the new bishopric to consist of a dean and twelve prebendaries, the chief minister of St. Giles to be the dean, and the chief ministers of Greyfriars, of Holy Trinity, of the south-east parish of Edinburgh, and of the churches of Holyroodhouse, Liberton, Tranent, Stirling, Falkirk, Linlithgow, Dalkeith, Haddington and Dunbar to be prebendaries. Moreover, to provide a patrimony and revenue for the bishop of Edinburgh we have endowed and mortified to the bishopric the temporalities within the precinct of Holyroodhouse, the superiorities of the barony of Dunrod, of the barony of Auldhame or White-kirk, and the teinds, parsonages and vicarages of twenty-three churches [all named] formerly pertaining to the Abbey of Holyroodhouse, together with the Abbey of New Abbey [Sweetheart] with all its lands, baronies, churches, teinds and patronages, its temporalities and spiritualities, together with other lands and superiorities [specified]—all to be united and annexed to the bishopric of Edinburgh in one free barony, with courts and the casualties thereof : the bishops of Edinburgh at their entry to render to us fealty and homage for the temporalities of the bishopric, to pay the stipends of the ministers of the churches named, and to make and do the duties of a faithful bishop.

R.M.S., 1620–33, No. 2225

CHARLES I's LITURGICAL POLICY [1]

In 1629 King Charles revived the project of liturgical revision which had been laid aside by his father ten years earlier. The Scottish bishops and clergy insisted that Scotland must have its own liturgy, distinct from that of England, while the king and his English Church advisers wanted the Scots to accept the English Prayer Book without modification ; and, owing to this tension, action was again deferred. The king's visit to Scotland, in 1633,

[1] On this subject, see G. Donaldson, *The Making of the Scottish Prayer Book of 1637.*

was made the opportunity to insinuate the use of the English Prayer Book and Anglican ceremonial, and at the same time the use of the surplice was enjoined.

1633.

The ordour appoyinted by his Majestie for the Apparrell off churchemen in Scotland, to be insert in the buiks off parliament conforme to the act off the late parliament maid thairanent.

It is our pleasure that all the lords Archbischops and Bischops within that our Kyngdome off Scotland sall in all publick places weare gownes with standing capes (such as they used at oure leite being there) and cassocks, And the inferiour clergie especiallie after they have taiken the degree off doctours or bachelours in divinitie or be preachours in any toune sall weare the same habite for faschioun bot for worth according to thair meanes, And no tippets unles they be doctours ; And furder our pleasoure is that the lords Arch-bischops and Bischops sall in all churches where they come in tyme of divine service or sermoun be in whytes, that is in a rochett and sleeves as they weare at the tyme off our coronatioun, And especiallie whensoever they administer the holy communioun or preach. And they sall lykewayes provide thame selffis a chymer (that is a sattyn or taffetie gowne without lyning or sleeves) to be worne over thair whytes at the tyme of thair consecratioun. And we will that all Archbischops and Bischops aforesaid that are off our Privie Counsaill or off our Sessioun sall come and sitt there in there whytes and mayntayne the gravitie off thair places. And for all inferiour clergymen we will that they preach in thair black gounes ; bot when they reade dyvine service, christen, burye or administer the sacrament off the lords supper, they sall weare there surplies, And if they be doctours there tippets over thame. And als weill Archbischops and Bischops as other ministers when they administer the holy communioun in our Chappell Royall or any cathedrall church within that our kyngdome sall

87

weare capes [1] And not onely they bot all inferiour preests and ministers sall at tymes and places befoir mentioned use thair squarr cappes especiallie in all our universities. Gevin att Whytehall the 15 off October 1633. *Et sic subscribitur* C.R. Sealed with the Court Signett

A.P.S., v, 21

When, shortly after this, the king gave the Scottish bishops a commission to compose a liturgy, he was still disinclined to permit deviation from the Book of England, and his instructions were that the liturgy was to be framed ' as near to this of England as might be.' There ensued a period of intensive work in Scotland, with successive drafts and correspondence passing backward and forward, and much coming and going between Edinburgh and the Court, as the book was hammered out in detail. The Scots were mainly concerned to bring the new book into line with their countrymen's beliefs, practices and prejudices, and they did secure substantial amendments to those ends ; but their most strenuous efforts could not prevail on the king to permit them to simplify the Kalendar and wholly to eliminate lessons from the Apocrypha. The king's attitude was not due merely to obstinacy or to High Church principles, but partly to the knowledge that the admission of certain modifications in the Scottish book would encourage the English puritans in their campaign against the Prayer Book in England.

Owing to the prolonged delay in bringing about agreement on the liturgy it was preceded by the Code of Canons which ought to have accompanied it. The Canons, ratified by the king in May 1635, were printed early in the following year under the title ' Canons and Constitutions ecclesiastical, gathered and put in form for the government of the Church of Scotland, ratified and approved by His Majesty's royal warrant and ordained to be observed by the clergy and all others whom they concern.' The more important of the nineteen chapters were the following :

(1) Excommunication was to be incurred by those who impeached in any part the king's supremacy in causes ecclesiastical or who maintained that the doctrine of the Church of Scotland, its Book of Common Prayer and

[1] i.e., copes

    its government, contained anything repugnant to the Scriptures.

(2) Ordination of presbyters and deacons was to be according to the Book of Ordination.

(9) No presbyter or reader was to conceive prayers extempore, or to use any other form than that prescribed.

(13) All baptisms, marriages and burials were to be registered.

(16) Every church was to have a Bible and a Book of Common Prayer, a Font (placed near the door), a Communion Table (placed at the upper end of the church or chancel), vessels reserved for sacramental use, a pulpit and an alms chest.

The canons were notable for their omissions—there was no mention of the discipline of the kirk sessions, none of the elder, none of the presbytery, none of the General Assembly. They prescribed the use of an ordinal and a prayer book which had not yet been published.

The Liturgy at last appeared in 1637. Careful examination would have shown the Scots how far the book was in accordance with their traditions and how many concessions had been made to their prejudices, but it had other features which rendered it wholly unacceptable, especially in the inflamed state of public opinion. It was notorious that it had not been authorised by Parliament or General Assembly, but was imposed solely by the royal prerogative, and it bore an initial proclamation by the king commanding men ' to conform themselves to the said public form of worship, which is the only form which we (having taken the counsel of our clergy) think fit to be used in God's public worship in this our kingdom ' ; the Kalendar contained more, and not fewer, festivals and saints' days than that in the English Prayer Book ; the directions concerning Morning and Evening Prayer referred to ' ornaments ' which ' are prescribed or shall be by his majesty or his successors according to the act of parliament provided in that behalf ' ; and the rubrics to the Communion Office, while directing that at the beginning of the service the presbyter should stand at the north side or end of the Holy Table, laid down that during the Prayer of Consecration he should stand ' at such a part of the Holy Table where he may with the more ease and decency use both his hands.'

Archbishop Laud, by whose name the book is known, had initially been opposed to a distinctive Scottish liturgy, but subsequently agreed to accept most of the Scottish proposals for amendments ; there is little in the book that emanated from him, and contemporaries were unanimous in attacking the Scottish bishops, and not Laud, as the authors of the Liturgy. There were, however, the following reasons for attaching Laud's name to the book : (i) A series of amendments to the English Prayer Book, authorised by the king in April 1636, were written, on the king's instructions, by Laud in person, and the evidence of his handwriting was regarded as proof of his responsibility for amendments which had in fact originated in Scotland. (ii) If the Scots suspected the truth, that the chief author of the book, outside Scotland, was the king himself, they could not say so as long as the fiction was maintained that Charles had been acting on evil advice—but they could accuse Laud. (iii) As Laud was already the bitter enemy of the English puritans, the attachment of his name to the Scottish Prayer Book provided a bond between the malcontents in the two countries.

1637. *The Proclamation and Preface in the Scottish Prayer Book*

A PROCLAMATION

for the authorising of the Book of Common Prayer to be used throughout the Realm of Scotland

CHARLES, by the grace of God, King of Great Britain, France, and Ireland, Defender of the Faith, To our Lovits [
]
Messengers, our Sheriffs in that part, conjunctly and sever- ally, specially constitute, greeting. Forasmuch as We, ever since our entry to the imperial Crown of this our ancient Kingdom of Scotland, especially since our late being here in the same, have divers times recommended to the Arch- bishops and Bishops here the publishing of a Public Form of Service, in the Worship of God, which we would have uniformly observed therein : And the same being now condescended upon, although We doubt not but all our subjects, both Clergy and others, will receive the said Public Form of Service with such reverence as appertaineth : Yet, thinking it necessary to make our pleasure known, touching the authorising of the Book thereof,

OUR WILL IS, and We charge you straitly, and command, that incontinent these our Letters seen, you pass, and in our Name and Authority command and charge all our subjects, both ecclesiastical and civil, by open Proclamation at the Market Crosses of the Head Burghs of this our Kingdom, and other places needful, to conform themselves to the said Public Form of Worship, which is the only Form which We (having taken the counsel of our Clergy) think fit to be used in God's Public Worship in this our Kingdom : Commanding also all Archbishops, and Bishops, and other Presbyters and Churchmen, to take a special care that the same be duly obeyed and observed, and the contraveners condignly censured and punished ; and to have special care that every Parish, betwixt and Pasch next, procure unto themselves two at least of the said Books of Common Prayer, for the use of the Parish. The which to do, we commit to you conjunctly and severally our full power, by these our Letters, delivering the same by you duly executed and indorsed again to the bearer.

Given under our signet, at Edinburgh, the twentieth day of December, and of our Reign the twelfth year, 1636.

Per actum Secreti Concilii

THE PREFACE

The Church of Christ hath in all ages had a prescript Form of Common Prayer, or Divine Service, as appeareth by the ancient Liturgies of the Greek and Latin Churches. This was done, as for other great causes, so likewise for retaining an uniformity in God's worship : a thing most beseeming them that are of one and the same profession. For by the Form that is kept in the outward worship of God, men commonly judge of Religion. If in that there be a diversity, straight they are apt to conceive the religion to be diverse. Wherefore it were to be wished, that the whole Church of Christ were one as well in form of Public Worship, as in doctrine : and that as it hath but one Lord, and one Faith, so it had but one heart, and one mouth. This would prevent many schisms and divisions, and serve much to the preserving of unity. But since that cannot be hoped for in the whole Catholic Christian Church, yet, at least, in the Churches that are under the protection of one sovereign Prince the same ought to be endeavoured.

It was not the least part of our late Sovereign King James of blessed memory, his care, to work this uniformity in all his dominions : but, while he was about to do it, it pleased God to translate him to a better kingdom. His Majesty that now reigneth, (and long may he reign over us in all happiness !) not suffering his father's good purpose to fall to the ground, but treading the same path, with the like zeal and pious affection, gave order, soon after his coming to the crown, for the framing of a Book of Common Prayer, like unto that which is received in the Churches of England and Ireland, for the use of this Church. After many lets and hindrances, the same cometh now to be published, to the good (we trust) of all God's people, and the increase of true piety and sincere devotion amongst them.

But as there is nothing, how good and warrantable soever in itself, against which some will not except ; so it may be, that exceptions will be taken against this good and most pious work, and, perhaps, none more pressed, than that we have followed the Service-Book of England. But we should desire them that shall take this exception, to consider, that, being as we are by God's mercy of one true profession, and otherwise united by many bonds, it had not been fitting to vary much from theirs, ours especially coming forth after theirs ; seeing the disturbers of the Church, both here and there, should by our differences, if they had been great, [have] taken occasion to work more trouble. Therefore did we think meet to adhere to their Form, even in the Festivals, and some other rites, not as yet received nor observed in our Church, rather than, by omitting them, to give the adversary to think that we dislike any part of their Service.

Our first Reformers were of the same mind with us, as appeareth by the ordinance they made, that in all the parishes of this Realm the Common Prayer should be read, weekly, on Sundays, and other Festival Days, with the Lessons of the Old and New Testament, conform to the order of the Book of Common Prayer ; (meaning that of England : for it is known that divers years after we had no other order for Common Prayer). This is recorded to have been the first head concluded in a frequent Council of the Lords and Barons professing Christ Jesus. We keep the words of the History ; *Religion was not then placed in rites and gestures, nor men taken with the fancy of extemporary prayers.*[1] Sure, the Public Worship of God in his Church, being the most solemn action of us his poor creatures here below, ought to be performed by a Liturgy advisedly set and framed, and not according to the sudden and various fancies of men. This shall suffice for the present to have said. The God of mercy confirm our hearts in his truth, and preserve us alike from profaneness and superstition ! Amen.

THE BEGINNINGS OF THE REVOLT : THE NATIONAL COVENANT

The reading of the Liturgy occasioned a tumult in the cathedral of St. Giles (23 July 1637), and in succeeding months there came from all parts of the country supplications directed not only against the nature of the ecclesiastical innovations but against the unconstitutional manner of their introduction. The authors of the supplications congregated in Edinburgh, and so overawed the Council that royal proclamations which commanded the lieges to disperse and ordered the removal of Council and Session from the capital were ineffective in allaying unrest. In November the Council gave its consent to the election by the supplicants of commissioners to represent them, and subsequently to the development of these commissioners into the body known as 'The Tables,' consisting of four delegates from each estate—an action almost tantamount to recognition of a rival administration.

[1] A marginal reference cites 'The History of the Church of Scotland, p. 218' (that is, Knox's *History of the Reformation*) as the evidence for the reformers' use of the Book of Common Prayer.

While the initial objective had been the Liturgy, it was soon apparent that there would be an attack on the bishops : not yet, indeed, as bishops, but as the authors and enforcers of the Liturgy and Canons and as the evil counsellors of the king. In December the Tables insisted that the bishops be excluded from the Council's deliberations on a dispute to which they were parties.

When an answer was at last vouchsafed to the supplicants, in February 1638, it took the form of a proclamation in which the king accepted personal responsibility for the Liturgy and repeated his command that it be used. The supplicants countered by a protestation rejecting the royal orders on the ground that the king had been misinformed by the bishops, to whom they persisted in attaching responsibility.

At this stage came the National Covenant, drawn up between 23 and 27 February and first signed on 28 February 1638. Already in the previous September, Johnston of Wariston, the principal author, had been interested in the Confession of 1581,[1] and in November he had been working on the law of the royal prerogative. These studies were reflected in the Covenant, which appealed from the liturgical innovations to the constitutional rights of parliaments and assemblies.

1637. *Supplication against the Service-Book*

My lords of secret counsell, unto your lordships humblie meanes and schawes we noblemen, barons, ministers, burgesses and commons occasionallie here present, being most desereous to testifie our loyaltie to our dread soveraigne and to give obedience to his majesties royall commandements, and considering that this new Book of Common Prayer (which all his majesties subjects, both ecclesiasticall and civill, by open proclamatioun ar commanded to receave with reverence as the onlie forme to be used in God's publik worschip in this kingdome, and the contravenars to be condignlie censured and punisched) is introduced and urged in a way which this kirk hath never bene acquainted with, and containeth manie verie materiall points contrarie to the Acts

---

[1] See *supra*, pp. 32–5, Johnston of Wariston, *Diary* (Scot. Hist Soc.), 269

of our Nationall Assemblies, his majesties lawes of this kingdome and to the religion and forme of worschip establisched
and universallie practised to the great comfort of all God's
people, his majesties subjects, since the Reformation, which
may tend to the great disquieting of there consciences and
to the hinderance of that harmonie and comfort which from
the influence of his majesties government all do pray for
and still expect ; we doe therefore in all humilitie supplicate
that your lordships, out of your care of religion so seriouslie
recommended to your lordships by his majestie, and out of
your compassion of our present case, wold be pleased fullie
to represent to his majestie these and the like considerations
knowne to your lordships, that this effaire of so great
importance may not appeare to his majestie a needless noise,
bot as it is indeed the verie desere of our hearts for the
preservation of true religion amongst us, which is dearer to
us then our lives and fortunes ; and, if this be refused, we
humblie crave a hearing of our just greavances before your
lordships conclusion, that by your lordships counsell some
way may be found quherby we may be delivered from the
feare of this and all other innovation of this kind and may
have the happienes to enjoy the religion as it hath bene by
the great mercie of God reformed in this land and is authorised by his majestie, quho may long and prosperouslie
reigne over us.

R.P.C., 2nd ser., vi, 699

1638. *The National Covenant*

The Confession of Faith of the Kirk of Scotland, subscribed
at first by the King's Majesty and his household in the year
of God 1580 [1581] ; thereafter by persons of all ranks in
the year 1581, by ordinance of the lords of the secret council
and acts of the general assembly ; subscribed again by all
sorts of persons in the year 1590, by a new ordinance of
council, at the desire of the general assembly ; with a
general band for the maintenance of the true religion and
the king's person, and now subscribed in the year 1638 by

us noblemen, barons, gentlemen, burgesses, ministers and commons under subscribing ; together with our resolution and promises for the causes after specified, to maintain the said true religion, and the King's Majesty, according to the confession aforesaid and acts of parliament :   the tenor whereof here followeth : [*Here follows the Negative Confession of 1581*].[1]

Like as many Acts of Parliament not onely in general do abrogate, annull, and rescind all Lawes, Statutes, Acts, Constitutions, Canons, civil or municipall, with all other Ordinances and practique penalties whatsoever, made in prejudice of the true Religion and Professours thereof ; Or, of the true Kirk-discipline, jurisdiction, and freedome thereof ; Or in favours of Idolatry and Superstition ; Or of the Papisticall Kirk ; As Act 3. Act 13. Parl. 1. Act 23. Parl. 11. Act 114. Parl. 12. of King James the sixt, That Papistry and Superstition may be utterly suppressed according to the intention of the Acts of Parliament repeated in the 5 Act Parl. 20. K. James 6.   And to that end they ordaine all Papists and Priests to be punished by manifold Civill and Ecclesiastical pains, as adversaries to Gods true Religion, preached and by Law established within this Realme, Act 24. Parl. 11. K. James 6. as common enemies to all Christian government, Act 18. Parl. 16. K. James 6. as rebellers and gainstanders of our Soveraigne Lords Authority, Act 47. Parl. 3. K. James 6. and as Idolators. Act 104. Parl. 7. K. James 6. but also in particular (by and attour the Confession of Faith) do abolish and condemne the Popes Authority and Jurisdiction out of this Land, and ordaine the maintainers thereof to be punished, Act 2. Parl. 1. Act 51. Parl. 3. Act 106. Parl. 7. Act 114. Parl. 12. K. James 6. do condemne the Popes erronious doctrine, or any other erronious doctrine repugnant to any of the Articles of the true and Christian religion publickly preached, and by law established in this Realme : And ordaines the spreaders and makers of Books or Libels, or Letters, or writs of that nature to be punished, Act 46. Parl. 3. Act 106. Parl. 7.

[1] See *supra*, pp. 32–5.

Act 24. Parl. 11. K. James 6. do condemne all Baptisme conforme to the Popes Kirk and the Idolatry of the Masse, and ordaines all sayers, willfull hearers, and concealers of the Masse, the maintainers and resetters of the Priests, Jesuites, traffiquing Papists, to be punished without any exception or restriction, Act 5. Parl. 1. Act 120. Parl. 12. Act 164. Parl. 13. Act 193. Parl. 14. Act 1. Parl. 19. Act 5. Parl. 20. K. James 6. do condemne all erroneous bookes and writtes containing erroneous doctrine against the Religion presently professed, or containing superstitious Rites and Ceremonies Papisticall, whereby the people are greatly abused, and ordaines the home-bringers of them to be punished, Act 25. Parl. 11. K. James 6. do condemne the monuments and dregs of by-gone Idolatry ; as going to the Crosses, observing the Feastivall dayes of Saints, and such other superstitious and Papisticall Rites, to the dishonour of God, contempt of true Religion, and fostering of great errour among the people, and ordaines the users of them to be punished for the second fault as Idolaters, Act 104. Parl. 7. K. James 6.

Like as many Acts of Parliament are conceaved for maintenance of Gods true and Christian Religion, and the purity thereof in Doctrine and Sacraments of the true Church of God, the liberty & freedom thereof, in her National, Synodal Assemblies, Presbyteries, Sessions, Policy, Discipline and Jurisdiction thereof, as that purity of Religion and liberty of the Church was used, professed, exercised, preached and confessed according to the reformation of Religion in this Realm. As for instance, The 99 Act Parl. 7. Act 23. Parl. 11. Act 114. Parl. 12. Act 160. Parl. 13. of King James 6. Ratified by the 4 Act of King Charles. So that the 6 Act Parl. 1. and 68 Act Parl. 6. of King James 6. in the Yeare of God 1579 declares the Ministers of the blessed Evangel, whom God of his mercy had raised up, or here-after should raise, agreeing with them that then lived in Doctrin, and Administration of the Sacraments, and the People that professed Christ, as he was then offered in the Evangel, and doth communicate with the Holy Sacraments, (as in the reformed Kirks of this Realm they were publickly administrat) according to the Confession of Faith, to be the true and Holy Kirk of Christ Jesus within this Realm, and decerns and declares all and sundry, who either gainsayes the Word of the Evangel, received and approved, as the heads of the Confession of Faith, professed in Parliament, in the Yeare of God 1560, specified also in the first Parliament of King James 6. and ratified in this present Parliament, more particularly do specify, or that refuses the administration of the Holy Sacraments, as they were then ministrated, to be no members of the said Kirk within this Realme, and true Religion, presently professed, so long as they keep themselves so divided from the society of Christs body : And the subsequent Act 69 Parl. 6. of K. James 6. declares, That there is none other Face of Kirk, nor other Face of Religion, then was presently at that time, by the Favour of God established within this Realme, which therefore is ever stiled, Gods true Religion, Christs true Religion, the true and Christian Religion, and a perfect Religion, Which by manifold acts of Parliament, all within this realme are bound to subscribe the articles thereof, the Confession of Faith, to recant all doctrine & errours, repugnant to any of the said Articles, Act 4 & 9 Parl. 1. Act 45, 46, 47, Parl. 3. Act 71 Parl. 6. Act 106 Parl. 7. Act 24 Parl. 11. Act 123 Parl. 12. Act 194 and 197 Parl. 14. of K. James 6. And all Magistrats, Sherifs, &c. on the one parte are ordained to search, apprehend, and punish all contraveeners ; For instance, Act 5 Parl. 1. Act 104 Parl. 7. Act 25 Parl. 11. K. James 6. And that notwithstanding of the Kings Majesty's licences on the contrary, which are discharged & declared to be of no force in so farre as they tend in any wayes, to the prejudice & hinder of the execution of the Acts of Parliament against Papists & adversaries of true Religion, Act 106 Parl. 7. K. James 6. On the other part in the 47 Act Parl. 3. K. James 6. It is declared and ordained, seeing the cause of Gods true Religion, and his highnes Authority are so joyned, as the hurt of the one is common to both : and that none shal be reputed as loyall

and faithfull subjects to our Soveraigne Lord, or his
Authority, but be punishable as rebellers and gainstanders
of the same, who shall not give their Confession, and make
their profession of the said true Religion, and that they
who after defection shall give the Confession of their Faith
of new, they shall promise to continue therein in time
comming, to maintaine our Souveraigne Lords Authority,
and at the uttermost of their power to fortify, assist, and
maintaine the true Preachers and Professors of Christs
Evangel, against whatsoever enemies and gainestanders of
the same ; and namely (against all such of whatsoever
nation, estate, or degree they be of) that have joyned, and
bound themselves, or have assisted, or assists to set forward,
and execute the cruell decrees of Trent, contrary to the
Preachers and true Professors of the Word of God, which
is repeated word by word in the Article of Pacification at
Perth the 23 of Februar. 1572, approved by Parliament the
last of Aprile 1573. Ratified in Parliament 1587, and related, Act 123 Parl. 12. of K. James 6. with this addition,
that they are bound to resist all treasonable uproars and
hostilities raised against the true Religion, the Kings
Majesty, and the true Professors. Like as all Lieges are
bound to maintaine the King Majesty's Royal Person, and
Authority, the Authority of Parliaments, without the which
neither any lawes or lawful judicatories can be established,
Act 130, Act 131 Parl. 8. K. James 6. and the subjects
Liberties, who ought onely to live and be governed by the
Kings lawes, the common lawes of this Realme allanerly,
Act 48 Parl. 3. K. James the first ; Act 79 Parl. 6. K. James
the 4. repeated in the Act 131 Parl. 8. K. James 6. Which,
if they be innovated or prejudged, the commission anent
the union of the two Kingdoms of Scotland and England,
which is the sole Act of the 17. Parl. of K. James 6. declares
such confusion would ensue, as this Realme could be no
more a free Monarchy, because by the fundamentall lawes,
ancient priviledges, offices and liberties, of this Kingdome,
not onely the Princely Authority of his Majesty's Royal
discent hath been these many ages maintained, but also the

peoples security of their Lands, livings, rights, offices, liberties, and dignities preserved, and therefore for the preservation of the said true Religion, Lawes, and Liberties of this Kingdome, it is statute by the 8 Act Parl. 1, repeated in the 99 Act Parl. 7, Ratified in the 23 Act Parl. 11. and 114 Act Parl. 12. of K. James 6. and 4 Act of K. Charles, That all Kings and Princes at their Coronation and reception of their Princely Authority, shall make their faithfull promise by their solemne oath in the presence of the Eternal God, that, enduring the whole time of their lives, they shall serve the same Eternal God to the uttermost of their power, according as he hath required in his most Holy Word, contained in the old and new Testament. And according to the same Word shall maintain the true Religion of Christ Jesus, the preaching of his Holy Word, the due and right ministration of the Sacraments now receaved and preached within this Realme (according to the Confession of Faith immediately preceeding) and shall abolish and gainstand all false Religion contrary to the same, and shall rule the people committed to their charge, according to the will and command of God, revealed in his foresaid Word, and according to the laudable Lawes and Constitutions received in this Realme, no wayes repugnant to the said will of the Eternall God ; and shall procure, to the uttermost of their power, to the Kirk of God, and whole Christian people, true and perfite peace in all time coming : and that they shall be careful to root out of their Empire all Hereticks, and enemies to the true worship of God, who shall be convicted by the true Kirk of God, of the foresaid crimes, which was also observed by his Majesty, at his Coronation in Edinburgh 1633, as may be seene in the order of the Coronation.

In obedience to the Commandment of God, conforme to the practice of the godly in former times, and according to the laudable example of our Worthy and Religious Progenitors, & of many yet living amongst us, which was warranted also by act of Councill, commanding a general band to be made and subscribed by his Majesty's subjects, of all ranks, for two causes : One was, For defending the true Religion, as it was then reformed, and is expressed in the Confession of Faith abovewritten, and a former large Confession established by sundry acts of lawful generall assemblies, & of Parliament, unto which it hath relation, set down in publick Catechismes, and which had been for many years with a blessing from Heaven preached, and professed in this Kirk and Kingdome, as Gods undoubted truth, grounded only upon his written Word. The other cause was, for maintaining the Kings Majesty, His Person, and Estate : the true worship of God and the Kings authority, being so straitly joined, as that they had the same Friends, and common enemies, and did stand and fall together. And finally, being convinced in our mindes, and confessing with our mouthes, that the present and succeeding generations in this Land, are bound to keep the foresaid nationall Oath & Subscription inviolable, Wee Noblemen, Barons, Gentlemen, Burgesses, Ministers & Commons under subscribing, considering divers times before & especially at this time, the danger of the true reformed Religion, of the Kings honour, and of the publick peace of the Kingdome : By the manifold innovations and evills generally conteined, and particularly mentioned in our late supplications, complaints, and protestations, Do hereby professe, and before God, his Angels, and the World solemnly declare, That, with our whole hearts we agree & resolve, all the dayes of our life, constantly to adhere unto, and to defend the foresaid true Religion, and (forbearing the practice of all novations, already introduced in the matters of the worship of God, or approbation of the corruptions of the publicke Government of the Kirk, or civil places and power of Kirk-men, till they be tryed & allowed in free assemblies, and in Parliaments) to labour by all meanes lawful to recover the purity and liberty of the Gospel, as it was stablished and professed before the foresaid Novations : and because, after due examination, we plainely perceave, and undoubtedly believe, that the Innovations and evils contained in our Supplications, Complaints, and Protestations have no warrant of the Word of God, are contrary to the Articles of the Foresaid Confessions, to the intention and meaning of the blessed reformers of Religion in this Land, to the above written Acts of Parliament, & do sensibly tend to the re-establishing of the Popish Religion and Tyranny, and to the subversion and ruine of the true Reformed Religion, and of our Liberties, Lawes and Estates, We also declare, that the Foresaid Confessions are to be interpreted, and ought to be understood of the Foresaid novations and evils, no lesse then if every one of them had been expressed in the Foresaid confessions, and that we are obliged to detest & abhorre them amongst other particular heads of Papistry abjured therein. And therefore from the knowledge and consciences of our duety to God, to our King and Countrey, without any worldly respect or inducement, so farre as humane infirmity will suffer, wishing a further measure of the grace of God for this effect, We promise, and sweare by the Great Name of the Lord our God, to continue in the Profession and Obedience of the Foresaid Religion : That we shall defend the same, and resist all these contrary errours and corruptions, according to our vocation, and to the uttermost of that power that God hath put in our hands, all the dayes of our life : and in like manner with the same heart, we declare before God and Men, That we have no intention nor desire to attempt any thing that may turne to the dishonour of God, or to the diminution of the Kings greatnesse and authority : But on the contrary, we promise and sweare, that we shall, to the uttermost of our power, with our meanes and lives, stand to the defence of our dread Soveraigne, the Kings Majesty, his Person, and Authority, in the defence and preservation of the foresaid true Religion, Liberties and Lawes of the Kingdome : As also to the mutual defence and assistance, every one of us of another in the same cause of maintaining the true Religion and his Majesty's Authority, with our best counsel, our bodies, meanes, and whole power, against all sorts of persons whatsoever. So that whatsoever shall be done to the least of us for that cause, shall be taken as done to us all in general, and to every one of us in particular. And that we shall neither directly nor indirectly suffer ourselves to be divided or withdrawn by whatsoever suggestion, allurement, or terrour from this blessed & loyall Conjunction, nor shall cast in any let or impediment, that may stay or hinder any such resolution as by common consent shall be found to conduce for so good ends. But on the contrary, shall by all lawful meanes labour to further and promove the same, and if any such dangerous & divisive motion be made to us by Word or Writ, We, and every one of us, shall either suppresse it, or if need be shall incontinent make the same known, that it may be timeously obviated : neither do we fear the foul aspersions of rebellion, combination, or what else our adversaries from their craft and malice would put upon us, seing what we do is so well warranted, and ariseth from an unfeined desire to maintaine the true worship of God, the Majesty of our King, and peace of the Kingdome, for the common happinesse of our selves, and the posterity. And because we cannot look for a blessing from God upon our proceedings, except with our Profession and Subscription we joine such a life & conversation, as beseemeth Christians, who have renewed their Covenant with God ; We, therefore, faithfully promise, for our selves, our followers, and all other under us, both in publick, in our particular families, and personal carriage, to endeavour to keep our selves within the bounds of Christian liberty, and to be good examples to others of all Godlinesse, Sobernesse, and Righteousnesse, and of every duety we owe to God and Man, And that this our Union and Conjunction may be observed without violation, we call the living God, the Searcher of our Hearts to witness, who knoweth this to be our sincere Desire, and unfained Resolution, as we shall answere to Jesus Christ, in the great day, and under the pain of Gods everlasting wrath, and of infamy, and losse of all honour and respect in this World, Most humbly beseeching the Lord to strengthen us by his holy Spirit for this end, and to blesse our desires and proceedings with a happy successe, that Religion and Righteousnesse may flourish in the Land, to the glory of God, the honour of our King, and peace and comfort of us all. In witnesse whereof we have subscribed with our hands all the premisses, &c.

A.P.S., v, 272–6 [1]

The National Covenant, with its appeal to the past, had been essentially a constitutional, and not a revolutionary, document. It had carefully refrained from an explicit condemnation of episcopal government, and some of the signatories made an express reservation to that effect, while others denied that they wished to condemn the Five Articles of Perth (which, unlike later innovations, had received constitutional authorisation). The document was successful in uniting almost the entire nation, but it may possibly be regarded as a formula which produced a deceptive appearance of unanimity.

At any rate, while the Covenant was still being signed, there were indications that the revolt was to go much farther than the Covenant itself expressed. Without any condemnation of episcopal government, there was an undermining of it, as presbyteries assumed the episcopal powers of ordaining and admitting ministers to parishes, so ' restoring that great liberty to the Church again.' [2] The following passage in Johnston of Wariston's *Diary* is illuminating as to the development of opinion during the ten months since the Prayer Book riot.

1638, May 4. *Johnston of Wariston on the development of opinion*

The Lord hes led us hitherto by the hand fra step to step ; and, at every step we wald haive stoodin at, maid our adversaries to refuise, and forced us to goe up a neu step of reformation ; so evin yet in this busines he wil not suffer any maner of composition or condiscendence til he bring us to the highest step of reformation ; and, instead of thos cautions and limitations of praelats nou conteined in our articles, suffer us not to settle til we speak plaine treuth according to the will of God, that is the utter overthrou

---

[1] The numerous MS. copies of the Covenant have minor variations in wording and spelling.   [2] Wariston's *Diary*, i, 338

and ruyne of Episcopacie, that great grandmother of al our corruptions, novations, usurpations, diseases and troubles.

Wariston's *Diary*, i, 347

THE GLASGOW ASSEMBLY : THE BISHOPS' WARS

In June the Marquis of Hamilton appeared in Scotland as the king's High Commissioner, but not until September did Charles give his assent to the summoning of a General Assembly and a Parliament ; at the same time he intimated that he would agree to the abrogation of Liturgy, Canons and Court of High Commission, and even to the withdrawal of the Five Articles of Perth.

The General Assembly which met at Glasgow in November 1638 was hardly the ' free ' assembly demanded by the Covenant, and it is doubtful whether circumstances permitted an assembly genuinely free, or at any rate recognised as such by all parties. Twenty years had passed since the last assembly, and considerably longer since the last one in which royal and episcopal influence had not been prominent. The composition of the assemblies since 1560 offered a variety of precedents, but the Tables appealed to an act of 1597 which provided that an assembly should consist of clerical and lay representatives of presbyteries, along with lay commissioners of the royal burghs. Partly because of the feeling against the supporters of the ' novations,' and partly because of the lack of conclusive precedents, there was ample opportunity for manipulation of the election of both clerical and lay commissioners, of which full advantage was taken by the dominant faction. Not only were members carefully selected, but they came briefed to support a predetermined policy. Even so, the legality of the appointment of elders was admitted only after some dispute.[1]

Before the Assembly entered on its central business, the High Commissioner withdrew and commanded the Assembly to dissolve, on the grounds that it was defective in composition and that its projected attack on the bishops was outwith its powers. In defiance of the Commissioner, the Assembly continued to sit, and its work was, in short, to restore the *status quo* of the 1590s. That its work could be regarded as restoration and not revolution would not have been apparent but for Johnston of Wariston's masterly stroke in producing the old registers of the assemblies.

[1] Baillie, *Letters and Journals*, i, 136, 138

The Glasgow Assembly

1638, November 23. *Production of the old registers*

[*To Archibald Johnston of Wariston, elected clerk of the Assembly*]
Mr. Thomas Sandilands, in face of the Assemblie, did
delyver two Registers, which contained the Acts of the Kirk
since the year 1590. . . . The Moderator required all
earnestlie to procure the production of any the Church-
Registers could be had ; for the losse of such a treasure as
the Church's evidents was pitifull. His Grace [the Com-
missioner] protested his willingness to doe his endeavour for
so good a work. Rothes intreated that the Bishops might be
caused delyver what they had ; for it was known that King
James had sent a warrand to Mr. Thomas Nicolsone, late
clerk, to deliver to the Bishop of St. Andrewes the Registers
of the Church. After much regrateing the irreparable losse
of these wrytes, the new Clerk declared, that by the good
providence of God, these books they spake off were come to
his hands, which there he produced to all our great joy :
Fyve books in folio, four written and subscryved and
margined with the known hands of ane Gray and Ritchie,
clerkes to the Generall Assemblie, containing the full
register from the Reformation in the [15]60 year, to the
[year 15]90, where Mr. Thomas Sandilands's books began,
except some leaves which Bishop Adamsone had riven out. . .

Baillie, *Letters and Journals*, i, 129

This day I produced for my first act the registers of the Kirk,
and can never sufficiently admire and adore the goodnes,
wysdome and providence of God in praeserving them and
bringing them to our hands at sutch a tyme—magnified be
His naime !—as this was a solid fondation to us, without the
quhilk we wald haive seimed to haive buildet upon sand. . . .
In the great committe, quhair my L. Argyle was sitting in
the Tolbooth, I cleired al thair mynds that Episcopacie was
condemned in this churche. I drew it up in a lairge treatise

by Gods assistance, as lykwayes anent the articles ; in the
Assemblee I scheu al the warrants and read the verry acts
themselves out of the registers and aunsuered al objections ;
and quhairas, both in the morning we heard of some wald
publikly disput for Episcopacie and many scores came to the
house rcsolut to voyte for it, yet the Lord maid the Acts so
to convince thair mynds that every mans mouth acknou-
ledgit that they had bein abjured and removed ; and, quhen
I was reading the roll and heard no word bot ' Abjured and
Removed,' I was struken with admiration . . . and yit my
ears sounds ever with thes words, ' Abjured and Removed.'

Wariston's, *Diary* 401–3

December 4. [The six late pretended Assemblies condemned.]
. . . The Assembly with the universall consent of all, after
the serious examination of the reasons against every one
of these six pretended Assemblies apart, being often urged
by the Moderatour to informe themselves throughly, that
without doubting, and with a full perswasion of minde, they
might give their voices, declared all these six Assemblies, of
Linlithgow 1606 and 1608, Glasgow 1610, Aberdeen 1616,
St. Andrews 1617, Perth 1618, and every one of them, to
have been from the beginning unfree, unlawfull, and null
Assemblies, and never to have had, nor hereafter to have,
any ecclesiasticall authoritie, and their conclusions to have
been, and to bee, of no force, vigour, nor efficacie : Prohibited all defence and observance of them, and ordained
the reasons of their nullitie to be insert in the Books of the
Assembly. . . .

December 6. [Condemning the Service-book, Book of
Canons, Book of Ordination, and the High Commission.]
1. The Assembly having diligently considered the Book of
Common Prayer, lately obtruded upon the reformed kirk
within this realme, both in respect of the manner of the
introducing thereof, and in respect of the matter which it

107

containeth, findeth that it hath been devised and brought in by the pretended prelats, without direction from the kirk, and pressed upon ministers without warrand from the kirk, to be universally received as the only forme of divine service under all highest paines, both civill and ecclesiasticall, and the book it self, beside the *popish* frame and forms in divine worship, to containe many *popish* errours and ceremonies, and the seeds of manifold and grosse superstition and idolatrie. The Assembly, therefore, all in one voice, hath rejected and condemned and by these presents doth reject and condemne the said book, not only as illegally introduced, but also as repugnant to the doctrine, discipline and order of this reformed kirk, to the Confession of Faith, constitutions of Generall Assemblies, and Acts of Parliament establishing the true religion : and doth prohibite the use and practise thereof : and ordaines presbyteries to proceed with the censure of the kirk against all such as shall transgresse.

2. The Assembly also, taking to their consideration the Book of Cannons, and the manner how it hath been introduced, findeth that it hath been devised by the pretended prelats, without warrand or direction from the Generall Assembly : and to establish a tyrannicall power in the persons of the pretended bishops, over the worship of God, mens consciences, liberties and goods, and to overthrow the whole discipline and government of the generall and synodall assemblies, presbyteries and sessions formerly established in our kirk. Therefore the Assembly all in one voice hath rejected and condemned . . . the said book, as contrare to the Confession of our Faith, and repugnant to the established government, the Book of Discipline, and the acts and constitutions of our Kirk. . . .

3. The Assembly having considered the Book of Consecration and Ordination, findeth it to have been framed by the prelats, to have been introduced and practised without warrand of authority, either civill or ecclesiasticall ; and that it establisheth offices in Gods house which are not warranded by the word of God, and are repugnant to the

discipline and constitutions of our Kirk, that it is an impediment to the entrie of fit and worthie men to the ministery, and to the discharge of their dutie after their entrie, conforme to the discipline of our kirk. Therefore the Assembly all in one voice hath rejected and condemned . . . the said book. . . .

4. The Generall Assembly, after due tryall, having found that the Court of High Commission hath been erected without the consent or procurement of the Kirk, or consent of the Estates in Parliament, that it subverteth the jurisdiction and ordinarie judicatories and assemblies of the kirk sessions, presbyteries, provinciall and nationall assemblies, that it is not regulate by lawes civill or ecclesiasticall, but at the discretion and arbitrement of the Commissioners ; that it giveth to ecclesiasticall persons the power of both the swords, and to persons meerly civill the power of the keys and Kirk censures : Therefore the Assembly all in one voice hath disallowed and condemned . . . the said court as unlawfull in it selfe, and prejudiciall to the liberties of Christs Kirk and Kingdome, the Kings honour in maintaining the established lawes and judicatories of the Kirk. . . .

December 13. [Sentence of deposition and excommunication against the Archbishops of St. Andrews and Glasgow and the Bishops of Edinburgh, Galloway, Ross, Brechin, Aberdeen, Dunblane, Moray, Orkney, Lismore, the Isles, Dunkeld and Caithness.]

The Assembly, having heard the lybels and complaints given in against the foresaids pretended Bishops . . . and finding them guiltie of the breach of the cautions agreed upon in the Assembly holden at Montrose, Anno 1600, for restricting of the minister voter in Parliament from incroaching upon the liberties and jurisdiction of this kirk,[1] which was set down with certification of deposition, infamie, and excommunication, specially for receiving of consecration to the office of Episcopacie, condemned by the Con-

[1] See *supra*, p. 54.

fession of Faith and acts of this Kirk as having no warrand, nor foundament in the Word of God, and by vertue of this usurped power, and power of the High Commission, pressing the Kirk with novations in the worship of God, and for sundrie other haynous offences and enormities, at length expressed, and clearly proven in their processe, and for their refusall to underly the tryal of the reigning slander of sundrie other grosse transgressions and crymes laid to their charge : Therefore the Assembly moved with zeal to the glorie of God, and purging of his Kirk, hath ordained the saids pretended Bishops to be deposed, and by these presents doth depose them, not only of the office of Commissionarie to vote in Parliament, Councell, or Convention in name of the Kirk, but also of all functions whether of pretended Episcopall or ministeriall calling, declareth them infamous ; And likewise ordaineth the saids pretended Bishops to be excommunicate, and declared to be of these whom Christ commandeth to be holden by all and every one of the faithfull as ethnicks, and publicanes ; and the sentence of excommunication to be pronounced by Mr. Alexander Henderson, Moderatour, in face of the Assembly in the High Kirk of Glasgow, and the execution of the sentence to bee intimat in all the kirks of Scotland by the Pastours of every particullar congregation, as they will be answerable to their Presbyteries and Synods, or the next Generall Assembly, in case of the negligence of Presbyteries and Synods.

In the cases of the Bishops of Moray, Orkney, Lismore and the Isles, the wording after ' Episcopall or ministeriall calling ' runs—

And likewise in case they acknowledge not this Assembly, reverence not the constitutions thereof, and obey not the sentence, and make not their repentance, conforme to the order prescribed by this Assembly, ordaines them to be excommunicated . . . and the sentence of excommunication to be pronounced upon their refusall, in the Kirks appointed, by any of these who are particularly named, to have the charge of trying their repentance or impenitencie. . . .

In the case of the Bishop of Dunkeld, the wording after 'Councell or Convention in name of the Kirk' runs—
And doth suspend him from all ministeriall function, and providing he acknowledge this Assembly, reverence the constitutions of it, and obey this sentence, and make his repentance conforme to the order prescribed, continueth him in the ministerie of St. Madoze ; And likewise, if he acknowledge not this Assembly *(etc. as in the cases of the Bishops of Moray, Orkney, Lismore and the Isles).*
In the case of the Bishop of Caithness, the wording after 'Councell or Convention, in name of the Kirk' runs—
And doth suspend him from the ministeriall function. And providing he acknowledge this Assembly, reverence the constitutions of it, and obey the sentence, and make his repentance conforme to the order prescribed by this Assembly, will admit him to the ministerie of a particular flock : and likewise, in case he acknowledge not this Assembly *(etc. as in the cases of the Bishops of Moray, Orkney, Lismore and the Isles).*

December 8. [Declaring Episcopacy to have been abjured by the Confession of Faith, 1580 (1581) ; And to be removed out of this Kirk.]
. . . All the members of the Assembly being many times desired and required to propone their doubts, and scruples, and every one being heard to the full, and after much agitation as fully satisfied ; the Moderatour at last exhorting every one to declare his minde, did put the matter to voicing in these terms :—' Whether according to the confession of faith, as it was professed in the year 1580, 1581, and 1590, there be any other Bishop, but a Pastour of a particular flock, having no preheminence nor power over his brethren, and whether by that Confession, as it was then professed, all other episcopacie is abjured, and ought to bee removed out of this Kirk ? ' The whole Assembly most unanimously, without contradiction of any one (and with the hesitation of one allanerly) professing full perswasion of minde, did voice that all episcopacie different

from that of a Pastour over a particular flock, was abjured in this Kirk, and to be removed out of it. And therefore prohibites under ecclesiasticall censure any to usurpe, accept, defend, or obey the pretended authoritie thereof in time coming.

December 10. [Declaring the Five Articles of Perth to have been abjured and to be removed.]
The Assembly remembring the uniformity of worship which was in this Kirk, before the Articles of Perth, the great rent which entered at that time, and hath continued since, with the lamentable effects that it hath produced, both against Pastours and professours. . . . The matter was put to voicing, in these words : ' Whether the five articles of Perth, by the confession of Faith, as it was meaned and professed in the year 1580, 1581, 1590, 1591 ought to be removed out of this Kirk ? ' The whole Assembly all in one consent, one onely excepted, did voice that the five articles above specified were abjured by this Kirk, in that Confession, and so ought to be removed out of it : And therefore prohibiteth and dischargeth all disputing for them, or observing of them, or any of them, in all time comming, and ordains Presbyteries to proceed with the censures of the Kirk against all transgressours.

December 19. [Against the civill places and power of kirkmen.]
. . . The Assembly most unanimously in one voice, with the hesitation of two allanerly, declared, that as on the one part the Kirk and the Ministers thereof are obligded to give their advise and good counsell in matters concerning the Kirk or the Conscience of any whatsomever, to his Majestie, to the Parliament, to the Councell, or to any member thereof, for their resolutions from the Word of God ; So on the other part, that it is both inexpedient, and unlawful in this Kirk, for Pastors separate unto the Gospel to brook civil places, and offices, as to be Justices of Peace ; sit and decerne in Councell, Session, or Exchecker ; to

ryde or vote in Parliament, to be Judges or Assessors in any Civill Judicatorie ; and therefore rescinds and annuls all contrarie acts of Assembly, namely of the Assembly holden at Montrose 1600, which being prest by authority, did rather for an *interim* tolerat the same, and that limitate by many cautions, for the breach whereof the Prelats have been justly censured, than in freedome of judgement allow thereof, and ordaineth the Presbyteries to proceed with the Censures of the Kirk, against such as shall transgresse herein in time comming.

December 20. [Concerning yearly General Assemblies.]
The Assembly having considered . . . the great benefite arysing to the Kirk from this one free and lawfull Assembly, finde it necessary to declare, and hereby declares, that by divine, ecclesiasticall, and civill warrands, this national kirk hath power and liberty to assemble and conveen in her yearly generall Assemblies, and oftner *pro re nata*, as occasion and necessity shall require. Appointeth the next Generall Assembly to sit at Edinburgh, the third Weddinsday of Julie 1639. And warneth all presbyteries, universities, and burghes to send their commissioners for keeping the same. Giving power also to the presbyterie of Edinburgh, *pro re nata* and upon any urgent and extraordinarie necessity (if any shall happen before the diet appointed in Julie) to give advertisement to all the presbyteries, universities, and burghes to send their Commissioners for holding an occasionall Assembly. And if in the meane time it shall please the kings Majestie to indict a Generall Assembly, ordaineth all presbyteries, universities, and burghes to send their commissioners for keeping the time and place which shall be appointed by his Majesties proclamation.

Peterkin, *Records of the Kirk of Scotland*, 24-40

The ' Bishops' Wars '

The king declined to ratify the acts of the Glasgow Assembly, and continued to play for time. The Covenanters, on their side, had already in 1638 been collecting money and munitions, and early in 1639, besides undertaking operations in the non-covenanting areas of the north-east, they seized a number of fortresses, including the castles of Edinburgh and Dumbarton. In May a fleet under Hamilton arrived in the Firth of Forth, but this had no result except to stimulate the Covenanters into action on land. A covenanting army marched to the Border, where it came within striking distance of a force raised by the king. Without giving battle, Charles agreed to the Scottish demands by the Pacification of Berwick (18 June 1639) : a General Assembly was to meet with his full sanction, and Parliament, previously summoned for May but since prorogued, was now to be allowed to proceed to business.

The Assembly, which met at Edinburgh in August, re-enacted, as of new, the measures passed at Glasgow in the previous year ; more than that, it prevailed on the Privy Council to pass an act imposing subscription to the Covenant with an express extension against episcopacy and the Five Articles.[1] At the Parliament there was contention on both constitutional [2] and ecclesiastical issues, and on 14 November, without having given statutory effect to the decisions of the Assembly, it was prorogued, without its own consent, until 2 June 1640.

The king was not prepared to surrender without another appeal to arms, and with that end in view he summoned the (English) ' Short Parliament' in April 1640. Consequently, when the Scottish estates, although again prorogued, met on 2 June without crown sanction and without a commissioner, a committee was appointed to organise military operations. As Charles gathered his forces in Yorkshire the Scots crossed the Tweed and took possession of Newcastle, where, in control of London's coal supply, they successfully insisted that they should remain in England at English expense until a settlement was reached. Negotiations, begun at Ripon, were continued in London and not concluded until August 1641. Meantime, under the financial pressure of the Scottish occupation, Charles had been compelled to summon the (English) ' Long Parliament' (November 1640), which in effect welcomed the Scots as its allies against the king.

Almost simultaneously with the conclusion of peace, Charles was in Edinburgh (August 1641), ready to give his ratification to

---

[1] See the later parliamentary ratification of this Assembly's acts, *infra*, pp. 117.   [2] See *infra*, pp. 120.

the acts of the parliaments of 1639 and 1640 and to the further
demands now made for the control of the executive and judicature
(see *infra*, pp. 246-7).

Parliamentary Ratification of the Covenanting Policy

1640. *Abolition of the clerical estate in Parliament*

The estatis of Parliament presentlie conveind by his
Majesties speciall authoritie, considering this present parliea-
ment was indicted by his Majestie for ratifieing of such actis
as should be concludit in the late assemblie of the kirke for
determining all civill materes and setling all such thingis
as may conduce to the publicte good and peace of this kirke
and kingdome, and considering the severall complaintis of
this kirke wnto parliamentis from tyme to tyme proceiding
from hir continouall experience of prejudice and ruine
throughe many persones and speciallie of prelates thair
attempting to voyce or doe any thing in name of the kirke
without ather beiring office in the kirke or haveing commissione from the kirke, and the actis of the lat Generall
Assemblie condemning the office of beshopis archebeshopis
and other prelatis and the civill power and places of
kirkmen, as thair voyceing and ryding in parliament, And
craveing the abolishing of these actis of parliament which
grantis to the kirke or kirkmen vote in parliament to be
abrogat as prejudiciall to hir liberties and incompatible
with hir spirituall nature ; Considering also that ther are
conveind in this present parliament by his Majesties speciall
indictione, warrand and authoritie [the] nobilitie, barrones
and burgess, the estatis of this kingdome, who have a full
and undoubted power to proceed and determine in all
matcris concerneing the publict good of this kingdome, and
that notwithstanding of the absence of the prelatis who by
former lawes ware appoynted to be memberis of parliament ;
and to the effect none presume to move any questione
thairanent : The saidis estatis now conveind as said is have
declaired and by these presents declaires this present

115

parliament, holdine be the nobilitie, barones and burgess and thair commissioneris, the trewe estatis of this kingdome, to be a compleit and perfyte parliament and to have the samene power, authoritie and jurisdictione as absolutlie and fullie as any parliament formerlie heath had within this kingdome in tyme bygone ; and ordeanes all parliamentis heireftir to be constitute and to consist onlie in all tyme comeing of the noblemen barronis and burgess as the memberis and thrie estatis of parliament ; and reschindis and annullis all former laws and actis of parliament mad in favouris of whatsoever beshopis, archbeshopis, abbotis, pryoris or other prelatis or churchmen whatsoevir for thair ryding, sitting or voceing in parliament either as church-men or as the clergie or in name of the Church or as representing the Churche as an state or member of parlia-ment by reassone of thair ecclesiasticall offices, titles, dignities or benefices. . . . And prohibits all personis whatsomevir to call in questione the authoritie of this present parliament wpon whatsoevir pretext, under the paine of treason.

A.P.S., v, 259, c. 2

1640. *Compulsory subscription of the Covenant*

The estates of parliament presentlie conveind by his majesties speciall authoritie, considering the supplicatione of the generall assembly at Edinburghe the 12 of August 1639 to his majesties heighe commissioner and the lordis of his majesties honorable privie counsell and the act of the counsell the threttie of August 1639 conteineing the answer of the said supplicatione and the act of the said generall assemblie ordeaneing by thair ecclesiasticall constitutione the subscriptione of the confessione of faith and covenant mentionat in thair supplicatione and withall haveing suppli-cated his majestie to ratifie and enjoyne the samen by his royall authoritie under all civill paines, as tending to the glorie of God, preservatione of religion, the kingis majesties honnour and the perfyte peace of this kirke and kingdome, doe ratifie and approve the said supplicatione, act of counsell and act of assembly, and conforme thairto ordeanes and commandis the said confessione and covenant to be subscryveit by all his majesties subjectis of what ranke and quality soevir under all civil paines, and ordeanes the said supplicatione, act of counsell and act of assembly with the whole confessione and covenant itselfe to be insert and registrat in the actis and bookis of parliament and also ordeanes the samene to be presented at the entrie of everie parliament and befor they proceed to ony uther act that the same be publicklie red and sworne by the whole memberis of parliament clameing voyce thairin, otherwayes the refuisseris to subscrybe and sweir the same shall have no place nor voyce in parliament, and suchlyke ordeanes all judges, magistratis and other officers of whatsoevir place, ranke or quality, and ministeris, at thair entrie to sweir and subscrybe the samene covenant, whairof and of the said supplicatione, act of counsell and act of assemblie the tennour falloweth : . . .

[*The Act of Assembly now ratified had contained the following clause :*] Ordeanes of new under all ecclesiasticall censure that all the maisteris of universities, colledges and schooles, all scolleris at the passing of thair degries, all persones suspect of papistrie or any other errour, and finally all the memberis of this kirke and kingdome subscrybe the same with theise wordis prefixed to thair subscriptione : ' The article of this covenant which was at the first subscriptioun referred to the determinatione of the generall assembly being determined and thairby the fyve articles of Pearth, the governement of the kirke by beshopis, the civill place and power of kirkmen upoun the reassones and groundis conteind in the actis of the generall assembly declaired to be unlawfull within this kirke we subscribe according to the determinatione foirsaid.'

A.P.S., v, 270, 272

This parliament, besides ratifying the acts of the Edinburgh General Assembly of August 1639, which *inter alia* abolished episcopal government (*A.P.S.*, v, 276–7), passed an ' act rescissory ' which revived the act of 1592 in favour of presbyterian government, annulled acts in favour of the bishops which had been passed from 1597 to 1621, and included the following clause formally transferring the episcopal functions to presbyteries.

And declaires that it is and shalbe lawfull to the presbyteries of this kirke to exact and receive frome subjects of all qualityes thair oath of the confessione of faith and covenant with the subscriptione therof, to examene pedagogues of the sones of noblemen passing out of the cuntrie, to give them testimoniellis according to former actes of parliament, to give and direct admonitionis privat or publicke to persones joyned in mariage for adherence, to designe manse and gleibes to ministeris, to appoynt stent maisteris for reparatione of kirke and kirkyairdis and for mentinance of the maisteris of schooles and to stent the parochineris conforme to the act of parliament, admit ministeris upon the presentationes from the lawfull patrons or *jure devoluto* . . . and to doe all and whatsoevir thingis which befor perteened to presbetries and ware usurped by the prelatis.

A.P.S., v, 277–8

One of the features of the ' Second Reformation ' now being carried through by the Covenanters was a drive to eliminate the remaining ' monuments of idolatry ' in churches. The destruction of buildings and their furnishings by the first reformers has been much exaggerated, and in 1640, after two generations and more of neglect, a great deal of fine medieval work in wood and stone still survived. An Act of Assembly, ratified in the following Act of Parliament, decreed that churches should be thoroughly purged.

1641. *Act for abolishing of monuments of idolatry*

Our soverane lord, with consent of the estates of parliament, understanding that the generall assembly of the kirke heath by there speciall act made the 30 of July 1640, sessione 3, ordeaned all idolatrous images, crucifixes, pictures of Christ and all other idolatrous pictures to be demolished and removed forth and from all kirkis, colledges, chappelles and other publict places, therfor ordeanes all presbetries to take diligent tryell of all idolatrous pictures and images being within kirkis [*etc.*] and eftir tryell intimat the same first to the owneres and pairties themselves that they may remove the same, and in caise they doe neither appeill presentlie from the presbetrie in the ordinarie way to the synod and generall assembly nor remove them within the space of three monethes, then to intimate the same to all shereffis, stewartes, baillies, magistrates of burghes and regalities within the which the same shall be fund, and ordeanes them upoun the requisitione to be mad to them by the saidis presbetries, moderator or brethren therof, to raz, demolishe, abolish, cast doune or deface all these idolatrous images [*etc.*] according as they shall be enjoyned and directed from the saidis presbetrie from tyme to tyme, ilke ane of them within there owne boundis and jurisdictione respective, except in the caise of appeallatione foirsaid. . . .

A.P.S., v, 351

The policy represented in these acts took effect at Aberdeen, where carved stone work in the cathedral, the church of St. Nicholas and elsewhere was destroyed or defaced in August 1640 and a reredos in the cathedral hewn down in June 1642 ; and at Elgin cathedral, where the screen between the nave and the choir, painted with the Crucifixion on one side and the Day of Judgment on the other, was demolished in December 1640 (Spalding, *History of the Troubles* [Bannatyne Club], i, 234-5, 286 ; ii, 57). The Synod of Argyll entered energetically on the task of eliminating all ' idolatrous monuments ' ; but the allegation that it was responsible for the destruction of numbers of stone crosses on Iona and of the library there must be regarded as not proven (J. R. N. MacPhail, ' The Cleansing of I colm kill ' in *S.H.R.*, xxii, 14-24 ; *Minutes of the Synod of Argyll* [Scot. Hist. Soc.], i, xx-xxi, 36, 45, 68).

DISSENSIONS AMONG THE COVENANTERS : ALLIANCE
WITH THE ENGLISH PARLIAMENT

Meanwhile, not only had anti-covenanting sentiment continued strong in the north-east (which again, in May 1640, required military action by the Covenanters), and also in Angus and the central Highlands (where Argyll, under a commission of fire and sword from the Covenanting Committee of Estates, had been devastating the lands of his hereditary and personal enemies), but there were indications that the initial unity of the covenanting movement itself had been disrupted. Dissension had emerged in the Parliament of 1639, when there was opposition to the abolition of the spiritual estate without the giving of some compensation to the Crown, and again in 1640, when opinion was not unanimous in favour of the estates' resumption of their meetings without royal authority. The views of the moderates, alienated by the revolutionary trends now apparent, were expressed by Montrose, probably in 1640, in a statement which, like the Covenant itself, stressed the mutual interdependence of royal prerogative and subjects' liberties.

Extract from a letter by Montrose on the Supreme Power in Government

The king's prerogative and the subjects' privilege are so far from incompatibility that the one can never stand unless supported by the other. For the Soveraign being strong, and in full possession of his lawfull power and prerogative, is able to protect his subjects from oppression and maintain their liberties entire ; otherwise, not. On the other side, a people, enjoying freely their just liberties and privileges, maintaineth the prince's honour and prerogative out of the great affection they carry towards him, which is the greatest strength against foreign invasion or intestine insurrection that a prince can possibly be possessed with.

Memorials of Montrose (Maitland Club), ii, 50

This incipient constitutionalism was possibly associated with personal rivalries ; at any rate, in August 1640 Montrose and a score of other peers and gentlemen signed the Cumbernauld Bond, in which they pledged themselves to maintain the ' public ends ' of the Covenant in opposition to the ' particular and indirect practicking of a few.' The bond was discovered and was publicly burned by order of the Committee of Estates (January 1641), and Montrose and two of his associates were imprisoned from June until November 1641.

1640. *Extract from the Cumbernauld Bond*

Whereas we under-subscribers, out of our duty to religion, king and country, were forced to join ourselves in a covenant for the maintenance and defence of eithers, and every one of other, in that behalf : Now, finding how that, by the particular and indirect practicking of a few, the country and cause now depending does so much suffer, do heartily bind and oblige ourselves, out of our duty to all these respects above mentioned, but chiefly and mainly that Covenant which we have so solemnly sworn and already signed, to wed and study all public ends which may tend to the safety both of religion, laws and liberties of this poor kingdom.

Memorials of Montrose (Maitland Club), i, 254–5

THE SOLEMN LEAGUE AND COVENANT

More serious division of opinion emerged over the question of Scotland's relations with the two parties in the English civil war, which began in August 1642. In November the parliamentary party appealed to the Scots for help, and in December came an appeal from the king. The Privy Council, by a majority of eleven to nine, decided to publish only the latter, but was subsequently prevailed on by a petition to publish the message from Parliament also, in spite of a counter-petition against this course. In September 1643 an alliance was concluded with the English Parliament—not the mere civil bond which the English would have preferred, but the Solemn League and Covenant, representing the policy of a presbyterian crusade for the imposition of uniformity in doctrine, worship, discipline and government on the three churches of Scotland, England and Ireland. Scotland was far from unanimous, yet the Committee of Estates and the Commission of Assembly proceeded to enforce subscription to the new Covenant on pain of excommunication and confiscation of goods.

1643. *The Solemn League and Covenant*

We Noblemen, Barons, Knights, Gentlemen, Citizens, Burgesses, Ministers of the Gospel, and Commons of all sorts in the Kingdoms of Scotland, England and Ireland, by the providence of God living under one King, and being of one reformed Religion, Having before our eyes the glory of God, and the advancement of the Kingdom of our Lord and Saviour Jesus Christ, the Honour and Happinesse of the Kings Majesty and his Posterity, and the true publick Liberty, Safety, and Peace of the Kingdoms, wherein every ones private condition is included ; And calling to minde the treacherous and bloody plots, conspiracies, attempts and practices of the Enemies of God against the true Religion and Professours thereof in all places, especially in these three Kingdoms, ever since the Reformation of Religion, and how much their rage, power and presumption are of late, and at this time increased and exercised ; whereof the deplorable estate of the Church and Kingdom of Ireland, the distressed estate of the Church & Kingdom of England, and the dangerous estate of the Church and Kingdom of Scotland are present and publick testimonies : We have now at last (after other means of Supplication, Remonstrance, Protestation and Suffering) for the preservation of our selves and our Religion from utter ruine and destruction, according to the commendable practice of these Kingdoms in former times, and the example of Gods People in other Nations, after mature deliberation, resolved and determined to enter into a mutuall and solemn League and Covenant : Wherein we all subscribe, and each one of us for himself, with our hands lifted up to the most high God, do Swear

1. That we shall sincerely, really and constantly, through the grace of God, endeavour in our several places and

callings, the preservation of the Reformed Religion in the Church of Scotland, in Doctrine, Worship, Discipline and Government, against our common Enemies ; The Reformation of Religion in the Kingdoms of England and Ireland, in Doctrine, Worship, Discipline and Government, according to the Word of God, and the example of the best Reformed Churches ; And shall endeavour to bring the Churches of God in the three Kingdoms, to the nearest conjunction and uniformity in Religion, Confession of Faith, Form of Church-government, Directory for Worship and Catechizing ; That we and our Posterity after us, may, as Brethren, live in Faith and Love, and the Lord may delight to dwell in the midst of us.

2. That we shall in like manner, without respect of persons, endeavour the Extirpation of Popery, Prelacy (that is, Church-government by Arch-bishops, Bishops, their Chancellours and Commissaries, Deans, Deans and Chapters, Arch-deacons, and all other Ecclesiasticall Officers depending on that Hierarchy), Superstition, Heresy, Schism, Prophanesse, and whatsoever shall be found to be contrary to sound Doctrine, and the power of Godliness ; Lest we partake in other mens sins, and thereby be in danger to receive of their plagues ; And that the Lord may be one, and his Name one in the three Kingdoms.

3. We shall with the same sincerity, reality and constancy, in our severall vocations, endeavour with our estates and lives mutually to preserve the Rights and Priviledges of the Parliaments, and the Liberties of the Kingdoms ; And to preserve and defend the Kings Majesty's Person and Authority, in the preservation and defence of the true Religion, and Liberties of the Kingdoms ; That the world may bear witnesse with our consciences of our Loyalty, and that we have no thoughts or intentions to diminish his Majesty's just power and greatnesse.

4. We shall also with all faithfulnesse endeavour the discovery of all such as have been, or shall be Incendiaries, Malignants, or evil instruments, by hindering the Reforma-

tion of Religion, dividing the King from his people, or one of the Kingdoms from another, or making any faction, or parties amongst the people contrary to this League and Covenant, That they may be brought to publick triall, and receive condigne punishment, as the degree of their offences shall require or deserve, or the supream Judicatories of both Kingdomes respectively, or others having power from them for that effect, shall judge convenient.

5. And whereas the happinesse of a blessed Peace between these Kingdoms, denyed in former times to our Progenitors, is by the good Providence of God granted unto us, and hath been lately concluded, and settled by both Parliaments, We shall each one of us, according to our place and interest, endeavour that they may remain conjoyned in a firme Peace and Union to all Posterity, And that Justice may be done upon the willfull Opposers thereof, in manner expressed in the precedent Article.

6. We shall also according to our places and callings in this Common cause of Religion, Liberty, and Peace of the Kingdoms, assist and defend all those that enter into this League and Covenant, in the maintaining and pursuing thereof ; And shall not suffer our selves directly or indirectly by whatsoever combination, perswasion or terrour, to be divided and withdrawn from this blessed Union and conjunction, whither to make defection to the contrary part, or to give our selves to a detestable indifferency or neutrality in this cause, which so much concerneth the Glory of God, the good of the Kingdoms, and honour of the King ; But shall all the dayes of our lives zealously and constantly continue therein, against all opposition, and promote the same according to our power, against all Lets and Impediments whatsoever ; And, what we are not able our selves to suppresse or overcome, we shall reveale and make known, that it may be timely prevented or removed : All which we shall do as in the sight of God.

And because these Kingdoms are guilty of many sins, and provocations against God, and his Son Jesus Christ, as is too manifest by our present distresses and dangers, the fruits thereof, We professe and declare before God, and the world, our unfained desire to be humbled for our own sins, and for the sins of these Kingdoms, especially that we have not, as we ought, valued the inesteemable benefit of the Gospel, that we have not laboured for the purity and power thereof, and that we have not endeavoured to receive Christ in our hearts, nor to walk worthy of Him in our lives, which are the causes of other sins and transgressions so much abounding amongst us, And our true and unfained purpose, desire, and endeavour for our selves, and all others under our power and charge, both in publick and in private, in all dutyes we owe to God and man, to amend our lives, and each one to go before another in the example of a real Reformation ; That the Lord may turn away his wrath, and heavy indignation, and establish these Churches and Kingdoms in truth and Peace. And this Covenant we make in the presence of Almighty God the Searcher of all hearts, with a true intention to perform the same, As we shall answer at that great Day when the secrets of all hearts shall be disclosed ; Most humbly beseeching the Lord, to strengthen us by his Holy Spirit for this end, and to blesse our desires and proceedings with such successe, as may be deliverance and safety to his people, and encouragement to other Christian Churches groaning under, or in danger of the yoke of Antichristian Tyranny, or to joyn in the same, or like Association & Covenant, To the Glory of God, the enlargement of the Kingdom of Jesus Christ, and the peace & tranquillity of Christian Kingdoms, and Common-wealths.

A.P.S., vi, 41

THE WESTMINSTER ASSEMBLY

On 12 June 1643 (that is, before the Solemn League and Covenant), the English Parliament, on the narrative that reform of the government and worship of the Church was required, and that reform of Church government should be such as would be ' most agreeable to God's holy word and most apt to procure and preserve the peace of the Church at home, and nearer agreement with the

Church of Scotland and other reformed churches abroad,'
appointed about a hundred and twenty ministers and thirty laymen to meet at Westminster on 1 July. The Scots were invited to
send representatives, and on 19 August the General Assembly gave
commission to Alexander Henderson, Robert Douglas, Samuel
Rutherford, Robert Baillie and George Gillespie, ministers, John,
Earl of Cassillis, John, Lord Maitland, and Sir Archibald Johnston
of Wariston, elders, or any three of them (two of the three being
ministers), to ' propone, consult, treat and conclude ' with the
Westminster Assembly or its commissioners ' in all matters which
may further the union of this island in one form of kirk government, one confession of faith, one catechism, one directory for
the worship of God.' The small band of Scots, being representatives of their Church, had influence out of proportion to their
numbers, but they were not incorporated in the Assembly, and its
productions were issued as those of ' The Assembly of Divines at
Westminster, with the assistance of commissioners from the Church
of Scotland.' Besides being predominantly English, the Assembly
was in Scottish eyes an Erastian body, under the domination of
Parliament ; yet the Scots accepted its formularies, which were
to remain the standards of presbyterian Scotland.

Letter of Robert Baillie [1 January 1644]

In the time of this anarchie the divisions of people weeklie
does much encrease : the Independent partie growes ; but
the Anabaptists more ; and the Antinomians most. The
Independents being most able men, and of great credit,
fearing no less than banishment from their native countrey
if Presbytries were erected, are watchful that no conclusion
be taken for their prejudice. It was my advyce which
Mr. Hendersone presentlie applauded, and gave me thanks
for it, to eschew a publick rupture with the Independents
till we were more able for them. As yet a Presbytrie to this
people is conceaved to be a strange monster. It was our
good therefore to go on hand in hand, so far as we did
agree, against the common enemie : hopeing that in our
differences, when we behooved to come to them, God would
give us light ; in the meantime we would assay to agree

upon the Directorie of Worship, wherein we expect no small help from these men, to abolish the Great Idol of England, the Service-Book, and to erect in all the parts of worship a full conformitie to Scotland in all things worthie to be spoken of. . . . This day [was] . . . assented to by all, that a sub-committee of five, without exclusion of anie of the committee, shall meet with us of Scotland for preparing a Directorie of Worship. . . .

Baillie, *Letters and Journals*, ii, 117

The Preface to the Directory for Public Worship

In the beginning of the blessed Reformation, our wise and pious ancestors took care to set forth an order for redress of many things which they then, by the Word, discovered to be vain, erroneous, superstitious and idolatrous, in the public worship of God. This occasioned many godly and learned men to rejoice much in the Book of Common Prayer, at that time set forth ; because the mass and the rest of the Latin service being removed, the public worship was celebrated in our own tongue : many of the common people also received benefit by hearing the scriptures read in their own language which formerly were unto them as a book that is sealed.

Howbeit, long and sad experience hath made it manifest that the Liturgy used in the Church of England . . . hath proved an offence, not only to many of the godly at home, but also to the reformed Churches abroad. . . . Sundry good Christians have been, by means thereof, kept from the Lord's Table ; and divers able and faithful ministers debarred from the exercise of their ministry. . . . Prelates, and their faction, have laboured to raise the estimation of it to such an height as if there were no other worship or way of worship of God amongst us but only the Service-book ; to the great hindrance of the preaching of the Word and (in some places, especially of late) to the jostling of it out as unnecessary, or at best as far inferior to the reading of

127

common prayer ; which was made no better than an idol by many ignorant and superstitious people, who, pleasing themselves in their presence at that service, and their lip-labour in bearing a part in it, have thereby hardened themselves in their ignorance and carelessness of saving knowledge and true piety. . . .

Upon these, and many the like weighty considerations in reference to the whole book in general, and because of divers particulars contained in it . . . that we may in some measure answer the gracious providence of God, which at this time calleth upon us for further reformation, and may satisfy our own consciences and answer the expectation of other reformed churches and the desires of many of the godly among ourselves, and withal give some public testimony of our endeavours for uniformity in divine worship, which we have promised in our Solemn League and Covenant : we have, after earnest and frequent calling upon the name of God, and after much consultation, not with flesh and blood, but with His holy Word, resolved to lay aside the former Liturgy, with the many rites and ceremonies formerly used in the worship of God ; and have agreed upon this following Directory for all the parts of public worship, at ordinary and extraordinary times.

Directory for Public Worship (reprinted in numerous editions of the *Confession of Faith*)

The Westminster Form of Church Government

The Form of Presbyterial Church-Government and of Ordination of Ministers ; agreed upon by the Assembly of Divines at Westminster, with the assistance of Commissioners from the Church of Scotland, as a part of the Covenanted Uniformity in Religion betwixt the Churches of Christ in the Kingdoms of Scotland, England and Ireland.

[Of the Officers of the Church]

The officers which Christ hath appointed for the edification of his church and the perfecting of the saints, are some extraordinary, as apostles, evangelists and prophets, which are ceased ; others ordinary and perpetual, as pastors, teachers and other church-governors, and deacons.

[Pastors]

The pastor is an ordinary and perpetual officer in the church. . . .

[Teacher or Doctor]

The scripture doth hold out the name and title of teacher, as well as of the pastor : who is also a minister of the word, as well as the pastor, and hath power of administration of the sacraments. . . . A teacher or doctor is of most excellent use in schools and universities. . . .

[Other Church-Governors]

As there were in the Jewish church elders of the people joined with the priests and Levites in the government of the church ; so Christ, who hath instituted government and governors ecclesiastical in the church, hath furnished some in His church, beside the ministers of the Word, with gifts for government, and with commission to execute the same when called thereunto, who are to join with the minister in the government of the church. Which officers reformed churches commonly call Elders.

[Deacons]

The scripture doth hold out deacons as distinct officers in the church : whose office is perpetual. To whose office it belongs not to preach the Word, or administer the sacraments, but to take special care in distributing to the necessities of the poor. . . .

[Of the Officers of a particular Congregation]

For officers in a single congregation, there ought to be one at the least, both to labour in the Word and doctrine and to rule. It is also requisite that there should be others to join in government. And likewise it is requisite that there be others to take special care for the relief of the poor. The number of each of which is to be proportioned according to the condition of the congregation.

These officers are to meet together at convenient and set times for the well ordering of the affairs of that congregation, each according to his office. It is most expedient that in these meetings one whose office is to labour in the Word and doctrine do moderate in their proceedings. . . .

[Of Church-Government, and the several sorts of Assemblies for the same]

Christ hath instituted a government and governors ecclesiastical in the church : to that purpose, the Apostles did immediately receive the keys from the hand of Jesus Christ, and did use and exercise them in all the churches of the world upon all occasions. And Christ hath since continually furnished some in His church with gifts of government, and with commission to execute the same when called thereunto.

It is lawful, and agreeable to the Word of God, that the church be governed by several sorts of assemblies, which are congregational, classical and synodical. . . .

[Of Congregational Assemblies]

The ruling officers of a particular congregation have power, authoritatively, to call before them any member of the congregation, as they shall see just occasion ; to enquire into the knowledge and spiritual estate of the several members of the congregation ; to admonish and rebuke.

[Of Classical Assemblies]

The scripture doth hold out a presbytery in a church. A presbytery consisteth of ministers of the Word and such other public officers as are agreeable to and warranted by the Word of God to be church-governors, to join with the

ministers in the government of the church. The scripture
doth hold forth that many particular congregations may
be under one presbyterial government. . . .

[Of Synodical Assemblies]

The scripture doth hold out another sort of assemblies for
the government of the church, beside classical and congregational, all which we call Synodical. . . . Synodical
assemblies may lawfully be of several sorts, as provincial,
national and oecumenical. It is lawful, and agreeable to
the Word of God, that there be a subordination of congregational, classical, provincial and national assemblies, for
the government of the church. . . .

Form of Church Government (reprinted in numerous editions of the
Confession of Faith)

[*This form of Church government was approved by the Scottish
General Assembly on* 10 *February* 1645.]

EMERGENCE OF A ROYALIST PARTY : THE ENGAGEMENT

The division of opinion over the question of participation in the
English civil war was so profound that civil war in Scotland became
unavoidable. Therefore, when Leslie, now Earl of Leven, led
a Scottish army across the Tweed (19 January 1644) in a campaign
to aid the Parliament which led to the great victory over the king
at Marston Moor (2 July 1644), the king granted a commission to
Montrose to raise forces in Scotland (1 February 1644), and
Montrose's campaign began seriously in August. His victories
were brilliant, but made only a slight contribution to the formation
of an effective royalist party. Moderate royalists were alienated
by the Highland and Irish descent on the Lowlands ; other nobles
were either hesitant or jealous ; and Huntly, dominant in the
non-Covenanting north-east, remained aloof. Montrose, on his
part, professed never to lose sight of the ends for which the Covenant had originally been undertaken, and shortly before his death
in 1650 he said, ' The Covenant which I took, I own it and adhere
to it. Bishops, I care not for them. I never intended to advance

their interest. But when the king had granted you all your desires, and you were every one sitting under his vine and under his fig tree—that then you should have taken a party in England by the hand, and entered into a league and covenant with them against the king, was the thing I judged my duty to oppose to the yondmost ' (Mark Napier, *Memoirs of Montrose*, ii, 787).

Montrose's victory at Inverlochy (2 Feb. 1645) was the occasion of the following letter. The battle of Kilsyth (15 August 1645) seemed to put Scotland in his control, but his Highland troops melted away and David Leslie, returning with tried forces from England, crushed him in a surprise attack at Philiphaugh (13 Sept. 1645).

Montrose to Charles I, 3 February 1645

. . . I have traversed all the north of Scotland up to Argyle's country ; who durst not stay my coming, or I should have given your Majesty a good account of him ere now. But at last I have met with him, yesterday, to his cost ; of which your gracious Majesty be pleased to receive the following particulars.

[*On learning that Argyll was assembling an army at Inverlochy*] I departed out of Argyleshire, and marched through Lorn, Glencow and [Loch]Aber, till I came to Loch Ness, my design being to fall upon Argyle before Seaforth and the Frasers could join him. My march was through inaccessible mountains, where I could have no guides but cow-herds, and they scarce acquainted with a place but six miles from their own habitations. If I had been attacked but with one hundred men in some of these passes, I must have certainly returned back, for it would have been impossible to force my way, most of the passes being so streight that three men could not march abreast. I was willing to let the world see that Argyle was not the man his Highlandmen believed him to be, and that it was possible to beat him in his own Highlands. The difficultest march of all was over the Lochaber mountains, which we at last surmounted, and came upon the back of the enemy when they least expected us, having cut off some scouts we met about four miles from Inverlochy. Our van came within view of them about five o'clock in the afternoon, and we made a halt till our rear was got up, which could not be done till eight at night. The rebels took the alarm and stood to their arms, as well as we, all night, which was moonlight and very clear. . . . . A little after the sun was up, both armies met, and the rebels fought for some time with great bravery, the prime of the Campbells giving the first onset, as men that deserved to fight in a better cause. Our men, having a nobler cause, did wonders, and came immediately to push of pike and dint of sword, after their first firing. The rebels could not stand it, but, after some resistance at first, began to run, whom we pursued for nine miles together, making a great slaughter, which I would have hindered, if possible, that I might save your Majesty's misled subjects. . . .

As to the state of affairs in this kingdom, the bearer will fully inform your Majesty in every particular. And give me leave, with all humility, to assure your Majesty that, through God's blessing, I am in the fairest hopes of reducing this kingdom to your Majesty's obedience. And, if the measures I have concerted with your other loyal subjects fail me not, which they hardly can, I doubt not before the end of this summer I shall be able to come to your Majesty's assistance with a brave army, which, backed with the justice of your Majesty's cause, will make the Rebels in England, as well as in Scotland, feel the just rewards of Rebellion. Only give me leave, after I have reduced this country to your Majesty's obedience, and conquered from Dan to Beersheba, to say to your Majesty then, as David's general did to his master, ' Come thou thyself, lest this country be called by my name.' . . .

Memorials of Montrose (Maitland Club), ii, 175–9

The emergence of a *strong* royalist party was delayed until after the surrender of the king to the Scots (May 1646) and their decision, on his refusal to take the Covenants, to hand him over to the English Parliament (8 January 1647). Developments were shaped by the course of events in England. The civil war had been an English war, a quarrel between the king and his English Parliament ; the quarrel in Scotland had long ago been settled by concessions from the king, and the objectives of the National Covenant achieved. Moreover, the declining authority of the English Parliament, which was favourable to presbyterianism, and the domination of the army, which stood for ' Independency ' in Church government, made it more than doubtful if the Solemn League and Covenant would ever take effect in England. Finally, there was anxiety about the ultimate fate of the king after his seizure by the English army in June 1647. Both Covenant and monarchy were threatened, and their joint preservation was the aim of the Engagement, secretly negotiated with the king by a section of the Scots.

The Engagement

1647. *Charles R.*

His Majesty giving belief to the professions of those who have entered into the League and Covenant, and that their intentions are real for preservation of his Majesty's person and authority according to their allegiance, and no ways to diminish his just power and greatness, his Majesty, so soon as he can with freedom, honour and safety be present in a free parliament, is content to confirm the said League and Covenant by Act of Parliament in both kingdoms, for security of all who have taken or shall take the said Covenant, provided that none who is unwilling shall be constrained to take it. His Majesty will likewise confirm by Act of Parliament in England, presbyterial government, the directory for worship and assembly of divines at Westminster, for three years, so that His Majesty and his household be not hindered from using that form of Divine Service he hath formerly practised ; and that a free debate and consultation be had with the Divines at Westminster, twenty of His Majesty's nomination being added unto them, and with such as shall be sent from the Church of Scotland, whereby it may be determined by His Majesty and the two Houses how the Church government, after the said three years, shall be fully established as is most agreeable to the Word of God : that an effectual course shall be taken by Act of Parliament, and all other ways needful or expedient, for suppressing the opinions and practices of Anti-Trinitarians, Anabaptists, Antinomians, Arminians, Familists, Brownists, Separatists, Independents, Libertines, and Seekers, and generally for suppressing all blasphemy, heresy, schism, and all such scandalous doctrines and practices as are contrary to the light of nature, or to the known principles of Christianity, whether concerning faith, worship or conversation, or to the power of Godliness, or which may be destructive to order and government, or to the peace of the Church and kingdom ; that in the next Session of Parliament after that the kingdom of Scotland shall declare for His Majesty in pursuance of this Agreement, he shall in person or by commission confirm the League and Covenant according to the first Article. Concerning the Acts passed in the last triennial Parliament of his kingdom of Scotland, and the Committees appointed by the same, His Majesty is content then also to give assurance by Act of Parliament that neither he nor his successors shall quarrel, call in question, or command the contrary of any of them, nor question any for giving obedience to the same ; and whereas after the return of the Scottish army to Scotland, the Houses of Parliament of England did resolve and appoint the army under command of Sir Thomas Fairfax to disband, and they having entered into an engagement to the contrary, His Majesty was carried away from Holdenby against his will by a party of the said army, and detained in their power until he was forced to fly from amongst them to the Isle of Wight ; and since that time His Majesty and the Commissioners of the kingdom of Scotland have earnestly pressed that His Majesty might come to London in safety, honour and freedom for a personal treaty with the two Houses and the Commissioners of the Parliament of Scotland, which hath not been granted : and whereas the said army hath in a violent manner forced away divers members of both Houses from the discharge of their trust, and possessed themselves

of the City of London and all the strengths and garrisons
of the kingdom, and, through the power and influence of
the said army and their adherents, Propositions and Bills
have been sent to His Majesty without the advice and consent of the kingdom of Scotland, contrary to the Treaty
between the kingdoms, which are destructive to religion,
His Majesty's just rights, the privileges of Parliament, and
liberty of the subject, from which Propositions and Bills the
said Scots Commissioners have dissented in the name of the
kingdom of Scotland ; and, forasmuch as His Majesty is
willing to give satisfaction concerning the settling of religion
and other matter in difference, as is expressed in this Agreement, the kingdom of Scotland doth oblige and engage
themselves first in a peaceable way and manner to endeavour
that His Majesty may come to London in safety, honour and
freedom for a personal treaty with the Houses of Parliament
and the Commissioners of Scotland upon such Propositions
as shall be mutually agreed on between the kingdoms, and
such Propositions as His Majesty shall think fit to make ;
and that for this end all armies may be disbanded, and in
case this shall not be granted, that Declarations shall be
emitted by the kingdom of Scotland in pursuance of this
Agreement, against the unjust proceedings of the two Houses
of Parliament towards His Majesty and the kingdom of
Scotland, wherein they shall assert the right which belongs
to the Crown in the power of the militia, the Great Seal,
bestowing of honours and offices of trust, choice of Privy
Councillors, the right of the King's negative voice in
Parliament ; and that the Queen's Majesty, the Prince, and
the rest of the royal issue, ought to remain where His Majesty
shall think fit, in either of the kingdoms, with safety, honour
and freedom ; and upon the issuing of the said Declarations,
that an army shall be sent from Scotland into England, for
preservation and establishment of religion, for defence of
His Majesty's person and authority, and restoring him to his
government, to the just rights of the Crown and his full
revenues, for defence of the privileges of Parliament and
liberties of the subject, for making a firm union between the

kingdoms, under His Majesty and his posterity, and settling a lasting peace ; in pursuance whereof the kingdom of Scotland will endeavour that there may be a free and full Parliament in England, and that His Majesty may be with them in honour, safety and freedom, and that a speedy period be set to this present Parliament, and that the said army shall be upon the march before the said peaceable message and Declaration be delivered to the House ; and it is further agreed that all such in the kingdoms of England or Ireland, as shall join with the kingdom of Scotland in pursuance of this Agreement, shall be protected by His Majesty in their persons and estates ; and that all such His Majesty's subjects of England and Ireland as shall join with him in pursuance of this Agreement may come to the Scotch army and join with them, or else put themselves into other bodies in England and Wales for prosecution of the same ends as the King's Majesty shall judge most convenient, and under such Commanders or Generals of the English nation as His Majesty shall think fit, and that all such shall be protected by the kingdom of Scotland and their army in their persons and estates, and where any injury or wrong is done to them therein, that they shall be careful to see them fully repaired so far as is in their power to do, and likewise, where any injury or wrong is done to those that join with the kingdom of Scotland, His Majesty shall be careful for their full reparation ; that His Majesty or any by his authority or knowledge shall not make nor admit of any cessation, pacification, nor agreement for peace whatsoever, nor of any Treaty, Propositions, Bills, or any other ways for that end, with the Houses of Parliament or any army or party in England and Ireland, without the advice and consent of the kingdom of Scotland ; nor any having their authority shall either make or admit of any of these any manner of way with any whatsoever without His Majesty's advice and consent ; that, upon the settling of a peace, there be an Act of Oblivion to be agreed on by His Majesty and both his Parliaments of both kingdoms ; that His Majesty, the Prince, or both shall come into Scotland upon the invitation of that kingdom and their declaration that they shall be in safety, freedom and honour, when possibly they can come with safety and conveniency ; and that His Majesty shall contribute his utmost endeavours both at home and abroad for assisting the kingdom of Scotland in carrying on this war by sea and land, and for their supply by monies, arms, ammunition, and all other things requisite, as also for guarding the coasts of Scotland with ships, and protecting all Scottish merchants in the free exercise of trade and commerce with other nations ; and His Majesty is very willing and doth authorise the Scots army to possess themselves of Berwick, Carlisle, Newcastle-upon-Tyne, Tynemouth, and Hartlepool, for to be places of retreat and magazine, and, when the peace of the kingdom is settled, the kingdom of Scotland shall remove their forces, and deliver back again the said towns and castles ; that, according to the large Treaty, payment may be made of the remainder of the Brotherly Assistance which yet rests unpaid ; and likewise of the £200,000 due upon the late Treaty made with the Houses of Parliament for the return of the Scots army, as also that payment shall be made to the kingdom of Scotland for the charge and expense of their army in this future war, together with due recompense for the losses which they shall sustain therein : that due satisfaction, according to the Treaty on that behalf between the kingdoms, shall be made to the Scottish army in Ireland, out of the land of that kingdom or otherwise ; that His Majesty, according to the intention of his father, shall endeavour a complete union of the kingdoms, so as they may be one under His Majesty and his posterity ; and, if that cannot be speedily effected, that all liberties, privileges, concerning commerce, traffic, and manufactories peculiar to the subjects of either nation, shall be common to the subjects of both kingdoms without distinction ; and that there be a communication of mutual capacity of all other privileges of the subject in the two kingdoms ; that a competent number of ships shall be yearly assigned and appointed out of His Majesty's navy, which shall attend the coast of Scotland for a guard and freedom of trade to his subjects of that nation ; that His Majesty doth declare that his successors as well as himself are obliged to the performances of the Articles and conditions of this Agreement ; that His Majesty shall not be obliged to the performance of the aforesaid articles until the kingdom of Scotland shall declare for him in pursuance of this agreement, and that the whole articles and conditions aforesaid shall be finished, perfected and performed before the return of the Scots army ; and that when they return into Scotland at the same time, *simul et semel*, all arms be disbanded in England.

Carisbrook, the 26th of December.

Gardiner, *Constitutional Documents of the Puritan Revolution*, 347-52

PRESTON, DUNBAR AND WORCESTER.   ENGAGERS AND ANTI-ENGAGERS.   RESOLUTIONERS AND PROTESTERS

Scotland was gravely divided over the Engagement.   While a clear majority in the Estates were in favour, the Assembly dis-approved and a powerful opposition maintained that, as the king's liberty was incompatible with security for the Covenants, hostility to the king must continue.   While the Estates authorised the raising of an army to implement the Engagement, most of the ministers did all in their power to obstruct recruitment.   The army of ' Engagers ' which invaded England on the king's behalf was cut to pieces by Cromwell at Preston (17–19 August 1648), an event which was disastrous, and not only in a military sense, to moderate and royalist policy.   The extremists of the south-west marched on Edinburgh in the ' Whiggamore Raid ' (5 September) ;   the Committee of Estates fled ;   and the anti-Engagers, led by Argyll and Cassillis, secured their position by coming to an understanding with Cromwell—a wholly unnatural alliance of rigid presby-terians with Independency.   One genuine bond of union was the hatred of the Engagers and all other ' Malignants ' which inspired the Act of Classes passed by the ' rump ' of the Scottish Parliament on 23 January 1649.

1649. *The Act of all Classes for purging the judicatories and other places of public trust*

The Estates of Parliament . . . declare, enact and ordane that all these officers of estate, members or clerks of the parlement, committeis theirof, Secreit Counsall, Session, Exchequer, Justice Courts, Commissioune for plantatioun of churches or conservatioun of the peace, Shirreff Courts, Stewart Courts, Baillie Courts, Commissar Courts, Baillies of regalitie Courts, Warden Courts of his Maiestie's Minthous, Admirall Court, Gild Court, Toun Counsall or any other publict judicature, or deacons of crafts and all who had any office, place or publict trust and all having deputatioun from or dependance upon any of the aforesaid who were guiltie of any of the faults conteined in any of the four severall classes eftermentioned shall be removed and secluded from publict trust according to the severall rules respective after following.

The First Classe

The estats declare all these to be comprehended in the first classe who wer generall officers who led and accompanied the army into England, and all those officers that continowed in the engagement who commanded the forces at Mauchline Moor or at Stirling, and all those who were principallie active in persuading or bringing over of the forces from Ireland, and all those persons who wer plotters, cheef actores, and pryme promotters of the late unlaufull engadgement from the beginning to the end therof in parlement, committeis or otherwise ; and sicklyk all these who were cheeff actoris and pryme promotters of the horrid rebellioun of James Grahame [Marquis of Montrose] and who since have either accepted of charge or joyned as volunteers in the said unlaufull engadgement or taken the oath in committeis or subscrived the band for themselves or others for the engadgement or sat in the committees or other meetings and gave ordour for prosequuting the said engadgement or who otherwise gave or received and execute orderis aganst others for prosequuting the engadgement, as also such clerkis of parlement, committeis theirof, Secreit Counsall or Session who wer guiltie of any of the faults contayned in any of the class at St. Andrews and retayning their former principles of malignancie, and have bene active in their places or imployments for promoving the late unlaufull engadgement.

The Second Classe

The estats also declar all these to be comprehended in the second classe who not being included in the first classe have bene formerlie classed or censured for malignancie or guiltie of the crymes contayned in the first and second classes at St. Andrews of the date at St. Andrewes the [blank] day of [blank] one thousand six hundred and [blank] yeires and since have ather accepted of charge or joyned as volunties in the said unlaufull engadgement ; . . . and siclyk all those persons, altho not formerlie classed and not being included in the first classe, who wer officers which wer upon any of the expeditions into England or Scotland for the said engagement ; and siclyk all these who concurred in petitions protestatiounes remonstrances or letters for moving the parliament or committeis to cary on the engagement ; and siclyk all these who protested aganst the caus of the fast or the kirks declaratiounes or petitions of the presbiteries or kirk sessions aganst the engadgement, or red, or caused read, at kirk doores the committeis observatiounes aganst the assemblies declaratioun, or interrupted Divyne service or magistrats and persons of quality, or who removed at the reading of the assemblies declaratioun ; sicklyk all those who not onlie took the oath injoyned by the last parlement for the engagement in committeis or subscryved the band and declared themselffis readie to doe the same, bot also seduced others or protested aganes others for not taking the oath or not subscribeing the band ; siclyk all these who injoyned and pressed others to subscryve the band or tak the oath for carying on the engagement ; and siclyk all these who concurred as members or clerks in acts of Parliament and Committee of Estats for prosecuteing the said engagement or for pressing others therunto, and such who consulted and gave advyse for penning or prosecuteing of the process aganst the honest ministers who were at Mauchline Moore or any others for thair opposing or not joyning in the engagement.

The Thrid Classe

The estats lykwise declares all these to be comprehended in the thrid classe who (not being included in the first or second classes) sat in parliament and committee of estats and took the oaths forsaid for the engagement, or sat as clerkis in any of these or any other judicatories and gave no publict testimony aganst the said engagement, caried on therin by thair service, or were any way knowne to have beene for the same in judgement manifested by thair expressions and actions ; siclyk all these persons who have taken the oath forsaid or subscryvit the band for the engagement or who in committeis of warre or other meetings, Toun Counsall or other courtis have refuised or opposed the desyres of any petitions from shyres, presbiteries, sessions or other kirk judicatories aganst the engagement, or concurred in acts to force the dissenters petitioners or others to concurre in the first or second Leavies or other accession to the said engagement, or with the forces under the earle of Crawford, earle of Lanark and George Monro ; and siclyk all such who were either forcers, urgers, or seducers of others to concurre in the said engagement or with the forsaid forces ; and siclyk all those who accepted commissions to be officers or joyned as voluntiers to the forces under the Duke of Hammiltoun or the earles of Crawford, Lanerk, or George Monro. Lykas all persons who in their speeches and actions did evidence thair judgement for and affectioun to that sinfull course, or who (in such a tyme of tryall after such petitions from the shires and such declaratiounes and warnings from the Church evidenceing to all

the unlaufulnes of the engagement aganst Covenant and
Treaties) did not give any countenance to the cause or
testimony of thair judgement and affectioun aganst such a
defection and dangerous war when and where they had the
opportunity to doe it with others.

The Fourth Classe

The estats of parlement in lyk maner declares all these to
be comprehended in the 4th classe who being members of
judicatories, clerkis and persons in publict trust as aforsaid
are given to uncleannesse, brybery, swearing, drunkennesse,
or deceiving, or are otherwise openlie profane and grosslie
scandalous in thair conversatioun or who neglect the
worship of God in thair families.

[*Those in the first class were excluded from office for life, those
in the second for ten years, those in the third for five years, and those
in the fourth for one. But readmission was in every case to be
preceded by satisfaction to the Kirk, which thus obtained a veto on
public appointments.*]

A.P.S., vi, pt. ii, 143-7

Seven days after the Act of Classes had been passed, Charles I
was beheaded. The effect in Scotland was to stimulate unity and
ultimately to weaken the grip of the extremists. Charles II,
taking the Covenants, was accepted as king of Scots, but none
except rigid adherents of the faction now in power were at first
permitted to fight for king and country against Cromwell. The
' purge ' of the army, in the very face of the enemy, contributed
to the disaster of Dunbar (3 September 1650).

But, as Preston had strengthened the extremists, so Dunbar
now produced a reaction in favour of the moderates. The
Assembly divided into the irreconcilables, who, in the Remonstrance (October 1650) denounced the understanding with the
king and contended that the Act of Classes had not been rigidly
enough applied, and a more moderate party, who were prepared
to co-operate with royalists and Engagers. Argyll reached an
accommodation with the king's party, who already had an armed
force in the Highlands ; the Committee of Estates condemned

the Remonstrance (25 November) ; a series of resolutions in favour
of admitting Engagers and even former supporters of Montrose
meant that the Act of Classes was virtually shelved. Thus the
Covenanting party was again divided, this time into Resolutioners
and Remonstrants or Protesters. The Remonstrant section of the
army was crushed at Hamilton (1 December) ; and Charles was
crowned at Scone (1 January 1651). An appeal for unity on a
basis of patriotism and royalism, signalised by the formal repeal
of the Act of Classes (2 June 1651),[1] produced a broadly based
force which slipped past Cromwell into England only to meet
with disaster at Worcester (3 September).

1650. *Extracts from the Remonstrance*

> To the Rt. Honorable the Committee of Estaites, the
> humble Remonstrance of the gentlemen, commanders
> and ministers, attending the forces in the west

Althoughe wee do not judge of the undertakings of the
Lords people by the successe, and be not shaken by the
dissipating of our armey, nor brought in question our causse,
yet wee thinke ourselves, and all the people of this land,
called by thesse late dispensations to searche and tray our
wayes ; wee doe therfor esteeme it our deutie . . . freelie
and faithfullie to make our thoughts knowen to your lordships concerning the causses and remedies of the Lords
indignation wich hath gone out aganist his people, quherin
wee supposse wee neid not insist upone the lait sinns conteined in the lait causses of the fast, published by the
Commissioners of the Kirke, relatting to the conducte and
carriage of our armie, and other thinges ; bot wee shall
speike to that wich most directlie concerns your lordships :—

That wiche is obvious, in the first place, amonge the sinns
of the land, is our late proceidings with the King ; quherin,
that wee be not mistakin, wee shall distinguish betuix our
deuty and our sinns. Wee owe and acknouledge for our
deutie to usse all lawfull wayes and means for reclaming
the King, and to owne his intrest according to oure
vocatione, so fare as he owns and prosecuttes the causse.

[1] *A.P.S.*, vi, pt. ii, 677

Bot we are convinced that it is our sinne, and the sin of the kingdome, that quhen the King had walked in the wayes of his fathers oppositione to the worke of reformation, and the soleme leauge and covenant . . . that after all this, commissioners should have beine warrandit to assure him of his present admissione to the exercisse of his royall power, upone his profession to joyne in the causse and covenant, not onlie without aney furder evidence of his repentance, unto the renewing of the Lord's contrawersie with his fathers housse, and without convincing evidences of the realitie of his profession and his forsaiking his former principalls and wayes ; but quhen ther was pregnant presumptions, if not cleir evidences, of the contrarey. . . .

Wee beseiche your lordships to consider wither in Gods sight, quho will not be mocket with declarations contrarie to intentions, ther be no just causse to charge some eminent persons in our counsaills and forces with suche ingagements and deseinges to invade England for the enforcing of the King upone that nation and for enriching themselves with ther spoyles. . . .

In the nixt place, the grate and mother sin of this nation wee conceave to be the backslydinge breache of covenant and engagements unto the Lord. . . . So wee humblie desyre your lordships to lay to heart :—

How unanswerable ye have walked to your soleme ingagement to purge the judicatories and armies, and to fill the places of truste and power with men of knowin good affection to the causse of God and of a blamles and Christian conversation. Have not some amongest you beine the cheiffe obstructors of the worke, by retarding conclusions, by studing to make them ineffectuall, quhen they have beine takin ; by your partiall dealling, differencing men according to ther intrests, countenancing, favoring, keiping in and helping to places of power and trust suche malignant and profane persons as might be subservient to your deseinges ; by your reckoning it qualificatione good aneuche if a man be free of accession to the ingagement, thoughe he were otherwayes malignant or prophaine ; by your sparing

145

of thosse in eminent places and truste in the judicatories and armies and taking no trayell of the qualifications, according to your vowis, quhill you wer doing some deutie upone them of lower degree, quherby it hath come to passe that ther remaine yet spots in your judicatories wich diminishes your crydit and authority, and occasione is given to the enimies to blaspheme the causse of God. . . .

Peterkin, *Records of the Kirk of Scotland*, 604-6 (from Balfour's *Annales*).

THE CROMWELLIAN OCCUPATION

Already before Worcester, the Committee of Estates had been captured by General Monck's cavalry at Alyth (27 August 1651), leaving Scotland without an organ of government, and the conquerors declined to recognise any authority not derived from the Parliament of England. Thus the representatives of shires and burghs who agreed to the union decided on by the Commonwealth Parliament were elected at the behest of the English administration ; there was no question of an independent Scottish legislature, meeting according to Scots usage, entering freely into agreement.

The administration of the country was in October 1651 entrusted to eight commissioners, mostly military men, and they arrived in Scotland in January 1652 ; in July 1655 they were superseded by a council of state of eight members. The Court of Session, as well as the Privy Council, did not act after July 1651. For a time justice could be obtained only from committees of officers, but in May 1652 seven commissioners of justice were installed, and to their efficient and impartial work there is ample testimony. Certain heritable jurisdictions were abolished, the power of baron courts restricted, justices of the peace appointed and attempts made to break down feudal ties and the power of the large landholders over their tenants.

Behind the administration lay the army of occupation, based latterly on five principal forts—Leith, Inverness, Inverlochy, Perth and Ayr—and a number of subsidiary posts [1]. It was inevitably an authoritarian government, with many restrictions on personal liberty, but it made much progress towards the establish-

[1] See *infra*, p. 465.

ment of order throughout the land, and not least in the Highland area influenced by the fort of Inverlochy under its able governors, Brayne and Hill.

The estates of Engagers and of supporters of Charles II were confiscated, some parts of the country were devastated by the wars, and the efficiency of the judicature was fatal to the many who had incurred debts in the cause for which they had fought. Many families were ruined, and financial desperation had a good deal to do with the outbreak of the royalist rising started in the Highlands by Glencairn in 1653 and subsequently led by Middleton. Adverse economic conditions were widespread. Scottish shipping had already suffered at the hands of royalist privateers, some was later confiscated by Cromwell, and the Scottish mercantile fleet suffered again as a result of the wars with Holland and Spain, which went far to disrupt Scottish trade. The application of English commercial and fiscal laws to the whole of Britain had the advantage of offering Scotland free trade with England and her plantations overseas, but Scotland was in no condition to take full advantage of the opportunity, and she was hard hit by the restrictions imposed on the use of foreign ships as carriers ; besides, the prohibition of the export of wool and hides upset the basis of Scottish commerce, while free trade permitted English manufactured goods to flood the market and ruin Scottish manufactures.

Taxation was by monthly assessment on personal and real estate. It was originally proposed that £10,000 a month should be raised, but in 1654 only £4,000 was coming in, and in 1657 the assessment was reduced to £6,000. (Monck, in pleading for the reduction, stated that people were paying up to a quarter of their incomes in taxation.) Even with this taxation, Scotland was occupied and governed only at a serious loss. The cost, in the last year of the protectorate, was £307,271, while the revenue was only £143,652 (£72,000 from the assessment, £49,000 from the excise and £15,000 from customs).

In the Church, the royalist and patriotic principles of the Resolutioners, which in 1651 had triumphed over the extremists, continued to be dominant, and inspired hostility to the Cromwellian administration. The government offered some countenance to the Protester minority, who, being as rigidly opposed as ever to co-operation with any ' malignants,' were anti-royalist,

but it gained little support from them, for Protesters and Resolutioners alike, being committed to the enforcement of presbyterianism, could have no sympathy with the government's policy
of toleration. Yet even the English occupation did little to heal
the breach between the two factions, and the Protesters were
virtually in a state of schism. The General Assembly was dissolved
by the military in July 1653, on the ground that it had no authorisation from the Commonwealth Parliament,[1] and it was not
permitted to meet again ; the comment of a presbyterian historian
was, ' They did not permit the General Assembly to sitt, and in
this I believe they did no bad office, for both the authority of that
meetting was denyed by the Protesters and the Assembly seemed
to be more sett upon establishing themselves than promoving
religion.' [2]

1651.   *Declaration of the English Parliament concerning Scotland*

. . . As to what concerns the advancement of the glory of
God, that their constant endeavours shall be to promote
the preaching of the Gospel there, and to advance the power
of true religion and holinesse, and that God may be served
and worshipped according to his mind revealed in his Word,
with protection and all due countenance and encouragement therein to the people of that nation from those in
authority under the parliament. . . .

Terry, *The Cromwellian Union* (Scot. Hist. Soc.), xxi

1652.   *Explanation and addition relating to the foregoing Declaration* [3]

We declare that for promoting of holiness and advancing
the power of godliness, all possible care shall be used for the
publishing of the Gospel of Christ in all parts of this land,
and provision of maintenance made and allowed to the
faithful dispensers thereof, together with such other encouragements as the magistrate may give, and may be
expected by them who demean themselves peaceably and

---

[1] Baillie, *Letters and Journals*, iii, 225
[2] Kirkton, *Secret and True History of the Church of Scotland*, 54
[3] Made by the Commonwealth's Commissioners in Scotland.

becomingly to the government and authority by which they receive the same. As also, that care shall be taken for removing of scandalous persons who have intruded into the work of the ministry, and placing others fitly qualified with gifts for the instructing of the people in their stead. And that such ministers whose consciences oblige them to wait upon God in the administration of spiritual ordinances according to the order of the Scottish Churches, with any that shall voluntarily join in the practice thereof, shall receive protection and encouragement from all in authority, in their peaceable and inoffensive exercising of the same ; as also shall others who, not being satisfied in conscience to use that form, shall serve and worship God in other Gospel way, and behave themselves peaceably and inoffensively therein. We shall likewise take care, as much as in us lies, that in places of trust throughout this nation, magistrates and officers fearing God may be set up, who, according to the duty of their places, may be a terror to all evil-doers, and even to them whose licentious practices (though under pretence of liberty and conscience) shall manifest them not to walk according to godliness and honesty.

Firth, *Scotland and the Commonwealth* (Scot. Hist. Soc.), xxxvi–xxxvii ;
   A.P.S., vi, part ii, 809

1652. *Scottish objections to the Cromwellian Union*

. . . It doth by necessary and cleir consequence establish in the Church a vast and boundles toleracion of all sorts of errour and heresies without any effectuall remedie for suppressing the same ; notwithstanding that there bee the same morall and perpetuall obligation upon us to suppress and extirpate heresie no less then profanenes : Lykeas this declaracion doe allow diverse wayes of worshipping God under the name of Gospell wayes. . . .

' Reasons for the dissent of Glasgow,' in Terry, *Cromwellian Union*, 35

. . . We conceive ourselves bound by the Law of God and oath of Covenant agreeable thereto to endeavour the

149   11

preservation of the liberties of this nation and just fundamentall lawes thereof, which we judge to be altogether
infringed be the forme of the now demanded incorporatioun
which tho carrieing along with it a change of the whole
fundamentall frame of governement and all thinges thereupon dependent is not presented to the full and frie deliberation of the people in their collectede bodie, but first concluded without their advyce and knowledge and now offered
in a divydit way without a previous condiscension in what
might preserve from the dangerous consequences that may
follow so great a change if not carefullie guarded against. . . .

We dar not add to nor diminish from the matteres of
Jesus Christ, dearer to us then all thinges earthlie, which is
so far from being seccured by any thing offered for that
effect that it is diverse wayes prejudiced and a fundation
laid downe in generall and doubtsome termes of a vast
tolleration. . . .

'Doubts and scruples of Lanark,' ibid., 74–5

The Commonwealth and Protectorate Policy of Toleration

1653. *The Instrument of Government*

Such as profess faith in God by Jesus Christ (though
differing in judgment from the doctrine, worship or discipline publicly held forth) shall not be restrained from, but
shall be protected in, the profession of the faith and exercise
of their religion ; so as they abuse not this liberty to the
civil injury of others and to the actual disturbance of the
public peace on their parts : provided this liberty be not
extended to Popery or Prelacy, nor to such as, under the
profession of Christ, hold forth and practise licentiousness.

Gardiner, *op. cit.*, 416

1657. *The Humble Petition and Advice*

That the true Protestant Christian religion . . . be held
forth and asserted for the public profession of these nations ;
. . . and such who profess faith in God the Father, and in

Jesus Christ His eternal Son, the true God, and in the Holy Spirit, God co-equal with the Father and the Son, one God blessed for ever, and do acknowledge the Holy Scriptures of the Old and New Testament to be the revealed Will and Word of God, and shall in other things differ in doctrine, worship or discipline, from the public profession held forth, endeavours shall be used to convince them by sound doctrine, and the example of a good conversation ; but that they may not be compelled thereto by penalties, nor restrained from their profession, but protected from all injury and molestation . . . ; so that this liberty be not extended to Popery or Prelacy, or to the countenancing such who publish horrible blasphemies, or practise or hold forth licentiousness or profaneness under the profession of Christ.

Ibid., 454–5

CHAPTER THREE

THE RESTORATION AND THE LATER COVENANTERS

THE RESTORATION SETTLEMENT

The settlement of church affairs after the Restoration was guided by considerations which were perhaps more apparent to contemporaries than they have been to posterity. Toleration, which had been so vehemently attacked during the Cromwellian period and which was to prove so unwelcome to the more rigid presbyterians and episcopalians alike when it was tried again in the shape of ' Indulgences,' was not a practicable policy ; the adherents to the Covenants wanted, not liberty for themselves, but freedom to coerce others. Equally, the Covenants could not receive official countenance. Although the National Covenant had not, initially, been either anti-monarchical or explicitly anti-episcopal, it was hopelessly compromised by the more extreme courses to which it had led, and it stood or fell along with the very different Solemn League, representing principles which the Scots could hardly be allowed to propagate as long as the two kingdoms were under one sovereign. Again, there could be no settlement by consent. Not only had the Cromwellian occupation done nothing to heal the breach between Resolutioners and Protesters, but on the part of the latter, at least, there was no disposition to accept majority decisions. Had a General Assembly been permitted to meet, it could hardly have failed to break up in disorder, if not indeed in violence. The Resolutioners, who were in a majority, would, once in power, have dealt with the Protesters as mercilessly as an episcopalian administration was to do.

The experiment of a presbyterian system without Covenants or General Assembly would not have satisfied a single Protester. On the other side, episcopacy still offered advantages from the point of view of the civil constitution, crown authority and political and social stability. Certain trends in opinion suggested that a moderate episcopalian settlement might prove almost as generally acceptable as it had under James VI. Yet in 1660 the restoration of episcopacy was not a foregone conclusion : the king, after all, had signed the Covenants ; and in a letter of 10 August 1660 [1] he undertook to ' preserve the government of the Church of Scotland as it is settled by law,' which was taken by some to mean that there would be a return to the system of 1639-53.

The Act Rescissory (March 1661), annulling all legislation since 1633, at once restored the ecclesiastical *status quo ante*. It was, however, accompanied by an act which stated that the king would maintain the church's doctrine and worship as they had been under his father and grandfather and that, while he would settle its government in the manner most agreeable to the Word of God, most suitable to monarchical government and most consistent with the public peace and quiet, yet kirk sessions, presbyteries and synods should continue in the meantime. By the end of the year bishops had been appointed and, as only one member of the old hierarchy survived, they were consecrated in England. When Parliament met again in May 1662 the bishops were invited to take their places, and acts were passed formally restoring episcopal government, declaring the covenants unlawful and prohibiting conventicles. Characteristic of the settlement, though not passed until 1669, was the Act of Supremacy, which curtly asserted the king's ' supreme authority and supremacy over all persons and in all causes ecclesiastical.' [2]

1661. *The Act Rescissory*

The Estates of Parliament, considering that the peace and happines of this Kingdome and of his Majesties good subjects therein doth depend upon the safety of his Majesties persone and the mantenance of his royall authority, power and greatnesse, and that all the miseries, confusions and disorders which this Kingdome hath groaned under these tuentie three yeers have issued from and been the necessary and naturall products of these neglects contempts and invasions which in and from the beginning of these troubles wer upon

[1] See page 499
[2] An oath of supremacy imposed in 1661 on all persons in public employment had acknowledged the king as ' supreme governor of this kingdom over all persons and in all causes ' (*A.P.S.*, vii, 44-5)

the specious (but false) pretexts of reformation (the common cloak of all rebellions) offered unto the sacred persone and royal authority of the King's Majestie and his Royall father of blessed memorie ; . . . and although the late Kings Majestie, out of his meer grace and respects to this his Native kingdome and the peace and quyet of his people and for preventing the consequences which such a bad example and practise might occasion to the disturbance of the peace of his other Kingdomes, was pleased in the yeer 1641 to come into this Cuntrie and by his oune presence at thair pretendit Parliaments and otherwayes to comply with and give way to many things neerly concerneing the undoubted interest and prerogative of the Croun, expecting that such unparalleled condiscentions should have made his subjects ashamed of their former miscariages, and the verie thoughts thairof to be hatefull to them and their posterity for ever ; yet such was the prevalency of the spirite of rebellion that raged in many for the tyme that, not content of that peace and happines which even above their desires wes secured unto them, nor of those many grants of honor and proffeit by which his Majestie endeavoured to endear the most desperate of them to their duety and obedience, they then, when his Maiestie had not left unto them any pretence or shadow of any new desire to be proposed either concerning themselffs or the Kingdome, did most un-worthily engadge to subvert his Maiesties Government and the publict peace of the Kingdome of England ; for which purpose, haveing joyned in a League with some ther, they for the better prosecution of the same did assume unto themselffs the Royall power, keept and held Parliaments at thair pleasure . . . ; and forasmuch as now it hath pleased Almighty God by the power of his oune right hand so miracoulously to restore the King's Majestie to the Govern-ment of his Kingdomes and to the exercise of His Royall power and Soveranity over the same, the estates of Parlia-ment doe conceave themselffs obleidged in dischairge of their duetie and conscience to God and the Kings Maiestie to imploy all their power and interest for vindicateing his

Maiesties Authority from all these violent invasions that have been made upon it . . . :

Thairfor the Kings Majestie and estates of Parliament doe heirby Rescind and annull the pretendit Parliaments keept in the years 1640, 1641, 1644, 1645, 1646, 1647 and 1648 and all acts and deids past and done in them and declare the same to be henceforth voyd and null ; and his Majestie, being unwilling to take any advantage of the failings of his Subjects dureing those unhappie tymes, is resolved not to retaine any remembrance thairof but that the same shall be held in everlasting oblivion and that, all differences and animosities being forgotten, his good subjects may in a happie union under his Royall Government enjoy that happines and peace which his Maiestie intends and really wisheth unto them as unto himselff, doth therfor by advice and consent of his estates of Parliament grant his full assureance and indemnity to all persones that acted in, or by vertew of the said pretendit Parliaments and other meitings flowing from the same to be unquestioned in their lives or fortunes for any deid or deids done by them in thair said usurpation or be vertew of any pretendit Authority deryved therfrom ; Excepting alwayes such as shall be excepted in a general act of indemnity to be past be his Maiestie in this Parliament.

A.P.S., vii, 86-87

Act concerning Religion and Church Government

Our soverane lord, being truely sensible of the mercies of Almighty God towards him in his preservation, in the times of greatest trouble and danger, and in his miraculous restitution to his just right and government of his kingdomes, and being desireous to improve these mercyes to the glorie of God and honour of his great name, doth with advice and consent of his estates of parliament declare that it is his full and firme resolution to maintaine the true reformed protestant religion in its purity of doctrine and worship as it wes established within this kingdome dureing the reigne of

155

his royall father and grandfather of blessed memorie ; and that his majestie will be cairfull to promote the power of godlinesse, to encourage the exercises of religion, both publict and private, and to suppresse all prophanesse and disorderlie walking, and for that end will give all due countenance and protection to the ministers of the gospell, they containing themselffs within the bounds and limites of their ministeriall calling and behaving themselffs with that submission and obedience to his majesties authority and commands that is suteable to the alledgeance and duety of good subjects. And as to the government of the church, his majestie will make it his care to satle and secure the same in such a frame as shall be most agreeable to the Word of God, most suteable to monarchicall government and most complying with the publict peace and quyet of the king-dome ; and in the mean tyme his majestie . . . doth allow the present administration by sessions, presbetries and synods (they keeping within bounds and behaveing them-selffs as said is) and that notwithstanding of the preceiding act rescissorie of all pretendit parliaments since the yeer 1633.

A.P.S., vii, 87–8

1662. *Act for Calling in the Bishops to the Parliament*

Forasmuch as the Kings Majestie hath been graciouslie pleased to restore the Church to its antient and right govern-ment be Archbishops and Bishops, dean and chapter, . . . and, considering that the clargie did alwayes in the right constitution of Parliaments represent the first state, and that now Archbishops and Bishops being restored it is fit the Parliament be returned to its antient constitution, and that the clargie have thair place and vote in Parliament as formerlie, thairfor his Majestie with advice forsaid gives Commission to the Earles of Kellie and Weymes, the Lord Torphichen, the Lairds of Crommerty, Blakbarronie and Prestoun, the commissioners for Edinburgh, Air and St. Andrewes to goe and in his Maiesties name invite the Archbishops and Bishops to come and take thair place and vote in Parliament as in former tymes befor these troubles (which wes accordinglie done).

A.P.S., vii, 370–1

1662. *Act for the Restitution and Re-establishment of the ancient Government of the Church by Archbishops and Bishops*

Forasmuch as the ordering and disposall of the externall government and policie of the church doth propperlie belong unto his majestie as ane inherent right of the croun, by vertew of his royall prerogative and supremacie in causes ecclesiasticall ; and in discharge of this trust his majestie and his estates of parliament takeing to their serious consideration that in the beginning of, and by, the late rebellion within this kingdome in the yeer 1637 the ancient and sacred order of bishops wes cast off, their persons and rights wer injured and overturned and a seeming paritie [1] among the clergie factiously and violently brought in, to the great disturbance of the publict peace, the reproach of the reformed religion and violation of the excellent lawes of the realme for preserveing ane orderlie subordination in the church ; and therwithall considering what disorders and exorbitancies have been in the church, what encroachments upon the prerogative and rights of the croun, what usurpations upon the authoritie of parliaments, and what prejudice the libertie of the subject hath suffered by the invasions made upon the bishops and episcopall government, which they find to be the church government most agreeable to the Word of God, most convenient and effectuall for the preservation of treuth, order and unitie and most suteable to monarchie and the peace and quyet of the state : Thairfor his majestie, with advice and consent of his estates of parliament, hath thought it necessar and accordingly doth heirby redintegrat the state of bishops to their antient places and undoubted priveledges in parliament, and to all their other accustomed dignities, priveledges and jurisdictions ; and doth heirby restore them

---

[1] Pairtie *in the printed record is an obvious misreading for* paritie

to the exercise of their episcopall function, presidencie in the church, power of ordination, inflicting of censures and all other acts of church discipline, which they are to performe with advice and assistance of such of the clergie as they shall find to be of knoun loyaltie and prudence ; [*reviving Acts of Parliament in favour of episcopal government ; rescinding acts by which* the sole and only power and jurisdiction within this church doth stand in the generall, provinciall and presbyteriall assemblies and kirk sessions, *particularly that of* 1592 ; *and restoring to the bishops the commissariot jurisdiction and their temporalities*].

A.P.S., vii, 372–4

1662. *Act against the Covenants*

The Estats of Parliament takeing into their consideration the miseries, confusions, bondage and oppressions this Kingdome hath groaned under since the yeer 1637, with the causes and occasions thairof, . . . and since the rise and progresse of the late troubles did in a great measure proceid from some treasonable and sedicious positions infused into the people, that it wes lawfull to subiects, for reformation, to enter into Covenants and leagues, or to take up armes against the King or those commisionated by him and suchlyke, . . . And considering that as the present aige is not fullie freed of those distempers, so posterity may be apt to relapse therein if timeous remeid be not provided : Therfor the Kings Majestie and Estates of Parliament doe declare that those positions, that it is lawfull to subjects upon pretence of reformation, or other pretence whatsoever, to enter into leagues and covenants or to tak up armes against the King ; or that it is lawfull to subjects pretending his Majesties authority to tak up armes against his person or those commissionated by him, or to suspend him from the exercise of his royall government, or to put limitations upon their due obedience and alledgeance, are rebellious and treasonable, and that all these gatherings, convocations, petitions, protestations and erecting and keeping of Councill Tables, that wer used in the begining and for carieing on of the late troubles, wer unlawfull and sedicious ; and particularly that these oaths wherof the one wes commonlie called The Nationall Covenant (as it wes sworne and explained in the yeer 1638 and therefter), and the other entituled a solemn League and Covenant wer, and ar, in themselffs unlawfull oaths and wer taken by and imposed upon the subjects of this kingdome against the fundamentall lawes and liberties of the same ; and that ther lyeth no obligation upon any of the subjects from the said oaths, or either of them, to endeavour any change or alteration of government either in Church or State ; and therfor annulls all acts and con-stitutions ecclesiastick or civill approveing the said pretended Nationall Covenant or League and Covenant, or makeing any interpretations of the same or either of them.

A.P.S., vii, 377–8

1662. *Act against Conventicles*

His Majestie, considering that under the pretext of religious exercises, diverse unlawfull meitings and conventicles (the nurseries of sedition) have been keept in private families ; hath thought fit, with advice [and consent of his estates conveened in this present Parliament], heirby to declare that as he doth and will give all due encouragement to the worship of God in families amongst the persons of the familie and others who shall be occasionally ther for the tyme, so he doth heirby discharge all private meitings or conventicles in houses which under the pretence of, or for, religious exercises, may tend to the prejudice of the publict worship of God in the Churches, or to the alienating the people from their lawfull pastors, and that duetie and obedience they ow to Church and State. And it is heirby ordained that none be heirafter permitted to preach in publict or in families within any diocesse, to teach any publict school, or to be pedagogues to the childrene of persons of qualitie, without the licence of the ordinary of the Diocesse.

A.P.S., vii, 379

1669.   *Act asserting his Majesties Supremacie over all Persons and
in all Causes Ecclesiasticall*

The Estates of Parliament, haveing seriously considered how
necessar it is, for the good and peace of the Church and
State, that his Majesties power and authority in relation to
maters and persons ecclesiasticall be more cleerlie asserted
by ane Act of Parliament, have therfor thought fit it be
enacted, asserted and declared, lykas his Majestie, with
advice and consent of his Estates of Parliament, doth heirby
enact, assert and declare, that his Majestie hath the Supream
Authority and Supremacie over all persons and in all causes
ecclesiasticall within this kingdom ; And that be vertew
therof the ordering and disposall of the externall government
and policie of the Church doth propperlie belong to his
Majestie and his successours as ane inherent right to the
Croun : And that his Majestie and his successours may setle,
enact, and emit such constitutions, acts and orders, concerning the administration of the externall government of
the Church, and the persons imployed in the same, and
concerning all ecclesiasticall meitings and maters to be
proposed and determined therin, as they in their royall
wisdome shall think fit.   Which acts, orders and constitutions, being recorded in the Books of Councill and dewly
published, are to be observed and obeyed be all his Majesties
subjects, any law, act or custome to the contrary notwithstanding.   Lykas his Majestie with advice and consent
forsaid, doth rescind and annull all laws, acts and clauses
therof, and all customs and constitutions, civill or ecclesiastick, which ar contrarie to, or inconsistent with his
Majesties supremacie as it is heirby asserted, And declares
the samen voyd and null in all tymecomeing.

A.P.S., vii, 554, c. 2

ORIGINS OF THE OPPOSITION

The moderation of the Restoration settlement was conspicuous,
especially if contrasted with the state of the Church immediately

before the National Covenant. A ' national synod,' although authorised,[1] never met, but kirk sessions continued to function as they had always done, and even presbyteries exercised important functions, while in the synods some at least of the bishops were modestly content with the position of *primus inter pares*.[2] Nor was the episcopacy founded on offensive claims to a divine right ; not only had the appeal been partly to expediency—the effectiveness of episcopacy for the preservation of law and order and its suitability to monarchy and the peace of the state—and the ' external government ' of the Church committed to the royal choice, but there was no general reordination of men in presbyterian orders, and presbyterian ordination was sometimes formally recognised as constituting ' admission to the holy ministry.' Finally, in the absence of a compulsory liturgy, services differed little from those held during the presbyterian regime and were often less liturgical than those prescribed in the old Book of Common Order. The aim, plainly, was a return to the moderate episcopalian regime of James VI before 1618, and not to the High Church Anglicanism of Charles I.

Conscientious presbyterians might cavil at the absence of a General Assembly, and claim that the Church was imperfect without it, and they were bound to object that even a moderate episcopacy infringed the sacred parity of pastors. A doctrinaire element objected that the synods and presbyteries were no longer true church courts, because they excluded elders and were dependent on the bishops' authorisation ; it was argued with some justice that whereas formerly an episcopal system had been superimposed on a presbyterian, now the presbyteries were supplementary to an episcopal system. Active opposition, however, was confined to extremists, whose complaints were ' prelacy,' ' Erastianism ' and the renunciation of the covenants ; the second complaint had most substance, because in the reaction against the rule of the covenanters the Restoration settlement went further than ever before in subjecting the Church to the control of the State.

Geographically, opposition was mainly in the South-West, and to some extent in Fife. The growing schism between presbyterian and episcopalian was following the lines already indicated

[1] *A.P.S.*, vii, 465
[2] See Roland Foster, *Bishop and Presbytery*

by the 'Aberdeen Doctors' and the Westland Whigs. The capital, which had been the centre of opposition to Charles I, gave no support to the malcontents and remained quiet until the cry of ' No Popery ' was raised by the policy of James VII. Socially, the contrast was equally marked : there were no noble or landed gentlemen to lead the insurgents this time. In so far as lay opinion generally was anti-clerical, it was now ranged against the High Presbyterian ministers, whereas under Charles I it had been alienated by High Anglican bishops.

The measure which proved to be most critical was one designed to regularise the position of clergy admitted to parishes since the abolition of lay patronage in 1649. They were required to seek presentation from the patron and collation from the bishops.[1] This act was restorative of old practice, for until 1649 admission had always been by presentation followed by collation, and the collation had been that of a bishop except during the brief periods when presbyteries had performed the function. It is illuminating as to the change brought about by the first Covenanting period that a procedure which had previously met with universal acquiescence should now be rejected by a large minority of the ministers ; on each occasion when episcopal government had previously been introduced, the unity of the Church had been preserved, but now for the first time a section of both clergy and people withdrew from the Church rather than accept the change of government. On 1 October 1662 the Council ordained that ministers who had refused to comply with the requirement to seek presentation and collation must remove by 1 November,[2] and, although an extension was subsequently given until February 1663, about 270 ministers, mainly in the Protester strongholds of the dioceses of Glasgow and Galloway, refused to comply.

1662. *Act concerning such Benefices and Stipends as have been possest without presentations from the lawfull Patrons*

The Kings most excellent Majestie . . . considering that notwithstanding the right of patronages be duely setled and established by the antient and fundamentall lawes and

---

[1] It is noteworthy that *ordination* was not in question : those to whom the act applied included clergy, episcopally ordained before 1638, who had been translated to a new parish since 1649.

[2] *R.P.C.*, 3rd ser., i, 270

constitutions of this kingdome, yet diverse ministers in this
Church have and doe possesse benefices and stipends in
their respective cures, without any right or presentation to
the same from the patrons ; and it being therfor most just
that lawfull and undoubted patrons of kirks be restored to
the possession of the rights of their respective advocations,
donations and patronages : Therfor his Maiestie, with
advice and consent of his Estates of Parliament, doth statut
and ordaine that all these ministers who entered to the cure
of any paroche in burgh or land within this kingdome in or
since the yeer 1649 (at and befor which time the patrons
wer most injuriously dispossessed of their patronages) have
no right unto nor shall receave uplift nor possesse the rents
of any benefice, modified stipend, mans or gleib for this
present cropt 1662, nor any yeer following, but their places,
benefices and kirks are *ipso iure* vacand. Yet his Maiestie,
to evidence his willingnes to passe by and cover the miscariages of his people, doth, with advice forsaid, declare
that this act shall not be prejudiciall to any of these
ministers in what they have possessed or is due to them,
since their admission ; and that everie such minister who
shall obtaine a presentation from the lawfull patron and
have collation from the bishop of the dyocie wher he liveth
betuixt and the tuentieth of September nextocome, shall
from thenceforth have right to, and enjoy his Church
benefice, manse and gleib as fully and freely as if he had
been lawfullie presented and admitted therto at his first
entrie or as any other minister within the Kingdome doth
or may doe. And for that end it is heirby ordained that
the respective patrons shall give presentations to all the
present incumbents who in due time shall make application
to them for the same. And in caice any of these Churches
shall not be thus duely provided befor the said tuentieth of
September, then the patron shall have freedome to present
another betuixt and the tuentieth day of March 1663, which
if he shall refuise or neglect, the presentation shall then fall
to the bishop *jure devoluto* according to former lawes. And
siclyk his Majestie with advice forsaid doth statute and

163

ordeane the Archbishops and Bishops to have the power of new admission and collation to all such Churches and benefices as belong to their respective sees and which have been vaiked since the yeer 1637, and to be carefull to plant and provide these their oune kirks conforme to this act.

A.P.S., vii, 376

The immediate problem was a direct outcome of the deprivations. The congregations of the south-west preferred the ministrations of the deprived clergy to those of their successors.[1] Meetings for worship outside the parish churches were already illegal by the act against conventicles,[2] but the ' Mile Act,' passed by the Council in August 1663, aimed at separating the deprived ministers from their flocks, by forbidding them to reside within twenty miles of their former parishes,[3] and a new Act of Parliament, known as ' the Bishops ' Drag Net,' imposed fines on those who separated themselves from the worship of the Established Church.

1663. *An Act against separation and disobedience to Ecclesiasticall Authority.*

. . . As his Majestie doeth expect from all his good and duetifull subjects a due acknowledgement and hearty complyance with his Majesties Government ecclesiasticall and civill as it is now established by law within this kingdome, and that in order therunto they will give their cheerfull concurrence, countenance and assistance to such Ministers as by publict Authority are or shall be admitted in their severall paroches, and attend all the ordinary meitings of divine worship in the same ; so his Majestie doth declare that he will and doth account a withdrawing from and not keeping and joyning in these meitings to be seditious and

---

[1] The ' curates ' who were appointed to serve the vacant parishes were slandered by contemporaries as young and ignorant, but the dispassionate pages of the *Fasti Ecclesiae Scoticanae* prove that nearly all of them were graduates and that they were no younger when ordained than the presbyterian ministers of the time (J. A. MacCulloch, in *The Scottish Guardian*, cited F. Goldie, *A Short History of the Episcopal Church in Scotland*, 24-5).   [2] *Supra*, p. 159   [3] *R.P.C.*, 3rd ser., i, 403-4

of dangerous example and consequence. And therfor and for preventing the same for the future His Majestie with advice and consent of his Estates in Parliament doth heirby statute ordean and declare that all and every such person or persons who shall heirafter ordinarly and wilfully withdraw and absent themselffs from the ordinary meitings of divine worship in their oune paroche church on the Lord's day (whither upon the accompt of poperie or other disaffection to the present government of the church) shall therby incur the paines and penalties underwritten, viz. each nobleman, gentleman and heritor the losse of a fourt parte of ilk yeers rent in which they shall be accused and convicted ; and every yeoman tennent or fermer the losse of such a proportion of their frie moveables (after the payment of their rents due to their master and landlord) as his Majesties Councill shall think fit, not exceiding a fourt parte thairof ; and every burgesse to losse the liberty of merchandizeing, tradeing and all other liberties within burgh and fourt parte of their moveables. . . .

A.P.S., vii, 455, c. 9

REPRESSION AND CONCILIATION

Conventicles became common in the south-west, and the only instrument at the Government's disposal for the purposes of breaking them up and of levying fines on absentees from church was military force,[1] which was applied with special severity when, after the outbreak of the war with Holland (1665), there was a fear of a Whiggamore rising in concert with the Dutch. A rebellion did indeed come, in the Pentland Rising (1666), but it was on a petty scale and received no support outside the area of its origin.

The first phase had been one of repression, parallel to the contemporary policy in England represented by the Clarendon Code, and directed mainly by the Earl of Rothes and Archbishop

[1] An act of 1663 authorised the raising of 20,000 infantry and 2,000 cavalry for forty days' service against either foreign invasion or insurrection (*A.P.S.*, vii, 480).

12

Sharp. Lauderdale, secretary for Scotland in London, believed the policy to be mistaken, but waited until it was discredited by the Pentland Rising. From 1667 there was a second phase, during which a conciliatory policy was pursued. In England, Clarendon was replaced by the Cabal (of which Lauderdale was a member) ; in Scotland, Sharp was denied the office of Lord Chancellor and his authority was diminished, Rothes—who had been Treasurer and Commissioner—was removed to the less influential post of Chancellor, and in 1669 Lauderdale himself came north as Commissioner. The new policy had been initiated by the disbanding of the army, except two troops of lifeguards and eight companies of foot (August 1667) and an amnesty for those involved in the late rebellion (October 1667). Conciliation could have taken either of two courses—'comprehension' of the presbyterians in the establishment by means of modifications which would have made the structure of the Church acceptable to all but the most intransigent ; or the toleration of presbyterians outside the national Church. Leighton, bishop of Dunblane, was energetic in schemes for 'accommodation,' and the disregard of the Government for determined episcopalian opinion was demonstrated when Archbishop Burnet of Glasgow, who strongly opposed concessions, was deprived (December 1669) and replaced by Leighton. The Act of Supremacy, passed in 1669,[1] was directed at least as much against the claims of *jure divino* episcopacy as against those of presbytery, and was designed to enable the Government to make such modifications as it thought fit in the episcopal regime.

Negotiations for 'accommodation' did not break down till 1671, but in the meantime the Government had experimented with something more like the alternative policy of toleration, in the first Declaration of Indulgence (1669), of which forty-two presbyterian ministers took advantage ; a second indulgence, in 1672, nominated about ninety nonconformists, mostly in pairs, to fifty-eight parishes, and about half of them accepted the appointment. The indulgences had the effect of splitting presbyterian opinion, both clerical and lay, and those who declined to accept them were more bitter against ' the indulged ' than they were against episcopalians. On the other hand, indulged ministers were precisely the more moderate men who, had they not received an indulgence, might have been enticed into an ' accommodation ' ; to the latter

[1] *Supra*, p. 160

policy, therefore, the indulgences were almost necessarily fatal. The final measure representative of the policy of conciliation was a Proclamation of Indemnity in March 1674.

The Declarations of Indulgence—1

1669, 7 June.

Wheras by the act of councill and proclamation at Glasgow in the year 1662 a considerable number of ministers were at once turned out and so debarred from preaching of the gospell and exercise of the ministry, wee are gratiously pleased to authorise yow our privy councill to appoynt so many of the outed ministers as have lived peaceably and orderly in the places where they have resided to return to preach and exercise other functions of the ministry in the paroch churches where they formerly served (provyded they be vacant) and to allow patrones to present to other vacant churches such others of them as yow shall approve of, and that such of these ministers as shall take collation from the bishop of the diocie and keip presbyteries and synods may be warranted to lift their stipends as other ministers of the kingdome, bot for such as are not or shall not be collated by the bishopes that they have no warrand to medle with the locall stipend, bot only to possesse the manse and glebe, and that yow appoynt a collectour for those and all other vacant stipends, who shall issue the same and pay a yearly mantinence to the saids not collated ministers as yow shall sie fitt to appoynt.

That all who are restored or allowed to exercise the ministry be . . . enjoyned to . . . keep presbyteries and synods . . . and that such of them as shall not obey our commands in keeping presbyteries be confyned within the bounds of the parishes where they preach ay and while they give assurance to keep presbyteries for the future.

That all who shall be allowed to preach be strictly enjoyned not to admitt any of their neighbour or other paroches into their communiones, nor baptise their childrein, nor mary any of them without the allowance of the minister of the paroch to which they belong, unless it be vacant. . . .

That such of the outed ministers who live peaceablie and orderly and are not re-entered or presented as aforsaid have allowed to them 400 merks Scotts yearlie out of the vacant church for their mantinence till they be provyded of churches, and that even such who shall give assurance to live so for the future be allowed the same yearly mantinence.·

And seing wee have by these orders taken away all pretences for conventicles and provyded for the wants of such as are and will be peaceable, if any shall be found here-after to preach without authority or keep conventicles, our expresse pleasur is that yow proceid with all severity against the preachers and hearers as seditious persons and con-temners of our authority.

R. P. C., 3rd ser., iii, 38–40

II

1672, 3 September.

The Lord Commissioner his grace and lordes of his majesties privy councill, considering the disorders which have latly bein by the frequent and numerous conventicles, and being willing to remeid so great ane evill in the gentlest maner could be thought on, . . . they doe order and appoint the ministers afternamed, outed since the year 1661, to repair to the paroches following and to remain therein confyned, permitting and allowing them to preach and exercise the other pairtes of the ministeriall function in the paroches to which they are or shall be confyned by this present act and commission after specifeid, viz. [*Then follows a list of parishes and ministers.*]

The Lord Commissioner his grace and lordes of his majesties privy councill, considering the extent of the indulgence given by this act and that if the same should be any further inlarged the regular ministers might be dis-couraged and the orderly and peaceably disposed people of this kingdom disquyeted, doe declare that hereafter they are not to extend the said indulgence in favoures of any other people or to any other paroches than to these mentioned. . . .

R. P. C., 3rd ser., iii, 586–9

1674, March 24. *Proclamation of Indemnity*

Charles [*etc.*] We have thought fit, as an act of our royal bounty, by our royal authority, with advice of our privy council, to declare our royal pleasure, for the ease and satisfaction of our good subjects, in manner following :

[*After remitting arrears of various taxations and impositions ;*] we, for a further proof of our affection to our good subjects of this our kingdom, do, with advice foresaid, freely and absolutely grant a general pardon and discharge of all arbitrary and pecunial pains incurred by any of our subjects before the date hereof through the contravening of any laws, penal statutes or public acts whatsoever, except such pecunial pains as are already inflicted or imposed by our privy council or any other competent judicatory for which bonds are given or money paid, and excepting all sentences of banishment, imprisonment or confinement ; declaring always that this pardon is not to be extended to any who were guilty of the rebellion in the year 1666 and are not admitted to the benefit of our indemnity, nor to such as are guilty of capital crimes ; and we having given, as said is, so full proof of our bounty and goodness to our subjects and of our full pardon of all arbitrary and pecunial pains, extending even to these against conventicles, withdrawing from ordinances, disorderly baptisms and marriages, we do expect that this our unparalelled grace and goodness will oblige all our good subjects to express their due sense of and thankfulness for the same by a more careful observance and due obedience to our laws, from which nothing is to be derogate hereby as to their due observance in time coming.

Wodrow, i, Appendix lxxvii (*R. P. C.*, 3rd. ser., iv, 167–8)

Renewed Repression : Bothwell Brig

The temporary absence of repressive action, combined with the bitterness of the extremists against the indulged clergy, led to a marked revival of conventicles, which became organised virtually as a schismatic church, with men ordained as field preachers who invaded the parishes of indulged ministers and held their services at the same hours as those of the parish churches. So serious was the situation that already in 1670, while the policy was still broadly one of conciliation, there was passed what Lauderdale called a ' clanking act ' against conventicles, though its penalty of death for field preaching was not imposed. Originally to endure for three years, it was renewed in 1672. The proclamation of indemnity in March 1674 gave further encouragement to conventicles.

From 1674 until 1679 there is a third phase, of renewed repression. Leighton retired to England, and Burnet was restored to Glasgow (September 1674). It became the law that heritors and masters should be responsible for the conformity of their tenants and servants, additional military forces were raised, and letters of intercommuning were issued against a number of rebels. In reaction against these measures, the conventicles of the south-west took on a new character, becoming every year larger and more frequent and more military in their nature. When, in 1677, the proclamation of 1674 on the responsibilities of heritors was re-issued, the heritors of Fife acquiesced, but those of the south-west intimated that to ask them to control their tenants was to ask the impossible. As the situation was completely out of hand, and none of the ordinary means of restoring order were reliable or adequate, recourse was had to the extraordinary device of the ' Highland Host,' which was quartered on the disaffected districts for some weeks early in 1678. In July 1679 a Convention of Estates voted a taxation of £1,800,000, over five years, to be used chiefly for the purpose of suppressing conventicles, and the lawfulness of paying this ' cess ' now became a further cause of dispute, widening the schism between the extreme and the moderate dissenters.

At the beginning of 1679 the new troops voted by the late convention were sent to the west. The answer of the conventiclers was to assemble in larger numbers than before and to maintain armed parties permanently in being. Almost at once there were clashes with the troops, and it was plain, even before the murder of Archbishop Sharp (3 May 1679) and the flight of his murderers to the west, that armed rebellion was bound to break out. On 29 May, the king's birthday, a body of rebels published a declaration at Rutherglen denouncing all violations of the Covenants from the Engagement to the Indulgences. On 1 June, Graham of Claverhouse was defeated at Drumclog by a large armed conventicle, and the rebels then rapidly gathered forces which were crushed at Bothwell Brig by the Duke of Monmouth (22 June).

During a brief interlude of conciliation, under Monmouth, the majority of the numerous prisoners from Bothwell Brig were allowed to return to their homes on pledging themselves not to rise in arms again, and only a minority were destined for Barbados, to perish by shipwreck in Orkney on the way. A third indulgence, of very wide scope, was issued on 29 June 1679.

1670. *Act against Conventicles*

[*It is enacted that*] no outed ministers who are not licenced by the councill and no other persons not authorized or tollerat by the bishop of the diocess presume to preach, expound scripture or pray in any meeting except in ther oune housses and to those of ther oune family, and that none be present at any meeting without the familie to which they belong wher any not licenced, authorized nor tollerat as said is shall preach, expound scripture or pray, . . . ; he or they who shall so preach, expound or pray within any house shall be seized upon and imprisoned till they find caution under the paine of fyve thousand merks not to do the lyk thereafter, or else enact themselves to remove out of the kingdom and never returne without his majesties licence, and that everie person who shall be found to have been present at any such meetings shall be *toties quoties* fined according to their qualities. . . .

And considering that these meetings are the rendezvous of rebellion and tend in a heigh measure to the disturbance of the publict peace, . . . that whosoever without licence or authoritie forsaid shall preach, expound scripture or pray at any of these meetings in the feild or in any house wher ther be moe persons nor the house contains so as some of them be without doors (which is heerby declared to be a feild conventicle) or who shall convocat any number of people to these meetings shall be punished with death and confiscation of ther goods. [*A reward of* 500 *merks is offered for the apprehension of any person present at a field conventicle. The act is to remain in force for three years.*]

A.P.S., viii, 9-10

1674, June 18. *Proclamation obliging Heritors and Masters to keep their dependents from Conventicles*

Charles [*etc.*] Forasmuch as . . . many persons continue so disloyal and disobedient as to frequent these unlawful and seditious conventicles and meetings, to the great scandal of the reformed religion professed within this kingdom, and great reproach and contempt of our authority and laws, and disturbance of the public peace ; and seeing the due observance of the foresaid act of parliament [i.e. *the 'clanking act' against conventicles*] is of great import and consequence (field-conventicles being declared by the law to be the rendezvous of rebellion, and house-conventicles the seminaries of separation ; and both of them tending to the subversion of all peace and order in the church) and that it might prove an effectual means for suppressing these disorders, if heritors, masters of families, and magistrates of burghs royal would employ that interest, power and authority which they have over their tenants, servants and inhabitants, in procuring their obedience to the law : We, therefore, with advice of the lords of our privy council, do hereby require and command all masters of families that they cause their domestic servants, chamberlains, grieves and others entertained by them [to] give obedience to the foresaid fifth act of the second session of our second parliament, in abstaining from all conventicles, either in houses or in fields, and that they retain none in their service but such for whom they will be answerable ; and in case of their disobedience that they remove them out of their service. As also, we do hereby require and command all heritors, landlords and liferenters in the country to require their rentallers and tenants, as well these who have tacks yet standing unexpired as moveable tenants, to subscribe the bond hereto subjoined. . . .

[The Bond]

I,   , bind and oblige me, that I, my wife, or any of my children in family with me, my cottars or servants, shall not keep, or be present at, any conventicles, either in houses or in the fields, as the same are defined by the fifth act of the second session of his majesty's second parliament, under the pains therein contained, being for ilk house-conventicle twenty-five pounds Scots for each tenant labouring land, twelve pounds for each cottar, and for each servant man a fourth part of his year's fee, and the husband the half of these fines for such of their wives or children as shall be at any house-conventicle, and the double of the respective fines for each of the said persons that shall be at any field-conventicle. . . .

Wodrow, i, Appendix, No. lxi (*R. P. C.* 3rd. ser., iv, 197–200)

1675, August 6.   *Letters of Intercommuning*

Charles [*etc.*].   Forasmuch as [*a large number of named persons have been put to the horn for attending conventicles, withdrawing from public ordinances and taking part in the invasion of parish churches :*] Our will is herefore, and we charge you straitly and command, that incontinent thir our letters seen ye pass to the market-crosses of Edinburgh, Haddingtoun, Lanerk, Cowpar, Perth, Dunfermling, Stirling, Glasgow, Linlithgow and other places needful, and thereat, in our name and authority, command and charge all and sundry our lieges and subjects that they, nor none of them, presume nor take upon hand to reset, supply or intercommune with any of the

173

foresaid persons, our rebels, for the causes foresaid, nor furnish them with meat, drink, house, harbour, victual nor no other thing useful or comfortable to them, nor have intelligence with them by word, writ or message or any other manner of way, under the pain to be repute and esteemed art and part with them in the crimes foresaid, and pursued therefor with all rigour, to the terror of others. . . .

Wodrow, i, Appendix lxxiii a.

1679, June 29. *The Third Indulgence*

Wee . . . have . . . suspended the execution of all laws and acts against such as frequent house conventicles in the low countreys on the south syde of the river of Tay only, excepting alwayes the towne of Edinburgh and two miles round about the same, with the lordships of Musleburgh and Dalkeith, the cities of St. Andrews and Glasgow and Stirling and a mile about each of them. . . . Wee hereby suspend all diligences for fynes upon the account of conventicles . . . and all letters of intercommuning and other executions. . . . We hereby ordaine all such as shall be suffered to preach, to have their names given in and surety found to our privy councill for their peaceable behaviour, only one preacher being allowed to a parish and none to be allowed who have appeared against us in this late rebellion.

R.P.C., 3rd ser., vi, 265

THE CAMERONIANS

The opposition had been for some time divided, and its main strength either broken by repression or reduced, through concessions, to acquiescence. Presently the more moderate elements were to be rendered still more amenable to the regime, as they were alienated by the excesses of the remnant of extremists who, with Cameron and Cargill as their preachers, alone remained actively in opposition. When Cargill and a lay companion were apprehended at Queensferry in 1680 a paper was found setting

forth their conception of government in Church and State as an
ecclesiastical oligarchy with no obligations to the Crown.

1680. *The Queensferry Paper*

We undersubscribers, for ourselves and all that shall adhere
to us, or join with us, being put to it by God, our own
consciences, and men, and following the examples of God's
people registrate in his word in such cases, we are resolved
(having acknowledged and obtained mercy, we trust, for
our former breaches of covenants with God), to bind
ourselves with a solemn and sacred bond. . . .

*   *   *

Thirdly. That we confess with our mouth and believe
with our hearts that the doctrine of the reformed churches,
especially that of Scotland, contained in the Scriptures,
summed up in our confessions of faith, and engaged to by
us in our covenants, is the only true doctrine of God, and
that we purpose to persevere in it to the end ; and that the
pure worship required and prescribed in the scriptures,
without the inventions, additions, adornings or corruptions
of men is the only true worship of God ; and the presbyterian government exercised by lawful ministers and elders
in kirk-sessions, presbyteries, synods, and general assemblies
is the only right government of the Church, and that this
government is a distinct government from the civil, and
ought distinctly to be exercised not after a carnal manner
by the plurality of votes, or authority of a single person,
but according to the word of God ; so that the word makes
and carries the sentence and not plurality of votes.

Fourthly. That we shall endeavour to our utmost, the
overthrow of the kingdom of darkness, and whatever is
contrary to the kingdom of Christ, especially idolatry and
popery in all the articles of it, as we are bound in our
national covenants ; superstition, will-worship and prelacy,
with its hierarchy, as we are bound in our solemn league
and covenant : and that we shall with the same sincerity
endeavour the overthrow of that power (it being no more

authority) that hath established and upholds that kingdom of darkness, that prelacy to wit and erastianism over the church, and hath exercised such a lustful and arbitrary tyranny over the subjects, taking all power in their hand, that they may at their pleasure introduce popery in the church, as they have done arbitrary government in the state. . . .

Fifthly. Seriously considering that the hand of our kings, and rulers with them, hath been of a long time against the throne of the Lord, and that the Lord upon this account has declared that he will have war with them for ever and has commanded his people utterly to root them out ; and considering that the line and succession of our king and rulers hath been against the power and purity of Religion and godliness, and Christ's reigning over his church, and its freedom, and so against God, and hath degenerate from that virtue, moderation, sobriety and good government which was the tenor and right by which their ancestors kept their crowns (for when they left that, they themselves were laid aside, as our chronicles and registers do record) into an idle and sinful magnificence where the all and only government is to keep up their own absoluteness and tyranny, and to keep on a yoke of thraldom upon the subjects, and to squeeze from them their substance to uphold their lustful and pompous superfluities ; we having no better nor greater way at this time of manifesting our public siding with and loving of God, nor seeing a more speedy way of relaxation from the wrath of God (that hath ever lain heavy on us since we engaged with him) but of rejecting of them who have so manifestly rejected God (especially of late) and his service and reformation . . . disclaiming the covenants with God and blasphemously enacted it to be burned by the hand of the hangman, governed contrary to all right laws divine and humane, exercised such tyranny and arbitrary government, so oppressed men in their consciences and civil rights . . . so that now it cannot be called a government but a lustful rage. . . .

We then being made free by God and their own doings

176

(he giving the law and they giving the transgression of that law which is the cause) and being now loosed from all obligations both divine and civil to them, knowing also, that no society of men, having corruption in them . . ., can be without laws and government, and withal desiring to be governed in the best way that is least liable to inconveniencies and least apt to degenerate into tyranny, we do declare that we shall set up over ourselves and over what God shall give us power of, government and governors according to the word of God . . . ; That we shall no more commit the government of ourselves and the making of laws for us, to any one single person or lineal successor . . ., this kind of government by a single person being most liable to inconveniencies, and aptest to degenerate into tyranny as sad and long experience has taught us. . . .

Eighthly. We bind and oblige ourselves to defend ourselves and one another in our worshipping of God, and in our natural, civil and divine rights and liberties, till we shall overcome or send them down under debate to the posterity that they may begin where we end ; and if we shall be pursued or troubled any farther in our worshipping, rights, and liberties, that we shall look on it as a declaring [of] war, and take all the advantages that one enemy doth of another, and seek to cause to perish all that shall in an hostile manner assault us, and to maintain, relieve and right ourselves of those that have wronged us, but not to trouble or injure any but those that have injured us. . . .

Wodrow, ii, Appendix xlvi

From this it was a simple step to the Sanquhar Declaration, in which Cameron and twenty of his associates renounced their allegiance to the king.

1680. *Sanquhar Declaration*

It is not amongst the smallest of the Lord's mercies to this poor land, that there have been always some who have given their testimony against every course of defection (that many are guilty of) which is a token for good, that he doth not as yet intend to cast us off altogether, but that he will leave a remnant in whom he will be glorious if they, through his grace, keep themselves clean still, and walk in his way and method, as it has been walked in and owned by him in our predecessors of truly worthy memory in their carrying on of our noble work of reformation in the several steps thereof from popery, prelacy, and likewise erastian supremacy so much usurped by him who (it is true so far as we know) is descended from the race of our kings, yet he hath so far deborded from what he ought to have been, by his perjury and usurpation in church matters, and tyranny in matters civil, as is known by the whole land, that we have just reason to account it one of the Lord's great controversies against us that we have not disowned him and the men of his practices (whether inferior magistrates or any other) as enemies to our Lord and his crown and the true protestant and presbyterian interest in thir lands, our Lord's espoused bride and church. Therefore, although we be for government and governors such as the word of God and our covenant allows, yet we for ourselves and all that will adhere to us, as the representative of the true presbyterian kirk and covenanted nation of Scotland, considering the great hazard of lying under such a sin any longer, do by thir presents disown Charles Stuart, that has been reigning (or rather tyrannizing as we may say) on the throne of Britain these years bygone, as having any right, title to, or interest in the said crown of Scotland for government, as forfeited several years since by his perjury and breach of covenant both to God and his Kirk, and usurpation of his crown and royal prerogatives therein, and many other breaches in matters ecclesiastic, and by his tyranny and breach of the very *leges regnandi* in matters civil. For which reason, we declare, that several years since he should have been denuded of being king, ruler, or magistrate, or of having any power to act or to be obeyed as such. As also, we being under the standard of our Lord Jesus Christ, Captain of salvation, do declare a war with such a tyrant and usurper and the men of his practices, as enemies to our Lord Jesus Christ, and his cause and covenants ; and against all such as have strengthened him, sided with, or any wise acknowledged him in his tyranny, civil or ecclesiastic, yea, against all such as shall strengthen, side with, or in any wise acknowledge any other in the like usurpation and tyranny, far more against such as would betray or deliver up our free reformed mother-kirk unto the bondage of Antichrist, the pope of Rome. And by this we homologate that testimony given at Rutherglen the 29th of May 1679 [1], and all the faithful testimonies of those who have gone before, as also of those who have suffered of late. And we do disclaim that declaration published at Hamilton, June 1679 [2], chiefly because it takes the king's interest, which we are several years since loosed from, because of the foresaid reasons, and others, which may after this (if the Lord will) be published. As also we disown, and by this resent the reception of the Duke of York, that professed papist, as repugnant to our principles and vows to the most high God, and as that which is the great, though not alone, just reproach of our kirk and nation. We also by this protest against his succeeding to the crown ; and whatever has been done, or any are essaying to do in this land (given to the Lord) in prejudice to our work of reformation. And to conclude, we hope after this none will blame us for or offend at our rewarding these that are against us, as they have done to us, as the Lord gives opportunity. This is not to exclude any that have declined, if they be willing to give satisfaction according to the degree of their offence.

Given at Sanquhar, June 22d. 1680.

Wodrow, ii, Appendix xlvii

Within a month, Cameron and some of his associates (including Hackston of Rathillet, one of Sharp's murderers) encountered a

[1] *Supra, p.* 171
[2] Apparently the Declaration of 13 June 1679 (Wodrow, ii, Appendix xxv).

party of dragoons at Aird's Moss, where Cameron was killed. Cargill was now the sole remaining field-preacher, and in September, at the Torwood in Stirlingshire, he formally excommunicated the King, the Dukes of York and Monmouth and the leading Scottish politicians. Stern action was necessarily taken against the adherents of this openly rebellious policy, and those who adhered to the Sanquhar Declaration and admitted their belief that it was lawful to kill the king were put to death. Cargill himself was executed in July 1681, leaving the party without a minister until James Renwick was ordained in Holland in 1683 for the purpose of ministering to them and reviving field-preaching.

The policy of renewed repression continued until, in the reign of James VII, toleration was granted as part of that monarch's papalist policy. The Government proceeded against some of the more moderate dissenters, whom it quite unjustifiably blamed for the Cameronian excesses. In 1682 Graham of Claverhouse was sent to the south-west with instructions to proceed against all persons implicated in the Bothwell Brig rebellion who had neglected to take the bond undertaking not to bear arms, and also all persons who had withdrawn themselves from the parish churches.[1] In April 1683 a proclamation was issued authorising proceedings against all persons suspected of having harboured rebels or conversed with them, whether by accident or design and whether or not the rebels had been denounced as such—an inquisitorial and vexatious measure, affecting hundreds of persons.[2]

Meantime, the Cameronians, now led by Renwick, had gone beyond mere resistance. In October 1684 they issued the Apologetical Declaration, in which they in effect declared war on all engaged in proceedings against them, and this proved to be no idle threat. The step provoked the government to proclaim that any person refusing to disown the Declaration should be put to death. Earlier declarations, from the Queensferry Paper onwards, had already adequately set down the Cameronian view of the monarchy, but the accession of James VII (February 1685) called forth the Sanquhar Protestation (28 May 1685), in which the 'contending, suffering remnant of the true presbyterians' protested against the proclamation of James as king and against the lawfulness of the parliament then in session.

---

[1] Wodrow, ii, Appendix lxxx   [2] Ibid., lxxxvii

1684. *Extracts from the Apologetical Declaration*

For preventing further mistakes anent our purposes, we do hereby jointly and unanimously testify and declare that as we utterly detest and abhor that hellish principle of killing all who differ in judgment and persuasion from us, it having no bottom upon the Word of God, or right reason, so we look upon it as a duty binding upon us to publish openly unto the world that forasmuch as we are firmly and really purposed not to injure or offend any whomsoever, but to pursue the ends of our covenants, in standing to the defence of our glorious work of reformation and of our own lives : yet (we say) we do hereby declare unto all, that whosoever stretcheth forth their hands against us, while we are maintaining the cause and interest of Christ against his enemies in the defence of our covenanted reformation, by shedding our blood actually, either by authoritative commanding, such as bloody counsellors (bloody we say) insinuating clearly by this and the other adjective epithets an open distinction betwixt the cruel and blood-thirsty and the more sober and moderate, especially that (so called) Justiciary, Generals of Forces, Adjutants, Captains, Lieutenants and all in civil and military power who make it their work to embrue their hands in our blood, or by obeying such commands, such as bloody Militia Men, malicious Troopers, Soldiers and Dragoons ; likewise, such gentlemen and commons who, through wickedness and ill will, ride and run with the foresaid persons to lay search for us, or who deliver any of us into their hands, to the spilling of our blood, by enticing morally, or stirring up enemies to the taking away of our lives, such as designedly and purposedly advise, counsel and encourage them to proceed against us, to our utter extirpation ; by informing against us wickedly, wittingly and willingly, such as viperous and malicious bishops and curates and all such sort of intelligencers who lay out themselves to the effusion of our blood, together with all such as, in obedience to the enemies their commands, at the sight of us raise the hue and cry after us ;

yea and all such as compearing before the adversaries their courts, upon their demands delate us and any who befriend us to their and our extreme hazard and suffering. We say all and every one of such shall be reputed by us enemies to God and the covenanted work of reformation, and punished as such, according to our power and the degree of their offence. . . .

Now let not any think that (our God assisting us) we will be so slack-handed in time coming to put matters in execution, as heretofore we have been, seeing we are bound faithfully and valiantly to maintain our covenants and the cause of Christ. Therefore, let all these foresaid persons be admonished of their hazard, and particularly all ye intelligencers who, by your voluntary informations, endeavour to render us up into the enemies their hands, that our blood may be shed ; for by such courses ye both endanger your immortal souls, if repentance prevent not, seeing God will make inquisition for shedding the precious blood of his saints, whatever be the thoughts of men ; and also your bodies, seeing you render yourselves actually and maliciously guilty of our blood, whose innocency the Lord knoweth. . . .

Wodrow, ii, Appendix xcix

1685. *The Sanquhar Protestation*

The protestation and apologetic admonitory declaration of the true Presbyterians of the Church of Scotland, against the proclaiming James, duke of York, king of Scotland, England, France and Ireland, the lawfulness of the present pretended parliament, and the apparent inlet of popery, etc., published at Sanquhar.

. . . A few wicked and unprincipled men of this kingdom having by open proclamation proclaimed James, duke of York, though a professed papist and excommunicate person and not yet received into the church, to be king of Scotland, England, France and Ireland : we the contending and suffering remnant of the true presbyterians of the Church of Scotland, calling to mind the many bonds and obligations that lie upon us from the Lord, and being desirous to be found faithful in this day of temptation . . . do here deliberately, jointly and unanimously protest against the foresaid proclamation of James, duke of York, to be king, as said is, in regard that it is the choosing a murderer to be a governor, who hath shed the blood of the saints of God ; in regard that it is the height of confederacy with an idolater, which is forbidden by the law of God ; in regard that it is contrary to the declaration of the general assembly of the Church of Scotland, of the date 27th July 1649 years ; in regard that it is contrary to many wholesome and laudable acts of parliament. . . . And in regard that it is inconsistent with the safety of the faith, conscience and Christian liberty of Christian people to choose a subject of Antichrist to be their (especially supreme) magistrate. . . . Our covenants and acts of parliament have put a bar upon the admission of any person, if either infidels or of a different religion, while such, to govern in Scotland : and the practice of our church confirms it, in refusing the crown to the late deceased tyrant Charles II until he subscribed such demands as were sent unto him. . . .

Also conceiving that this pretended parliament is not a lawful parliament, in regard that the election of commissioners is limited and prejudged, in the due liberty thereof, by their acts and laws : in regard that the members are convicted of avowed perjury . . . in regard they are men of blood, the chief being convicted of avowed murder, whereby they are under the lash of the law ; and in regard of their carrying on apostasy and making way for the man of sin : we do in the like manner . . . protest against the validity and constitution of this present parliament, as not being free and lawful. . . .

And further seeing bloody papists, the subjects of Antichrist, become so hopeful, bold and confident, under the perfidy of the said James, duke of York, and popery itself to [be] eminent and (oh lamentable !) like to be intruded again (if God's mercy and power meeting together in a wonderful way prevent it not) upon these covenanted lands, an open door being made thereunto, by its accursed and abjured harbinger Prelacy, which these three kingdoms are equally sworn against. We do in the like manner protest against all kind of popery in general and particular heads. . . .

Moreover, taking to our serious consideration the low, deplorable and obscured state of the churches of England and Ireland, and that we are all bound in one covenant and solemn league together, we . . . do in like manner hereby admonish you our brethren in these our neighbouring and covenanted lands that ye remember how far ye have sadly failed in pursuing the ends of our covenants. . . . Stretch your hands to the helping, strengthening, encouraging and comforting a poor wasted, wronged, wounded, reproached, despised and bleeding remnant (with whom you are in covenant) setting ourselves against all the injuries and affronts done to our blessed Lord Jesus Christ, against the man of sin, the kingdom of Antichrist and all the limbs and parts thereof. . . .

Given at   the 28th day of May 1685

Testimony-Bearing Exemplified (Paisley, 1791), pp. 260 *et seq.*

CHAPTER FOUR

THE REVOLUTION

THE PARLIAMENT OF 1681

A new element had entered into Scottish ecclesiastical politics in the last years of Charles II's reign. James, Duke of York, the Roman Catholic heir to the throne, had come to Scotland in November 1679, as High Commissioner, and he returned as High Commissioner to the Parliament of 1681. That Parliament's first statute, passed on 13 August, ratified all acts in favour of the protestant religion,[1] but its second secured the indefeasible hereditary succession to the crown. On 31 August followed the Test Act, imposing on a wide variety of persons an oath which was much criticised on the grounds of its internal inconsistency : for instance, it was difficult to reconcile the Scots Confession of 1560 with the terms in which the royal supremacy was now recognised, or the undertaking to maintain the existing settlement of the Church with an implied acknowledgment of the king's power to alter it. A much more serious matter was the association of this act with the Duke of York's right to the succession ; for this meant that a papist would be supreme governor of the Church. In consequence of refusal to ' take the Test,' a number of ministers were deprived, Sir James Dalrymple was removed from the Presidency of the Court of Session, and the Earl of Argyll was condemned for treason.

1681. *Act acknowledging and asserting the Right of Succession to the Imperial Crown of Scotland*

The Estates of Parliament, considering that the Kings of this Realme, deryving their royall power from God Almightie alone, doe succeid lineallie therto according to the known degrees of proximitie in blood, which cannot be interrupted, suspended or diverted by any act or statute whatsoevir, and that none can attempt to alter or divert the said succession

[1] *A.P.S.*, viii, 238

without involving the subjects of this kingdom in perjurie and rebellion, and without exposing them to all the fatall and dreadfull consequences of a civil warr : Doe therfore from a heartie and sincere sense of their duty, recognize, acknowledge and declare that the right to the Imperiall Croune of this Realme is by the inherent right and nature of the Monarchie, alsweil as by the fundamentall and unalterable laws of this Realme, transmitted and devolved by a lineal succession according to the proximitie of blood : And that upon the death of the King or Queen who actuallie reignes, the subjects of this kingdome are bound by law, duty and allegiance to obey the nixt immediat and laufull heir either male or female upon whom the right and administration of the Government is immediatlie devolved, and that no difference in religion nor no law nor act of Parliament made or to be made can alter or divert the Right of Succession and lineal descent of the Croun to the nearest and laufull heirs according to the degrees foirsaids, nor can stop or hinder them in the full, frie and actuall administration of the Government according to the laws of the kingdom. Lykeas our Soveraigne Lord, with advice and consent of his saids Estates of Parliament, doe declare it is high treason in any of the subjects of this kingdom by writeing, speaking or any other manner of way to endeavour the alteration, suspension, or diversion of the said right of Succession, or the debarring the nixt laufull Successor from the immediat, actual, full and free administration of the Government, conform to the laws of the kingdom ; and that all such attempts or designes shall inferr against them the pain of treason.

A.P.S., viii, 238, c. 2

1681. *Act anent Religion and the Test*

[*To maintain and preserve the Protestant religion, the laws against Popery and against sayers and hearers of the Mass, etc., are to be put to full and vigorous execution ; the ministers of the parishes are to give in lists to the bishops of all papists and schismatical with-*

186

drawers from public worship, and the bishops are to give in copies of the lists to the sheriffs and other magistrates so that they may proceed against offenders ; the bishops are also to send copies of the lists to the Clerks of the Privy Council so that the diligence of the sheriffs and other judges may be examined and controlled :] And to cut off all hopes from Papists and phanaticks of their being imployed in offices and places of publict trust it is hereby statute and ordained that the following Oath shall be taken by all persons in offices and places of publict trust, civill, ecclesiastical and military, especially by all Members of Parliament and all electors of Members of Parliament, all Privy Councellors, Lords of Session, Members of the Exchequer, Lords of Justitiary, and all other members of these courts, all Officers of the Croune and State, all Archbishops and Bishops, and all preachers and ministers of the Gospell whatsoever, all persons of this kingdom named or to be named Commissioners for the Borders, all members of the Commission for Church-affairs, all Sheriffs, Stewarts, Balyies of Royalties and Regalities, Justices of the Peace, Officers of the Mint, Commissars and their deputs, their clerks and fiscalls, all advocats and procurators before any of these courts, all Writers to the Signet, all publict notars and other persons imployed in writeing or agenting, the Lyon King at Armes, Heraulds, Pursevants and Messingers at Armes, all Collectours, Subcollectors and farmourers of his Majesties Custome and Excise ; all Magistrats, Deans of Gild, Counsellours, and Clerks of Burghs Royal and Regalitie ; all Deacons of Trades, and Deacon-Conveeners in the saids burghs ; all Maisters and Doctors in Universities, Colledges, or schools ; all chaplanes in families, pedagogues to children ; and all officers and souldiers in Armies, Forts, or Militia, and all other persons in publick trust or office within this kingdom, who shall publikely swear and subscribe the said Oath as follows. . . . And ordains that all who shall hereafter be promoted to or imployed in any of the forsaids offices, trusts or imployments, shall at their entry into and before their exerceing therof, take and subscribe the said Oath in manner foresaid, to be recorded in the Registers of these respective courts, and reported to his Majesties Privy Councill within the space of fourty dayes after their taking the same : And if any shall presume to exercise any of the saids offices or imployments or any publict office or trust within this kingdom (the Kings lawfull brothers and sons only excepted) until they take the oath foresaid and subscribe it to be recorded in the registers of the respective courts, They shall be declared incapable of all publict trust thereafter and be further punished with the loss of their movables and liferent escheat, the one half wherof to be given to the informer and the other half to belong to his Majestie. And his Majestie with advice foresaid recomends to his privy Council to see this Act put to due and vigorous execution.

Follows the tenor of the Oath to be taken by all persons in publick trust.

I A:B: Solemnlie swear in presence of the Eternal God, whom I invocat as judge and witness of my sincere intention of this my oath, That I own and sincerely profess the true protestant religion contained in the Confession of Faith recorded in the first Parliament of King James the Sixth, And that I beleive the same to be founded on and agreeable to the written word of God. And I promise and swear that I shall adhere therto during all the days of my lifetime, And shall endeavour to educat my children therin : And shall never consent to any change nor alteration contrary therto : And that I dissown and renunce all such principles, doctrines, or practises, whether Popish or Phanaticall, which are contrary unto and inconsistent with the said Protestant Religion and Confession of Faith. And for testification of my obedience to my Most Gracious Soveraigne Charles the Second, I doe affirm and swear by this my solemn oath that the Kings Majesty is the only Supream Governour of this Realme, over all persons and in all causes as weill Ecclesiastical as Civill ; And that no forraigne Prince, Person, Pope, Prelate, State, or Potentat, hath or ought to have any jurisdiction, power, superiority, preheminency, or authority ecclesiastical or civil within this Realme ; And therfore I doe utterly renunce and forsake all forraigne jurisdictions, powers, superiorities, and authorities, And doe promise that from henceforth I shall bear faith and true allegiance to the Kings Majestie his heirs and laufull successors. And to my power shall assist and defend all rights, jurisdictions, prerogatives, privileges, preheminencies and authorities belonging to the Kings Majestie his heirs and laufull successors. And I farder affirm and swear by this my solemn oath that I judge it unlauful for subjects upon pretence of reformation or any other pretence whatsoever, to enter into Covenants or Leagues, or to convocat, conveen or assemble in any Councills, Conventions or Assemblies, to treat, consult or determine in any mater of State, civil or ecclesiastick without his Majesties special command or express licence had thereto, Or to take up arms against the king or those commissionated by him : And that I shall never so rise in arms or enter into such Covenant or Assemblies : And that ther lyes no obligation on me from the National Covenant or the Solemn League and Covenant (so commonlie called) or any other manner of way whatsoever, to endeavour any change or alteration in the Government, either in Church or State, as it is now established by the Laws of this kingdom. And I promise and swear that I shall with my utmost power defend, assist and mantein His Majesties jurisdiction foresaid against all deadly : And I shall never decline his Majesties power and jurisdiction, As I shall answer to God. And finally I affirm and swear that this my solemn oath is given in the plain genuine sense and meaning of the words without any equivocation, mental reservation, or any manner of evasion whatsoever ; And that I shall not accept or use any dispensation from any creature whatsoever. So help me God.

A.P.S., viii, 243, c. 6

THE POLICY OF JAMES VII

Apart from the Cameronian remnant, the country of which James VII became king in February 1685 was not merely at peace but was effusively loyal. His first parliament, in April 1685, passed statutes imposing the death penalty for mere attendance at a conventicle, declaring it treason to take or own the covenants, and, with a fulsome preamble expressive of loyalty, annexing the excise to the Crown in perpetuity.[1] The utter failure of Argyll's rising (May-June 1685) demonstrated the unreadiness of the country to resort to rebellion.

Yet it would have been plain enough to any intelligence less obtuse than the king's that there was one issue on which the political and ecclesiastical fabric so carefully fostered by his predecessors could be shaken, and that was its use in the interests of the Roman Church. Already in 1680, while James was resident at Holyrood, there had been an anti-papal demonstration in Edinburgh, and now, after the Earl of Perth (chancellor of the kingdom) and his brother, Lord Melfort (a secretary of state), had announced their conversion to Roman Catholicism, the citizens of the capital rioted against the appearance of the apparatus of Roman Catholic worship (January 1686).

1685. *Preamble to the Act annexing the Excise to the Crown*

The estates of parliament . . . taking into their consideration how this nation hath continued now upwards of two thousand years in the unaltered form of our monarchical government, under the uninterrupted line of one hundred and eleven kings, whose sacred authority and power hath been upon all signall occasions so owned and assisted by Almighty God that our kingdom hath been protected from conquest, our possessions defended from strangers, our civil commotions brought into wished events, our laws vigorously executed, our propertys legally fixed and our lives securely preserved, so that we and our ancestors have enjoyed those securitys and tranquillities which the greater and more flourishing kingdoms have frequently wanted, those great

[1] A.P.S., viii, 459–61

blessings we owe in the first place to divine mercy, and, in dependance on that, to the sacred race of our glorious kings and to the solid, absolute authority wherwith they were invested by the first and fundamentall law of our monarchy, nor can either our records or our experience instance our being deprived of those happy effects but when a rebellious party did by commotions and seditions invade the kings soveraign authority, which was the cause of our prosperity, . . . Therfor the estates of parliament . . . declare . . . that they abhor and detest not only the authors and actors of all preceeding rebellions against the soveraign, but likways all principles and positions which are contrary or derogatory to the kings sacred, supream, absolute power . . . and as their dutie formerly did bind them to owne and assert the just and legall succession of the sacred line as unalterable by any human jurisdiction, so now they hold themselves on this occasion obliged for themselves and the whole nation represented by them in most humble and dutifull maner to renew the hearty and sincere offer of their lives and fortunes to assist, support, defend and mentain King James the Seventh, their present glorious monarch, and his heirs and lawfull successors, in the possession of their crowns, soveraignty, prerogatives, authority, dignity, rights and possessions against all mortalls, and withall to assure all his enemies who shall adventure on the disloyalty of disobeying his laws or on the impiety of invading his rights, that such shall sooner weary of their wickedness then they of their dutie, and that they firmly resolve to give their entire obedience to his majestie without reserve, and to concurr against all his enemies, forraign or intestine, and they solemnly declare that as they are bound by law so they are voluntarly and firmly resolved that all of this nation, betuixt sixty and sixteen, armed and provyded according to their abilities, shall be in readiness for his majesties service where and as oft as it shall be his royal pleasure to require them.

A.P.S., viii, 459-60

A year later, to the Parliament of April 1686 James in effect offered free trade with England as a bribe for the relief of Roman Catholics from the laws against them. There was strong opposition even in the Committee of Articles, and the indignation of the estates was such that their reply amounted to a rebuff to the king. Parliament was first adjourned (June) and later dissolved. The king had to pursue his policy by other means.

The conversions of Perth and Melfort were followed by others, while officials who adhered to the reformed faith were dismissed and replaced by Roman Catholics. Thus Queensberry lost the commissionership and was removed from the treasury, which was put into commission with Melfort as principal commissioner ; Sir George Mackenzie, the lord advocate, was likewise dismissed. The Duke of Gordon, another Romanist, was appointed to the command of Edinburgh Castle.

While the law was thus being dispensed with in individual cases, its general suspension had to be brought about by Privy Council ordinance or royal proclamation. In September 1686 the Council was instructed to embody in an ordinance the measure of protection to Roman Catholics in the private exercise of their religion which had been offered by the Parliament of the preceding April,[1] and at the same time the king intimated his intention to fit up the Chapel Royal at Holyrood for Roman Catholic worship.[2] Subsequently a Jesuit school and a Roman Catholic printing press were established at Holyrood.

1686. *James VII's Proposal for Toleration*

A letter from his Majesty to the Parliament being presented was twice read and ordained to be recorded : . . .

James R

My Lords and Gentlemen :

Wee have considered your interest as much as our distance from you could bring into our prospect, and those things which wee found proper for it whether in relation to trade and commerce or easing some things uneasie to you amongst your selves. Wee have fully instructed our Commissioner (with your advice and consent) to conclude soe as

[1] *A.P.S.*, viii, 580   [2] Wodrow, iv, 389

may be most for the general good of that our ancient Kingdom. We have made the opening of a free trade with
England our particular care and are proceeding in it with
all imaginable application, and are hopefull in a short tyme
to have considerable advances made in it.

Wee have considered the truble that many are putt to
dayly by prosecutions befor our judges or the hazard that
they lye under for their accesion to the late rebellions :
And to show the world (even our greatest enemies themselves) that mercy is our inclination, and severity what is
by their wickedness extorted from us, Wee have sent doun
to be past in your presence our full and ample Indemnity
for all crymes committed against our royal persone or
authority. And whilst wee show these Acts of mercy to the
enemies of our person, Croun and royal dignity, We can
not be unmindfull of others our innocent subjects, those of
the Roman Catholick religion, who have with the hazard of
their lives and fortunes been alwayes assistant to the Crown
in the worst of rebellions and usurpations, though they lay
under discouradgements hardly to be named. Them wee
doe heartily recommend to your care to the end that as they
have given good experience of their true loyalty and peaceable behaviour, soe by your assistance they may have the
protectione of our lawes and that security under our government which others of our subjects have, not suffering them
to lye under obligations which their religion can not admitt
of. By doeing whereof you will give a demonstration of the
duety and affection you have for us and do us most acceptable service. . . .

Soe not only expecting your complyance with us but that
by the manner of it you will show the world your readiness
to meet our inclinations, Wee bid you most heartily farewell.
Given at our Court at Whitehall the 12th day of April 1686
and of our Reigne the 2nd year.

*   *   *

The draught of a letter from the Parliament to the King
in answer to his Majesties Letter being brought in by the

Lords of the Articles and several tymes read, sundry members of Parliament did object against the words of the Letter ' subjects of the Roman Catholick religion ' as ane designation not fitt to be given by the Parliament to these of the Romish persuasione, and after debate it being putt to the vote if the letter as it was brought in by the Lords of the articles containing the forsaid words, should be approven or amended, the letter was approven, this not being ane publict act of Parliament but a letter written in answer to his Majesties letter containing the forsaid expression and this letter only resuming the same, which was ordained to be marked in the Minuts and it was ordered that the letter should be signed by the Lord Chancellar in name of the Parliament, wherof the tenor followes :

. . . Your Majesties care of the trade of this kingdome (which is at present exceedingly decayed) and particularly your royal endeavours to procure us a free trade with your kingdome of England will very much enable us to make these supplies effectual which wee have soe heartily and willingly undertaken for the security of the Croun and safety of the kingdom. . . .

As to that pairt of your Maiesties letter relating to your subjects of the Roman Catholick religion, wee shall in obedience to your Majesties commands and with tendernes to their persones take the same into our serious and duetifull consideration and goe as great lengths therin as our conscience will allow, not doubting that your Maiesty will be carefull to secure the Protestant religion established by law.

A.P.S., viii, 579–81

While ready enough to enlarge the privileges of his co-religionists beyond protection for the exercise of their religion in their own homes, James was reluctant to extend concessions to the presbyterians and to accept the policy of a general toleration. His first proclamation of toleration, in February 1687, was accompanied by a letter to the Council inveighing against ' those enemies of Christianity as well as government and human society, the field conventiclers, whom we recommend you to root out with all the severities of our laws,' and, while granting toleration to Romanists and Quakers, provided only that they did not worship in the fields, make public processions in the high streets of royal burghs or invade protestant churches, allowed presbyterians to meet only in private houses with ministers who would accept the indulgence.[1] In June, however, these distinctions were withdrawn, and a proclamation permitted all the king's subjects ' to meet and serve God after their own way, be it in private houses, chapels or places purposely hired or built for that purpose.'

James's indulgence undid at one stroke all the work of a genera-tion of efforts, with a measure of success, to weld the presbyterians into the established church. It also went far to unite the nation in opposition. The presbyterians, reinforced by exiles returning from Holland, rapidly built up an organisation which offered an alternative to the existing establishment ; the bishops and clergy generally were almost equally hostile to the toleration of the presbyterians and the toleration of the Roman Catholics, and two bishops were deprived for their opposition ; peers and politicians were alienated by the freedom accorded to the Romanists and by the king's disregard for the statutes securing the reformed church.

1687, February. *James VII's Indulgences*

James [*etc.*]. We having taken into our royal consideration the many and great inconveniencies which have happened to that our ancient kingdom of Scotland of late years through the different persuasions in the Christian religion, and the great heats and animosities amongst the several professors thereof, to the ruin and decay of trade, wasting of lands, extinguishing of charity, contempt of the royal power and converting of true religion, and the fear of God, into animosities, name, factions and sometimes into sacrilege and treason ; and being resolved, as much as in us lies, to unite the hearts and affections of our subjects to God in religion, to us in loyalty and to their neighbours in Christian love and charity, have therefore thought fit to grant, and by our sovereign authority . . . do hereby give and grant

---

[1] A further condition imposed was an oath of non-resistance, but it was withdrawn in May.

our royal toleration to the several professors of the Christian religion afternamed, with and under the several conditions, restrictions and limitations aftermentioned. In the first place, we allow and tolerate the moderate presbyterians to meet in their private houses and there to hear all such ministers as either have or are willing to accept of our indulgence allanerly, and none other, and that there be not anything said or done contrary to the weal and peace of our reign, seditious or treasonable, under the highest pains these crimes will import ; nor are they to presume to build meeting-houses, or to use out-houses or barns, but only to exercise in their private houses, as said is. In the mean time it is our royal will and pleasure that field-conventicles and such as preach or exercise at them, or who shall any wise assist or connive at them, shall be prosecuted according to the utmost severity of our laws made against them. . . . In like manner we do hereby tolerate Quakers, to meet and exercise in their form, in any place or places appointed for their worship. And considering the severe and cruel laws made against Roman catholics (therein called Papists) . . . we, of our certain knowledge and long experience knowing that the Catholics, as it is their principle to be good Christians so it is to be dutiful subjects, and that they have likewise on all occasions shewn themselves good and faithful subjects to us and our royal predecessors . . . do therefore . . . suspend, stop and disable all laws or acts of parliament, customs or constitutions made or executed against any of our Roman Catholic subjects in any time past, to all intents and purposes, making void all prohibitions therein mentioned, pains or penalties therein ordained to be inflicted, so that they shall, in all things, be as free, in all respects, as any of our protestant subjects whatsoever, not only to exercise their religion but to enjoy all offices, benefices and others which we shall think fit to bestow upon them in all time coming : nevertheless it is our will and pleasure and we do hereby command all catholics, at their highest pains, only to exercise their religious worship in houses or chapels, and that they presume not to preach in the open fields or to invade the protestant churches by force . . . nor shall they presume to make public processions in the high streets of any of our royal burghs. . . .

Wodrow, ii, Appendix cxxix ; cf. *R.P.C.*, 3rd. ser., xiii, 123–4

1687, June.

James VII [*etc.*]. . . . We will protect our archbishops and bishops, and all our subjects of the protestant religion, in the free exercise of their protestant religion as it is by law established, and in the quiet and full enjoyment of all their possessions, without any molestation or disturbance whatsoever. And we do likewise . . . suspend, stop and disable all penal and sanguinary laws made against any for nonconformity to the religion established by law in that our ancient kingdom, or for exercising their respective worships, religions, rites and ceremonies, all which laws are hereby stopt, suspended and disabled to all intents and purposes. . . . As we do give them leave to meet and serve God after their own way and manner, be it in private houses, chapels or places purposely hired or built for that use, so that they take care that nothing be preached or taught among them which may any ways tend to alienate the hearts of our people from us or our government, and that their meetings be peaceable, openly and publicly held, and all persons freely admitted to them, and that they do signify and make known to some one or more of the next privy councillors, sheriffs, stewarts, bailies, justices of the peace or magistrates of burghs royal, what place or places they set apart for these uses, with the names of the preachers. . . . Provided always that their meetings be in houses, or places provided for the purpose, and not in the open fields, for which now after this our royal grace and favour shewn . . . there is not the least shadow of excuse left ; which meetings in fields we do hereby strictly prohibit and forbid, against all which we do leave our laws and acts of parliament in full force and vigour, notwithstanding the premisses. . . .

Ibid., Appendix cxxxiv (*R.P.C.*, 3rd ser., xiii, 156–8)

The Events of 1688–9

Scottish opinion was ripe for a revolution, but there were no indications whatever that any initiative in that direction would have been taken north of the Border, even when the birth of James's son, on 10 June 1688, seemed to assure the permanence of the existing regime. In the events which led to the arrival in England of William of Orange (5 November 1688) and the flight of James to France (22 December), although some part was played by Scottish exiles, Scotsmen in Scotland had no part at all. William undertook the provisional government of England on 28 December 1688, a convention met there on 22 January 1689, and on 13 February the crown of that country was offered to, and accepted by, William and Mary.

James had summoned to England most of the Scottish troops— the horse commanded by Viscount Dundee (Graham of Claverhouse)—and the Privy Council lacked the means to maintain order. In the south-west the Whigs declared for William and drove out the curates ; in the capital the mob sacked the chapel at Holyrood and drove out the Jesuits. Scottish peers and gentlemen, to the number of over a hundred, flocked to London, where, on 7 January, they were invited to meet William, who, a week later, agreed at their request to undertake the administration of Scotland provisionally and to send out letters calling a convention to meet on 14 March.

In the composition of the convention, the Test Act, although still law, was dispensed with, and the burgh representatives were popularly elected, but, on the other hand, the sworn supporters of James obtained his permission to attend. That the body contained a Williamite majority was shown when the Duke of Hamilton (who had been chosen as their leader by the lords and gentlemen who had met William in London) was elected as president in preference to the Jacobite nominee. A more important trial of strength came when a letter from King James arrived and it was moved that it be read ; Hamilton produced a letter from William, and obtained a majority in favour of its being read first. Lest James's letter might contain a message dissolving the convention, a resolution was signed by all present that ' this lawful convention of estates' would continue to meet in spite of anything in the letter.

When the letter was opened, it proved to contain not, indeed, an order to dissolve, but an assertion of a completely uncompromising attitude and threats of punishment against disloyal subjects. The Jacobites, discouraged, left the convention and even abandoned the idea of a rival meeting at Stirling. The Whig and Williamite rump were able to proceed unrestrained by the Tory moderation which had influenced the proceedings of the English convention ; and, although Edinburgh Castle was held for King James until 14 June and Dundee was presently in arms in the Highlands, the convention enjoyed comparative security, especially with the raising of an armed force from among the Cameronians and the arrival, on 25 March, of the Scots regiments from Holland under Mackay. The subsequent military operations in the Highlands were of little importance in deciding the future of Scotland ; the rout of Mackay's force at Killiecrankie (27 July) was an action on too small a scale to have determined the issue even had Dundee survived, but his death was an almost irreparable disaster to the Jacobite cause, and his victory was in any case offset by the Cameronians' successful defence of Dunkeld (21 August).

On 26 March the convention had appointed a committee of eight nobles, eight shire commissioners and eight burgesses to frame measures. On 4 April it was resolved that James had forfeited the crown and that the throne was vacant ; on 11 April the Claim of Right was adopted ; and two days later the supplementary Articles of Grievances. Without waiting for the acceptance of the crown by William and Mary, the estates ordered that they should be proclaimed and should be prayed for as king and queen, and they also drew up a coronation oath.

Perhaps because the Revolution was English made, the emphasis was laid on constitutional issues in language adapted from that used in the corresponding English documents. William's proclamation to Scotland, dated at the Hague on 10 October 1688, was mainly a shortened version of the proclamation which he issued to England on the same day ; its emphasis was on the illegality of the government's proceedings, which had changed ' the constitution of the monarchy regulate by laws, into a despotic or arbitrary power,' on the predominance under James of ' evil counsels and counsellors' and on the suspension of the penal laws ; a paragraph was, indeed, devoted to the oppression of the covenanting counties, but no hint was given that the issue there was ecclesiastical—the prosecutions had taken place ' for no other reason but because they would not answer or satisfy them in such questions as they proposed to them, without any warrant of law and against the common interest of mankind, which frees all men from being obliged to discover their secret thoughts.' [1]

The Claim of Right was likewise coloured by the precedent of the English Bill of Rights, and followed it closely in structure. But there were two important deviations from the English model : (1) The English declared that James, by his flight, had abdicated ; the Scots repeated their resolution, arrived at a week earlier, that by his misdeeds he had forfeited the crown. (2) It was decided, by a majority, to insert a clause condemning ' prelacy.' This ' grievance ' might more fittingly have been included in the Articles of Grievances, adopted two days after the Claim of Right, since they were concerned with matters technically legal but now considered undesirable ; and it has been suggested that the inclusion of the clause about ' prelacy ' in the Claim of Right was an attempt to commit William to the overthrow of episcopacy by virtually making that a condition of his acceptance as king. The most important of the Articles of Grievances were those denouncing the Committee of Articles and all committees for initiating legislation which were not freely elected by the estates,[2] and condemning the Act of Supremacy of 1669.

1689. *The Claim of Right*

Declaration of the Estates of the Kingdom of Scotland, containing the Claim of Right, and the offer of the Crown to their Majesties King William and Queen Mary.

Whereas King James the Seventh, being a profest Papist, did assume the regal power, and acted as King, without ever taking the oath required by law, whereby the King at his access to the Government, is obliged to swear, to maintain the Protestant religion, and to rule the people according to the laudable laws ; And did, by the advice of wicked and evil counsellors, invade the fundamental constitution of this Kingdom, and altered it from a legal limited monarchy, to an arbitrary despotic power ; And in a

---

[1] Wodrow, ii, 647   [2] cf. *infra*, p. 236

public proclamation, asserted an absolute power, to cass, annul and disable all the laws, particularly arraigning all the laws establishing the Protestant religion, and did exercise that power, to the subversion of the Protestant religion, and to the violation of the laws and liberties of the Kingdom.

By erecting public schools and societies of the Jesuits ; and not only allowing the Mass to be publicly said, but also inverting Protestant chappels and churches to public Mass-houses, contrary to the express laws against saying and hearing of Mass.

By allowing Popish books to be printed and dispersed by a gift to a Popish printer ; Designing him printer to His Majesty's Household, College and Chappel, contrary to the laws.

By taking the children of Protestant Noblemen and Gentlemen, sending and keeping them abroad, to be bred Papists, making great fonds and dotations to Popish schools and colleges abroad ; bestowing pensions upon priests ; and perverting Protestants from their religion, by offers of places, preferments, and pensions.

By disarming Protestants, while at the same time he imployed Papists, in the places of greatest trust, civil and military, such as Chancellor, Secretaries, Privy Counsellors, and Lords of Session, thrusting out Protestants, to make room for Papists, and entrusting the forts and magazines of the Kingdom in their hands.

By imposing oaths contrary to law.

By giving gifts and grants for exacting money, without consent of Parliament, or convention of Estates.

By levying or keeping on foot a standing army in time of peace, without consent of Parliament, which army did exact locality, free and dry quarters.

By imploying the officers of the army, as Judges through the Kingdom, and imposing them where there were Heretable offices and jurisdictions, by whom many of the Leidges were put to death summarly, without legal tryal, jury or record.

By imposing exorbitant fines, to the value of the parties' estates, exacting extravagant bale ; and disposing fines and forfaultures before any process or conviction.

By imprisoning persons without expressing the reason, and delaying to put them to tryal.

By causing persue and forefault several persons upon stretches of old and obsolete laws, upon frivolous and weak pretences, upon lame and defective probations : As particularly the late Earl of Argyle, to the scandal and reproach of the justice of the Nation.

By subverting the right of the Royal Burghs, the third Estate of Parliament, imposing upon them not only Magistrats, but also the whole Town-council, and Clerks, contrary to their liberties, and express Charters, without the pretence either of sentence, Surrender or Consent, so that the Commissioners to Parliaments being chosen by the Magistrats and Council, the King might in effect als well nominat that entire Estate of Parliament ; and many of the saids Magistrats put in by him, were avowed Papists, and the Burghs were forced to pay money for the Letters imposing these illegal Magistrats and Councils upon them.

By sending letters to the chief Courts of Justice, not only ordaining the Judges to stop and desist *sine die* to determine causes ; but also ordering and commanding them how to proceed, in cases depending before them, contrary to the express laws ; and by changing the nature of the Judges' Gifts *ad vitam aut culpam*, and giving them Commissions *ad bene placitum*, to dispose them to complyance with arbitrary courses, and turning them out of their Offices, when they did not comply.

By granting personal Protections for civil debts, contrary to law.

All which are utterly and directly contrary to the known laws, statutes and freedoms of this Realm.

Therefore the Estates of the Kingdom of Scotland, Find and Declare that King James the Seventh being a professed Papist, did assume the Regal power, and acted as King, without ever taking the oath required by law, and hath by the advice of evil and wicked counsellors, invaded the fundamental constitution of the Kingdom, and altered it from a legal limited Monarchy, to an arbitrary despotick Power, and hath exercised the same, to the subversion of the Protestant religion, and the violation of the laws and liberties of the Kingdom, inverting all the ends of Government, whereby he hath forefaulted the right to the Crown, and the Throne is become vacant.

And Whereas His Royal Highness, William then Prince of Orange, now King of England, whom it hath pleased the Almighty God to make the Glorious Instrument of delivering these Kingdoms from Popery and arbitrary power, did, by the advice of several Lords and Gentlemen of this Nation, at London for the time, call the Estates of this Kingdom to meet the Fourteenth of March last, in order to such an Establishment as that the Religion, Laws and Liberties might not be again in danger of being subverted ; And the saids Estates being now assembled in a full and free Representative of this Nation, taking to their most serious consideration the best means for attaining the ends aforesaid, Do, in the first place, as their Ancestors in the like cases have usually done, for the vindicating and asserting their ancient rights and liberties, Declare,

That by the law of this Kingdom, no Papist can be King or Queen of this Realm, nor bear any office whatsoever therein ; nor can any Protestant Successor exercise the Regal Power, until He or She swear the Coronation Oath.

That all Proclamations asserting an absolute power, to cass, annull, and disable laws, the erecting schools and colledges for Jesuits, the inverting Protestant Chappels & churches to public Mass-houses, and the allowing Mass to be said, are contrary to law.

That the allowing Popish books to be printed and dispersed, is contrary to law.

That the taking the children of Noblemen, Gentlemen and others, sending and keeping them abroad to be bred Papists, the making fonds and dotations to Popish schools and colledges, the bestowing pensions on priests, and the perverting Protestants from their religion, by offers of places, preferments, and pensions, are contrary to law.

That the disarming of Protestants, and imploying of Papists in the places of greatest trust, both Civil and Military, the thrusting out of Protestants, to make room for Papists, and the intrusting Papists with the Forts and Magazines of the Kingdom are contrary to law.

That the imposing Oaths without the Authority of Parliament, is contrary to law.

That the giving gifts or grants, for raising of money, without the consent of Parliament, or Convention of Estates, is contrary to law.

That the imploying the officers of the Army as Judges through the Kingdom, or imposing them where there were heretable offices and Jurisdictions, and the putting the Leidges to death summarly without Legal tryal, Jury, or record are contrary to law.

That the imposing of extraordinary fines, the exacting of exorbitant bale, and the disposing of fines and forfeitures before sentence, are contrary to law.

That the imprisoning persons, without expressing the reason thereof, and delaying to put them to tryal, is contrary to law.

That the causing pursue and forfault persons, upon stretches of old and obsolete laws, upon frivolous and weak pretences, upon lame and defective probation, as particularly the late Earl of Argyle, are contrary to law.

That the nominating and imposing the Magistrats, Councils, and Clerks upon Burghs, contrair to their liberties and express Charters, is contrary to law.

That the sending letters to the Courts of Justice, ordaining the Judges to stop or desist from determining causes, or ordaining them how to proceed in causes depending before them, and changing the nature of the Judges' Gifts *ad vitam aut culpam* into Commissions *durante bene placito*, are contrary to law.

That the granting personal protections for civil debts, is contrary to law.

That the forcing of the Leiges to depone against themselves in capital crimes, however the punishment be
restricted, is contrary to law.

That the using Torture without evidence, or in ordinary
crimes is contrary to law.

That the sending of an army in an hostile manner, upon
any pairt of the Kingdom in a peaceable time, and exacting
of Locality, and any manner of free quarters, is contrary
to law.

That the charging of the Leiges with Law-borrows at the
King's instance, and the imposing of Bonds without the
authority of Parliament, and the suspending Advocats from
their imployment, for not compearing when such Bonds
were offered, were contrary to law.

That the putting of garisons in privat men's houses in time
of peace, without their consent, or the authority of Parliament, is contrary to law.

That the opinions of the Lords of Session in the two cases
following, were contrary to law, viz. 1. That the concealing
the demand of a supply for a forefaulted person, although
not given, is treason. 2. That persons refusing to discover
what are their private thoughts and judgements in relation
to points of treason, or other men's actions, are guilty of
treason.

That the fyning husbands for their wives withdrawing
from the Church was contrary to law.

That Prelacy and the superiority of any office in the
Church above Presbyters, is, and hath been a great and
insupportable grievance and trouble to this Nation, and
contrary to the inclinations of the generality of the
people, ever since the Reformation (they having reformed
from Popery by Presbyters), and therefore ought to be
abolished.

That it is the right and privilege of the Subjects to protest
for Remeed of law to the King and Parliament, against
sentences pronounced by the Lords of Session, providing the
same do not stop execution of these sentences.

That it is the right of the subjects to petition the King,

and that all imprisonments and prosecutions for such petitioning, are contrary to law.

That for redress of all grievances, and for the amending, strengthening and preserving of the laws, Parliaments ought to be frequently called, and allowed to sit, and the freedom of speech and debate secured to the members.

And they do claim, demand and insist upon all and sundry the premisses as their undoubted rights and liberties, and that no declarations, doings, or proceedings, to the prejudice of the people, in any of the said premisses, ought in any ways to be drawn hereafter, in consequence or example, but that all forefaultures, fines, loss of offices, imprisonments, banishments, pursuits, persecutions, tortures and rigorous executions be considered, and the parties lesed be redressed.

To which demand of their rights, and redressing of their grievances, they are particularly encouraged by His Majesty the King of England, his declaration for the Kingdom of Scotland, of the . . . day of October last, as being the only means for obtaining a full redress and remedy therein.

Having therefore an entire confidence, that His said Majesty the King of England, will perfect the deliverance so far advanced by Him, and will still preserve them from the violation of their rights which they have here asserted, and from all other attempts upon their Religion, Laws, and Liberties.

The said Estates of the Kingdom of Scotland, Do resolve that WILLIAM and MARY, King and Queen of England, France and Ireland, Be, and Be Declared King and Queen of Scotland, to hold the Crown and Royal Dignity of the said Kingdom of Scotland, to them the said King and Queen, during their lives, and the longest liver of them, and that the sole and full exercise of the Regal power be only in, and exercised by Him the said King, in the names of the said King and Queen during their joynt lives ; and after their decease, the said Crown and Royal Dignity of the said Kingdom, to be to the Heirs of the body of the said Queen ; which failing to the Princess Anne of Denmark, and the

Heirs of her body ; which also failing, to the Heirs of the body of the said William King of England.

And they do pray the said King and Queen of England to accept the same accordingly.

And that the oath hereafter mentioned, be taken by all Protestants, of whom the oath of allegiance, and any other oaths and declarations might be required by law, instead of them, and that the said oath of allegiance, and other oaths and declarations may be abrogated :

' I, A.B. Do sincerely promise and swear, That I will be faithfull, and bear true allegiance to their Majesties King William and Queen Mary. So help me God.'

A.P.S., ix, 37

1689. *Articles of Grievances*

The greivances prepaired and brought in by the committee for setleing the government [1] being read, after argueing upon the severall articles they were voted and approven, wherof the tenor followes :

The estates of the kingdome of Scotland doe represent that the committee of parliament called the Articles is a great greivance to the nation, and that there ought to be no committees of parliament but such as are freely chosen by the estates to prepare motions and overtures that are first made in the house.

That the first act of parliament [of 1669] [2] is inconsistent with the establishment of the church government now desyred and ought to be abrogated.

That forefaulters in prejudice of vassalls, creditors and aires of entail are a great greivance.

That the oblidging the leidges to depone upon crymes against delinquents utherwayes then when they are adduced in speciall processes as witnesses is a great greivance.

That assyses of error are a greivance, and that juries be considered by parliament.

---

[1] i.e. the committee of twenty-four elected on 26 March (*supra*, p. 199)
[2] The Act of Supremacy (*supra*, p. 160)

That the eighteinth act of parliament [of 1681] declareing a cumulative jurisdiction is a greivance.[1]

That the commissariot courts as they are now constitute are a greivance.

That the twenty seventh act of parliament [of 1663] giveing to the king power to impose custome at pleasure upon forraigne import and trade is a greiveance and prejudiciall to the trade of the nation.

That the not takeing ane effectuall course to repress the depredations and robberies by the Highland clannes is a greivance.

That the banishment by the councill of the greatest pairt of the advocates from Edinburgh without a proces was a greivance.

That most of the lawes enacted in the parliament anno [1685] are impious and intollerable greivances.

That the marriage of a king or queen of this realme to a papist is dangerous to the protestant religion and ought to be provyded against.

That the levieing or keeping on foot a standing army in tyme of peace without consent of parliament is a greivance.

A.P.S., ix, 45

1689. *The Oath taken by William and Mary on their acceptance of the Crown of Scotland*

Wee, William and Mary, King and Queen of Scotland, faithfully promise and swear, by this our solemne oath, in presence of the Eternall God, that dureing the wholl course of our life wee will serve the same Eternall God to the utermost of our power according as He has required in His most Holy word, revealed and contained in the New and Old Testaments, and according to the same word shall maintaine the

---

[1] An ' Act asserting his majesties prerogative in point of jurisdiction ' declared that as all government and jurisdiction in the kingdom originally resided in the king, therefore the jurisdictions granted to subjects were not privative of the king's jurisdiction and he could, by himself or commissioners, take cognisance of any cases or causes he pleased (*A.P.S.*, viii, 352).

208

true religion of Christ Jesus, the preaching of His Holy word and the due and right ministration of the Sacraments now receaved and preached within the realm of Scotland, and shall abolish and gainstand all false religion contrary to the same and shall rule the people committed to our charge according to the will and command of God, revealed in his aforesaid Word, and according to the loveable lawes and constitutiones receaved in this realm, nawayes repugnant to the said word of the Eternall God, and shall procure, to the utmost of our power, to the Kirk of God and wholl Christian people true and perfect peace in all tyme comeing ; That we shall preserve and keep inviolated the rights and rents with all just priviledges of the Crown of Scotland, naither shall wee transferr nor alienate the same ; That we shall forbid and repress in all estates and degrees reife, oppression and all kind of wrong, and we shall command, and procure that justice and equity in all judgments be keeped to all persons without exception, as the Lord and Father of all mercies shall be mercyfull to us ; And we shall be carefull to roote out all heretiks and enemies to the true worship of God that shall be convicted by the true Kirk of God of the forsaids crymes, out of our lands and empire of Scotland. And wee faithfully affirme the things above writen by our solemne oath signed by us at Whitehall the eleventh day of May j^mvi^c fourscore and nyne years.

WILLIAM R.   MARIE R.

Nat. MSS. Scot., iii, No. cvii

THE CONSTITUTIONAL SETTLEMENT

The programme of a constitutional revolution had been stated or implied in the Claim of Right and the Articles of Grievances —the abolition of prelacy (which was as important in the civil constitution as in the Church), the freedom of burgh councils, the independence of the judicature, the appellate power of Parliament, the right of petitioning, the frequency and freedom of parliaments, the suppression of the Committee of Articles—and most of this programme was put into effect.

Two archbishops and seven bishops were present in the Convention, but when that body reassembled as a Parliament on 5 June 1689 they absented themselves, and episcopal government was abolished in July.[1]

The removal of the bishops opened the way for a return to the covenanting precedent of a freely elected Committee of Articles, genuinely representative of each estate. The retention of the committee in some modified form was strongly favoured by William, but the opposition contended that all standing committees had been condemned. A further issue was raised by the condemnation of the presence of any officer of state on a committee unless he was chosen thereto by his estate. It was in vain that arguments were advanced, based on precedent and policy, in favour of the reform of the committee rather than its abolition, and that Hamilton, the Commissioner, proposed that the committee should consist of eleven representatives of each estate, subject to periodic election, along with the officers. The majority in the estates desired to abolish the organ entirely and to transact all business ' in plain parliament,' with only *ad hoc* committees.

This dispute was only one of several which strained the relations between the government and the Parliament. Jealousy of William's ministers—Lord Melville, Secretary, Lord Stair, Lord President and Sir John Dalrymple (Stair's son), Lord Advocate—on the part of the unsuccessful candidates for office provided a personal element of discord, and the opposition organised themselves effectively as ' The Club.' William's reluctance to follow up the abolition of episcopal government with the establishment of presbyterianism added an ecclesiastical element which intensified the dispute, and the opposition asserted themselves by declining to grant supply. On 2 August Hamilton prorogued Parliament.

When the estates reassembled, on 25 April 1690, now with Melville as Commissioner, the government gave way on the points at issue. On 8 May the Committee of Articles was abolished ; Parliament might appoint special committees at its discretion, and on these committees the officers of state should have power to propose and debate but not to vote.[2]

---

[1] See *infra*, p. 213   [2] See *infra*, p. 240

The Church Settlement

In Holland, William had been in the hands of presbyterian exiles, but he soon found that they had misrepresented the state of opinion in Scotland, where sentiment in favour of the existing church settlement was not to be ignored. Various considerations prompted him to adopt a favourable attitude to the episcopalion cause. He fully realised the value to the crown in England of the support of the established church there, and was prepared to accept, if it would be given, similar support from the Scottish episcopalians ; he was also aware that, while a presbyterian church was unlikely to acquiesce in crown control of ecclesiastical affairs, the bishops had been in large measure crown instruments for the government of the state as well as the church. There was the further point that the Scottish presbyterians, if they achieved power, were certain to demand retaliatory measures against the episcopalians ; whereas William was opposed to persecution—and indeed qualified his acceptance of the coronation oath on that ground—and he knew that if the Scottish episcopalians were ill used the Church of England might in its turn reject the toleration of English nonconformists. For these reasons, the king long declined to commit himself, despite the clause on prelacy in the Claim of Right, which had attempted to make the abolition of episcopacy one of the conditions of his acceptance of the crown. There seems to be little doubt that the principal factor in moving William finally to acquiesce in the establishment of presbyterianism was the incurable Jacobitism of the Scottish bishops and many of the clergy, revealed in the attitude of the Bishop of Edinburgh to William's offer to maintain the episcopal church and subsequently in the refusal of a large number of the clergy to pray for the new king and queen.

The attitude of the Bishops and Clergy

The Scottish bishops, on 3 December 1688, had appointed Rose, Bishop of Edinburgh, and Bruce of Orkney to go to London to represent the interests of the Scottish Church. Bruce fell ill and Rose proceeded south alone. The Bishop of London informed him of William's views :

The king bids me tell you that he now knows the state of Scotland much better than he did when he was in Holland ; for while there he was made believe that Scotland generally all over was presbyterian, but now he sees that the great body of the nobility and gentry are for episcopacy, and 'tis the trading and inferior sort that are for presbytery : wherefore he bids me tell you, that if you will undertake to serve him to the purpose that he is served here in England, he will take you by the hand, support the church and order and throw off the presbyterians.

Next day Rose had an interview with William which he relates as follows :

Upon my being admitted to the prince's presence, he came three or four steps forward from his company and prevented me, by saying, ' My Lord, are you going for Scotland ? ' My reply was, ' Yes, Sir, if you have any commands for me.' Then he said, ' I hope you will be kind to me, and follow the example of England.' Wherefore, being something difficulted how to make a mannerly and discreet answer without intangling myself, I readily replied, ' Sir, I will serve you so far as law, reason or conscience shall allow me.' How this answer pleased I cannot well tell, but it seems the limitations and conditions of it were not acceptable, for instantly the prince, without saying anything more, turned away from me and went back to his company.

Keith, *Scottish Bishops*, 1824, pp. 69–71

1689, 13 April. *Proclamation appointing Prayers for William and Mary*

The estates of this Kingdome of Scotland haveing proclaimed and declaired William and Mary, King and Queen of England, France and Ireland, to be King and Queen of Scotland, they have thought fitt by publick proclamatione to certifie the leidges that . . . all the ministers of the gospell within the kingdome publickly pray for King William and Queen Mary as King and Queen of

this realme ; and the estates doe require the ministers
within the city of Edinburgh, under the pain of being
depryved and loseing ther benefices, to read this proclamation publickly from their pulpits upon Sunday nixt [*and the
ministers in other parts of the country to do so on succeeding Sundays*].

A.P.S., ix, 43

A few deprivations followed shortly after this proclamation ; but,
on 6 August following, members of congregations were invited to
denounce to the Council such ministers as did not comply with
the proclamation,[1] and by 7 November the number of deprivations
had risen to a hundred and eighty-two.

The Establishment of Presbyterian Government

In 1689 the King agreed to abolish episcopal government, but not
yet to substitute presbyterian government for it.

1689.   *Act abolishing Prelacy*

Wheras the estates of this kingdome in their Claime of Right
of the eleavinth of Apryll last declaired that prelacie and
the superioritie of any office in the Church above presbyters
is and hath been a great and unsupportable greiveance to
this nation and contrair to the inclinationes of the generalitie
of the people ever since the Reformation, they having
reformed from poperie by presbyters, and therfor ought to
be abolished, our soveraigne lord and lady the king and
queens majesties with advyce and consent of the estates of
parliament doe hereby abolish prelacie and all superioritie
of any office in the church in this kingdome above presbyters,
and hereby rescinds, casses and annulls the first act of the
second session of the first parliament of King Charles II,
and the second act of the third session of the first parliament
of King Charles II, and the fourth act of the third parliament
of King Charles II, and all other acts, statutes and constitutiones in so farr allennerly as they are inconsistent with this
act and doe establish prelacie or the superioritie of church

[1] *R.P.C.*, 3rd ser., xiv, 19–20

officers above presbiters, and the king and queens majesties doe declair that they, with advyce and consent of the estates of this parliament, will settle by law that church government in this kingdome which is most agreeable to the inclinationes of the people.

A.P.S., ix, 104

The Convention, after being turned into a Parliament, exerted pressure by withholding supply. William therefore had ultimately to authorise his Commissioner, when Parliament met again in 1690, to approve legislation establishing presbyterian government and if necessary abolishing patronage. Two measures which had been rejected in 1689 were now passed, one annulling the act of suprem- acy of 1669 and the other restoring to their parishes, whether or not they were vacant, the surviving ministers who had been ejected in 1662 (*A.P.S.*, ix, 111). And the long delayed vote of supply was passed on the day when presbyterian government was at last established.

1690, June 7. *Act establishing Presbyterian Government*

Their majesties, with advyce and consent of the saidis three estates, doe hereby revive, ratifie and perpetually confirme all lawes, statutes and acts of parliament made against popery and papists and for the maintenance and preserva- tion of the true reformed protestant religion and for the true Church of Christ within this kingdom, in swa far as they confirme the same or are made in favours thereof ; lykeas they by these presents ratifie and establish the Confession of Faith now read in their presence and voted and approven be them as the publick and avowed con- fession of this church . . . :

As also, they doe establish, ratifie and confirme the presbyterian church government and discipline, that is to say the government of this church by kirke sessions, presby- teries, provinciall synods and generall assemblies, ratified and established by the 114 Act Ja. 6 parl. 12 anno 1592, entituled Ratification of the liberty of the true kirke etc., and thereafter received by the generall consent of this nation

to be the only government of Christs Church within this
kingdome ; reviveing, renewing and confirmeing the forsaid
act of parliament in the haill heids thereof, except that part
of it relateing to patronages, which is hereafter to be taken
into consideration ; [*and annulling several acts in favour of
episcopal government and prejudicial to presbyterianism*].

Their majesties doe hereby appoint the first meeting of
the generall assembly of this church as above established to
be at Edinburgh the third Thursday of October nexttocome
in this instant yeare [1690]. And becaus many conforme
ministers either have deserted or were removed from
preaching in their churches preceiding the 13 of April 1689,
and others were depryved for not giveing obedience to the
act of the estates made the said 13 day of Apryle 1689
. . . ,[1] therefore their majesties . . . doe hereby declare all the churches either deserted or from which the
conforme ministers were removed or depryved, as said is,
to be vacant [*and that presbyterian preachers who have been
irregularly installed in such parishes should continue in possession*].
Their majesties . . . doe hereby allow the generall meeting
and representatives of the forsaid presbyterian ministers and
elders in whose hands the exercise of the church government
is established . . . to try and purge out all insufficient,
negligent, scandalous and erroneous ministers.

A.P.S., ix, 133–4

1690. *The transfer of Patronage*

Our soveraigne lord and lady . . . considering that the
power of presenting ministers to vacant churches of late
exercised by patrons hath been greatly abused and is
inconvenient to be continued in this realme, doe therefore
with the advyce and consent of the estates of parliament
heirby discharge, cass, annull and make void the aforsaid
power heretofore exercised by any patrone, of presenting
ministers to any kirke now vacant or that shall hereafter
happen to vaike within this kingdome, with all exercise of

----
[1] See *supra*, p. 212.

the said power, and also all rights, gifts and infeftments, acts, statuts and customes, in sua far as they may be extended or understood to establish the said right of presentatione. . . . And to the effect the calling and entering ministers in all tyme comeing may be orderly and regularly performed, their majesties with consent of the estates of parliament doe statute and declare that in case of the vacancie of any particular church and for supplyeing the same with a minister the heretors of the said parish (being protestants) and the elders are to name and propose the persone to the whole congregatione to be either approven or disapproven by them, and, if they disapprove, that the disapprovers give in their reasons to the effect the affair may be cognosced upon by the presbytery of the bounds ; [*and in the event of failure to present within six months the right to appoint devolves to the presbytery*]. It is alwayes hereby declared that this act shall be bot prejudice of the calling of ministers to royall burghs by the magistrats, toune counsell and kirke sessione of the burgh where there is no landward parish, as they have been in use before the yeare 1660, and where there is a considerable part of the parish in landward, that the call shall be by the magistrats, toune counsell, kirke sessione and the heretors of the landward paroch. . . .

A.P.S., ix, 196–7

The settlement was based on the act of 1592, which had been essentially a compromise measure, and not on either the full programme of Andrew Melville or the demands of the later covenanters. Not only was there no mention of the covenants, but an act condemning them was left unrepealed ; while the rights of individual patrons were abolished, popular election of ministers was not substituted ; the civil consequences of excommunication were swept away. The settlement was founded, not on the divine right of presbytery, but on the ground that prelacy had been found contrary to the inclinations of the generality of the people ; and, as was to be amply demonstrated in succeeding years, the Church was still subject to the Crown-in-Parliament. As the Revolution settlement of the Church was not a victory for the covenanting cause, the Cameronians refused to accept it, and remained outside the new establishment.

THE SETTLEMENT WITH THE EPISCOPALIANS

The essential moderation of the settlement was somewhat impaired by the measures taken to put it into force throughout the country. The General Assembly which met in October 1690 numbered only some one hundred and eighty ministers and elders, none of them from the country beyond the Tay, but this small body, many of them men who had been evicted in 1662 and were advanced in years, were in full control. Commissions appointed to purge the Church [1] deposed many ministers on frivolous charges, and, although it was plain that the presbyterians could not themselves staff the Church, some time elapsed before they were convinced of the need to come to terms with the episcopalian incumbents or at least the less intransigent among them.

To the second General Assembly (January 1692) there came a petition from those episcopalian ministers who were ready to submit to presbyterian government and to subscribe the Westminster Confession and Catechisms. They had the support of the king, who took the view that, as the parts of the country which wanted presbyterian ministers had now been supplied with them, there was no need for harsh treatment of the episcopalian clergy in the rest of the country, and who observed with some justice that the Assembly could not claim to be fully representative, since the ministers excluded were as numerous as those present, and that the continuance of the government of the Church in the hands of an oligarchy was contrary to presbyterian principles. The refusal of the Assembly to entertain the idea of an inclusive policy led to its being dissolved.

A more liberal policy was embodied in statutes passed by Parliament in 1693 and 1695. In 1693 it was provided that ministers should be admitted who (a) took the oaths of allegiance and assurance, (b) subscribed the Confession of Faith and (c)

---

[1] The universities also were dealt with. An act of July 1690 imposed on all university teachers the requirements of acknowledging the Confession of Faith and submitting to presbyterian government, and a commission was appointed to deprive the recalcitrant (*A.P.S.*, ix, 163–4). See *S.H.R.*, xiii, 1–15.

acknowledged presbyterian government and undertook not to subvert it ; and that presbyteries should be represented in the General Assembly in proportion to the number of ministers in each.[1] While conscientious episcopalians were as yet excluded from recognition, a considerable number of them were still *de facto* ministers of parishes. In 1695 there came a further act, somewhat in the nature of an act of indulgence to episcopalians.

1693. *Oath of Allegiance*

I, A.B., do sincerely promise and swear that I will be faithfull and bear true allegiance to their majesties King William and Queen Mary. So help me God.

The Assurance

I, A.B., do in the sincerity of my heart assert, acknowledge and declare that their majesties King William and Queen Mary are the only lawfull undoubted soveraigns of this realm as well *de jure*, that is, of right, king and queen, as *de facto*, that is in the possession and exercise of the government, and therefore I do sincerely and faithfully promise and ingage that I will with heart and hand, life and goods, maintain and defend their majesties title and government against the late King James and his adherents and all other enemies who either by open or secret attempts shall disturb or disquiet their majesties in the possession and exercise therof.

A.P.S., ix, 264

1695. *Act in favour of Episcopalian clergy*

Our soveraign lord, being sensible of the hurt and mischieffe that may ensue upon the exposing of the peoples' minds to the influence of such ministers who refuse to give the prooffs required by law of their good affection to the government, and withall desirous that in the first place all gentle and easie methods should be used to reclaim men to their duty whereby the present establishment of this church may be

[1] *A.P.S.*, ix, 303

218

more happily preserved . . ., hath thought good to allow
. . . to all ministers that were at the time of his majesties
happy accession to the crown, and have since continowed,
actual ministers in particular churches, and no sentence
either of deposition or deprivation past against them, and
have not yet qualifyed themselves conform to the act [*of
1693, referred to above*], a new and farther day [*1 September
1695*] to come in and take the said oath of alleagiance . . .,
declaring that all such as shall duly come in and qualify
themselves as said is and shall behave themselves worthily
in doctrine, life and conversation as becomes ministers of
the gospel, shall have and enjoy his majesties protection as
to their respective kirks and benefices, or stipends, they
allwayes containing themselves within the limits of their
pastural charge within their said paroches, without offering
to exerce any power, either of licenceing, or ordaining
ministers or any part of government in generall assemblies,
synods or presbytries, unless they be first duly assumed by
a competent church judicatory. [*Ministers who do not avail
themselves of this offer are to be deprived.*]

A.P.S., ix, 449–50

Over a hundred episcopalian incumbents took advantage of this
act. A good many more retained their parishes because it proved
impracticable to dispossess them, and it is said that as late as 1707
there were still 165 episcopalian incumbents in parishes. The
legislation had not, of course, done anything either for the many
episcopalian ministers who had been ejected from their parishes
at or since the Revolution, or for those who declined to acknowledge William ; they, and their following, remained outwith the
Church of Scotland, the non-Jacobites receiving toleration in 1712
but the Jacobites or non-jurors not until 1792.

SETTLEMENT OF THE HIGHLANDS : GLENCOE

The Jacobite force which had remained in being in the Highlands
after Killiecrankie and Dunkeld was dispersed after an encounter
with government troops under Sir Thomas Livingston at Crom-
dale in May 1690, and General Mackay built a fort at Inverlochy

(Fort William) from which Colonel Hill could exert pressure on the western clans. But the Highlands remained in a disturbed state, and many of the chiefs declined to acknowledge William and Mary. In 1691 an attempt at a settlement by negotiation was conducted by the Earl of Breadalbane, apparently at considerable expense but with little result except a meeting at Achallader when King James's officers and a number of chiefs agreed to an armistice—with, however (so at least it was alleged), a secret undertaking by Breadalbane to join them if their terms were not accepted by William. A sterner policy was represented by a proclamation, on 27 August 1691, which, while offering pardon, also threatened the utmost extremity of the law against chiefs who did not take the oath of allegiance by 1 January following. Sir John Dalrymple, Master of Stair, as Secretary of State, was bitterly hostile to the clans and already before the end of the year was planning punitive measures, especially against the MacDonalds of Glencoe, who were a small clan, vulnerable to attack from Fort William and from the territories of their hereditary foes the Campbells.

The chief of the MacDonalds, after delaying until the end of the year and then offering the oath to Colonel Hill at Fort William, was sent to Inveraray, where two or three more days elapsed before the sheriff, Campbell of Ardkinglas, arrived and acceded to MacDonald's entreaties that he would administer the oath to him (6 January). The Privy Council was apparently in some doubt as to whether the oath could be accepted, and Glencoe's name was at first entered on the list of those who had taken the oath, but was afterwards deleted. On 11 January King William authorised action against recalcitrant chiefs, and Dalrymple entered zealously on the issue of instructions for the Massacre of Glencoe, which took place on 13 February.

The massacre might have been numbered among many other tragedies of Highland history but for the existence of interests determined to embarrass an administration which had earned unpopularity on other grounds. Jacobites, Cameronians, episcopalians, all had reasons for antipathy to King William, and there were also those, like Johnston, the joint-Secretary, who were moved by rivalry to Dalrymple. An investigation into the massacre was authorised in 1693,[1] but a formal commission of

---

[1] *Papers Illustrative of the Highlands* (Maitland Club), 90

inquiry was not set up until 1695.[1] Its findings exonerated the king, and attached most blame to Stair, who was removed from the secretaryship but received from his master a remission for ' any excess, crime or fault done or committed in that matter of Glencoe '; Colonel Hill was exculpated, and the subordinates who were accused were absent on military service and escaped punishment. At the same time, the Earl of Breadalbane was committed to Edinburgh Castle on account of his alleged treasonable dealings in 1691, but was never brought to trial.

Extracts from Letters of the Master of Stair

1691, December 2 (*to the Earl of Breadalbane*)

. . . I think the clan Donell must be rooted out, and Lochiel. Leave the McLeans to Argyll. . . . God knows whether the 12,000 l. sterling [2] had been better employed to settle the Highlands, or to ravage them ; but, since we will make them desperate, I think we should root them out before they can get that help they depend upon. . . .

Papers Illustrative of the Highlands (Maitland Club), 49–50

1691, December 3 (*to Lt.-Col. Hamilton*) [3]

. . . The McDonalds will fall in this net. That's the only popish clan in the kingdom, and it will be popular to take severe course with them. Let me hear from you with the first whether you think that this is the proper season to maul them in the cold long nights, and what force will be necessary. . . . Write your thoughts on the whole with the first, for all must be in readiness by the first of January. . . .

Ibid., 52–3

---

[1] Ibid., 98
[2] That is, the money expended by Breadalbane in his negotiations
[3] Subordinate to Hill at Fort William

1692, January 11 (*to Sir Thomas Livingston*) [1]

. . . Just now, my Lord Argile tells me that Glenco hath not taken the oathes, at which I rejoice, it's a great work of charity to be exact in rooting out that damnable sect, the worst in all the Highlands. . . . Ibid., 62

Extracts from the King's Instructions

1692, January 11 (*to Sir Thomas Livingston*)

Sic supra scribitur, William R.

1. You are hereby ordered and authorized to march our troops, which are now posted at Inverlochy and Inverness, and to act against these Highland rebells who have not taken the benefite of our indemnity, by fire and sword, and all manner of hostility ; to burn their houses, seiz or destroy their goods or cattell, plenishing or cloaths, and to cutt off the men. . . . 4. That the rebells may not think themselves absolutely desperate, wee allow to [our] own powers to give tearmes and quarters ; but wee are so convinced of the necessity of severity, and that they canot be reclaimed, that wee will not allow you to give any other tearmes to Chiftans, Heretors or Leaders, but to be prisoners of war, whereby their lives are safe ; but for all other things they must render on mercy, and take the oath of alleadgance. . . . Given under our Royal hand and signet, at our Court of Kensingtoun, the 11th day of January 169$\frac{1}{2}$, and of our reign the 3d year. Sic subscribitur, W.R. Ibid., 60-1

[1692, January 16] (*to the same*)

Sic suprascribitur, William R.

. . . 4. If McKean of Glencoe, and that tribe, can be well separated from the rest, it will be a proper vindication of the publick justice to extirpate that sect of thieves. . . .

Sic subtur. W.R.

Ibid., 65

[1] Commanding in the Highlands

1692, February 12.   *Robert Duncanson* [1] *to Captain Robert Campbell of Glenlyon*

Sir,

Yow are herby ordered to fall upon the rebells, the McDonalds of Glenco, and to putt all to the sword under 70. You are to have a speciall care that the old fox and his sones doe not escape your hands. Yow are to secure all the avenues, that no man escape. This you are to putt in execution at fyve of the clock precisly. And by that time, or very shortly after it, I will strive to be at yow with a stronger party. If I do not come to yow at fyve, you are not to tarry for me, butt to fall on. This is by the King's speciall commands, for the good and safety of the countrey, that these miscreants be cutt off root and branch. So that this be put in executione without feed or favour, as yow may expect to be dealt with as one not true to King nor countrey, nor a man fitt to carry commission in the King's service. Expecting ye will not faill in the fullfilling herof, as yow love yourselfe, I subscryve this with my hand at Ballacholis, 12 Febrry 1692.

Robert Duncanson.

Ibid., 72

[1] Major in Argyll's Regiment

SECTION II

Chapter Five

PARLIAMENT

Composition

County Commissioners

James I's attempts (vol. ii, 2nd edn., 37–8) to bring the small barons and freeholders into Parliament had failed. Attendance at Parliament was still regarded as a burden ; and by the middle of the sixteenth century it could be said ' there were no lairds in Parliament.' The Reformation movement, however, had been strongly supported by the small barons and freeholders, and in 1560 the ' Reformation Parliament ' was thronged with over a hundred lairds claiming a right to ' be heard, to reason and vote . . . in Parliament' according to an old Act of Parliament of the time of James I. The constitutional position of these members was not then regularised ; the ' Concessions ' granted to the Congregation at the time of the Treaty of Edinburgh (vol. ii, 2nd edn., 183) had laid down that ' it shall be lawful for all those to be present at that meeting [of the Estates] who are in use to be present ' ; and since it could hardly be said that the small barons and freeholders were ' in use to be present,' the validity of that Parliament was not unnaturally later called in question. Again, however, in the important Parliament of December 1567 a goodly number of lairds once more appeared ; and this time an act was passed that ' by law and reason, the barons of this realm ought to have vote in Parliament as a part of the nobility ' and that therefore one or two of the wisest barons were in future to be chosen from each shire to act as shire commissioners ; but, like the Act of 1428, it was apparently inoperative.

The Act of 1567, however, had spoken of the necessity for ' safety of numbers ' in every Parliament, and, if the Protestant religion were to be maintained, the safety of a *Protestant* majority (and the lairds were largely Protestant) was necessary ; indeed it became more than ever necessary with the assassination of William the Silent (1584), the proclamation of the ' Catholic League '

(1585) and the conclusion of a defensive and offensive alliance with England. Moreover, James VI and his secretary, Maitland of Thirlestane, may have been anxious to strengthen the representative nature of Parliament in view of the power of the more representative General Assembly of the Church.[1] It is significant, too, that the small barons and freeholders now petitioned the king for a revival of the ' gude and lovable ' Act of 1428 ; more than that, they made an offer of £40,000 towards the king's immediate ' necessities.' With the growth of political consciousness arising out of the Reformation the small men were now willing to make a ' handsome contribution ' to secure a right which had been rejected as a burden when it had been freely offered a century and a half before.

The king's attitude was favourable, and the Act of 1587 ratified, approved and gave full effect to the Act of 1428, which was recited in full in its preamble. It would appear, however, that there was some delay in the payment of the ' contribution,' and precepts summoning commissioners of the shires were first issued for the parliament of 1594. Even then, the lists of sederunt show that only gradually did the shires take full advantage of their rights of representation.

Modifications in electoral qualifications were made in 1661 and 1681. In June 1690 Parliament passed an act whereby certain of the larger shires were to ' add to their former representation,' some to have two additional members, others one ; and in April 1693 additional representatives compeared from a number of the larger counties (*A.P.S.*, ix, 152, 239–40).

1587.

Oure Souerane lord considering the act of his hienes parliament haldin at Linlythgow the tent day of December the yeir of god i^{M} v^{c} foure scoir fyve yeiris Makand mentioun how necessar it is to his hienes and his estaittis to be trewly informit of the nedis and causis pertening to his loving

---

[1] The so-called ' Black Acts ' of 1584 had included one affirming the ' dignity and authority ' of the Three Estates which had been ' of lait yeris callit in sum doubt ' (*A.P.S.*, iii, 293, c. 3). See *supra*, p. 39.

subjectis in all estaittis speciallie the commonis of the realme,[1]
And remembering of ane gude and lovable act maid be his
hienes progenitour king James the first of worthie memorie.[2]
. . . That his Majestie and his saidis estaittis wald ratefie
and approve the same, To have full effect and to be put to
executioun in tyme cuming, And of new statute and ordane
for the mair full explanatioun of the same act, and certane
executioun thairof, That preceptis suld be direct furth of
the Chancellarie to ane barroun of ilk schire first to convene
the frehalders within the same schire for chesing of the Commissioners as is contenit in the said act, Quhilkis commissioners being anys chosin and send to parliament the
preceptis of parliament for convening of frehalders to the
effect foirsaid to be directit to the last commissioners of ilk
schire quhilkis sall caus cheis twa wyse men, being the kingis
frehalders resident induellaris of the schire, of gude rent and
weill estemit as commissioners of the same schire, To have
pouer and be authorisit, as the act proportis, under the
commissioners seill in place of the schireffis, And that all
frehalders of the king under the degre of prelattis and lordis
of parliament be warnit be proclamatioun to be present at
the chesing of the saidis commissioners, and nane to have
voit in thair electioun bot sic as hes fourty schilling land in
fre tenandrie haldin of the king, and hes thair actuall
duelling and residence within the same schire : Quhilk mater
being remittit be the saidis estaittis convenit in the said
parliament haldin at linlythgow to the will and gude
consideratioun of oure said souerane lord To do and ordane
thairin as his hienes suld think maist requisite and expedient
betuix and his nixt parliament. And now his Majestie
intending, godwilling, to tak ordoure for the finall setling
and establesching of that gude forme and ordoure maist
meit and expedient to stand in perpetuitie in this behalff,
according to the effect of the said act of parliament maid
at linlythgow in consideratioun of the great decay of

[1] That is, the petition of 1585 referred by Parliament ' to the will and
good consideration ' of the king (*A.P.S.*, iii, 422, c. 74)
[2] That is, the Act of 1428

the ecclesiasticall estate and utheris maist necessar and wechty considerati004es moving his hienes THAIRFORE his Majestie, now efter his lauchfull and perfeit aige of xxj yeiris compleit, sittand in plane parliament, Declaris and decernis the said act maid be king James the first to tak full effect and executioun, and ratefeis and apprevis the same be thir presentis, and for the bettir executioun thairof ordanis the commissioners of all the schirefdomes of this realme according to the nowmer prescrivit in the said act of parliament to be electit be the frehalders foirsaidis at the first heidcourt efter Michaelmes yeirlie, or failyeing thairof at ony uther tyme quhen the saidis frehalders plesis convene to that effect, or that his Majestie sall require thame thairto, Quhilkis conventionis his Majestie declaris and decernis to be lauchfull. And the saidis commissioners being chosin as said is for ilk schirefdome, Thair names to be notefeit yeirlie in write to the directoure of the chancellarie be the commissioners of the yeir preceding : And thairefter quhen ony parliament or generall conventioun is to be haldin, that the saidis commissioners be warnit at the first be virtew of preceptis furth of the chancellarie, or be his hienes missive lettres or chargeis, And in all tymes thairefter be preceptis of the chancellarie as salbe direct to the utheris estaittis. And that all frehalders be taxt for the expensis of the Commissioners of the schires passing to parliamentis or generall counsellis ; And lettres of poinding or horning to be direct for payment of the sowmes taxt to that effect upoun ane simple charge of sex dayes warning allanerlie. And that the saidis Commissioners, authorizit with sufficient commissionis of the schirefdome fra quhilk thay cum, seillit and subscrivit with sex at the leist of the baronis and frehalders thairof, salbe equall in nowmer with the commissioners of burrowis on the articles and have voit in parliamentis and generall counsellis in tyme cuming. And that his Majesties missives befoir generall counsellis salbe directit to the saidis commissioners, or certane of the maist ewest [1] of thame, as

---

[1] *nearest*, or *most convenient*

to the commissioners of burrowis in tyme cuming. And that the lordis of counsell and sessioun sall yeirlie direct lettres at the instance of the saidis commissioners for convening of the frehalders to cheis the Commissioners for the nixt yeir and making of taxationis to the effect abonewrittin : And that the comperance of the saidis commissioners of the schires in parliamentis or generall counsellis sall releif the haill remanent small baronis and frehalders of the schires of thair sutes and presence aucht in the saidis parliamentis. Providing alwayes that the saidis small baronis observe thair promise and conditioun maid to his Majestie.[1] Upoun the quhilk declaratioun and ordinance maid and pronuncit be oure souerane lord sittand in plane parliament as said is, Johnne Murray of tullybardin askit actis and instrumentis, And David erll of craufurd lord lyndesay, for him selff and in name and behalff of utheris of the nobilitie, protestit in the contrair.

A.P.S., iii, 509, c. 120

1661.

The kingis majestie . . . doe therfor with advice and consent of his estates of parliament statute, enact and declare that beside all heritors who hold a fourtie shilling land of the kings majestie in capite, that also all heritors lyverenters and wodsetters holding of the king, and others who held their lands formerlie of the bishops or abbots and now hold of the king and whose yeerly rent doth amount to ten chalder of victuall or one thousand pund, all few dewties being deducted, shall be and are capable to vote in the election of commissioners to parliament and to be elected commissioners to parliaments, excepting always fra this act all noblemen and their vassals. [*And provision is made for a ' daily allowance ' to commissioners of £5 Scots during their attendance at and in travelling to and from parliaments.*]

A.P.S., vii, 235, c. 253

[1] That is, to furnish the king with a ' contribution ' of £40,000

1681.

His majesty with advice and consent of his estates of parliament statuts and ordains that none shall have vote in the elections of commissioners for shires or stewartries which have been in use to be represented in parliament and conventions, but those who at this time shall be publicklie infeft in property or superiority and in possession of a fourty shilling land of old extent holden of the king or prince distinct from the few duties in fewlands, or wher the said old extent appears not shall be infeft in lands lyable in publick burden for his majesties supplies for four hundred punds of valued rent, whether kirk-lands now holden of the king or other lands holding few, waird or blensh, off his majestie as king or prince of Scotland, . . . and likewise proper wodsetters having lands of the holding, extent or valuation foresaid . . ., appeirand heirs being in possession by vertue of their predicessors infeftment of the holding, extent and valuation foresaid, and lykways liferenters and husbands for the freeholds of their wyves. . . .

Likeas his majesty ordaines the whole freeholders of each shire and stewartry having election of commissioners to meet and conveen at the head burghs thereof, and to make up a roll of all the freeholds within the same . . . according as the same shall be instructed to be of the holding, extent or valuation foresaid, containing the names and designations of the fiars, liferenters and husbands having right to vote . . . and expressing the extent or valuations of the saids freeholds. . . . Likeas the saids freeholders shall meet and conveen at the head burghs of the saids shires and stewartries respective at the Michaelmes head court yearly thereafter and shall revise the said roll of election. . . .

A.P.S., viii, 353, c. 87

The Spiritual Estate

(i) *Bishops.* Bishops in possession of sees in 1560, and those appointed between 1560 and 1567 (either by simple crown gift or, in defiance of the law, by crown nomination followed by papal provision), took their places in parliaments, whether or not they accepted the reformed faith. In 1572 it became the law that as vacancies occurred they should be filled by ministers (p. 10), and these new protestant bishops inherited the right of parliamentary attendance. For some years after 1587 no bishops were appointed (though the surviving holders of episcopal titles still took their places in Parliament), but in 1597 it was agreed that ministers should be appointed to the titles of sees and should represent the Kirk in Parliament (p. 53). From 1600 onwards the bishoprics were once more filled by ministers, and in 1606 the Act for Restitution of the Estate of Bishops (p. 57) completed the process of restoring this part of the spiritual estate. Then in 1638 and 1639 the whole episcopal structure established by James VI was swept away (pp. 111, 114) ; the bishops did not take their places in the parliament of 1639 ; and the parliament of June 1640 declared the nobility, the small barons and the burgesses to be ' the true Estates of this Kingdom ' and proscribed ' bishops, archbishops, priors or other prelates or churchmen whatsoever ' from ' sitting or voicing ' in Parliament as ' an estate or members ' (p. 115). With the General Act Rescissory of 1661, however (p. 153), episcopacy was restored as the established form of Church government, and bishops again sat in the parliament of 1662. Finally, in 1689, with the act abolishing episcopacy in the established church, the clerical estate in Parliament came to an end, for the General Assembly of 1638 had forbidden any minister of the presbyterian church to ' ride or vote ' in Parliament and in 1690 the Assembly maintained its opposition to the representation of the Church in Parliament. Thus, after 1707, the British House of Lords contained English bishops but no Scottish ecclesiastics ; and in 1801 ministers of the Church of Scotland were disqualified by statute (41 Geo. III, c. 63) from becoming members of parliament.

(ii) *Commendators.* The abbots and priors were succeeded, either before or after the Reformation, by commendators who, although laymen, formed part of the spiritual estate. In the early years of the seventeenth century, however, it became the regular practice to ' erect ' such commendatorships into temporal lordships (p. 57n) and when this took place the ' lords of erection ' joined the estate of nobles.

The Committee of the Articles

It would appear that at one time, in the election of the Lords of the Articles, the spiritual lords had chosen the temporal lords, and the temporal lords had chosen the spiritual lords [1] ; upon other occasions the committee of the Articles had been chosen by the whole estates ; and, upon other occasions again, each estate had chosen its own representatives.

After his accession to the English throne, however, James VI strove to secure a close relationship between the members of the Articles, the members of the Privy Council and the Senators of the College of Justice. With a small group of his own ' men ' serving on all three bodies he could control, from London, the Scottish legislature, executive and judiciary, and thereby govern Scotland ' with his pen.' To achieve this, some royal control over the election of the Lords of the Articles was essential ; and with that end in view James revived the earlier method of election—for the bishops, being of his own creation, could be trusted to elect noblemen who would be acceptable to the king, and the noblemen could not fail to elect bishops who were ' king's men ' ; and if the prelates and nobles so elected were then to elect the representatives of the commissioners of the shires and of the burghs, royal control would be assured—even though the commissioners of the more important burghs could not easily be passed by.

Some such method of election can be traced in 1612, and possibly in 1617 at the time of James VI's visit to Scotland (p. 236), though in neither case do we know how the representatives of the small barons and of the burghs were chosen. In 1621, however, Calderwood's account clearly states that the bishops and the nobles who had been elected to the Articles chose the representatives of the other two estates (p. 237), and the Earl of Melrose, James's secretary, wrote to the King that ' the Lords of the Articles were chosen with such dexterity that no man was elected (one only excepted) but those who by a private roll were selected as best affected to your Majesty's service.' [2] This method was also followed in 1633 (p. 239–40, *anno* 1663).

The Committee of the Articles, moreover, had now established complete control over the legislation to be introduced ; no measure

[1] A.P.S., ii, 289   [2] *Melrose Papers*, ii, 416

could be brought before the House save through the Articles. Thus the Scottish Parliament had become the ' registrar of conclusions reached elsewhere.' It met ; it elected the Committee of the Articles ; it dispersed ; and then it met again to approve the ' articles ' or ' bills ' which were placed before it. As one English critic observed, ' Their parliaments hold but three days ' ; [1] and, if Row's account is to be accepted, at the parliament of 1633 all the articles were presented to the House for approval *en bloc*, while Charles I, with his own pen, noted how the members cast their votes (p. 237-8).

In the parliament of 1639, there being no bishops to elect the representatives of the nobility (p. 233), the royal commissioner, the Earl of Traquair, upon Charles's instructions, claimed that right for himself ; and although the nobility then gave way they demanded the introduction of a measure whereby each estate would elect its own representatives (p. 238). Such a measure was introduced in 1640 when Parliament (which sat in defiance of the king's prorogation by proclamation) asserted that it could ' choose or not choose ' a Committee of the Articles as it thought expedient ; that if it decided to choose a Committee of the Articles, each estate was to elect its own representatives ; and, finally, that the Lords of the Articles were to concern themselves solely with the ' articles ' submitted to them by the whole House (p. 238-9). Although Charles I gave his royal assent to this act in 1641, there was no occasion for it to become operative. The rapidly developing crisis between Charles and his people led instead to the appointment of a Committee of Estates (p. 242-5), a body which enjoyed full parliamentary powers and which was regularly appointed throughout the period of the Civil War until 1651 when General Monck captured nearly all its members.

With the Restoration, the Committee of the Articles was revived in the parliament of 1661 ; but, there being no bishops in that parliament, each of the other three estates chose its own representatives ' without prejudice ' to any subsequent method which might be approved. Then, in the second session of the parliament, in 1662 (when bishops again took their places—p. 156), nine bishops were added to the Committee of the Articles by the royal commissioner ; and in the third session, in 1663, an act was passed whereby ' at this session and in all time coming ' the representatives

---

[1] Hume Brown, *Early Travellers in Scotland*, 102

of the noblemen were to be chosen by the bishops, the representatives of the bishops were to be chosen by the noblemen, and the representatives of the county commissioners and of the burgh commissioners were to be chosen by the elected representatives of the bishops and noblemen (p. 239-40). And, once again, the Lords of the Articles secured control over the business of the House.

Nevertheless, there is evidence that the body of the House was beginning to assert itself, and was no longer willing to be merely the ' registrar ' of conclusions reached by the Lords of the Articles (p. 252-3) ; opposition to the Articles, as a tool of royal absolutism, grew ; and in the Articles of Grievances (p. 207) it was declared, ' The Committee of Parliament called the Articles is a great grievance to the Nation.'

William would have liked to continue the Committee of the Articles, with each Estate choosing its own representatives ; and, with adequate controls, it was obviously a useful body ' to prepare matters and acts for the Parliament.' But, despite strenuous attempts to retain the Committee, the opposition to the Articles was too strong, and in 1690 the Committee of the Articles was finally discharged and abrogated in all time to come (p. 240). (See, in general, Rait, *Parliaments of Scotland*, 367–91)

Election of the Lords of the Articles

1617.

The tyme being thus spent till foure of the afternoone, they proceedit to the choosing of the Lords of the Articles. The noblemen, speciallie suche as feared a prejudice to their estate, and namelie touching the dissolution of the erectiones and of the right they had to the tythes, were not content that they sould be chosen as the king and the bishops wold have them. The king purposed once to dissolve the parliament and the lords were readie to depart. At last they were chosen, but not altogether to the king and the bishops' contentment. But the king would in noe case suffer the Laird of Dunipace to be one of the number becaus he had found him his opposite at the assize of Linlithgow, where the ministers were convict of treasone.

The king and the estates came out of the Tolbuith after ten houres at night, and went doun to the palace in great confusion, some ryding in their robes, others walking on foote and the honours not caried as before. The Lords of the Articles satt everie day, except the Lord's day, and the king himself was ever present.

Calderwood, vii, 250

1621.

The Grand Commissioner, the noblemen and the prelats, the chancelour, the thesaurer, the secretarie, and clerk of register went into the Inner-House to choose the Lords of the Articles. The choise was not made of persons most indifferent, of best judgment and noe wayes partiallie affected to anie partie, as beseemeth free parliaments and counsels. The bishops choosed eight of the nobilitie, Anguse, Mortoun, Niddisdaill, Wigtoun, Roxburgh, Balcleugh, Scoone, Carnegie. These choosed eight bishops, St. Androes, Glasco, Dunkeld, Aberdeen, Brechine, Dumblaine, Argile, Orkney, and these together choosed eight barons and eight burgesses. . . . The officers of estate, the chancellour, the thesaurer, privie seale, justice clerk, the king's advocate, and the clerk of register, men readie to serve the king's humour for the benefite they had by their offices, and hopes of greater preferments, satt and voted with them, howbeit not chosen.

Calderwood, vii, 490

1633.

. . . the Parliament did ryde and end upon Fryday the 28th of June. And when the articles came to be voted, the King perceaveing that there would be some contrare to them, taketh a pen, and with his awin hand (an uncouth practise) noted the votes, whereby (no doubt) many were afraid to vote as otherwise they intended to doe. Albeit, some (as by an holie Ἀντιπερίστασις) were the more encouraged to vote according to their conscience. Some

237

of the nobilitie voted speciallie aganis the Articles concluded anent the Kirk's bussiness ; but would have consented to other articles anent annuel rents and taxations etc. : it being all put together (a frequent Satanical trick of Bishops) they behoved either to vote aganis all or then consent to all.

Row, *Historie of the Kirk of Scotland*, 366

1639.

The Lord Commissionars grace and haill noblemen above namit being reteired by themselves into ane inner roume for choosing of the lordis of the articles, the erle of Argyle protestite that albeit for many reasones at this tyme . . . they gave way to the commissionaris for electing the noblemen who are to be upon the articles, yit that this act doe not introduce ane custome or preparative prejudiciall to thair reight and libertie of ane frie parliament, but that now presentlie at this same parliament thair be ane article presented and ane act mad accordinglie for setling ane perfyte order of electione of the articles in all tyme comeing quhairby the noblemen by themselffis, the barrones by themselvis, and the burrows by themselffis, may elect such of thair owne nomber as shall bee upon the articles. [*And a similar protestation came from the barons and burgesses.*]

A.P.S., v, 252

1640.

The estates of parliament . . . have statute and declaired that according to the libertie of all frie judicatories anent thair owne preparatorie committies all subsequent parliamentis may, according to the importance of effaires for the tyme, either choose or not choose severall committies for articles as they shall thinke expedient ; and that any subsequent parliamentes, makeing electioun of committies for articles to prepair materis for them, shall proceed in maner falloweing, to wit that these of the noblemen shall be named and choosine by the noblemen themselves out of thair nomber, and by the barrones commissioneris of shyres by themselves out of ther nomber, and the burgess commissioneris of burrous by themselves out of there nomber, the names of the which persones so named and choosine out of everie estate (not exceeding for every committie the nomber prescryveit by the act of parliament 1587 [1]) being openlie red and mad knowne to the whole estatis sitting in plaine parliament, the said estates . . . by ane act shall authoreize the said persones with power to treat reason or consult upoun the expediencie of such articles allenerlie as shall be commited and recommendit unto them be the estates, and to set doune such reasones and motives as they can devyse wherby to enforce either the passing or rejecting of the samene in parliament, to be reported with the said articles to the remanent of the said estates assembled in parliament that they may deliberat and advyse therupon.

A.P.S., v, 278–9

1663. *Restoration of the Articles*

The which day the Earle of Rothes his Majesties Commissioner represented to the Estates of Parliament that it wes his Majestie's express pleasure that, in the constitution of Parliaments and choiseing of Lords of the Articles at this session, and in all time comeing, the same forme and order should be keeped which had been used befor these late troubles, especially in the Parliament holden in the yeer 1633. And the manner of the election of the Lords of the Articles at that time being now seen and considered be the Estates of Parliament, they did, with all humble duetie, acquiesce in his Maiesties gracious pleasure thus signified unto them. And in prosecution therof, the clergie retired to the Exchequer Chamber and the nobilitie to the Innerhouse of the Session (the barrons and burgesses keeping their places in the Parliament House). The clergie made choise of eight noblemen to be on the Articles . . . and the nobilitie made choise of eight bishops . . . which being

---

[1] *A.P.S.*, iii, 343 : the estates to be equally represented and the numbers to be not less than six and not more than ten for each estate.

done the clergie and nobilitie met together in the inner Excheckquer house, and, haveing shoune their elections to other, the persons elected, at least so many of them as were present, stayed together in that room (whilst all others removed) and they jointly made choise of eight barrones and eight commissioners of burrowes . . . and then represented the whole elections to His Maiesties Commissioner : who, being satisfied therof, did then with the clergie and nobility return to the Parliament House, where the list of eight bishops, eight noblemen, eight barrons and eight burgesses being read, it was approven and his Majesties Commissioner did add to the list the Officers of Estate and appointed the Lord Chancellour to be president in the meitings of the Lords of the Articles who are to proceid in discharge of their trust in prepareing of lawes, acts, overtures, and ordering all things remitted to them by the Parliament and in doeing every thing else which by the law or practick of the Kingdom belonged or were propper to be done by the Lords of the Articles at any tyme bygon.

A.P.S., vii, 449

1690, 8 May. *Abolition of the Articles*

Our soverayne lord and lady the king and queens majesties, with advyce and consent of the estates of parliament, doe heirby discharge and abrogate in all tyme comeing the forsaid committie of parliament called the Articles, and further cass and annull and rescind the 1st Act, 3rd Session, Parliament first, Charles the 2nd, anent the way and manner of election of the lords of the articles,[1] with all other acts, lawes and constitutions establishing the said committie or lords of articles, lykeas their majesties, with advyce and consent forsaid, doe heirby enact and declare that this present and all succeiding parliaments and three estates thereof may choise and appoint committies of what numbers they please, there being alwayes ane equall number of each estate to be chosen, viz. the noblemen by the estate of

[1] That is, the act printed *supra*, p. 239.

noblemen, the barrons by the estate of barrons, and the burrowes by the estate of burrowes, for prepareing all motions and overtures first made in the house, and they may alter and change the saids committies at their pleasure, without prejudice alwayes to the estates of parliament to treate, vote and conclude upon matters proponed or brought before them in plaine parliament without committies as they shall think fitt, and alsoe provydeing that in all committies to be hereafter appointed some of the officers of state may be present by their majesties or their commissioners appointment as to them shall seeme necessary, and that to the effect and with power to the saids officers of state present in the saids committies freely to propose and debate allennarly but not to vote, declareing lykeas it is hereby declared that no officers of state shall be other wayes admitted in any committie of parliament but as it is here allowed, but prejudice alwayes to the estate of the noblemen to choise such of their owne bench as are officers of state to be members of the committies if they thinke fit.

A.P.S., ix, 113

THE TRIENNIAL ACT

Parliament met in answer to a royal summons; but the king might refrain from summoning a parliament, or a parliament, when it met, might be continued or prorogued. How then could the people give public voice to their ' grievances and complaints ' ?

A parliament had met in Edinburgh on 15 September 1628, only to be immediately continued to April 1629, then to September 1629, then to June 1630, then to August 1630, then to April 1631, then to August 1631, and then to April 1632. Not until June 1633 did Charles's first parliament hold its first effective sitting.

Again there was a long interval until 1639 when, at the Pacification of Berwick (p. 114), Charles agreed to summon another parliament. This, his second parliament, met in August 1639, but when the full House assembled in November 1639, expecting to hear the articles, it was prorogued to June 1640 (despite certain protests that the king could not lawfully prorogue a parliament without its own consent) and, when June approached, Charles issued a proclamation for a further prorogation. But parliament had never previously been prorogued solely by proclamation [1] and, in defiance of the king's proclamation, the parliament met, asserted its authority as a valid assembly, and, *inter alia*, passed a Triennial Act, which received an unwilling royal assent in the following year and which provided an example for the English Triennial Act of February 1641. Under this Triennial Act a parliament was to be held at least once every three years, and, in accordance with the Act, parliaments were held in 1644 and 1648. [The Act must be clearly distinguished from the later English Triennial Act of 1694 and the British Septennial Act of 1716, which limited the life of any one parliament to a maximum of three years and seven years respectively. Under the Parliament Act of 1911 the life of any one parliament is now limited to five years.]

The ' Restoration Parliament ' re-affirmed that ' no Parliament can be lawfully keept without the speciall warrand and presence of the King's Majesty or his commissioner ' and repealed all acts inconsistent with that doctrine ; [2] and the General Act Rescissory rendered the Triennial Act null and void.

1640.

The estates of parliament . . . have statute and ordeant that everie thrie yeir once at least a full and frie parliament shall be holdine (and oftner as his majestie shall be pleased to call them) within the boundis of this kingdome in the most commodious place and convenient tyme to be thought upon, appoynted and affixed by his majestie and his commissioner for the tyme and the estatis of parliament befor the ending and closing of everie parliament and to be the last act thairof. . . .

A.P.S., v, 268

THE COMMITTEE OF ESTATES

The parliament of 1640, in addition to passing the Triennial Act and legislating on the Committee of the Articles (p. 238), passed,

[1] Prorogation had always hitherto been made in parliament.
[2] *A.P.S.*, vii, 10, c. 7

on 8 June, three days before it continued its sitting to 19 November,[1] the following act appointing a Committee of Estates with wide powers. This was, in effect, the appointment of a ' commission ' with full powers of parliament (cf. vol. i, p. 173), and the word ' commission ' is used in the act itself, but, exceptionally, the Committee of Estates included certain lairds and burgesses who were not members of the parliament.[2]

1640, June.

The thrie estates of parliament . . ., considering how necessar it is for the good of the publicke wealle of the cuntrey and mentinance of the armies lifted and to be uplifted and outreiked [3] both by sea and land and for ordering, directing and governeing of the whole body of this cuntrey and kingdome that a setled, grave and solid committe from the estates be elected, nominat, constitute and authoreized by this present parliament, . . . heerby nominat . . . the persones afterspecified . . . to be commissioners :
. . . to whom the estates and body of this present parliament gives and commites full power, warrand and commissione to doe, order, direct, act and put in executione everie thing necessar, expedient and incombent alsweell for the preservatioune and mentinance of the armyes both of horse and foot by sea and land as for ordering the cuntrie and whole body and inhabitants therof, deceiding of questiones and debaites which shall happine to aryse or fall out in any bussines which shall occasione or offer in this kingdome concerneing the peace and quyet therof, . . . with full power to them to barrow, uptake and levy moneyes for the use of the publict and to give and prescribe orderes and directiones for depursing therofe, . . . to give orderis

[1] Only to be continued to 14 January 1641, then to 13 April 1641, then to 25 May 1641, and then to 15 July 1641 when it began a full session.
[2] Four of the burgess members, for example, came from Edinburgh : of these four, one represented Edinburgh throughout the parliament, one had sat only in 1639, the third did not sit until November 1640, and the fourth was never a member of the parliament (Rait, op. cit., 377, *note*).   [3] equipped

and directiones to collectores, commissioneres and all
otheres persones who shall happine to be employed or have
chairge or place either in the army or in the contrey in the
publicke bussines . . . and to call them to accompt alse
oft as they please, . . . to prescrybe, enjoyne and set doune
reules and wayes for the defrayment of the same burthenes
and for payment and releefe therof to the creditoures and
otheres who lye and shall lye under the burthen of the same,
. . . to impose the payment and releefe therof upoun the
estat and inhabitantes of the cuntry according to the ren-
talles, rolles and valuationes of the rentes of the kingdome,
. . . to cast a proportionall pairt thereof upoun everie
shereffdome, presbytery, parochine and burghe within this
kingdome conforme to the saidis valuationes, and which
shereffdomes, presbytries and burghes shall devyd the same
among the particular persones lyable thereine, . . . to set
doune wayes for exsyses to be laid on wivers for the weall of
the cuntrey, . . . to give orderis, instructiones and directiones to all inferiour committies, shyres, burghes, presbetries, stewartries, regalities and others whatsoevir within this
kingdome in everie thing which concernes the publicke and
for the mentinance of the armeys and other necessar em-
ploymentes through the whole kingdome, . . . to nominate
and constitut commissioneris, overseeres and all other
officeris asweell in the army as in the cuntrey so oft as
occasioun and necessity shall requyre. . . . There shall be
two constante places of there residence, wherof the one shall
be at Edinburgh or any other convenient place wher they
may most convenientlie and saiflie sit and resid and the
other shall be constantlie at the army. . . . And it is
ordeaned that there shall be twelve of everie estate for both
committies, making eighteine for everie committie [1]. . . .
And this commissioune to indure ay and whill the nixt
meeting of estates ather in conventione or parliament.

A.P.S., v, 282–4

---

[1] That is, twelve members from each of three estates would provide
thirty-six members—eighteen members for each of the two sections, one
at Edinburgh and the other with the army.

During the session of 1641 various expedients were adopted, and the precedent of the Committee of Estates as appointed in 1640 was not followed.[1] The Convention of 1643, however, revived the Committee, and the same practice was then followed not only during prorogations but after the dissolution of the triennial parliament of 1644–7 and so on down to 1651. Generally these Committees of Estates included a considerable proportion of men who were not members of the House. They were given executive powers, but, unlike the earlier commissions, they had no legislative powers. The following rule for election was made in 1644 :

1644.

The estates . . . declaires that the electione of any that shall be chosine commissioneres out of the nomber of the barrones or burrowes in all tyme comeing in any commissioun that shall be granted in parliament or conventioune of estates for quhatsomevir bussines or effaires shall be chosine by the parliament out of ane list to be set doune by the commissioneris of parliament for ilke ane of the saides two estates respective, and if ony of the other two estates shall desyre to add any to that list they are ather to name them of any of the present memberes of parliament or other wayes that they shall be such as are capable to be commissioners for each estate respective. . . .   *A.P.S.*, vi, pt. i, 215

The members of the last Committee of Estates, appointed on 3 June 1651, were captured by General Monck at Alyth some three weeks later, and therewith the Committee ceased to function until August 1660 when the Committee of June 1651 was summoned to meet and sat until December 1660. ' The Parliament which appointed it had originally received a royal summons for its meeting, and the act of appointment, duly ratified by Charles II, authorised the commission to meet " until the next session of Parliament," or until a full Parliament reclaimed the powers thus delegated ' (Rait, op. cit., 380). The ' first parliament ' of Charles II met in January 1661.

Finally, and again in revolutionary times, the meeting of the

[1] Parliament, however, approved ' ther proceedingis and cariage therin ' (*A.P.S.*, v, 396, c. 79).

estates called in March 1689 by ' circular letters from his Highness the Prince of Orange ' appointed, on 29 April, a Committee of Estates with full executive power to carry on the government.[1] The first parliament [2] of William and Mary met on 5 June 1689.

PARLIAMENT OBTAINS CONTROL OF THE EXECUTIVE AND THE JUDICIARY

With the conclusion of the ' Second Bishops' War,' parliament in 1641 soon went far beyond the question of an ecclesiastical settlement. It was determined to ensure that henceforth power should lie, not with the Crown, but with Parliament (which then meant the party of the Covenant). In that respect, and in its legislation, the Scottish Parliament was following a course similar to that of the ' Long Parliament ' then sitting in England, but in its method of settling the ' unlucky differences ' between Charles and his people the Scottish Parliament anticipated the work of the English Parliament and (despite the humble wording of its enactments) was in many respects more forthright.

The demand that Privy Councillors, Officers of State and Senators of the College of Justice should be chosen ' with the advice and approbation ' of Parliament—a demand to which Charles was forced to accede in his assent to the following act—broke the royal control which had been so carefully established by James VI (p. 234), and, indeed, could be said to rest on earlier constitutional practice prior to the union of the crowns.

Following this act, a new Privy Council and new Lords of Session (ordinary and extraordinary) were appointed in parliament on 13 November 1641 [3]—Charles's nominations for the offices of Chancellor and Treasurer being rejected, his proposed list of Privy Councillors being amended, and new Senators of the College of Justice being appointed in the places of others who were adjudged corrupt.

The control thus gained by parliament, however, was voted away by parliament itself in January 1661 (*A.P.S.*, vii, 10, c. 6), and Scotland returned ' to the good old form of Government by his Majesty's Privy Council,' appointed by his Majesty.

[1] *A.P.S.*, ix, 79, c. 80
[2] This was a ' convention ' which was ' turned into a parliament ' by royal letters (*A.P.S.*, ix, 95, c. 97).   [3] *A.P.S.*, v, 388–9

1641 September 16.

Oure soverane lord and the estates of parliament considering that as there was ane article in the treaty [1] anent the maner of choosing and placeing of officeres of stat, counselloures and sessioneres wherof the answer was remitted to be determined by his majestie and this parliament, and his majestie being willing to give this his ancient and native kingdome all sattisfactione possible that fit and qualified persones shall ever fill these places and considering that his majesties residence (because of his great effaires) will be more ordinarie in England than heir, wherby the qualificatione of persones may not at all tymes be so weell knowne to him, therfor his majestie with advyse and consent of the estates of parliament declaires for himselffe and his successoures that he will nominat and make choise of such able and qualified persones to fill these places as shall be fittest for his service and may give most contentment to the estates of parliament, which nominatione and choise his majestie will make with the advyse and approbatione of the saides estates of parliament dureing there sitting and if any of the saidis places shall happine to vaike and must be provydit in the intervall betuixt parliamentes his majestie will choose and nominat officeres of state and counselloures with the advyse and approbatione of the counsell, all that nomber being warned upoun fyftene dayes calling to meit theranent and most pairt of the whole consenting, and in lyke maner the sessioneris with the advyse and approbatione of the most pairt of that house ; which electiones mad in the intervall shall be allowed or disallowed in the next ensueing parliament as the kingis majestie and the parliament shall thinke expedient. And the officeres of state, counsellouris and lordis of sessione so nominat and chosine by his majestie and the parliament or allowed by his majestie and them shall be provided *ad vitam aut culpam*, and they all shall be lyable to the censure of the kingis majestie and parliament.

A.P.S., v, 354–5

[1] Treaty of Ripon

Scottish Representation in the Parliaments of the Cromwellian Union

The ordinance for the union of the peoples of Scotland and England into one Commonwealth was based on the Instrument of Government ; [1] it was passed by Cromwell and his Council on 12 April 1654 ; and it was confirmed and given statutory authority by Cromwell's second (united) parliament in 1656. By its provisions Scotland was incorporated into one Commonwealth with England, and was to be represented by thirty members (compared with four hundred members for England, and another thirty members for Ireland) in a united parliament of the Commonwealth of England, Scotland and Ireland. A second ordinance, of June 1654, determined the electoral districts of the thirty Scottish representatives.

Although this new constitution was coldly received in Scotland, it is to be noted that Scotland was not treated as a subject nation but as an independent assenting party to a mutual agreement—though indeed the people of Scotland had little choice otherwise. It should also be noted, however, that the Scottish representation in the united parliament was even smaller than thirty members, for, as the table (p. 251) shows, many English army officers and government officials served as Scottish representatives.

1654

His Highness the Lord Protector of the Commonwealth of England, Scotland and Ireland, &c., taking into consideration how much it might conduce to the glory of God and the peace and welfare of the people in this whole island, that after all those late unhappy wars and differences, the people of Scotland should be united with the people of England into one Commonwealth and under one Government, and finding that in December, 1651, the Parliament then sitting did send Commissioners into Scotland to invite the people of that nation unto such a happy Union, who

[1] Gardiner, *Constitutional Documents of the Puritan Revolution* (3rd edn.), 405–17

proceeded so far therein that the shires and boroughs of Scotland, by their Deputies convened at Dalkeith, and again at Edinburgh, did accept of the said Union, and assent thereunto ; for the completing and perfecting of which Union, be it ordained, and it is ordained by his Highness the Lord Protector of the Commonwealth of England, Scotland and Ireland, and the dominions thereto belonging, by and with the advice and consent of his Council, that all the people of Scotland, and of the Isles of Orkney and Shetland, and of all the dominions and territories belonging unto Scotland, are and shall be, and are hereby incorporated into, constituted, established, declared and confirmed one Commonwealth with England ; and in every Parliament to be held successively for the said Commonwealth, thirty persons shall be called from and serve for Scotland.

[*All the people of Scotland discharged of all service and allegiance to any of the issue of Charles Stuart, late King of England and Scotland ; and all issue of Charles Stuart disabled from holding the Crown of Scotland or from enjoying any of the honours or possessions thereof.*

The office, style, dignity, power and authority of the King of Scotland, and all right of the three Estates of Scotland to assemble in any general Convocation or Parliament, and all Parliamentary authority in Scotland, discharged.

The St. Andrew's Cross to be received into the Arms of the Commonwealth ; and the Arms of the Commonwealth to be used on all seals which previously bore the Arms of the Kings of Scotland.]

And be it further ordained by the authority aforesaid, that all customs, excise and other imposts for goods transported from England to Scotland, and from Scotland to England, by sea or land, are and shall be so far taken off and discharged, as that all goods for the future shall pass as free, and with like privileges and with the like charges and burdens from England to Scotland, and from Scotland to England, as goods passing from port to port, or place to place in England ; and that all goods shall and may pass between Scotland and any other part of this Commonwealth or the dominions thereof, with the like privileges, freedom, charges and burdens as such goods do or shall pass between England and the said parts and dominions, any law, statute, usage or custom to the contrary thereof in any wise notwithstanding, and that all goods prohibited by any law now in force in England to be transported out of England to any foreign parts, or imported, shall be and hereby are prohibited to be transported or imported by the same law, and upon the same penalties, out of Scotland to any foreign parts aforesaid, or from any foreign parts into Scotland.

And be it further ordained by the authority aforesaid, that all cesses, public impositions and taxations whatsoever, be imposed, taxed and levied from henceforth proportionably from the whole people of this Commonwealth so united.

[Apart from yearly rents, boons and annual services, no other duty, service, vassalage or demand to be rendered for lands other than heriots, fines upon the death of the lord or upon the death or alienation of the tenant, and suit and service to such Court and Courts Baron as shall be constituted in Scotland.

All heritors, proprietors and possessors of lands discharged from all fealty, homage, vassalage and servitude, and from all suit and presence at their lords' or superiors' courts of justiciary, regality, stuartry, barony, bailiary, heritable sheriffship [and] heritable admiralty, all of which are abolished ; and all heritors, proprietors and possessors of lands discharged from all military service and personal attendance upon any their lords or superiors in expeditions or travels. All feudal casualties abolished.

And all forfeitures and escheats which previously fell to the King, lords of regality, or other superiors, henceforth to fall to the Lord Protector of the Commonwealth for the time being.]

Passed 12th April, 1654. Confirmed Anno 1656, Cap. 10.

A.P.S., vi, pt. ii, 816–7

In the immediately following Ordinance for Elections in Scotland (27 June 1654) the distribution of the thirty members from Scotland to be elected to the Parliament of the Commonwealth was prescribed as :

Shires : one member, from Orkney, Shetland and Caithness ; from

Sutherland, Ross and Cromarty ; from Inverness ; from Elgin and Nairn ; from Banff ; from Aberdeen ; from Kincardine and Forfar ; from Fife and Kinross ; from Perth ; from Linlithgow , Stirling and Clackmannan ; from Dumbarton, Argyle and Bute ; from Ayr and Renfrew ; from Lanark ; from Midlothian ; from the Merse ; from Roxburgh ; from Selkirk and Peebles ; from Dumfries ; from Wigton ; and from East Lothian. Total of shire members, 20.

Burghs : one member, from each of the following groups—Dornoch, Tain, Inverness, Dingwall, Nairn, Elgin and Fortrose ; Banff, Cullen and Aberdeen ; Forfar, Dundee, Arbroath, Montrose and Brechin ; Linlithgow, Queensferry, Perth, Culross and Stirling ; St. Andrews, Dysart, Kirkcaldy, Cupar, Anstruther East, Pittenweem, Crail, Dunfermline, Kinghorn, Anstruther West, Inverkeithing, Kilrenny and Burntisland ; Lanark, Glasgow, Rutherglen, Rothesay, Renfrew, Ayr, Irvine and Dumbarton ; Dumfries, Sanquhar, Lochmaben, Annandale, Wigton, Kirkcudbright, Whithorn and Galloway ; Peebles, Selkirk, Jedburgh, North Berwick, Dunbar and Haddington ; and *two* from Edinburgh. Total of burgh members, 10.

A.P.S., vi, pt. ii, 823–4

Scottish Representatives in the Parliaments of the Protectorate

	First Protectorate 1654	Second Protectorate 1656	Richard Cromwell's 1659
Lairds	8	7	5
Burgesses	2	2	—
Peers	2	2	2
Army Officers	6	9	7
Government Officials	3	10	7
TOTAL	21	30	21

Note : Some figures are approximate.
The officers and officials included some Scots.

GROWTH OF PARLIAMENTARIANISM

The following extracts show that despite the royal control of the Articles, the Scottish Parliament during the period immediately preceding the Revolution Settlement was beginning to assert itself as an assembly of the nation and was no longer subserviently accepting the articles placed before it or bowing to the will of the King's Commissioner.

1669.

Upon this debate many members spoke . . . but at last the Commissioner rose in a passion, and swore that though the Parliament stopt the Act, yet they should gain nothing by it. . . .

There was another Act past the same day . . . but this was vehemently oppos'd by many. . . .

Yet so averse were the members of Parliament . . . that the Commissioner durst not put it to a vote.

Sir George Mackenzie, *Memoirs of the Affairs of Scotland*, 169, 171, 178

1672.

And thus this Act was past in Parliament, after much debate. . . .

Mr. William Moor [Moir], Advocate, and burgess of Inverurie, added, that it was fit that the members might be allow'd some time to advertise their constituents, as was the laudable custom of England; whereupon the Commissioner, chaff'd by the former speeches, resolving to vent his passion upon the weakest, and hoping here to terrify others, desir'd that he might be sent to the bar, for offering to impose the customs of England upon the Parliament of Scotland. . . .

Ibid., 222, 230. See also Additional Documents, No. 2, p. 501

1673.

After reading of this letter [a letter from Charles II, of 16 October 1673, appointing Lauderdale as his Commissioner for the new session of Parliament and asking, *inter alia*, for further supplies for a continuance of the Dutch War], it was propos'd that a Committee should be nam'd for bringing in an answer to it ; whereupon the Duke of Hamilton, and after him with the same breath twenty moe, desir'd that their grievances might be first consider'd : Which did astonish so Lauderdale's friends, that only the Earl of Kincardine debated, ' that this delay was most derogatory to that high respect we owed to the King ; and the motion for a Committee of Grievances, was an innovation of all our old customs, which had never allowed a Committee of Grievances ; the legal way of motioning any new thing to our Parliaments being by the Lords of Articles.'

Ibid., 256

1674

[After the adjournment of Parliament, William, 3rd Duke of Hamilton, Lieut.-Gen. Drummond and John, 1st Marquess of Tweeddale, proceeded to London, when] At their arrival, the King charg'd them with having endeavor'd to undermine the very foundation of his authority, by offering to bring in things in plain Parliament, without bringing them first to the Articles ; which Articles he lookt upon as the securest fence of his government.

Ibid., 263

1681.

There were many tart and bitter reflections past betwixt several members, in the heat of their debates, especially betwixt Duke Hamilton, and the King's Advocate, and some of the Barons, and the Burrows, which are not to be keeped on record.

Fountainhall, *Decisions*, i, 152

1686.

This being put to the vote, was carried *negativè*, by the votes of the Barons and Burrows, who, in most things in this Parliament, adhered *mordicus* one to the other.

The Burrows . . . were obstinate against the Court party
. . . they never being so unanimous in any Parliament as
in this, but formerly depending on Noblemen ; and therefore some called this an independent Parliament.

Ibid., i, 417–18

Following the Revolution and the final disappearance of the Committee of the Articles the members of the Scottish Parliament for
the first time came into their own. No longer was the House
merely called upon to say ' Yes ' or ' No ' to conclusions reached
elsewhere. This naturally necessitated immediate changes in
legislative procedure.

At first, ' overtures,' or proposals for legislation, were usually
remitted to a committee (either one of the Standing Committees,[1]
or a committee appointed *ad hoc*) which, if it approved of the overture, drafted an act for submission to the whole House. The
draft act was then debated, amendments made, and a final version
put to the vote. In 1693, however, overtures submitted by individual members were sometimes debated immediately, without
submission to a committee ; and then in 1695 it became customary
to order them to ' lie on the table ' so that the other members
might have more time to consider them. In 1696 Parliament not
only ordered certain overtures to be printed ' for the better
information of members ' but also passed the following act that
' no Law pass at the first reading.'[2] In 1700 committees were
precluded from initiating legislation and could make ' motion or
overture ' only upon ' matters first remitted to them by the Parliament.'[3] Finally, in 1703 the House, distrustful of government
influence upon committees,[4] elected none of the Standing Com-

[1] From 1690 to 1702, in accordance with the Act of 1690 which,
while abolishing the Committee of the Articles, enabled the House to
choose committees—of equal numbers of each estate, chosen by each
estate separately—for particular business, three Standing Committees
were elected at the beginning of each session : for the Security of the
Kingdom ; for Trade ; and for Controverted Elections.

[2] For the technical significance gradually acquired by ' reading,' see
Rait, *Parliaments of Scotland*, 430–3   [3] *A.P.S.*, x, 207*b*

[4] By the act of 1690 anent committees, the Officers of State could sit
on committees with power ' freely to propose and debate,' but ' not to
vote ' (*A.P.S.*, ix, 113, c. 3).

mittees, and thereafter legislation in the Scottish Parliament was discussed and conducted through all its stages by the whole House. Four years later, however, 'the United Kingdom of Great Britain' was 'represented by one and the same Parliament . . . styled the Parliament of Great Britain.'

1696. *Act that no Law pass at the first Reading.*

Our Soveraign Lord with advice and consent of the Estates of Parliament Statutes Enacts and Declares That any Law to be made for hereafter shall not be concluded and voted in that Sederunt in which it is first read, but that the same shall ly on the table till another Sederunt that the Members of Parliament may consider theron in the mean time.

A.P.S., x, 35, c. 10

CONVENTIONS OF ESTATES

Formality and publicity were the keynotes of Parliament; it was a 'much-advertised-in-advance' occasion for all men to claim the royal justice; it had a particular competence in cases of treason; and, working with its committee appointed *ad judicia contradicta*, it was the ultimate court of appeal and decision wherein it 'declared the law.' The General Council, on the other hand, had no competence either in treason cases or as a supreme court of law; but, although little more than a meeting of the King's Council, augmented by the attendance of additional persons called thereto at the king's will, it had equal competence with Parliament in decisions of State, in legislation and in taxation.[1]

In the reign of David II representatives of the burghs had been called to General Councils—to consider ways and means of meet-

[1] cf. i, 2nd edn., 194. The formality of a meeting of the 'Court of Parliament' is stressed by the open proclamation and by the summons, upon forty days' notice, by *precept*, at first, apparently, under the Great Seal, later under the Quarter Seal (known as 'The Testimony of the Great Seal'). The informality of a meeting of a General Council is stressed by the absence of proclamation, by the shortness of notice, and by the calling of the meeting by the issue of *letters close* (addressed to those invited by the king), at first under the Privy Seal, later under the Signet.

ing the instalments of the king's ransom ; and, arising out of the
economic difficulties caused by the drain of the ransom, burgh
representatives were summoned to Parliament in 1366 and
regularly thereafter. But, since the composition of a General
Council was decided by the king (doubtless with the advice of those
big lords who were in his immediate attendance), and since the
burgesses were looked upon askance by the feudatories, burgess
members, although regularly attending Parliament, were
apparently now seldom called to General Councils. On the other
hand, from the reign of James I, it appears to have been customary
to call all prelates and lords to General Councils.[1] Thus, in
composition, although a General Council was usually smaller
than a Parliament it tended to differ from a Parliament mainly
in the absence of representatives of the burghs.

But although the burghs were now regularly summoned to
Parliament, their right of representation in Parliament might mean
little if decisions, and notably decisions to impose taxation, or to
follow a foreign policy which might entail taxation, were to be
taken in General Councils at which they were not represented.
Accordingly the burghs had now to win a right to be regularly
called to General Councils, and particularly so if their interests
were likely to be affected by the decisions which were there made.

In 1504 it was enacted that ' commissaris and hedismen of
burrowis ' were to be ' warnyt, quhen taxtis or contributiones ar
gevin, to haif thair avise thairintill as ane of the thre estatis
of the Realme ' [2] ; and, since the burghs would automatically be
' warned ' of a meeting of Parliament (if only through its proclamation), this statute must mean that they had now gained
a right to be called to General Councils whenever a taxation was
under consideration.

This change in the composition of a General Council to include
' the thre estatis ' may have resulted in the appearance of the
new name ' Convention of Estates '—a ' coming-together-by-
invitation ' of the Estates, as opposed to a formal summoning to
Parliament—which, in the reign of James V, supersedes the old
name ' General Council.' [3] And in 1563 and 1567 the burghs

---

[1] This appears to be implicit in the Acts of 1426 and 1428 (ii, 2nd
edn., 37–8).   [2] *A.P.S.*, ii, 252, c. 30

[3] In the County Franchise Act of 1587 (*supra*, p. 228), ' general convention ' and ' general council ' are used synonymously.

gained the further rights to be called to Conventions whenever ' peace or war ' or ' weighty affairs of the realm ' were to be decided.

1563

The Quenis grace being of will and mynde that all Provestis Aldermen Baillies counsall and communitie and inhabitantis of Burrowis of this Realme be rather augmentit in thair privilegeis maid be hir grace and hir predecessouris to thame nor diminisit thairintill, Hes statute and ordanit . . . that fyve or sax of the principallis Provestis Aldermen and Baillies of this Realme sall in all tymes tocum be warnit to all conventiounis that sall happin the Quenis grace and hir successouris to conclude upone peax or weir with quhatsumever hir hienes confederatis or inimeis or making or granting of generall taxatiounis of this Realme ; And that hir hienes or counsall sall not conclude nor decerne upone peax weir nor taxatiounis foirsaidis without fyve or sax of the saidis principallis Provestis Aldermen and Baillies of Burrowis be warnit thairto lauchfullie as effeiris.

A.P.S., ii, 543, c. 20

1567

Item that in all tymes cuming quhane thair salhappin ane generale conventioun tobe for the wechtie effaris of the realme that the provestis of burrowis or thair com-missaris be requirit thairto, and thair consentis had to the samyn ; And in speciale for generale taxtis or extentis. . . .

A.P.S., iii, 42, c. 64

Then, in 1587, the County Franchise Act [1] applied to both Parliaments and Conventions ; and, with commissioners both of the burghs and of the shires attending Conventions, a meeting of a Convention of Estates was becoming more representative, less subject to the king's pleasure, and almost as full as a meeting of Parliament. This can be seen by comparing the composition

---

[1] *Supra*, p. 228.

of the Convention of 1630 [1] with that of the very full Parliament
of 1633 [2]

	Convention 1630	Parliament 1633
Lords spiritual and temporal and Officers of State	62	87
Commissioners of shires	30	45
	(from 19 shires)	(from 27 shires)
Commissioners of burghs	32	51
	(from 31 burghs)[3]	(from 50 burghs)[3]
Total number of members	124	183

In 1597, moreover, when certain acts of a Convention were to be
proclaimed at the market crosses of the head burghs that ' none
pretend ignorance thereof,' and were also to be printed for a like
reason,[4] a tendency towards publicity had also appeared. But
the idea that only those ' whom the king wills ' were to be called
to a Convention still persisted. In 1616, for example, with a
letter to James VI advising the calling of a Convention, the Privy
Council sent ' a list of those whom we think meet to be written
for.' [5] Nevertheless, when, in 1621, James called only the nobility,
seeking a tax from them, he was told that supply ' can not be
but by a taxation to be imposed upon the whole body of the
estate [i.e. upon all the estates of the realm] without respect to any
man's privilege ' ; and the lords attending the Convention informed the provost and bailies of Edinburgh of the king's demand,[6]
who, in turn, stated that the matter should be communicated to
the ' consideration ' of all the burghs.[7]

Then in May 1643 it was agreed to *proclaim* a Convention in
the king's name (though contrary to his wishes). The post-
Restoration Conventions of 1665, 1667 and 1678, moreover, were
all publicly proclaimed ; there was no selection of members by

[1] *A.P.S.*, v, 208   [2] *A.P.S.*, v, 7–9

[3] Edinburgh sending two representatives, the other burghs sending
one each   [4] *A.P.S.*, iv, 119, 122

[5] *Melrose Papers* (Abbotsford Club), i, 266. In 1609 a letter from the
Privy Council to the king reported that a Convention was ' most solemnly
kept by the noblemen and others selected by Your Majesty for that
purpose ' (Denmilne MSS., Nat. Lib. Scotland, iii, fo. 1).

[6] In view of the rights now enjoyed by the burghs

[7] *A.P.S.*, iv, 589–90

the king ; all were fully attended representative meetings of the Estates ; and the final Convention of 1689 was converted (simply by letter from William) from a Convention of ' the full Representatives of the Nation ' into a Parliament.

The financial difficulties of James VI had tended to associate Conventions with taxation and the provision of supply. The post-Restoration Conventions of 1665, 1667 and 1678 were called solely for supply ; and for the Conventions of 1665 and 1678 it was expressly stated in the king's letter that that was all the Convention was to do.

1665

. . . Now sieing Our Parliament of Ingland have so francklie and so verie liberallie . . . givin so extraordinary supplies. . . . And sieing Our Parliament of Ireland ar also ready to give according to their abilitie, Wee thought it heighly concernd the honor of that Our ancient kingdome to witnes also according as they are able their zeale for Our service. This was the onlie reason of Our Calling yow togither. . . . This is the only bussines yow are to doe in this convention. . . .

A.P.S., vii, 528–9

1667

. . . We thought it necessary to call yow together, that you may provyde suteable remedies And prepare for the defence of the kingdome. . . . Thairfore We earnestlie Recommend it to yow To take the most easie and expedite way of raiseing money for this so necessary a work. . . .

A.P.S., vii, 538–9

1678

. . . And considering that all Kings and stats doe at present carefully secure themselves and their people by provyding against all such forreigne invasions and intestine commotions as may make them a prey to their enemies : It is not fitt that our Kingdome should only of all others

259

remaine without defence. . . . These are the only reasons of calling yow together at this tyme . . . wee doubt not but yow will chearfully give such a supply as may be effectuall for the ends proposed, such as the Kingdome can bear. . . . This is the only bussines yow are to doe in this Convention. . . .

A.P.S., viii, 218–9

A Convention of Estates, accordingly, had now lost (or been deprived of) its legislative powers.

Finally, James VII's attempt in 1689 to call a rival Convention illustrates ' the persistence of the conception of Convention as an enlarged Council, in spite of its approximation to Parliament. On 17th May 1689 James authorised such of his Privy Council as were with Viscount Dundee to act as a committee for the management of public affairs, and entrusted them with the power of the whole Council, " by which authority," he added, " you may turn yourselves into a convention of states." Dundee was empowered to " call as many to that assembly of the states " as were usually summoned " by proclamation or letters," avowed rebels or traitors excepted.' [1]

[1] Rait, *Parliaments of Scotland*, 160

CHAPTER SIX

LAW AND ORDER

THE HIGHLANDS AND ISLANDS

In the *Basilikon Doron* James VI had written :

As for the Highlands, I shortly comprehend them all in two sorts of people : the one, that dwelleth in our mainland, that are barbarous for the most part, and yet mixed with some show of civility : the other, that dwelleth in the Isles, and are utterly barbarians, without any sort or show of civility. For the first sort, put straitly to execution the laws made already by me against their overlords and the chiefs of their clans ; and it will be no difficulty to danton them. As for the other sort, follow forth the course that I have intended, in planting colonies among them of answerable inland subjects, that within short time may reform and civilise the best inclined among them : rooting out or transporting the barbarous and stubborn sort, and planting civility in their rooms.

The ' laws already made ' by James included that known as the ' General Band,' enacted in 1587, whereby chiefs of clans and ' landlords and bailies of the lands on the Borders and in the Highlands where broken men have dwelt or presently dwells ' were to find sureties (landed men in the Lowlands) for the peaceful and orderly conduct of those beneath them ; and anyone thereafter suffering injury from ' broken men ' could pursue the sureties who had been found, and the ' chief ' or ' landlord ' in addition to being bound to satisfy his sureties was to be mulcted in a heavy fine to the crown.[1] This was followed in 1597 by two further acts—the

[1] *A.P.S.*, iii, 461-7. The Act is followed by an interesting ' roll ' of the landlords and bailies of the lands where there are broken men, and of the clans that have captains, chiefs and chieftains on whom the clans depend ' oft times against the will of their landlords.' For a graphic description of the ' Band ' at work, see A. A. W. Ramsay, *The Arrow of Glenlyon* (London, 1930), pp. 108 ff.

18

first stating that, since the inhabitants of the Highlands and Islands had neglected to pay their yearly rents and due service to the Crown, therefore all ' landlords, chieftains and leaders of clans, principal householders, heritors and others possessing, or pretending right to possess, any lands in the Highlands and Isles ' were to produce their titles before the Lords of Exchequer before 15 May 1598 and then to find sureties for regular payment in future and for the observance of law and order in their respective parts, with the penalty that those who failed to produce their titles and to find sureties would forfeit their lands ; [1] and the second (here printed) authorising the erection of three burghs—in Kintyre, in Lochaber, and in Lewis—which were to be government outposts of ' civility and policy.'

1597.

Oure Soverane Lord [with avise] of the estaitis of this present Parliament For the bettir intertening and continuing [of] civilitie and polecie within the hielandis and iles hes statut and ordanit that thair be erectit and buildit within the boundis thairof thre brughtis and burrow tounes in the maist convenient and commodius pairtis meit for the samyn To wit ane in Kintyre Ane uthair in Lochaber and the thrid in the Lewis To the quhilk brughtis and inhabitantis thairof our Soverane lord and estaittis foirsaidis Sall grant and be thir presentis his grantis [2] all privelegeis quhilkis his hienes or predicessouris hes grantit to onie uthair brughtis or inhabitantis thairof within this realme And that it salbe lesum to oure Soverane lord be the advise of the lordis of his majesties cheker to gif grant and dispone to everie ane of the saidis brughtis samekill land and grund furthe of his hienes annexit propertie as may serve to beig the saidis tounis upoun the samyn with samekill land and fischeingis nixt adjacent thairto in commoun gude to everie ane of the saidis thre tounes as may sustene the commoun chairgeis thairof To be haldin in frie burgage of his hienes in sic forme and maner as his majesteis maist nobill progeni-

---

[1] *A.P.S.*, iv, 138, c. 33   [2] *Rectius* hes grantit

touris of worthie memorie hes grantit of auld to the erectioun of uthair brughtis of this realme.

A.P.S., iv, 139, c. 34

Although no immediate steps were taken to put this second act to execution, burghs were in due course erected at Lochhead (or Campbeltown), Fort William and Stornoway, of which only Campbeltown can be really associated with the act, and only Campbeltown eventually attained the status of a royal burgh.[1]

But while the act is important as showing James's belief in ' plantation ' and ' settlement,' there was also in the background a royal hope of some revenue from hitherto unremunerative areas : a hope which may not be unconnected with the act ordering the production of titles. It must have been evident that few chiefs would be able to produce their title-deeds ; and failure to do so could then be seized upon by the king as an excuse for further ' plantation ' with the prospect of further revenue. Thus it would appear that when certain of the MacLeods failed to produce their titles, the Isles of Lewis and Harris and the lands of Dunvegan and Glenelg were declared to be at the king's disposal and were granted by him to an association of Lowlanders (who, coming mainly from Fife, became known as ' The Gentlemen Adventurers of Fife ') to colonise and improve those parts.[2] The ' Adventurers ' first endeavoured to ' colonise ' Lewis, but disease, lack of supplies and the not unnatural hostility of the people (who were to be ' rooted out ' as ' barbarous inhabitants ') forced them, after three attempts, to abandon the project.

James now tried a policy of conciliation—though his terms were to be laid down with the backing of force. A commission was granted in April 1608 to Andrew, Lord Stewart of Ochiltree, and Andrew Knox, Bishop of the Isles, with minute instructions designed to reduce the power of the chiefs and to ' civilise ' them ;[3] but the commissioners were to be accompanied by a powerful force.[4]

[1] See Andrew McKerral, *Kintyre in the Seventeenth Century*, 23–31

[2] cf. *A.P.S.*, iv, 160, c. 4 (where the contract speaks not only of the ' evil disposition and barbarity ' of the people but also of the king's desire to make the islands ' profitable ') ; Register of the Privy Seal lxxix, fo. 252   [3] *R.P.C.*, viii, 737

[4] It is important to note that although for long the Islesmen had helped the Irish chieftains in their rebellions against the English government, and the Irish had helped the Islesmen in their rebellions against

A veritable armament sailed to Mull in August and, doubtless impressed by such a display of strength, many of the Island chiefs came to Aros to present themselves to the King's Commissioners. There, by a ruse, all but one were trapped on board one of the ships, taken to Edinburgh, and imprisoned in the castles of Dumbarton, Blackness and Stirling. Subsequently, as a result of communications between the King, the Bishop of the Isles, and the Island chiefs, Bishop Knox again sailed to the Isles in July 1609, this time as sole commissioner, and the imprisoned chiefs were liberated partly on their undertaking to give him all their support. At Iona most of the principal chiefs attended a court held by Knox and there, in a new atmosphere (doubtless largely the result of Andrew Knox's personality and knowledge of the way to approach the Islesmen), the ' Statutes of Iona ' were accepted by the chiefs on 23 August 1609. On the following day, moreover, the chiefs subscribed a ' band ' accepting the ' true religion,' acknowledging the King's supreme authority ' in all causes . . . both spiritual and temporal,' and promising ' dutiful obedience to the wholesome laws, acts of parliament, and constitutions ' of the Kingdom of Scotland.

the Scottish government, now, after the union of the crowns in 1603, there was close co-operation between the Scottish Privy Council and Sir Arthur Chichester, Lord Deputy of Ireland. Sir Arthur Chichester was at this time engaged in crushing O'Dogherty's rebellion in Ulster, and the Scottish Privy Council had already called out the ' fencibles ' of the south-west lest the Irish rebellion ' albeit of litill begynning ' should ' haif a forder grouth and progress over mony other pairtis of his Majesteis dominionis,' had forbidden aid to the Irish under pain of death, and had even sent a small force to the aid of the Lord Deputy. Then came the arrangements for the expedition to the Western Isles, and various suggestions were put forward for co-operation between Ochiltree and Chichester ; and, with the collapse of O'Dogherty's rebellion in July 1608, Chichester wrote to the Scottish Privy Council offering his aid on the ground that his task and their task were but two parts of one and the same work.

This co-operation was more important in its spirit and principle than in its effectiveness. But the ' Plantation of Ulster,' following the collapse of O'Dogherty's rebellion, was, in effect, an attempt to establish a loyal Protestant buffer between the Celts of Ireland and the Celts of the Scottish Highlands and Islands. Many Scots took estates in the plantation of Ulster, and possibly some ten thousand men, women and children from Scotland settled there. Ochiltree himself was one of the ' undertakers.' (See *R.P.C.*, viii, 79, 82, 511-13).

The Statutes of Iona made no attempt to alter the social structure of the clans ; instead, abuses were to be checked and there was to be reformation through religion and education. Of their immediate result one Highland historian has written : ' The lords of Sleat and Harris forgot mutual injuries . . . and entered into a contract of friendship. Seven chiefs formed a League of Clans, binding themselves to assist with their whole strength the king's Lieutenants of the Isles ; to live together in future " in peace, love, amytie " ; and to settle all disputes between them, not by the sword but by the ordinary course of law and justice. A transformation seemed to have been wrought in the temper of the wild chiefs : they had acquired apparently a " new heart." ' [1] The more lasting results of Bishop Andrew Knox's work may perhaps be seen in a comparison between conditions in the Isles at the beginning of the seventeenth century and the conditions described by Martin in his *Western Islands* published at the beginning of the eighteenth century.

1609, August 23. *The Statutes of Iona*

The Court of the South and North Illis of Scotland haldin at Icolmekill be ane Reverend Father in God, Andro, Bischop of the Illis, haveand speciall pouer and commissioun to that effect of his Majestie and Counsell the twenty thrie day of August the yeir of God j^{m}vj^c and nyne yeiris . . .

The quhilk day in presence of the said reverend father the speciall barronis and gentilmen of the saidis Yllis undirwrittin, viz. Angus McDonald of Dunnoveg, Hector McCleane of Dowart, Donald Gorme McDonald of Slait, Rorie McCloyd of Hareis, Donald McAllane VcEane of Ilanterane, Lauchlane McCleane of Coill, Rorie McKynnoun of that Ilk, Lauchlane McClane of Lochbowie, Lauchlane and Allane McCleanis brether german to the said Hectour McClane of Dowart, Gillespie McQuirie of Ullowa, Donald McFie in Collonsaye, togidder with the maist pairt of thair haill speciall freindis, dependairis and tennentis. . . .

[1] W. C. Mackenzie, *The Highlands and Isles of Scotland* (1949), 207

[I] Undirstanding and considering the grite ignorance unto the quhilk not onlie thay for the maist pairt thameselffis, bot also the haill commonalitie inhabitantis of the Illandis, hes bene and are subject to, quhilk is the caus of the neglect of all dewtie to God and of his trew worschip . . . ffor remeid quhairof thay haif all aggreit in ane voice, lyk as it is presentlie concludit and inactit, that the ministeris alswele plantit as to be plantit within the parrochynis of the saidis Illandis salbe reverentlie obeyit, thair stipendis dewtifullie payit thame, the ruynous kirkis with reasounable diligence repairit, the sabothis solemplie keipit, adultereis, fornicationis, incest, and sic uther vyle sklanderis seveirlie punist, mariageis contractit for certane yeiris simpliciter dischairgit and the committaris thairof haldin, repute and punist as fornicatouris, and that conforme to the lovable Actis of Parliament of this realme and disciplein of the Reformit Kirk. . . .

[II] The quhilk day the foirsaidis personis, considering and haveing found be experience the grite burdyne and chairges that thair haill cuntreymen, and speciallie thair tennentis and labourairis of the ground, hes sustenit be furnissing of meit, drink, and intertenyment to straingeris, passingeris and utheris idill men without ony calling or vocatioun to win thair leiving, hes, for releif of passingeris and straingairis, ordanit certane oistlairis to be set doun in the maist convenient placeis within every Ile, and that be every ane of the foirnamit speciall men within thair awne boundis as thay sall best devyse ; quhilkis oistlairis sall haif furnitoure sufficient of meit and drink to be sauld for reasonable expensis.

[III] And also thay consent and assentis, for releif of thair said intollerable burdyn, that na man be sufferit to remaine or haif residence within ony of thair boundis of the saidis Iles without ane speciall revenew and rent to leive upoun, or at the leist ane sufficient calling and craft quhairby to be sustenit. And, to the intent that na man be chairgeable to the cuntrey be halding in houshold of ma gentilmen nor his proper rent may sustene, it is thairfore aggreit and

266

inactit, with uniforme consent of the foirsaidis personis,
barronis and gentilmen within-nameit, that thay and ilkane
of thame sall sustene and interteny the particular number of
gentilmen in houshald undirwrittin,—to wit, the said Angus
McDonald six gentilmen, the said Hectour McCleane
of Dowart aucht gentilmen, the saidis Donald Gorme
McDonald, Rorie McCloyde, and Donald McCawne
VcEane, ilkane of thame sex gentilmen, the saidis Lauchlane
McCleane of Coill and Rorie McKynnoun ilkane of thame
thrie gentilmen, the said Lauchlane McCleane, bruther to
the said Hectour, thrie servandis ; and the saidis gentilmen
to be sustenit and interteneit be the foirnamit personis ilkane
for thair awne pairtis as is above rehersit, upoun thair awne
expensis and chairges, without ony supplie of thair cuntreyis.

[IV] And, finalie, to the intent that the inhabitantis of
the saidis Illandis haif na caus to complene of ony oppressioun or that the fruit of the labouris of the puir tennentis
and labouraris of the ground within the samyn (as thay haif
bene heirtofoir) be eitting up be soirnaris and idill belleis,
thay haif all aggreit in ane voice . . . that quhatsumevir
persone or personis, strangearis or inborne within the
boundis of the saidis Yllis, salhappin to be found soirning,
craveing meit, drink or ony uther geir fra the tennentis and
inhabitantis thairof be way of conyie as thay terme it, except
for reasonable and sufficient payment fra the oistlairis to be
appointit as is foirsaid, thay salbe repute and haldin as
thevis and intollerable oppressouris, callit and persewit
thairfore before the judge competent as for thift and
oppressioun. . . .

[V] The quhilk day, it being foundin and tryit be appeir-
ance that ane of the speciall causis of the grite povertie of
the saidis Ilis, and of the grite crueltie and inhumane
barbaritie quhilk hes bene practisit be sindrie of the inhabitantis of the samyn upoun utheris thair naturall freindis and
nychtbouris, hes been thair extraordinair drinking of strong
wynis and acquavitie brocht in amangis thame, pairtlie be
merchandis of the maneland and pairtlie be sum trafficquaris
indwellaris amangis thame selffis, ffor remeid quhairof

it is inactit . . . that no persone nor personis indwellairis within the boundis of the saids haill Iles bring in to sell for money ather wyne or acquavitie, undir the pane of tinsale of the samyn. . . . And forder, gif it salhappin ony merchand on the mainland to bring ather wyne or acquavitie to the saidis Iles or ony of thame, it is lykwyse inactit that quhatsumevir persone or personis indwellairis thairof that salhappin to buy ony of the samyn fra the said merchand sall pay for the first fault fourty pundis money, the secund fault ane hundreth pundis, and the thrid fault the tinsale of his haill rowmes, possessiounis, and moveable goodis . . . without prejudice alwyse to ony persone within the saidis Illis to brew acquavitie and uthir drink to serve thair awne housis, and to the saidis speciall barronis and substantious gentilmen to send to the Lawland and thair to buy wyne and acquavitie to serve thair awne housis.

[VI] The quhilk day, it being undirstand that the ignorance and incivilitie of the saidis Iles hes daylie incressit be the negligence of guid educatioun and instructioun of the youth in the knowledge of God and good letters for remeid quhairof it is inactit that everie gentilman or yeaman within the said Ilandis, or ony of thame, haveing childreine maill or famell, and being in goodis worth thriescore ky, sall put at the leist thair eldest sone, or haveing no childrene maill thair eldest dochter, to the scuillis on the Lawland, and interteny and bring thame up thair quhill thay may be found able sufficientlie to speik, reid, and wryte Inglische.

[VII] The quhilk day, the said reverend father with the foirsaidis barronis and gentilmen consisddering ane lovable Act of Parliament of this realme be the quhilk . . . it is expreslie inhibite, forbiddin and dischairgit that ony subject within this his Majesteis kingdome beir hagbutis or pistolletis out of thair awne housis and dwelling places, or schuit thairwith at deiris, hairis, or foullis . . . undir certaine grite panes thairin specifeit ; quhilk Act of Parliament, in respect of the monstrous deidlie feidis heirtofoir intertenyit within the saidis Yllis, hes nawyse bene observit and keipit amangis thame as yit, to the grite hurte of the maist pairt of

the inhabitantis thairof ; for remeid quhairof it is inactit ...
that na persone nor personis within the boundis of the saidis
Iles beir hagbutis nor pistolletis furth of thair awne housis
and dwelling places, nathir schuit thairwith at deiris, hairis,
foullis, nor na uther maner of way, in tyme cuming, undir
the panes contenit in the said Act. And, gif it salhappin ony
man to contravene the same, that the speciall man undir
quhome the contravenair dwellis execute the said Act and
panes contenit thairintill upoun him, the contraventioun
alwyse being sufficientlie tryit, or at the leist produce him
before the Judge ordinair.

● [VIII] The quhilk day, it being considerit that amangis
the remanent abuses quhilkis without reformatioun hes
defylit the haill Iles hes bene the intertenyment and beiring
with idill belleis, speciallie vagaboundis, bairdis, idill and
sturdie beggaris, expres contrair the lawis and loveable
Actis of Parliament, for remeid quhairof it is lykwyse inactit
. . . that na vagabound, baird, nor profest pleisant pretending libertie to baird and flattir, be ressavit within the
boundis of the saidis Yllis be ony of the saidis speciall barronis
and gentilmen or ony utheris inhabitantis thairof, or interteneit, be thame or ony of thame in ony soirt ; but, incais
ony vagaboundis, bairdis, juglouris, or suche lyke be apprehendit be thame or ony of thame, he to be tane and put in
suir fe[n]sment and keiping in the stokis, and thairefter to
be debarit furth of the cuntrey with all guidlie expeditioun.

[IX] And, for the bettir observeing, keiping and ful-
filling of the haill actis, lawis, and constitutiounis within-
writtin and ilkane of thame, it is aggreit unto, concludit, and
inactit, seing the principall of every clan man be ansuerable
for the remanent of the samyn, his kin, freindis, and dependairis, that, gif ony persone or personis of quhatsumevir clan,
degrie or rank, within the boundis of the saidis Yllis, salhappin to contravein the actis, lawis and constitionis within-
writtin or ony of thame, or dissobey thair schiref or superiour
foirsaid, that then and in that caice thir presentis salbe ane
sufficient warrand to the barroun and speciall man within
quhais boundis the contravenair makes his speciall residence,

to command him to waird, and in caice of disobedience to
tak and apprehend the persone or personis disobeyairis, and
eftir dew tryall of thair contraventioun in maner foirsaid to
sease upoun thair movable guidis and geir, and to be
ansuerable for the samyn to be brocht in to his Majesteis use,
and to produce lykwyse the malefactouris before the judge
competent quhill his Majestie tak forder ordour thairanent.
Lykeas it is specialie provydit that na cheif of ony clan,
superiour of ony landis, or principall of ony familie, recept
or mantene ony malefactour fugitive and dissobedient to his
awne naturall kyndlie cheif and superiour. In witness
quhairof the foirsaidis barronis and speciall gentilmen abovewritten hes subscryvit thir presentis with our handis as
followis in taikin of thair presentis [consentis ?] thairto. Sic
subscribitur : Angus McConeill of Dunivaig, McClane of
Dowart, Donald Gorme of Slait, McCleud, McKynnoun,
McClane of Coill, Donald McDonald of Ilentyram, McClane
of Lochbuy, McQuirie.

R.P.C., ix, 26-30

1609, August 24.   *The Band of Iona*

We and everie ane of us, principall gentilmen indwellairis
within the West and North Illis of Scotland, undirsubscry-
varis, acknowledgeing and now be experience finding that
the speciall caus of the grite miserie, barbaritie and povertie
unto the quhilk for the present our barrane cuntrie is subject
hes proceidit of the unnaturall deidlie feidis quhilkis hes bene
foisterit amangis us in this lait aig, in respect that thairby
not onlie the feir of God and all religioun, bot also the cair
of keiping ony dewtie or geveing obedience unto oure gratious
soverane the Kingis Majestie and his Heynes lawis, for the
maist pairt wes decayit : and now, seing it hes pleasit God
in his mercie to remove thair unhappie distractionis, with
the causis of thame all, frome amangis us ; and undirstanding that the recoverie of the peace of oure conscience, our
prosperitie, weill, and quietnes consistis in the acknowlege-
ing of our dewtie towardis our God and his trew worschip,

and of oure humble obedience to our dreid soverane and
his Heynes lawis of this his Majesteis kingdome : and also
being perswadit of mercie and forgivenes of all our bygane
offensis of his Majesteis accustomet clemencie : Bindis and
obleisis ourselffis, be the faith and treuth of oure bodyis,
under the pane of perjurie and defamatioun for evir, and
forder undir sic uther civile penulteis as it sall pleis his
Majestie and his honnourable Counsale to subject us unto
at our nixt compeirance before thair Lordschippis : —That,
as we presentlie profes the trew religioun publictlie taucht,
preitchit and professit within this realme of Scotland, and
imbracet be his Majestie and thre Estaitis of this realme,
as the onlie and undoubtit treuth of God, sua be his grace we
sall continew in the professioun of the samyn without hypo-
cracy to our lyves end, and sall dewtifullie serve his Majestie
in mantenance of the treuth, libertie of the samyn, and
of all the lawis and previlegeis of ony pairt of his Heynes
dominionis, with our bodyis and goodis, without excuis or
weyring to oure last breath. Lyke as alsua we and everie
ane of us protestis in the sicht of the evirliving God that we
acknowlege and reverence our soverane Lord his sacred
Majestie allanerlie supreame judge undir the Eternall God
in all causis and above all personis, both spirituall and
temporall, avowing our loyaltie and obedience to his Heynes
onlie, conforme to his Majesteis most lovable Act of Supremacie, quhilk we imbrace and subscryves unto in our hairtis.
And forder, under the samyn aith and panes, we faithfullie
promeis dewtifull obedience to the halsome lawis, Actis of
Parliament, and constitutionis of this his Heynes kingdome
of Scotland, and to observe and keip everie point and
ordinance of the same as thay ar observit and keipit be the
rest of his Majesteis maist loyall subjectis of this realme, and
to be ansuerable to his Heynes and his Majesteis Counsale
as we salbe requirit upoun our obedience thairto, and forder
as salbe mair particularlie injoinit unto us, for our weill and
reformatioun of this our puir cuntrey, be his Majestie and
Counsale, haveing consideratioun quhat it may beir and we
ar able to performe, and also as mair speciallie we haif

271

aggreit unto, set doun, and establischit as necessar lawis to be keipit amangis ourselffis in our particulair courtis haldin be his Majesteis Commissionair, Andro, Bischop of the Illis, and subscryvit with all oure handis in his presence. And, finalie, we bind and obleis ourselffis undir the aith and panes foirsaid that, in caice ony of us, or oure freindis, dependairis, or servandis, upoun ony evill or turbulent motioun (as God forbid thay do), dissobey ony of the foirsaidis ordinanceis or be found remis or negligent in observeing of the speciall pointis of oure obligatioun above writtin, and being convict thairof be the judge ordiner of the cuntrey, spirituall or temporall, that then and in that cais we sall afauldlie concur togidder, conjunctlie or severalie, as we salbe imployit be his Heynes or the said judge ordiner or schireff, and sall concur with the said schireff or judge quhatsumevir haveing warrand of his Majestie to persew, tak, apprehend and present to justice the said dissobedient persone, intromet with his landis, guidis and geir, and dispone thairupoun, as we sall haif commissioun of his Majestie. And heirto we and everie ane of us faithfullie promitt, bind, and obleis us, be oure grite aithis, as we salbe savit and condempnit upoun the grite day of the grite Judge of the world, to observe, keip, and fulfill the premisis. And, for the mair securitie gif neid beis, we ar content and consentis that thir presentis be insert and registrat in his Heynes buikis of Secrite Counsale of this realme, and the samyn to haif the strenth of ane act and decrite of the Lordis thairof interponit theirto, with executoriallis to be direct heirupoun in forme as effeiris. . . . In witnes quhairof we haif subscryvit thir presentis with our handis as followis (writtin be Johnne Henrysoun, noter publict, commissair of the Illis) in Icolmakill the xxiiij day of August the yeir of God j^{m}vj^{c} and nyne yeiris before thir witnesses : Johnne Hammiltoun of Wodhall, Johnne Stewart of Ascok, Johnne Colquhoun younger of Camstrodane, Mathew Semple, servitour to Robert lord Semple, Aulay McCaulay of Stuck, and Mr Malcome Colquhoun. Sic subscribitur :—Angus McConeill of Dunivaig, McClane of Dowart, Donald Gorme of Slait, McCleud, McKynnowne, McClane of Cole, Donald McDonald of Ilintyrim, McClane of Lochbowy, McQuirie.

R.P.C., ix, 25–6

ORKNEY AND SHETLAND

Just as Bishop Andrew Knox, as the king's commissioner, ' brought in ' the Western Isles, so James Law, Bishop of Orkney (later Archbishop of Glasgow), again as the king's commissioner, ' brought in ' Orkney and Shetland. But the local conditions were vastly different. As late as 1567 the Scottish Parliament had specifically ' found ' that Orkney and Shetland should continue to enjoy their own laws and should not be subject to the common laws of Scotland ; [1] but the Stewart earls, taking advantage of their remote lordship, had turned the udal laws of the islands to their own advantage and had forced the people to perform ' works and services ' hitherto unknown. In 1609, however, Earl Patrick Stewart was warded in the castle of Edinburgh ; in 1611 the Privy Council ' discharged ' the ' foreign laws ' in Orkney and Shetland (which had been used for ' private gain and commodity ') and brought the islands beneath the ' proper laws ' of the kingdom of Scotland ; and, in December 1611, the Privy Council abrogated certain exactions and hardships of which the people had complained.

1611.   *The Abolition of the Norse Law in Orkney and Shetland*

Forsamekle as the kingis majestie and his predicessouris of famous memorie with the consent and auctoritie of thair esteatis of parliament hes statute and ordanit that all and sindrie the subjectis of this kingdome sould lieve and be governit under the lawis and statutis of this realme allanarlie and be no law of foreyne cuntreyis, as in the actis maid thairanent at lenth is contenit, nochtwithstanding it is of treuthe that some personis beiring power of magistracie within the boundis of Orknay and Yetland hes thir divers yeiris bigane maist unlauchfullie tane upoun thame for thair awne privat gayne and commoditie to judge the inhabitantis

[1] *A.P.S.*, iii, 41, c. 48

273

of the saidis cuntreyis be foreyne lawis, making choise
sometymes of foreyne lawis and sometymes of the proper
lawis of this kingdome as thay find mater of gayne and
commoditie, in heich contempt of our soverane lord and
to the grite hurte and prejudice of his majesteis subjectis :
Thairföir the lordis of secreit counsaile hes dischargeit and
be the tennour heirof dischargeis the saidis foreyne lawis,
ordaning the same to be no forder usit within the saidis
cuntreyis of Orknay and Yetland at ony tyme heirefter, and
that letters of publicatioun be direct heirupoun commanding
and inhibiting all and sindrie personis beiring office of
magistracie and judicatorie within the same that nane of
thame presome nor tak upoun hand at ony tyme heirefter
to judge or censure the inhabitantis within the saidis
boundis be foreyne lawis nor to proceid in ony actioun or
caus criminal or civile according to foreyne lawis, bot to
use the proper lawis of this kingdome to his majesteis
subjectis in all thair actionis and caussis as thay and ilk ane
of thame will answer upoun the contrarie at thair heichest
perrell.

MS. Registrum Secreti Concilii, Acta, 1610–12, fo. 53 (cf.
R.P.C., ix, 181–2)

It is clear, however, that the situation which had been created by
the oppressions of the Stewart earls was now turned by the government to its own advantage. In 1612 the islands of Orkney and
Shetland were permanently annexed to the Crown [1] and, following
a brief and unsuccessful revolt by Robert Stewart, a natural son
of Earl Patrick, the earl and his son were executed in Edinburgh
(1615). Then Bishop Law, holding the king's commission, held a
court at Scalloway in Shetland at which it was enacted as follows :

1615, August.

There has been great ignorance of his most sacred Majesty's
royal and supreme authority in [the] practising of foreign

---

[1] *A.P.S.*, iv, 481, c. 15. Again the Act of Annexation speaks of the
' augmentation of the patrimony and revenues of the Crown.'

and uncouth laws contrary to the tenour of the Acts of Parliament and secret council made thereanent, And likewise that there has been great desolation in the commonweal, trouble and disorder, injuries and wrongs amongst the inhabitants of the lands for lack of government, administration of justice, and putting of the same to execution, Therefore it is statute and ordained . . . that all manner of persons . . . shall honour their dread Sovereign the King's Majesty and submit themselves with all reverence to his authority, obey his laws, [and] disclaim and renounce all foreign laws, acts, statutes and constitutions whatsoever observed heretofore.

Maitland Club Miscellany, ii, part i, 169–70

In the immediately following November an identical decree was registered in the rolment of a court held at Kirkwall in Orkney (ibid., 179–80). Orkney and Shetland were now administered by royal officials enforcing the king's law, though local ' acts ' (known as ' Country Acts ') to meet local needs and to temper Scots law to the usages of the past were still made ' with the advice and consent of the gentlemen suitors of court and commons ' or with the advice and consent of the suitors of court and ' Bailies of Parishes.' Today, however, the old udal law survives only in certain foreshore and fishing rights.

THE BORDERS

Although there had been a long period of peace between Scotland and England, Border raids and forays had still continued. In 1597, on the West March alone, the damage done by the Scots in England during the last ten years was assessed at £12,000, and that by the English in Scotland at £13,000 ;[1] in the Middle March, for the same period, the damage done by the Scots in England was alleged to be between £16,000 and £20,000.[2] Revenge and reprisal were still the order of the day.

With James's accession to the English throne, however, the Borders were now the ' Middle Shires ' and ' as it were the harte of

[1] *Calendar of Border Papers*, ii, 606–7   [2] Ibid., ii, 410

his empire ' ; [1] and now it was possible to take combined measures against the lawless clans.

On 7 March 1605 the King ordained a commission under the great seal bearing that, having a special care that the shires of Berwick, Roxburgh, Selkirk, Peebles, Dumfries, Kirkcudbright and Annandale should be reduced to obedience, he appointed five justices for those districts ; [2] and on 14 March 1605 he added to the five Scottish justices five English justices to form a conjoint commission to suppress all deadly feuds, to bring outlaws and rebels to justice and to ' remove ' all those from whom ' can be expected no hope of amendment ' in the seven Scottish Border counties already mentioned and in the English counties of Northumberland, Westmorland and Cumberland.[3]

The Border Commission, moreover, was not left without arms to put its decrees to execution. On 14 March, under the king's authorisation, the Privy Council appointed twenty-five horsemen to serve under Sir William Cranston as a body of mounted police to carry out the directions of the commissioners.[4] Nor did Cranston and the commissioners do their work half-heartedly. So thoroughly were the old Border thieves and ' broken men ' harried, driven out, or executed, that in 1609 the ' Middle Shires ' were declared (though with some exaggeration) to be ' as lawful, as peaceable, and as quiet as any part in any civil kingdom in Christianity.'

The main instructions of the commissioners were as follows :

1605. *The Border Commission*

That thay have ane speciall cair and regaird for removing of deidlie feidis within the saidis boundis and for preventing of sic occasionis as may ather renew bigane feidis or mak new inimiteis to aryse within the cuntrey, and utherwayis with all haist possibill to suppres, sa fer as in thame lyis, that unnaturall and barbarous custome.

That they caus delyverie to be maid of all personis fugitive fra the one cuntrey to the uther, or that utherwayis ar suspect guiltie, and that to the ordinar officer and minister that sall demand thame to justice.

[1] *R.P.C.*, vii, 701–2   [2] Ibid.
[3] *R.P.C.*, vii, 706–7   [4] Ibid., vii, 704

That thay caus extract the names of all outlawis, rebellis, fugitives and outlawis, and utheris unanswerable to the lawis, and tak ordour how that ather thay may be maid furthcummand to justice, or then the cuntrey be voydit of thame.

That thay inquyre for the registeris and nottes maid be the Lieutennantis clerkis on ather syde of all souerteis found for any personis to be ansuerable to justice, that accordinglie thay may demand thair entrie from thair cautioner, and that thairby also thay may understand the Lieutennantis procedingis.

That lykwayis all actis of cautioun and generall bandis that hes bene gevin be any duelling within these boundis may be consider it of, and the pairteis band to be burdynit to mak thair men ansuerable according thairto.

That speciall cair be had for expelling furth of the saidis boundis of all idle vagaboundis quhais meanis to leif and sustene thameselffis being unknawne caryis ane presumptioun of thair unlawfull purchase for thair mantenance.

That all these in quhome thair can be expectit na houpe of amendement and ar thocht incorrigible may be removit furth of that cuntrey to some uther place, quhair the change of air will mak in thame ane exchange of thair maneris.

That the armour quhilk hes servit the brokin people within these boundis in thair lewd actionis may be takin frome thame, and that nane of thame quhais bipast behaviour makis thame suspect be permitted to have horses for any uther use or of better valew then ordinarie wark horses for the lauboring of the ground.

That thay exact ane particular accompt of the commissioneris that salbe apointit for administratioun of justice and causing of executioun to be done upoun the offendouris, and that thay sett doun the formes how the saidis commissioneris sall proceid in the justice courtis to be haldin be thame, and utherwayis baith be thair authoritie and advyse assist thame as thair salbe occasioun.

R.P.C., vii, 703

19

THE ADMINISTRATION OF JUSTICE

Justices of the Peace

In 1587 an act of parliament had decreed that commissions should be given in every shire to certain ' honorable and worthie personis being knawin of honest fame. . . erlis lordis baronis knichtis and speciale gentilmen landit, experimentit in the lovable lawes and custumes of the realme . . . [to be] kingis commissioneris and justices in the furtherance of justice peax and quietness ' to prepare ' executionis and arreistments ' for the justice ayres (which were henceforth to be held regularly twice a year [1]) and to ' do justice thame selffis at thair courtis and metingis to be keipit foure tymes every yeir ' for lesser crimes and defaults.[2]

The provisions of this act, however, never became generally effective. Then, six years after his accession to the English throne, James once more turned to the idea of Justices of the Peace on the English model, and the following act, confirming and extending the act of 1587, was passed :

1609. Act establishing Justices of the Peace

Forsamekle as . . . [the] brutall custome of deadlie feadis . . . wes become sa frequent in this realme as the subjectis of greatest rank and qualitie upoun everie nauchtie occasioun of base and unworthie controverseis of neighbourheid for turves, foldykis, furris [3] or marches of landis, foolishe wordis or drunken discordis betwene thair meanest servandis and dependeris and ony uther in the countrey did so readelie imbrace the protectioun of thair injust and unnecessarie querrellis as did mony tymes involve thameselffis and thair haill freindschip in maist bludie and mortall trubles whilk they did prosecute with sic malice and crueltie as . . . did distract the kingdome in opposite factiounis and mony tymes furnessit mater of maist pernicious seditious and civill warris, . . . yit the corruptioun wes sa universall that the

---

[1] See *infra*, pp. 283–5
[2] *A.P.S.*, iii, 458, c. 57, printed *infra*, pp. 283–5   [3] furrows

greatest pairt prevailing aganis the best that cruel barbaritie hath baith continuance and daylie incresce untill his majestie bending the excellent wisdome and rare graces of his royall mynd (wheirwith God hes indewit him mair abundantlie than any king that evir did regne in this iland) aganis that godles unnatural and bestlie custome did devyse and establishe a maist godlie just and prudent law and ordinance [1] for the course to be observed for removeing upoun equitable and just conditiounes the deadlie feadis whilk then stude in great number betwene the maist powerfull subjectis in this kingdome and thair kinsmen assisteris and partakeris in the executioun wheirof God haveing miraculouslie assistit his majesteis maist halie and just intentioun eftir exceding great cair and panis tane by his majestie in tryell of all the originall caussis of the saidis discordis . . . his majesteis admirable constancie hes sa ouercome all difficulteis that the haill knawin feadis within the kingdome being now removed . . . his majesteis haill subjectis findis sic joy and happines in the sweit fruittis of his wisdome and providence expressed in that caise that they earnestlie wische that his majestie wha hes sa cairfullie exterminat that abhominable pest of deadlie feedis may in his singular wisdome find meanis for evir to prevent the reviveing of that monster wheirin his majestie considering that naithing gaif sa great grouth and strenth to that bipast barbaritie as the slouth of magistratis in nocht suppressing the first seidis of these dissentionis whilk being small and weak in the beginning . . . were then easilie to be satlit gif diligence and authoritie had bene joynit for repressing thairof . . . his majestie and estaittis foirsaidis ratefeis and appreves the former act maid by his hienes for abolischeing of deadlie feedis in everie heid, clause and article thairof and forther statutis and ordanis that in everie schyre within this kingdome thair sall be yeirlie appointit by his majestie some godlie, wyse and vertuous gentilmen of good qualitie,

---

[1] The Act ' anent removeing and extinguischeing of deidlie feidis ' passed by a Convention of Estates in 1598 (*A.P.S.*, iv, 158, c. 1) and ratified by Parliament in 1600 (*A.P.S.*, iv, 233, c. 31).

moyen and reporte, making residence within the same, in sic number as the boundis of the schire sall require, to be commissionaris for keiping his majesties peace, to quhome his majestie with advyse of the lordis of his privie counsell shall give power and commissioun to oversie, trye and prevent all sic occasionis as may breid truble and violence amongis his majesteis subjectis or forceable contempt of his majesteis authoritie and breache of his peace, and to command all personis in quhome they sall sie manifest intentioun to mak truble or disordour ather by gathering togidder of idill and disordourlie persones or by publict bearing or wearing of pistolettis or uther forbiddin weaponis and sic uther ryottous and swaggering behaviour to bind themselffis and find cautioun under competent panis to observe his majesteis peace and for thair comperance befoir his majesteis justice or lordis of privie counsaill to undirly sic ordour as sall be foundin convenient for punishing of thair transgressionis or staying of trublis and enormiteis, and gif neid sall be to require the duetefull and obedient subjectis of the schyre to concur with them in preventing all sic contemptis and violences or for taking and warding of the wilfull and dissobedient authouris, committeris and fostereris of these crymes and disordouris under sic competent arbitrarie paynis as his majestie and lordis of his privie counsaill shall appoint for the offenderis, and sic of the countrey as being requirit shall nocht gif thair readie and afauld [1] concurrence to his majesteis commissioneris in the premissis quhairby the ordiner magistratis and officiaris within the schyres may be the better assistit and thair absence imploymentis or uther impedimentis mair commodioslie supplyit without derogatioun of thair jurisdictioun or want of readie conforte and justice to the obedient subjectis within the boundis thairof, ordaning alsua the saidis commissionaris to gif true advertesment and informatioun to the lordis of his majesteis privie counsaill, justice generall and his deputtis his majesteis thesaurar and other magistratis and officeris quhome it efferis off the names of

[1] honest, sincere

sic faithfull and unsuspect witnessis and assyssouris to be summonit in all crymes and disordouris whilkes salhappin to fall furth within the saidis shyres as salbe knawin to be maist meit and hable for tryell and probatioun of the samin and for eschewing that sic as ar ather aged, seiklie or unhable to travell or ignorant of the factis to be tryit be nocht unjustlie vexit or unnecessarlie drawin frome thair awin houssis and affaris for materis whereof they ar nocht hable to gif ony light.

A.P.S., iv, 434

It is noticeable that in this act James refers to his successful efforts to remove the ' deadly feuds ' which had done so much to distract the realm, and that the main function of the justices of the peace was ' to oversie, trye and prevent . . . truble and violence.' Earlier, in his *Basilikon Doron*, James had written :

The natural sickness that I have perceived this estate [the nobility] subject to in my time hath been a feckless arrogant conceit of their greatness and power ; drinking in with their very nouris-milk [1] that their honour stood in committing three points of iniquity : to thrall, by oppression, the meaner sort that dwelleth near them to their service and following, although they hold nothing of them ; to maintain their servants and dependers in any wrong, although they be not answerable to the laws (for anybody will maintain his man in a right cause) ; and for any displeasure that they apprehend to be done unto them by their neighbour to take up a plain feud against him and (without respect to God, King, or Commonweal) to bang it out bravely, he and all his kin, against him and all his . . .

In the same book he had referred to heritable sheriffdoms and regalities as being ' the greatest hindrance to the execution of our laws ' for, ' being in the hands of the great men ' they ' do wrack the whole country.'

Thus it was probably part of James VI's intention that the

----

[1] nurse's milk

justices of the peace should act as a counterbalance to the heritable jurisdictions in the hands of the nobility ; and immediately following the statute of 1609 justices of the peace were appointed for the different shires by the king and the privy council.[1] But old traditions die hard. Not only were the nobility and the holders of franchise jurisdictions included among the justices for each shire, but in 1611 the position of the justices of the peace, as holders of a new jurisdiction, was aptly summarised by one privy councillor who incautiously remarked that there was no reason why the new jurisdiction ' as ane sone, sould overschaddow and obscure all the uther jurisdictions of the kingdome, and that the realme had many hundredth yeiris bene weill governed without Justices of Peace.' [2]

Nevertheless the authority and position of the justices of the peace was gradually established ; equally gradually they were steadily burdened (like their English counterparts) with further and further duties. An act of 1617 [3] gave them jurisdiction in a host of minor offences ; and their hey-day was probably reached during the Cromwellian administration when the ' Instructions to Justices of the Peace,' issued in December 1655 to define their functions and powers,[4] brought them closely into line with the justices of the peace in England. The justices of the peace were now burdened, *inter alia*, with breaches of the peace, idle beggars, roads and bridges, forestallers and regraters, the wages of labourers and servants, the maintenance of prisons, the fixing of prices for craftsmen's work, swearing, profaning the Sabbath, drunkenness and the relief of the poor.

With the Restoration, the act of 1617 was confirmed,[5] and the confirmation included the new duties imposed under the Cromwellian ' Instructions.' After the Union, the statute 6 Anne c. 6 gave the Scottish justices of the peace all powers with regard to the preservation of ' the peace ' which were enjoyed by the English justices. But then came a gradual shedding of their powers ; and most of their administrative duties were transferred to the county councils by the Local Government (Scotland) Act of 1889 (52 & 53 Vict. c. 50).

[1] R.P.C., ix, 75–80
[2] R.P.C., xiv, 621 (from the Haddington MS.)
[3] A.P.S., iv, 535, c. 8
[4] Scotland and the Protectorate (Scot. Hist. Soc.), 403–5
[5] A.P.S., vii, 306, c. 338 (1661).

The High Court of Justiciary

In 1514 Colin, third Earl of Argyll, had received a commission as Lord Justice General, and in 1524 Parliament had enacted that the Justice (or his depute) should remain continually in Edinburgh, or ' with the king's grace,' for the hearing of criminal actions.[1] This act resulted in the centralisation of criminal justice in Edinburgh. In 1566 and 1567 there is evidence of attempts, or intentions, to revive the justice ayres (under which, according to ' old custom,' justiciars had passed through the shires twice a year hearing criminal actions at the *caput* of each shire), but nothing came of them ; and significantly in 1567 the Justice Criminal Court is included in a statement of those courts which sit in Edinburgh.[2] Then, in 1587, ' through the not holding of justice ayres ' and because ' judgment in criminal causes is only now at Edinburgh,' a new system was devised. By the following act the country was to be ' quartered ' and two justices depute were to be appointed for each quarter to hold justice ayres twice a year, while ' crimes and defaults in the second degree ' were to be heard before officers similar to the English justices of the peace (*supra*, p. 278).

1587.

Becaus of the grite delay in actionis criminall throw the not halding of justice airis twyis in the yeir according to the auncient and lovable ordour established be divers guid lawes and actis of parliament maid of befoir, Considering the ordiner judgement in criminall caussis is only now at Edinburgh quhair particular dyettis ar sett for certane speciall and heichast crymes, The punishment of uther offensis quhairby the commoun weill is greitlie grevit left to the justice airis that verie senedill [3] haldis and thairthrow ar becumin contemptable ; Thairfoir and for eise and releif of the subjectis that ar sa frequentlie inquieted be cuming in convocatioun to dayes of law and to pas upoun assysis in Edinburgh, quhair the courtis ar oftymes continewit in hinderance of justice, and to the grite truble and neidles

expensis of the kingis lieges: It is thairfoir statute and ordanit
be our soverane lord with avise of his thre estaittis convenit
in this present parliament, That justice airis salbe haldin
twyis everie yeir in tyme cuming ower all the schires of this
realme in the monethis of Aprile and October, begynnand
in the moneth of October nixtocum gif convenientlie it may
be. And be ressoun the mater can not be orderit and overtane
attanis [1] be ony few number to pas successivelie our all the
haill realme from ane schyre to ane uther, that our soverane
lord sall caus his justice generall mak aucht deputis, or ellis
his hienes sall mak sa mony be his awin commissionis under
the testimoniall of the grite seill, of sum of the senatouris of
the college of justice or certane weill experimentit advocattis
that ar maist able for travell, appointand tua our everie
quarter of the realme quhilk contenis sevin serefdomes or
thairby with ane depute of the thesaurairis and ane uther
of the justice clerkis. And . . . befoir the cuming of the
quhilkis justices deputtis dittayes salbe uptakin and the
personis inditit arreistit. . . . And to the effect that all
executionis and arreistmentis requisite may be dewlie pre-
pairit befoir the cuming of the saidis justice deputis, It is
statute and ordanit that our soverane lord with avise of his
chancellair thesaurair and justice clerk sall nominat and
gif commission to honorable and worthie personis being
knawin of honest fame . . . and in degree erlis lordis baronis
knichtis and speciale gentilmen landit experimentit in the
lovable lawes and custumes of the realme actuall induellaris
in the same shires [14 for Orkney and Shetland ; 21 for Inverness and Cromarty ; 7 for Nairn ; 7 for Elgin and Forres ;
7 for Banff ; 21 for Aberdeen ; 7 for Kincardine ; 14 for
Forfar ; 14 for Fife ; 7 for Kinross ; 7 for Clackmannan ;
21 for Perth ; 7 for Stirling ; 7 for Dunbarton ; 7 for Linlithgow ; 7 for Mid-Lothian ; 7 for Haddington ; 7 for
Berwick ; 14 for Roxburgh ; 7 for Selkirk ; 7 for Peebles ;
14 for Lanark ; 7 for Renfrew ; 7 for Argyll ; 7 for Bute ;
21 for Ayr ; 7 for Wigtown ; and 21 for Dumfries] Quhilkis
salbe kingis commissioneris and justices in the furtherance of

[1] at once

justice peax and quietnes, Togidder with foure of the counsall of every burgh within the selff quhilkis salbe constant
and continewall uptakeris of dittay : Gevand grantand and
committand to thame full power to tak inquisitioun and
mak dittay be thair awin knawlege or be a sworne inqueist
or sworne particulcr man of all personis suspectit culpable
of the crymes and defaultis contenit in the table to be maid
be the thesaurair justice clerk and advocate annext to this
present act, devidit in tua sortis, And all personis dilatit as
culpable in the first degree the saidis juges and commissioneris sall othir apprehend and commit to ward (gif
convenientlie thai can) or ellis sall deliver thame in portuus
to the crowner of the schire every moneth anis to be arreistit
and put under suirtie be him or his deputtis to the nixt
justice air . . . And upoun all personis dilaitit and suspect
as culpable of the uther crymes and defaultis in the secund
degree the saidis justices and commissioneris in the schyris
sall proceid and do justice thame selffis at thair courtis and
metingis to be kepit foure tymes every yeir, That is to say at
the first day of May at the first day of August at the first day
of November and at the first day of Februare or utherwayes
at ony tyme, thrie of thame being togidder and alwayes
sitting in the tolbuyth of the heid burgh of the schire, and
that thai remane at every ane of the saidis foure tymes in the
yeir thre dayes togidder or langair or schortair as they find
occasioun; With power to thame to direct thair preceptis and
portuus to the crowneris and thair preceptis to sereffis or
officiaris of armes to summound assyises, ilk persoun under
the pane of ten pundis, As alsua to send thair extractis to the
thesaurair efter cverie ane of thair four metingis to the effect
the panes and unlawis thairin contenit may be takin up,
quhairof compt rakning and payment salbe maid at the nixt
chekker and the charges and expenssis of the saidis justices
and commissioneris allowit thairin. . . . And the saidis
justices of bayth sortes for the space of ane yeir and further
induring our soverane lordis will to induir.

There is no evidence, however, that this act was effective. The central criminal court still sat in Edinburgh, and throughout the localities criminal justice was administered haphazardly by local deputes appointed by the Lord Justice General or through special commissions of justiciary granted to local earls or barons and often grossly abused.

Finally, in 1671, the present High Court of Justiciary was established. As ratified by the following act of 1672, the new court consisted of the Lord Justice General and the Lord Justice Clerk together with five Lords of Session. It was to sit in Edinburgh every Monday during the session, and it was to hold ' circuit courts,' once a year in April or May, in three circuits with two Lords for each circuit. The Lord Justice General was to be the President of the court or, in his absence, the Lord Justice Clerk. No circuits appear to have been held until 1708.

1672.

. . . That the office of Deputes in the Justice-court be suppressed, and that five of the Lords of Session be joyned to the Justice-Generall and Justice-Clerk, and all of them invested with the same and equall power and jurisdiction in all criminall causes ; that the Justice-Generall being present preside, and in his absence the Justice Clerk, and in absence of both that these present elect one of their number to preside. . . .

That they be appointed to meit each Monday . . . in time of Session, and oftner if business soe require. . . .

That once a yeir in the moneth of Aprile or May, Circuit Courts be keiped, two of their number appointed to goe and keep courts at Dumfreis and Jedburgh, Two at Stirling, Glasgow and Aire, and the other two at the tounes of Perth, Aberdein and Inverness ; the Justice-Generall being all-wayes super-numerary in anie of these Circuit-Courts.

A.P.S., viii, 87–88

In 1746 it was enacted that the circuit courts should be held twice a year. By the act of 1808 (48 George III c. 151) the Lord Justice Clerk was appointed to preside over the newly constituted Second

Division of the Court of Session (see vol. ii, p. 51) ; and by the act of 1830 (1 Will. IV c. 69) the Lord President of the Court of Session became *eodem officio* Lord Justice General. Under the Criminal Procedure (Scotland) Act, 1887, the High Court of Justiciary was reconstituted to consist of the Lord Justice General, the Lord Justice Clerk and all the remaining Lords of Session—every Senator thus becoming a ' Lord Commissioner of Justiciary.' By the Circuit Courts and Criminal Procedure (Scotland) Act of 1925 (15 and 16 Geo. V c. 81) the Lords Commissioners of Justiciary, by Act of Adjournal, can alter their circuits, or change the boundaries of circuits, or form new circuits, and can fix and determine the number of circuit courts to be held, and their places and times.

Act Anent Wrongous Imprisonment

See Additional Documents, No. 3, p. 502.

The Public Register of Sasines

See Additional Documents, No. 4, p. 505.

CHAPTER SEVEN

FINANCE AND TAXATION

CROWN FINANCE AFTER THE REFORMATION

The mediaeval theory that the king ' can and ought to live of his own ' [1]—that is, that the royal revenues derived from the crown lands, the royal burghs, the great customs, profits of justice, feudal casualties, escheats, forfeitures and so forth should and ought to be sufficient to meet the expenses of ' government '—persisted until the sixteenth century. Taxation was regarded as ' extraordinary ' revenue, to be exacted only upon extraordinary occasions—as, for example, the ransom of the king (as in the cases of William, David II and James I), or to meet the expenses of royal marriages or important embassies. Exceptionally, an annual ' tenth penny ' had been granted to Bruce, in 1326, owing to the impoverishment of the crown revenues through the wastings and harryings of the war with England.

In Scotland taxation had certainly been exceptional ; for Scotland, unlike England, had no expensive continental wars. Hence, in Scotland, there was no development of the constitutional check, ' No supply without redress of grievances ' : in Scotland ' supply ' was not necessarily voted by parliament, usually it was voted by convention.[2] Unfortunately, however, the royal revenue was not always efficiently collected ; and James I had re-organised the ' revenue department,' superseding the chamberlain (the principal financial officer) by the comptroller and the treasurer. Unfortunately, too, crown lands, escheats and other revenues were apt to slip out of the king's hands ; and in 1455 (at the time of the enormous forfeitures following the fall of the Black Douglases) parliament, remembering that previous endeavours to prevent the alienation of crown lands (in rewards and favours) had proved unavailing, and striving to secure an adequate revenue without the ' inconvenience ' of taxation, had ' annexed ' to the crown the great customs, certain lordships and

[1] cf. vol. i, 2nd edn., 184   [2] cf. *supra*, pp. 255-60

certain strategic centres which henceforth were to be alienated only with the consent of parliament and only then for great and reasonable causes.[1]

But the expenses of ' government ' were growing fast ; and the expenses of waging war (particularly with the development of artillery and the rise of a navy) were growing fast also.[2] To meet the increasing financial burden, recourse was had to ' feuing '[3] ; and in the period immediately preceding the Reformation some money was obtained from the Church—notably from the arrangements for financing the College of Justice,[4] and partly from semi-voluntary payments made by the prelates for the prosecution of the war against ' heretical ' England. Nor, in contrast with England, did the crown immediately benefit from the Reformation. The nobility had already ' greedily gripped ' many monastic lands ; no churchmen were deprived of their offices or revenues ; and although for a few years after 1562 more and more of the ' Thirds '[5] found its way to the ' support of the queen's majesty, above her own proper rents, for the common affairs of the country ' (or, as Knox put it, for ' the guard, and the affairs of the kitchen '), the amount so received by the crown made little appreciable difference to crown needs.

In 1587, however, in addition to a sweeping Act of Revocation[6] and an act endeavouring in various ways to limit governmental expenditure and to conserve income,[7] James VI secured from parliament an act of annexation whereby, with certain stated exceptions, all ecclesiastical lands and all revenues derived from ecclesiastical lands (excluding teinds) were annexed to the crown and were declared to be ' the property and patrimony ' thereof ' after the form, tenour and order ' of the act of 1455.[8] This act of annexation proceeded on the preamble that the crown ' had not sufficient means to bear forth the honour ' of the royal estate, and that the king, ' for the great love and favour which he bears to his subjects ' was unwilling to burden them with ' importable taxations specially for his royal support.' But, quite apart from the fact that most of the church lands were soon erected by James into temporal lordships and, as such, granted to various

[1] cf. vol. ii, 2nd edn., 16–18   [2] cf. vol. ii, 2nd edn., 76–82
[3] cf. vol. ii, 2nd edn., 238–42   [4] cf. vol. ii, 2nd edn., 48–51
[5] cf. vol. ii, 2nd edn., 191–4   [6] A.P.S., iii, 439, c. 14
[7] A.P.S., iii, 456, c. 54   [8] Supra, p. 44 (A.P.S., iii, 431, c. 8)

members of the nobility,[1] the position had long been reached that only by taxation could the expenses of government be met. In the very next year, 1588, there was a taxation of £100,000 for the expenses of the king's marriage,[2] followed by further large taxations in 1594 and 1597.

TAXATION UNDER JAMES VI AND CHARLES I

In 1599 James informed a Convention of Estates, small in numbers, that his ' rents and casualties ' were not able to entertain his estate and weighty affairs, that he recognised how grievous taxations had been and was resolved never to impose them, and that therefore he would appreciate ' some favourable relief of their benevolence.' But the convention, in its reply, referred to the ' shortness of time ' and the ' few number of the estates presently convened.'

1599.

The Kingis Majestie haifing exponit and declairit to his nobilitie and estaittis how that the necessar charges of his honorable effairis and adois daylie incresse, and that his majesties rentis and casualities ar not able to interteny his present estait in that honour and royall port quhilk his place and apperance dois requyre, and how that besyde and attour the intertinement of thair majesties houssis and bairnis his hienes palaceis and castellis ar altogidder ruynous and at the point of decay, his munitioun and ordinance unmountit without provisioun of pulder and bullet, his majesties movabillis waisted worne and consumit, Besydis divers utheris his majesties extraordiner charges in his maist wechtie effairis at mair lenth declairit befoir the saidis estaittis, Quhilkis the offices of thesaurie comptrollarie and collectorie ar nocht able to defray ; And how that the default of moyane hes bene ane greit lat and impediment to his majestie in the dew prosequutioun and punischement of the avowit contempt rebellioun and dissobedience sa

---

[1] So forming part of the background to Charles I's Act of Revocation with all its far-reaching results (see *supra*, pp. 66 *et seq.*).   [2] *A.P.S.*, iii, 523

publict and complenit upoun in all the land : Considdering lykewayes how grevous the burden of taxationis hes bene to his majesties subjectis and how litill profittable ather to the supplie of the foirsaidis defectis or ony uther his majesties necessar serviceis ; Quharupoun his majestie is resolvit in his tyme never to impone ony taxatioun heirefter upoun his pepill bot rather to expect at thair handis sum favourable releiff of thair benevolence without ony grudge.   The saidis estaittis haifing hard and being surelie informit of his majesties gracious resolutioun foirsaid, thay haif all aggreit in ane voice that his majesties honorable necessities salbe suppliet be ilkane of thame at thair uttermost powar.   Bot becaus of the schortnes of the tyme and thair langsum tarying, besydis the few nowmer of the estaittis presentlie convenit, the supplie of his majesties necessitie and maist feit moyane for prosequuting of the best remeid therof is be all thair consentis remittit to ane mair frequent conventioun to be apointit at his majesties guid plesur sa convenientlie as it may be.   At the quhilk tyme the estaittis presentlie convenit hes faithfullie promeist to hald hand and concur to sie the necessitie of his majesties effairis suppliet be sic meanis as may be best fund out to his hienes greittest weill and smallest greif to his subiectis.

A.P.S., iv, 185–6.

This was both a refusal and an indication that taxation was a matter for parliament or for a full and representative convention. James was too good a politician not to take the hint ; and thereafter his taxations were voted either by parliament or by a full convention—notably in 1606, 1612, 1617 and 1621.[1]   Nor was James averse to seeking ' benevolences ' in other ways, as the following letter to Sir Walter Dundas aptly illustrates :

1600.   *Letter of James VI to Sir Walter Dundas*

Richt traist freind we greit you hertlie wele.   The solempnitie of the Baptismc of our dearest sone being appointit at

[1] *A.P.S.*, iv, 289, c. 18 ;   475, c. 12 ;   581 ;   597, c. 2

Halyruidhous upoun the xxiij day of December instant,
quhairat sum princis of France strangearis with the speciallis
of our nobilitie being invyted to be present : Necessar it
is that great provisioun, guid cheir, and sic uther thingis
necessar for decoratioun thairof be provydit : Quhilkis can
not be had without the help of sum of our loving subjectis
quhairof accompting you ane of the speciallis, We have
thocht gude to requeist you effectuusly to propyne us with
vennysoun, wyld meit, brissell foulis,[1] caponis, with sic uther
provisioun as is maist seasonabill for that tyme, and earand [2]
to be send in to Halyruidhous upoun the xx day of the said
moneth of December instant. And heirwithall to inveit
you to be present at that solempnitie to tak pairt of your
awne guid cheir ; As ye tender our honnour and the honnour
of the cuntrey. Swa we commit you to God from Linlychtqw
this vj of December 1600.

JAMES R.

Walter MacLeod (ed.), *Royal Letters etc. from the Family
Papers of Dundas of Dundas*, No. 33.

With the increase in the number and the burden of taxations,
however, it became necessary to legislate for a more equitable
incidence. In the past, taxation had been borne by the clergy,
the barons (i.e. those holding direct of the crown) and the burghs.
Church lands were taxed upon the valuation made by Baiamund
(Bagimond) in the second half of the thirteenth century,[3] and
although revised valuations of all secular lands were carried out,
or authorised, for the taxations to meet the ransoms of David II
and James I, the assessment of secular lands known as ' Old
Extent ' was still used.[4] Then, in 1472, parliament adopted for
the first time the method of fixing the sum to be brought in by the
tax, and leaving each estate responsible for its own share in the
proportions of two-fifths of the total amount from the clergy, two-
fifths from the barons and one-fifth from the burghs [5]—these proportions being maintained until shortly before the Reformation

---

[1] possibly *turkeys*   [2] *in advance*
[3] See *Scottish History Society Miscellany*, vi, 3–77
[4] See *Thomas Thomson's Memorial on Old Extent* (ed. J. D. Mackie,
Stair Soc., 1946). See also *A.P.S.*, iv, 51*a*, 143*a*.   [5] *A.P.S.*, ii, 102*b*

when they were changed to one-half from the clergy, one-third from the barons and one-sixth from the burghs. Bagimond's roll was still used for church lands, Old Extent for secular lands, and a roll, adjusted from time to time by the Convention of Royal Burghs, decided the amounts due from individual burghs. In due course the general phraseology employed was a tax of x shillings on ' each pound land of Old Extent ' with proportional sums to be provided by the prelates and the burghs.

But the incidence of payment was obviously unfair. Taxation was a land tax and nothing more. Already, in 1597, feuars of crown lands and of church lands annexed to the crown had been made liable to tax,[1] and in 1621 a further extension was made whereby, for the next four years, annualrents were to be subject to a tax of five per cent (' the twenty penny of all annualrents '), though this was regarded as something ' extraordinary.'

1621. *Taxation of Annualrents*

. . . besyidis the ordiner taxatioun abonewrittin the saidis estaittis have, for the space of four yeiris nixt and immediatlie following the terme of Martinmes nixtocum, voluntarlie and frielie grantit to his Majestie a yeirlie extraordiner taxatioun of the tuentie pennye of all annuelrentis wheche any persoun or persounes within this Kingdome have frielie dew and payable to thame yeirlie or termelie (thair awin annuelrent quharin they ar addettit to utheris being first deducit).

A.P.S., iv, 598

This was, in effect, a new taxation upon personal incomes. Taxes of five per cent upon annualrents (and apparently, despite the opposition of the merchants in the burghs, also upon the interest derived from bonds) were again voted, in the reign of Charles I, in 1625, 1630 and 1633—while in 1633 the ' twenty penny ' (5%) was raised to the ' sixteen penny ' ($6\frac{1}{4}$%) [2] and a separate act ordered payment to the Crown of all interest taken above eight per cent.[3] To the first convention of his reign, moreover, Charles

---

[1] *A.P.S.*, iv, 142–6   [2] *A.P.S.*, v 13–14
[3] Called colloquially ' the tua of ten ' (see R. K. Hannay, ' The Building of the Parliament House ' in *Book of Old Edinburgh Club*, xiii, 15–16)

had proposed a new custom upon coal exported in foreign vessels, which was clearly to be an additional tax, without any easing of the burdens already imposed, and which was politely refused in letters sent to him from the convention :

1625.

. . . If this new custome be imposed, it wilbe a scar and hinder to strangearis to come heir for coale whairunto thay ar allured more be the ease thay haif in the pryce nor for ony necessitie they haif of our coale. And if the trade fall, without the whilk the awnaris ar not able to interteny thair workis and coalheughis, the same will perishe without ony possibilitie of recoverie . . . not onlie to the utter undoing of the awnaris, bot to the extreame hurt and prejudice of the cuntrey, whilk by this occasioun will be destitute of all the sea coale within the kingdome . . . Besydis the miserable wraik of manie hundreth families of poore people whose onlie mantenance dependis upoun thir workis . . . The estaittis haveing at lenth hard the saidis awnaris upoun this poynt, and the treuth of thair affirmatioun being knawne to sindrie of thame, and the matter being putt to voitting, It wes fund that without a sein and evident hurt to the cuntrey this new custome could not be imposed upoun the coale.

A.P.S., v, 186

More important, it is to be noted that taxations were now being voted for a number of years. In 1606 the vote of a land tax meant payment annually for the next four years ; the tax on annual-rents voted in 1621 was to be paid annually for the next four years (and that precedent was followed in 1625, 1630 and 1633) ; and the land tax voted in 1633 was to be paid annually over each of the next six years. In effect, taxation, far from being an exceptional and ' extraordinary ' source of revenue, was now becoming annual, and its scope had been extended. The burden of taxation played no small part in the opposition to Charles I.[1]

[1] See the note (*supra*, p. 83) in relation to Edinburgh and the National Covenant

TAXATION IN THE CIVIL WAR PERIOD

The Bishops' Wars, followed by Scotland's participation in the Civil War, necessitated new and heavier taxations to finance the struggle against the king. In 1640 parliament confirmed a proposal of a tax of ten per cent on profits and income of every kind, to be raised on a new valuation to landward by assessors appointed locally for each presbytery—the presbyteries and the burghs to form the units of collection.[1] The new unit of the presbytery, however, was quickly abandoned in favour of the shire. In 1643 when the convention voted a ' compulsory loan ' of 1,200,000 merks (with a further 100,000 merks for expenses), of which the burghs were to pay 'one sixth part ' (their old proportion), a fixed sum was assigned to each shire,[2] and local committees were appointed to make new valuations. Moreover, because the loan was raised wholly from land and the burghs, a relief of six per cent was allowed from all payments of annualrents :

1643.

. . . The sowme of tuelff hundreth thousand merkis Scottis money Togidder with the sowme of ane hundreth thowsand merkis . . . as allowance for charges . . . To be upliftit be way of loane out of the severall shereffdomes and borrowis . . . The saidis borrowes [to pay] one sixt part of the principall sowme, extending to 200,000 merkis, and the severall shereffdomes . . . to pay the remnent of the saidis sowmes . . . And becaus the sowmes of money presently to be lent are not to be ingathered aff the shyres, as taxatiounes have bein, or by the devisiounes of temporalities and spiritualities, but rather is thoucht fitt that the samen may be uplifted out of the landis, teindis and utheres as they lye locallie in every shereffdome promiscuously . . . Thairfoir it is thoucht necessarie that severall subcollectoures be appoynted, through the wholl kingdome, in ilk shyre or

[1] *A.P.S.*, v, 280, c. 23
[2] The roll of the shires, with the sums to be furnished by each, is given at the end of the arrangements and regulations for the ingathering of the loan.

shyres one or more, which subcollectour or collectoures so to be appoynted shalbe chargit with the wholl sumes of moneyes to be lent by the shyre or shyres wher he or they shalbe collectoure.

[*To aid the collectors commissioners are named for each shire*] who shall convein with the wholl heritoures, lyferenters, taksmen [*of teinds*], titulares propper, wodsetteres, pensiouneres, conjunctfieres, lady terceres, and uthers . . . who brooke any benefeitt to landward wherby any proffet or commoditie aryseth, And by consent of them, or most pairt of them . . . shall mak choyse of a select number of persounes to be joyned with the foirsaidis commissioners [*with power to*] . . . direct out summons at thair awin instance against any persone or persounes within the said shyre To compeir befoir them and give them informatioune upon oath [*under penalty of £40 for contempt or refusal and*] . . . use all legall way to informe themselffes of the just and trew worth of every persoune, or persounes, thair present yeares rent of this crope and yeir 1643 to landward, as weill of landis and teinds as of any uther thing wherby yeirlie proffeit and commoditie aryseth . . .

And for inbringing of the burrowes pairt of the said loane . . . the provost and baillies of ilk burgh to mak payment of thair part thairoff (conforme to ane roll to be submittit by the clerk of the burrowes [1] or conforme to the old roll) . . . and the provost baillies and counsell within each burgh to convein and elect certane persounes to stent thair nichtbouris . . . and to mak a stent roll . . .

And becaus the foirsaidis wholl sowmes of money alsweill to burgh as landward extendis to a greate sume of money and wilbe considerable burthein upon this Kingdome, and that the same is wholly payed out of the land rentis, trade, burrow landis, and other land rent and yeirly commoditie without consideratioun or laying any burding upon money, bank, or annualrent : Thairfoir it is statute and ordained . . . that everie debtour of money upon annualrent, alsweill

---

[1] That is, the clerk to the Convention of Royal Burghs

to burgh as landward, shall have retention . . . of sex of
each hundreth merkes or pundis quharin he is lyable of
annualrent to his creditoures. . . .

A.P.S., vi, pt. i, 27–36

Continuing financial difficulties led in 1644 to an excise duty on
the English model upon ale, beer and whisky, slaughtered cattle
and sheep, imported wines, tobacco and textiles, and exported
coal.[1]

Then, under the Cromwellian administration, Scottish taxation,
customs and excise were brought more or less into line with their
English counterparts. The eight commissioners appointed, after
the battle of Worcester, to settle the civil government of Scotland
and to prepare the way for a union [1] were also empowered to
determine the Scottish taxation. The burden of this taxation at
about £10,000 sterling a month (*supra*, p. 147 ; *infra*, p. 467), was
reduced by abatements to some £8,500 (1653), to be raised upon
the valuations already in force,[3] of which sum a large part
went towards the cost of the English army of occupation, though,
even then, a far larger part of that cost fell upon England.

But £8,500 sterling a month was more than Scotland could raise
—especially after the further disruption caused by Glencairn's
rising in 1654, a rising joined by many who thought they had
been so reduced to beggary that they had nothing more to lose—
and, after many representations from Monck, the Scottish assessment (or ' cess ') was fixed in June 1657 at £6,000 sterling a month,
a figure at which it remained until the Restoration.

In addition to the ' cess,' excise and customs duties, on the
English model, were fixed in the autumn of 1655 [4] and by 1659
were bringing in about £45,000 sterling a year.

TAXATION AFTER THE RESTORATION

Excise had now come to stay—and so also, as it was to be proved,
had the ' cess.' In 1661, in the first flush of the Restoration, the

---

[1] *A.P.S.*, vi, pt. i, 76–7.   [2] *Supra*, p. 146
[3] Firth, *Scotland and the Commonwealth* (Scot. Hist. Soc.), 172–9
[4] See *Report by Thomas Tucker upon the settlement of the Revenues of Excise
and Customs in Scotland, 1656* (Bannatyne Club, and *Burgh Records Society
Miscellany*)

Estates made a ' humble and cheerfull ' offer to the king of *a yearly annuity* of £40,000 sterling (or £480,000 Scots) to be raised as to £96,000 (Scots) from excise duties on inland salt and a long list of imported foreign commodities, and the remainder from excise duties on beer, ale, *aquavitæ* and ' strong waters '—a fixed quota being assigned to each shire and the burghs therein.[1] The burden of the excise was, indeed, ' cheerfully ' continued.

In addition, in 1665, with the excise duties still continuing, a taxation based on the rate of forty shillings on every pound land of Old Extent, with proportional amounts from the other estates, was voted for each of the five years 1666-70. This was a reversion to the old traditional method ; but it was the last time that method was used. The tax was voted by a convention summoned for the sole purpose of granting supplies for the Dutch War.[2]

1665.

[*The temporal estate grants*] That there sall be uplifted of everie pound land of old extent within this Kingdome, pertaineing to Dukes, Marquesses, Earles, Viscounts, Lords, barrons and free holders, and fewers of his Majesties proper lands, the soume of fourtie shillings Money at everie one of the fyve termes following [*annually, at Whitsunday,* 1666-70] And the Archbishopes and bishopes, for the spirituall estate have granted that ther sall be uplifted of all archbishopricks, bishopricks, abbacies, priories, and uther inferior benefices within this kingdome, at everie one of the fyve termes above-specifeit, the just taxation thairof proportionallie . . . as they have been accustumed to be taxed unto in all tyme bygone . . . And the Commissioners of burghs for their estate have granted that there sall be uplifted of all the burghs of this kingdome, at everie one of the fyve termes above specifiet, the just taxation therof proportionally . . . as they have been accustomed to be taxed unto in all tyme bygone. . . . And inregard that his Majestie hath erected sundrie prelacies and temporall lordships, wherby the ouners therof may claime to be taxed with the barrons of the temporall estate, and therby his Majestie would be

[1] *A.P.S.*, vii, 78, 88-9   [2] See *supra*, p. 259

defrauded of a great pairt of the said taxation, Therfor the said Estates ordaines that all erections of prelacies and uther small benefices, in whole or in pairt, in temporall lordships, sall, in payment of the said taxation, pay to the collector therof so much of the samen taxation (pro rata) as if they wer nowayes erected and as they wer subject to do befor the erection of the same [*and all ' desolved benefices ' to be subject to pay likewise*] And that those pairties who have gotten any pairt or portion of any prelacies or uther inferiour benefices, desolved, and new securities made unto them by his Majestie, of that pairt and portion therof so desolved shall be subject in payment of the taxation therof to the prelate or uther beneficed person, for his releefe of the same taxation, as they would have been so the same had not been desolved.

A.P.S., vii, 530–31

1667.

In 1667, however, a convention, adopting the former Cromwellian method, granted a new and additional supply (over and above the taxation voted in 1665) of £72,000 (Scots), or £6,000 sterling, monthly, for the period of a year :

. . . To be raised and payed be the severall shyres and burghs of this kingdome, according to the valuationes in the yeir of God one thousand six hundreth and sixtie and at the proportiones underwrittin respective [a *sum specified for each shire and burgh*] . . . And to the effect this supplie so cheerfullie offered to his Majestie by his good subjects may be equallie and justlie laid on, proportioned and raised upon all persones lyable, and who have any reall rent in lands, teynds, or otherwayes within the said shyres and burghs belonging to them, and that no persone may have just reason to complain that they pay more nor ther just proportion, the Kings Majestie, with advyce of his Estates, doth heirby nominat and appoint the Lords of his Majesties privie Counsell and the Senators of the Colledge of Justice within the severall respective shyres, wher any part of ther

lands and estates doeth ly, and also the persones underwrittin within the severall shyres, to be commissioners to
the effect afterspecifeit [*commissioners listed for each shire*] And
for the burghs the magistrates of the same for the tyme being
with power to them to choose stent-masters within ther
respective bounds. . . .
[*The commissioners to call for valuations ; to make new valuations
where necessary ; to value the rents of benefices ' in so far as they
exceid the ordinarie value of modified stipends.*']
. . . And the Kings Majestie, considering that the land
and reall rent of the Kingdome is lyable to his Majestie for
this supplie, and that the said land rent is under many other
great burdens, and his Majestie being desireous to ease the
same so far as is possible, doeth therfore, and for releif
therof, with advyce of his estates, Statute and ordaine that
all persones inhabitants within the severall shyres past
sixteen yeirs of age [*with certain exceptions*] be taxed and pay
into the heretors and others lyable for reall rent, under
quhom they live and for ther releif the soumes of money
aftermentioned. . . . Each gentleman above the qualitie
of ane tennent, the soume to be appointed by the heretor
not exceiding six punds scotts for himselfe his wyfe and
children, and each tennent and other inhabitant above the
qualitie of ane tradesman, cotter, or servant, for themselves
and ther wyves any soume not exceiding four pounds scotts,
and each tradesman, cottar, or servant, any soume not
exceiding the soume of twentie shilling scottis ; And the
burghs royall are, for ther releif, heirby impowered to tax
all ther burgesses, constant inhabitants, tradesmen, and
servants conforme to the above mentioned rules, excepting
as is before excepted in relation to the shyres. . . .

A.P.S., vii, 540 *et seq.*

This taxation of 1667 became the model for all subsequent taxations
up to the Union ; the old Cromwellian figure of £72,000 (Scots),
or £6,000 sterling, a month, became a standard rate, and the
English word ' cess ' (i.e. assessment) became the accepted term.
The commissioners appointed for each shire were soon known as

the ' county commissioners of supply,' and their duties of assessing the land-tax were later extended to include such administrative duties as the control of vagabonds, the maintenance of roads and the erection of schools—all because, in modern parlance, they administered the ' county rate.'

One sixth of the cess was still charged to the burghs ; the remainder was levied upon lands and land rents. But it had been realised for a long time that the incidence was unfair ; [1] various expedients for the ' relief of heritors ' had been tried ; and now, in 1667, a new expedient of poll money made its appearance. In 1672, however, there was a return to the old expedient of allowing every debtor, in the payment of his annualrent, to retain one-sixth part of his payment. In 1678 no relief was granted ; in 1681 poll money was re-imposed.

Taxations were henceforth granted as ' cess ' for a stated number of months in the year. In 1678, for example, a convention granted ' five months cess ' annually for five years.[2]

After the Revolution, parliament, in 1690, voted ' eight months cess ' for that year and ' five months cess ' for each of the years 1691–4. The expenses of the war against France, however, meant not only that cess had to be voted virtually every year and that the excise duties had to be raised, but also that other financial expedients had to be adopted. A hearth-tax of fourteen shillings was imposed for the year 1691,[3] but never re-imposed ; and in 1693 poll money gave way to a poll tax, falling upon all classes and not intended for the ' relief of heritors.' [4] The poll tax was re-imposed in 1695, and again in 1698 (for two years) ; but in 1701 a proposal for a further poll tax was defeated on a vote.

After 1701 direct taxation again became solely a land-tax, the cess being levied upon land, the income from land and the burghs. The burghs continued to pay one-sixth of every cess. The method of assessment had changed, and the division of the landward areas into spirituality and temporality had disappeared ; otherwise there was no change from the principles of taxation in the reign of James VI. Only the excise, now an indirect tax on ale, beer and liquors, was new.

In the Treaty of Union, the cess was still reckoned as yielding £6,000 sterling a month, and it was agreed that, when taxations

---

[1] cf. *supra*, p. 293   [2] See *supra* p. 170
[3] *A.P.S.*, ix, 236, c. 5   [4] *A.P.S.*, ix, 266, c. 17

were imposed, eight months cess (£48,000) in Scotland should be regarded as equivalent to an English land-tax of four shillings in the pound (yielding nearly £2,000,000).[1] The excise duties in Scotland were then stated to bring in £33,500 a year, and the customs £30,000 a year.

[1] *Infra*, p. 482

CHAPTER EIGHT

COMMERCE AND INDUSTRY

IMPORTS AND EXPORTS

Scottish trade in the second half of the sixteenth century and in the first half of the seventeenth century followed the mediaeval pattern.[1] Exports were mainly wool, skins, fish (barrelled herring and salmon), cattle, and some coal and lead ; imports were either necessities like iron (for the Scottish ores were as yet unexploited), timber and salt (for fish-curing), or manufactured articles, like fine cloths, and luxuries. In a ' Table of Scottish Produce exported yearly ' the figures for the year 1614 show that the value of ' commodaties of the land ' exported was £375,085, and of fish £153,354, while the value of manufactures exported (mainly cloth and plaiding and linen yarn) was only £169,097 [2]—though all these figures excluded trade with England. In 1656 Thomas Tucker [3] reported that the Scottish exports were still ' pladding, coal, salt, herring and salmond '—though again he took no reckoning of the trade with England because Scotland was then part of the Commonwealth.

Trade lay predominantly with France, the Low Countries, the Baltic, Ireland and England. In France Scotsmen had long enjoyed special privileges and, following Mary Stewart's marriage to the Dauphin, all Scotsmen were made naturalised subjects in France, and all Frenchmen naturalised subjects in Scotland— concessions which theoretically carried certain economic advantages not always enjoyed in practice ; in the Low Countries Scotland still maintained a ' staple port ' [4] ; and all trade was exclusive to the royal burghs under the supervision and general guidance of the Convention of Royal Burghs. There was no

[1] cf. vol. ii, 2nd edn., 228 et seq.

[2] Theodora Keith, Commercial Relations between England and Scotland, 1603–1707, pp. 1–2, citing Hist. MSS Comm., Mar and Kellie Papers, 70–4.

[3] See supra, p. 297, note 4

[4] At Campvere (cf. vol. i, p. 213). See Davidson and Gray, The Scottish Staple at Veere.

participation in the expanding trade with the new world, and ' companies ' had as yet no part in the commercial structure.

The 'Shipping Lists of Dundee, 1580–1618,'[1] detailing the cargoes of ships discharging at Dundee, are exceedingly valuable as showing the foreign countries with which Scotland traded, the places from which the different kinds of goods were imported, the different measures in use, the quantities officially declared (for payment of harbour dues), and the capacities of the ships. Charter-parties were very simple ; the skipper of a vessel was usually also the supercargo, and might be instructed to sell ' quhair he hapnit to mak mercat,' and might undertake to lay out any monies received as carefully as if they were his own.[2]

To the year 1612 belongs a Book of Rates of Customs and Valuation of Merchandises in Scotland, giving long lists of goods imported into and exported out of Scotland.[3] It is a significant document, but evidently the compilers were primarily concerned to make it comprehensive, and it gives no indication of the volume of the traffic in the commodities listed.

1598. *Fynes Moryson's Account of Scottish Trade*

.   Since the Scots are very daring, I cannot see why their Marriners should not bee bold and courageous, howsoever they have not hitherto made any long voyages, rather for want of riches, then for slothfulnesse or want of courage. The inhabitants of the Westerne parts of Scotland, carry into Ireland and Neighbouring places, red and pickeled Herrings, Sea coales, and Aquavitae, with such like commodities, and bring out of Ireland Yarne and Cowes hides or Silver. The Easterne Scots carry into France course cloathes, both linnen and woollen, which be narrow and shrinkle in the wetting. They also carry thether Wooll, Skinnes of Goates, Weathers, and of Conies, and divers kindes of Fishes, taken in the Scottish Sea, and neere other Northerne Ilands, and after smoked, or otherwise dried and salted. And they bring from thence Salt and Wines :

---

[1] Printed in the *Compt Buik of David Wedderburne* (Scot. Hist. Soc.), 195–302.   [2] Ibid , xxxiv–xxxvi, 78–9, 101

[3] *Ledger of Andrew Halyburtoun*, ed. C. Innes, 279 *et seq.* ; *R.P.C.*, ix, pp. lxix–lxxiii

but the cheefe trafficke of the Scots is in foure places, namely at Camphire in Zetland (i.e., Zealand), whether they carry Salt, the Skinnes of Weathers, Otters, Badgers and Martens, and bring from thence Corne. And at Bordeaux in France, whether they carry cloathes, and the same skinnes, and bring from thence Wines, Prunes, Walnuts, and Chessenuts. Thirdly, within the Balticke Sea, whither they carry the said Clothes and Skinnes, and bring thence Flaxe, Hempe, Iron, Pitch and Tarre. And, lastly, in England, whether they carry Linnen cloathes, Yarne, and Salt, and bring thence Wheate, Oates, Beanes and like things.

Hume Brown, *Early Travellers in Scotland*, 87

1614. *Cargoes landed at Dundee*

18 May.

Swane

Quhilk day comperit Colene crokat maister of the goode schip callit the swane And entered the said schip laitlie cum frome norroway Contenand sex hunder dealls xxxviij doubill dealls fourtie aucht fourtene elnes Tua dussone auchtene elnes ane hundreth Twelff elnes tua hundreth nyne elnes thrie thowsand steingis [1] with sum bills of aikin tymer and thrie faldomes of wood.

1 November.

Grace of God

Quhilk day comperit walt bannerman and entered ane bark of Dundie callit the grace of god and entered the said bark laitlie arryvit frome flanderis contenand sex score barellis ingeounis [2] and appllis thairof fyve score twelff barell Ingeounis & aucht barrell apills.

Shipping Lists of Dundee, 245, 251

---

[1] poles   [2] onions

The Cloth Industry

It will be seen that Scotland's exports, apart from fish and cattle, were essentially raw materials. Hence industries could be developed only at the expense of the old export trade, and exports had paid for many real necessities—iron, timber, salt, pitch and hemp. Moreover, in times of dearth the Privy Council had usually found it necessary to forbid the export of cattle and grain.

Clearly, however, the manufacture of cloth from native wool would not only help to satisfy the home demand, but would also improve the export position—providing always that the manufactured cloth was of a high enough quality and that a market for Scots cloth could be found.

This position was realised by Sir Thomas Craig :

1605. ' Export or Die '

If the harvest is a good one we are in a position to export considerable quantities of grain to foreign countries, and also wool, hides, skins and fish in great abundance. This is of advantage to the whole nation, and provides the means wherewith to import wine, silks, and French and English cloth, although the cloth produced by ourselves suffices for our needs. . . . In future our people must pay very particular attention to the manufacture of cloth, for thence will proceed our ability to import wines, merchandise, and those things on which men set store. Otherwise we shall find it hard to raise the money to pay for our imports.

Sir Thomas Craig, *De Unione Regnorum Britanniae*
(Scot. Hist. Soc.), 448

Already some attempts had been made to help and to improve the manufacture of cloth. The export of wool had been forbidden in 1581 [1] ; the inbringing of foreign craftsmen had been made permissible in 1582 ; and the Edinburgh burgh records show that Flemings were brought to Edinburgh in 1588.[2] In

[1] *A.P.S.*, iii, 221a. cf. *infra*, p. 308
[2] A second attempt made shortly afterwards appears to have been unsuccessful (1594. *A.P.S.*, iv, 85, c. 72).

1597 the 'hame-bringing off Inglis claith' was prohibited, and the same meeting of the Convention of Estates renewed the ban on the export of wool and again urged the introduction of ' craftsmen strangearis ' for the working of the wool within Scotland.

1588.

Ordanis Edward Mawchan, thesaurer, to pay to the Flemyng wobsters, walkers and litsters, laitly brocht hame furth of Flanders, the sowm of threscoir aucht pund sex schillings aucht penneis for thair charges and expenssis in transporting thame, thair wyffes, childerein and famely, to this burgh, for exerceing thair said craft thairinto. . . .

Edinburgh Burgh Records, iv, 530

1597. *Act anent the Restreaning off the hame-bringing off Inglis claith*

The Kingis Majestie, his nobilitie counsale and Esteatis presentlie convenit, foirseing the grite hurte and inconvenient quhilk the commounwele of this realme dalie sustenis throu the unproffitable trade usit be maircheantis in the hamebringing of Inglis claith and utheris inglis wairis and maircheandice maid of woll, The same claith haveand onlie for the maist parte ane outwarde shaw, wantand the substance and strenth quhilk oftymes it appeiris to have, and being ane of the cheiff caussis of the transporting of all gold and silver furth of this realme, and consequentlie of the grite scarsitie and present derth of the cunyie now current within the samin, Seing that kynd of exchange cannot weill be intertenyit be ony lauchfull trade or uthiris wairis or marcheandice to be transportit furth of this realme, quhilkis be the lawis of the samin ar not alreddy prohibite and forbiddin : And thairfoir his majestie with avise of his nobilitie counsale and Esteatis foirsaidis hes thocht meit and convenient To restreane the hamebringing within this Realme off all inglis claith, or utheris inglis wairis or marcheandice maid of woll, in tyme cuming ; And ordanis lettres to be direct chargeing officeris of armes to pas and

mak publicatioun heirof be oppin proclamatioun at the
mercat croceis of the heid burrowis of this realme and
uthiris placeis neidfull quhairthrow nane pretend ignorance
thairof, And to command and charge all his hienes liegis off
quhat estate qualitie or degree that evir thay be of that nane
of thame tak upoun hand to by or bring hame within this
realme tobe sauld ony kynd of Inglis claith or uthiris inglis
wairis or marcheandice maid of woll at ony tyme heireftir,
Undir the pane of confiscatioun of the same claith and
marcheandice and all uthiris the movable guidis of the
hamebringaris to his majesteis use Certifeing thame and
thay failyie or do in the contrair that the same claith and
movable guidis salbe confiscat and intrommettit with all
rigour and extremitie in example of utheris.

A.P.S., iv, 119

[This Act of the Convention of Estates at Dundee, 13 May
1597, was confirmed in the Parliament of 16 December 1597,
' to stand as ane law in all tym cumming ' (*A.P.S.*, iv, 136, c. 23) ;
but, owing to the inability of the Scottish manufacture to meet
even the home demand, it was of necessity repealed two years
later (*R.P.C.*, vi, 32–3).]

1597.

The kingis maiestie with avise of his nobilitie counsaill and
esteatis presentlie convenit ratifeis apprevis and confirmis
the act of parliament maid be his hienes and his esteatis for
the tyme anent the restreaning and retening within this
realme of all the woll quhilk growis within the same . . .
and ordanis . . . that craftismen strangearis be brocht
hame within this cuntrey for workeing of the said woll
within the same for the commoun wele and proffeit thairof
in tyme cuming.

A.P.S., iv, 119

Similar methods to encourage a home manufacturing cloth
industry continued until the middle of the seventeenth century.
The export of raw materials was restricted and the import of

manufactured cloth was prohibited ; foreign cloth-workers were to be encouraged to settle in Scotland ; and, since the home-grown wool was not of a good enough quality for the manufacture of fine cloths, Spanish and other foreign fine wools (together with dyes and oils) were to be imported free of custom.[1] Most of this economic legislation was by ' act ' of the Privy Council, but the very repetition of re-enactment [2] shows the difficulty of enforcement. In any case, total enforcement was made impossible by the frequent grants of royal licences to export—the crown preferring the immediate financial gain to the possibility of future economic advantage.

MONOPOLIES

Attempts to improve, or to establish and protect, particular industries by the granting of ' patents of monopoly ' have a certain contemporary economic justification ; and in some cases the recipients of grants of monopoly undertook to bring in skilled workers from abroad to introduce better methods and to train native workmen. On the other hand, the crown tended to regard a grant of monopoly as a useful source of revenue, or as a convenient method of reward, and the burghs were in constant protest against the monopolies held by private individuals.

Lord Erskine's patent for the tanning of leather was particularly opposed by the burghs ; but as it was estimated that the undertaking would cost at least £20,000, the system of monopoly was probably the only way of furthering the venture—and, in return, Erskine was granted a levy of only four shillings (Scots) on every hide tanned by the new process for the first twenty-one years of his monopoly, and only one shilling (Scots) a hide for the remaining ten years : if, indeed, he could collect it. Erskine undertook to bring in skilled tanners from England, and the records show that four months after the granting of his patent he had brought seventeen English tanners to Edinburgh, each of whom took an oath to be honest and faithful in the instructing of Scottish tanners.

It is less easy to justify a monopoly such as that held by James Primrose for the sale of *God and the King*, a manual inculcating passive obedience to monarchs, which in 1616 was ordered

[1] *A.P.S.*, v, 412a (1641)
[2] cf. *R.P.C.*, vi, 123, 520–21 ; ix, 409 ; x, 273

by the Privy Council to be used in schools and private families, and later prescribed in a like way by the General Assembly.[1] In 1623 the burgh of Aberdeen held ' fourscoir and some ma [copies] undistribute that we have payed for,' and was being pressed, under penalty, to purchase more—in the end, as often happened, endeavouring to escape from the burden by payment of ' a compositioun ' for ' ane absolute discharge from him in all tyme cumming.' [2]

Despite much opposition, however, there was no Scottish dispute over monopolies comparable with that which took place in England, though the burdens and abuses were always equally apparent. At least fifty monopolies were granted in Scotland in the reigns of James VI and Charles I, but, of these, only a small proportion were actually exercised.

1620. The Leather Project

In the parliament of 1617 an act was passed ' for reforming of the abuse used by tannaris and barkaris of leather,' and on 22 January 1619 the king instructed the council to determine what steps should be taken to remedy the said abuse (*R.P.C.*, xii, 159).

On 1st February 1620 *the following missive was approved by the Council for despatch to the King :*
According to the commissioun and warrand of the lait parliament and your majesteis command and directioun following thairupoun, we have haid diverse meiteingis and conferrenceis upoun that subject recommendit unto us anent the reformeing of the abuse of tanning of ledder within this kingdome, and we callit befoir us some of the principall tannaris of the cheif burrowis and certaine cordonaris of gode credeit, knowledge and experience in that trade ; be whome we ar trewlie and sufficientlie informed that the said abuse proceidis frome the ignorance and unskilfulnes of the tannaris thame selffis, and that thair is a necessitie of inbringing of strangeris for instructing of thame in the right forme of tanning. . . .

---

[1] *R.P.C.*, x, pp. cvii–cix, 522*n*, 530–1, 534–8, 600*n*
[2] *Aberdeen Council Letters*, i, 203

A draft patent was also submitted to the king for his signature :
The saidis lordis [of the council] . . . have . . . resolveit
upoun certane heidis, articleis, and conditionis, bothe anent
the inbringing of the strangeris, thair intertenyment and
furnissing during the tyme of thair aboade heir, the dis-
tributioun of thame throughoute the countrey for instructing
of the countrey people, the conditionis quhairunto thay
salbe tyed and in this service, and upoun certane utheris
poyntis toucheing the advancement of the said service, and
thay have appoynted and prefixt a certaine terme, to witt
the first day of Januar in the yeir of God j^{m}vj^c and tuentie
tua yeiris, within the quhilk the barkaris, yf thei be willing,
may have convenient tyme to learne the trew and perfyte
forme of tanning, and after the expyreing of that terme thay
have ordaneit that no hydis sould be presentit to mercatt,
sauld, or putt in worke till the sufficiencie thairof be approvin
be a seale to be sett and stampit thairon ; and thay have
maid sindrie provisionis and cautionis aganis the keiparis of
the seale for thair dewytifull cariage in that charge. . . .

Thairfoir his majestie . . . committis the charge . . .
of the saidis strangeris and of the keiping of the said seale to
. . . Johnne, Lord Erskene . . . for . . . threttie ane
yeiris. . . . And his majestie, considering that the said
Johnne, Lord Erskene, wilbe drivine in verry grite chargeis
and expenssis upoun occasioun of this service, not only be
the inbringing and intertenying of strangeris dureing the
appoyntit tyme of thair aboade heir and in directing of
thame through the countrey and appoynting of deputeis in
all convenient placeis to attend that charge and service, bot
through ane nomber of uther occasionis . . ., thairfoir . . .
hes givin . . . to the said Johnne, Lord Erskene, his airis
and assigneyis, dureing the first tuentie ane yeiris of this
patent, the sowme of four schillingis Scottis money upoun
the hyde as the pryce of the seale . . . and, the said
tuentie ane yeiris being expyreit, becaus the service will then
become facile and easie, . . . allowis . . . dureing the
last ten yeiris of this patent, the sowme of tuelf pennyis
Scottis upoun the hyde allanerlie. . . .   *R.P.C.*, xii, 190–3

[On 2 June 1620 there appeared before the council seventeen English tanners who 'gaif thair greit and solemne oathe to instruct the tannaris and barkaris of ledder in this kingdome in the trew and perfyte forme of tanning' (ibid., 294), and four days later the council submitted to them a *questionnaire* concerned with the technical processes of tanning, to which the Englishmen gave detailed answers (ibid., 296–8).]

1619-21. *Patent for the Manufacture of Soap*

On 2 November 1619 *the privy council granted to Mr Nathaniel Udwart, son of the deceased Nicol Udwart, provost of Edinburgh, the sole right of making and selling soap within the kingdom for the space of twenty-one years.* The soap previously used in Scotland had been imported soap, compoised of such pestiferous and filthie ingredientis as no civile kingdome, yea the verry rude barbarianis, will nocht allow nor permitt the lyk to be sauld amongis thame, *yet brought into Scotland by merchants who prefer* thair awne privat gayne to the honnour, credite and reputatioun of thair native countrey ; . . . quhairthrow not only ar the moneyis of this kingdome transportit yeirlie in greit aboundance, and bestowit and wairit [1] upoun ane most filthie and noysome commoditie, . . . bot withall the use of this pestiferous and noysome saip within this kingdome produceis mony schamefull and havie imputationis aganis the same, especiallie be strangeris hanting and frequenting this kingdome, quha may not abide the stinking smell of the naiprie and lynning clothes waschin with this filthie saip.

R.P.C., xii, 106–7

On 26 *June* 1621 *the council heard a petition from Udwart* quhairby he craved ane restreante to be maid of importatioun of foreyne soape according to the tennour and conditioun of his patent, seeing, as he affermed, he wes able to furneis the cuntrie abundantlie and sufficientlie within the self with goode and holesome soape maid be him at easie

[1] i. e., expended

and reasonable pryceis. *A commission was therefore appointed, consisting of six counsellors and six merchants of Edinburgh* to trye and examine the sufficiencie of the soape maid be the said Mr. Nathanaell, and how it haldis and answeris in goodnes with foreyne soape, yf the said Mr. Nathanaell be able to furneis the cuntrie abundantlie and sufficientlie thairwith, and upoun quhat prices the same may and salbe sauld . . . and generallie to informe thame selffis in all and everie thing whilk in the prosequutioun and halding fordwart of this worke may tend to the weele and benefeit of the cuntrey ; and to mak ane formall reporte thairof in write to the saidis lordis, to the effect thay may accordinglie grant or refuse the said restreant.

Ibid., xii, 505–6

Next day the commissioners convenit and mett in the toun of Leythe, within the said Mr. Nathanaell his workehous thair . . . and thair thay sighted and considderit the greene and quhyte soape maid be the said Mr. Nathanaell and conferrit the same with some examplis of Flanderis soape. . . .

Ibid., xii, 508

On 4 July 1621 *the commissioners reported to the council that* haveing fund his [Udwart's] greene soape to be als goode and sufficient as the soape of that kynd broght frome Flanderis, thay find it expedient for the better tryeing of the continewance of the said soape in the present fynnes that the provost and baillies of Edinburgh be thame selffis or some otheris to be nominat be thame, sall tuyse or thrise everie yeir, or ofter as thay sall think meete, trye the sufficiencie of the soape maid be the said Mr. Nathanaell at unawars quhen the soape is boylled, and sall confer the same with the Flemis soape, and yf thay sall find ony defect in the fynnes thay sall acquent his majesteis counsell thairwith.

Ibid., xii, 516–17

Coal

Meantime the export of coal was steadily expanding, and the fuel requirements of the growing towns and, particularly, of a rapidly growing London, provided a ready market. This trade, moreover, was not hampered by the trading monopoly of the royal burghs, and was carried on by the individual owners of 'coal heuchs.' Seventeenth-century acts bound the colliers and other workers in the coal mines to their employment in order to maintain and develop the coal industry.[1]

1618. *A Description of Sir George Bruce's mine at Culross*

The mine [of Sir George Bruce at Culross] hath two ways into it, the one by sea and the other by land ; but a man may goe into it by land, and returne the same way if he please, and so he may enter into it by sea, and by sea he may come forth of it : but I for varieties sake went in by sea, and out by land. Now men may object, how can a man goe into a mine, the entrance of it being into the sea, but that the sea will follow him and so drown the mine ? To which objection thus I answer, That at low water, the sea being ebd away, and a great part of the sand bare ; upon this same sand (being mixed with rockes and cragges) did the master of this great worke build a round circular frame of stone, very thicke, strong and joined together with glutinous and bitumous matter, so high withall, that the sea at the highest flood, or the greatest rage of storme or tempest, can neither dissolve the stones so well compacted in the building, or yet overflowe the height of it. Within this round frame (at all adventures) hee did set workmen to digge with mattockes, pick-axes, and other instruments fit for such purposes. They did dig forty foot downe right, into and through a rocke. At last they found that which they expected, which was sea-cole : . . . so that in the space of eight and twenty, or nine and twenty yeeres, they have

[1] cf. *infra* p. 386

digged more then an English mile under the sea, that when men are at worke belowe, an hundred of the greatest shippes in Britaine may saile over their heads. Besides, the mine is most artificially cut like an arch or a vault, all that great length, with many nookes and by-wayes ; and it is so made, that a man may walke upright in the most places, both in and out. Many poor people are there set on work, which otherwise through the want of employment would perish. . . .

The sea at certaine places doth leake, or soake into the mine, which, by the industry of Sir George Bruce, is all conveyed to one well neere the land, where he hath a device like a horse-mill, that with three horses and a great chaine of iron, going downeward many fadomes, with thirty-sixe buckets fastened to the chaine ; of the which eighteene goe downe still to be filled, and eighteene ascend up to be emptied, which doe emptie themselves (without any man's labour) into a trough that conveyes the water into the sea againe. . . .

Besides he doth make every weeke ninety or a hundred tunnes of salt, which doth serve most part of Scotland ; some he sends into England, and very much into Germany.

Hume Brown, *Early Travellers in Scotland*, 116–17

THE CROMWELLIAN UNION

The constitutional union between England and Scotland, implied in the Instrument of Government, and given effect and detailed regulation in the Ordinance for Union on 12 April 1654,[1] brought with it complete economic union. A uniform system of customs, excise, protection and taxation [2] brought freedom of trade with England and her colonies, but, by disrupting the traditional commercial pattern, had a detrimental effect on Scotland's economy. Taxation for a military government brought an unprecedented burden and kept the country in a state of poverty ; and Cromwell had seized and appropriated the greater part of the Scottish merchant fleet. Old and new industries alike languished, and trade was almost at a standstill. Moreover, customs and import-

[1] *Infra*, pp. 463–5   [2] *Supra*, p. 297

export regulations were not geared to the needs of Scottish trade, and, to crown all, Cromwell's Dutch War ruined, for a time, the old-established trade with the Low Countries. The six years' duration of Cromwellian union did not provide sufficient time for economic adjustment, and the Restoration was hailed as a welcome relief.

The interlude is interesting as illustrating the problems of commercial union and as anticipating the post-1707 economic troubles.

POST-RESTORATION TRADE AND INDUSTRY

With the abolition of the Cromwellian union there was urgent need of economic reorganisation (and of government aid and encouragement) to recover from the depression of the previous six years. The new government activity and legislation in encouraging trade and manufactures, although mainly a reassertion of past policy, was now greeted with more enthusiasm than in the past ; also new ventures in ' manufactories ' were increasingly more spontaneous in the closing decades of the century.

The new government's first important act to promote trade and industry was that establishing a Council of Trade.

1661. *Act appointing a Council of Trade*

The Kings most excellent Majestie, takeing to his Royall consideration of how great consequence it may be for the good and honour of this kingdome and for the benefite and advantage of his people that care be had for encourageing and right ordering of trade, And that the trust therof be committed to persones of knoune abilities, integritie and fitnes for such ane affaire, Therfor his Majestie, with advice and consent of his Estates of Parliament, have thought it necessarie that a Councill of Trade be established, And accordingly doth heirby give full power and Commission to [blank] to be of the Councill for ordering of trade within this Kingdome, With power to them or any [blank] of them, [blank] being alwayes present, to meit at such tymes and places as they shall think fit And ther to make and set doun rules, acts and ordinances for regulateing, improveing and advanceing of trade, navigation and manufactories, rectifie- ing of abuses, And to give orders for putting the same in execution, And with power to them to establish severall companies and impower them with such priviledges, liberties and immunities as shall be fittest for the good of the service and are not contrarie to the positive lawes of this kingdome, And to prescryve such rules as none of the saids companies incroach upon or prejudge another, And that they give out orders and directions to all Scots factors and Staples abroad, And generallie with power to them to doe everie thing con- cerneing trade, manufactories and navigation Which they shall find to be necessarie or fit for the right ordering pro- moveing and advancing therof; And in caice any just ground of grieveance occurre betuixt the said Councill and any of the Royall burrowes His Majesties Privie Councill is heirby impowered to determine therintill : And this Commission to endure ay and whill the same be discharged be his Majestie . . .

A.P.S., vii, 273, c. 292

This act empowered the Council of Trade to establish companies and to confer upon them privileges, liberties and immunities ; and the privileges which the companies were to enjoy were enumerated in the Act for erecting of Manufactories which, at the same time, reimposed the old provisions forbidding the export of wool and other raw materials suitable for manufactures. Specific acts were passed prohibiting the export of linen yarn and the import of ' made work ' which could be ' made ' (manu- factured) in Scotland. That is, restraint of the export of raw materials suitable for manufacture was accompanied by the com- plementary restraint of the import of manufactured articles. In addition, an attempt was to be made to use the new ' companies ' for the relief of poor children, vagabonds and the unemployed,[1] and foreign craftsmen were to be made naturalised subjects of the realm.

The stress, at first, was upon the manufacture of linen and cloth, though an act ' discharging the exportation of skins and

[1] See *infra*, p. 382

hides' showed that the policy of protection was likely to be extended.

1661. *Act for erecting of Manufactories*

Our soverane lord, considering how many great advantages this kingdome and the subjects thairof may have by the erecting, cherishing and mantaining of manufactories, therby keeping in the cuntrie great sumes of money dayly exported by bringing in such commodities as may be made at home and bringing in money for such commodities as may be made and wroght within the same, and exported to forrane nations, besids that therby many poore people and idle persones and vagabounds will be set at work and intertained, wherby vertew will be increased and idleset crubed[1] and restrained, . . . hath therfor thought fit, with advice and consent of the estates of parliament, heirby to grant to all such persones as have or shall undertake to set up any manufactories the priviledges following, viz. if any stranger shall come or be brought into this kingdome by natives to set up work and teach his arte in makeing cloath, stuffs, stockings, soap or any other kynd of manufactorie, he shall enjoy the benefite of the law and all other priveledges that a native doth enjoy, with power to erect manufactories either in burgh or landward as they shall think fit, and ther to dwell and exerce their trade without any stop or trouble : And for their further encouragement declared all oyll, dying stuffs, forrane wooll, pottashes or any other materialls whatsoever usefull for manufactories that shall be imported to be frie of custome, excise and other publict dues, and that all cloath, stuffs, stockings or any other commodity to be made and exported by them be frie of custome and excise for nyntein yeers after January 1662 yeers ; and if any stock shall be imployed for erecting or intertaining of any manufactories of any kind the same is to be frie of all publict and private taxes whatsoever, lykas all customers, collectors, fermerers of customes or excise and others are heirby discharged to demand any custome, excise or any other im-

[1] i.e., curbed

position whatsoever for such materialls befor mentioned and belonging to manufactories as they will be answerable.

And in regaird of the great prejudice to the kingdome by exportation of wooll, and skins and wooll upon them, and of other native commodities and materialls fit for manu-factories ; thairfor his majestie with advice forsaid doth heirby discharge all and everie persone whatsoever native or stranger to export out of this kingdome any wooll or skins with wooll upon them or skins of any kynd or any materialls usefull for manufactories untill they be made in work or put to the best availl for the good of the kingdome. . . .

Lykas his majestie for the further encouragement of the saids manufactories doth . . . discharge all quarterings or leveying of souldiers upon manufactories or the masters therof and that no persone whatsoever intyse resset or inter-teane any of the servants or apprentises of the manufactories without consent of their master under the paines contained in the acts of parliament against coallhewers, salters and their resetters. . . . And because many things may occur heirafter which may be necessary for advancement of manu-factories, thairfoir his majestie . . . doth impower the lords of his majesties privy councill or exchequer or such as shall be appointed by his majestie dureing this present parliament or therafter to consider such overtures as shall be offered for the good of manufactories and to make such orders and grant such further liberties and priveledges to them as they shall think just. . . .

A.P.S., vii, 261–2

1661. *Act discharging the exportation of linen yarn*

Considering that it would tend more to the advantage of his majesties subjects and promoveing of manufactories to restraine the libertie that merchants have taken to export lining yearn (one of the choicest commodities of this his majesties auncient kingdome) then still to suffer them to carie the same into other places and kingdomes, thairfor his majestie with advice and consent of his estates of parliament discharges any merchant or others whatsoever to transport out of this kingdome any lining yearne under the paine of confiscation of the same, the one halffe to his majesties use and the other halff to the use of the attatcher and apprehender of the said yearn.

A.P.S., vii, 257

1661. *Act dischargeing tradesmen to import made work*

The Kings Majestie considering the great discouragement given to manufactories and trades by tradesmens bringing home from forrane places such commodities as may be made within the kingdome by these of the same trade ; Doth therfore with advice and consent of the Estates of Parliament inhibite and discharge all tradsmen and mechanicks to import from forrane partes any made worke belonging to that trade or calling wherof they are freemen or to vend the same or any such ware brought home by merchants in their shops or otherwise, under the paine of confiscation the one halffe to his Majesties use and the other to the apprehender or pursuer of the same.

A.P.S., vii, 284, c. 310

1661. *Act Establishing Companies and Societies for Makeing Lining Cloth Stuffs &c.*

Oure Soverane Lord Considering that all the lawdable lawes and statuts made be his Majesties ancestors anent Manufactories for inriching of his Majesties antient kingdome putting of poore children ydle persons and vagabounds to work, for the mantenance and releiff of the cuntrie of the burden of such unproffitable persones, have been hitherto rendered ineffectuall, And that many good spirites haveing aimed at the publict good, have for want of sufficient stocks councill and assistance been crushed by such undertakeings, Doe conceave it necessar to create and erect companies and societies for manufactories that what wes above the capacity of single persons may be carried on by the joynt assistance councill and means of many ; And therfor his Majestie with advice and consent of his Estats of Parliament doth establish particular societies and companies in the persones of such as shall enter themselffs in the said societies . . . for makeing of lining cloath, worstead stockings, searges, baises, sayes, cottons, sempeternums, castilians, perpetuanaes and all uther wollen stuffs and cloath ; And for their encouragement and good of his hienes kingdome . . . prohibites and discharges any of his Majesties leidges to carie and transport into Spain, Portugall, Biscay, Russia, France or any place beyond seas any [such wollen stuffs or cloths] except they be frie and of one of the societies forsaid ; And it is heirby declared that all materialls imported for the use of the said manufactories, and that all the saids stuffs or cloaths exported by the said companie shall be frie of all custome excise or any other imposition whatsoever for the space of nyntein yeers . . . And that this pious charitable and proffitable designe may be no longer frustrat, nor poore childreen, vagabounds or idle persons continew to be burdensome to their cuntrie, It is statute and ordained that ther be in each paroche one or moe persons provided and appointed upon the charges and expences of the heritors thairof for instructing of the poore childreen vagabounds and other idlers to fine and mix wooll, spin worstead, and knit stockings . . . And for the encourageing of skillfull artizans to come from abroad for traneing up the persones forsaids and workeing for the use of the saids companies, It is heirby declared that all such as shall be brought home and imployed for the saids companies shall be frie to set up and worke in burgh and landward wher the companies shall think fit without payeing any thing whatsoever to any persone or persones under whatsoever culour or pretext for their freedome, and shall be frie of taxes publict burdings or exactions dureing their lifetyme. . . .

A.P.S., vii, 255, c. 275

1661. *Act dischargeing the exportation of skines and hyds etc.*

The kings majestie considering how necesser it is that all former lawes for improveing of native commodities be revived, and understanding that the deacons and remanent tradsmen of the skinners have upon their oune charges brought from forrane places perfumers, makers and pre- parers of lether, by whose pains and arte the kingdome may be furnished with gloves at easier rates and able to furnish other nations abroad with made worke, doth therfor . . . ratifie and approve the 178 act of the 13 Par. of K. Ja. 6 [*apparently A.P.S., iii, 579, of date* 1592] . . . dischargeing the exportation of skins and others thairin contained . . . and also . . . doth . . . discharge all merchants tradsmen and others to transport any calff skin, kid skin, hudderon or shorling skins or any goat skins, hart, buck, deer or any other wilde beasts skins forth of the kingdome under paine of confiscation of the same ; and for the further encourage- ment of the skinner trade and manufactorie licence is heirby given to export gloves made within the kingdome frie of all custome and excise for the space of nyntein yeers after the date heirof.

A.P.S., vii, 259

The Navigation Act

An English Navigation Act of 1651 endeavoured to encourage the carrying trade of the Commonwealth at the expense of the Dutch. The Act forbade the importation into the British Isles of the pro- duce of Asia, Africa and America except in British ships or those belonging to the Plantations, and required that the majority of each crew should be subjects of the Commonwealth. In 1660 a further Navigation Act passed by the English Parliament extended the restrictions to *exports* as well as imports ; added that imports from Russia and Turkey were to be carried either in English-built ships, with three-quarters of the crew English, or in ships built in the country of origin of the imports and navigated by crews of whom three-quarters were natives of the country of origin ; and further added that no ' alien ' could exercise the trade or occupa- tion of a merchant or factor in the Plantations, and that certain specific exports from the Plantations were to be carried to English ports.

Whereas the Act of 1651 had regarded England and Scotland as one, the Act of 1660 now referred throughout to *England*, to

English ships and *English* trade. Moreover, free trade between Scotland and England had come to an end with the end of the Cromwellian Union ; Scotland soon began to suffer from the enforcement of the 1660 Act ; and the English refused to exempt Scotland from its operation.

Accordingly, Scotland replied with her own Navigation Act of 1661, roughly copying the restrictions of the English Act, but leaving the door open for mutual concessions.

The working of the English Act, however, virtually excluded Scotland from the fertile field of colonial and foreign trade, and was thus one of the factors leading to the Darien Scheme. But after the Union of 1707 Scotland benefited by the Navigation Act (and its amendments) in that Scottish shipbuilding was encouraged and Scottish vessels could now carry Scottish products to the Plantations and bring back colonial produce, notably tobacco, molasses and cotton—all leading to the development of industrial Glasgow.

1661. *Act for encourageing of Shiping and Navigation*

Our Soverane Lord, Considering that the wealth, safety and strenth of this his Kingdome are very much concerned in the increase of shiping and encouradgement of trade and navigation, both which are much decayed if not wholly ruined by the late unhappie wars, and the sad effects that have followed therupon, And perceaveing the present low condition of trade and the small number of Ships and seamen within this Kingdome, Hath thoght expedient out of his Princely zeale for the publict good, with advice and consent of his Estates of Parliament now presently conveened, to Statute and Ordaine, And by these presents Statuts and Ordaines, That from and after the [*blank*] day of [*blank*] and thenceforward no goods nor commodities whatsoever that are of forrane grouth, product or manufactorie which are to be broght into Scotland or any of the yles thereto belonging shall be shiped or brought from any other place or places Cuntrie or Cuntries But only from those places wher the saids Commodities doe grow, are produced or made or from the ports wher the saids goods and commodities commonly are or usually have been first shipped for transportation, and from no other place or Cuntrie, and in no other ships or vessells but such as doe truely and only belong to his said Kingdome ; and whairof the Master and three fourt parts of the mariners are natives and inhabitants within the same, Or at least in such ships and vessells as doe truely and only belong unto, and are of the build of these Kingdomes or Cuntries wher the saids Commodities doe grow, are made or produced, and whairof the Master and three fourt parts of the mariners are natives and inhabitants within the same . . . under the paine of confiscation of all such goods . . . as also of the ship in which they shall happin to be imported . . . And further it is Statute and ordained by his Majestie, with advice and consent forsaid, That all goods or commodities whatsoever produced or shipped as is above exprest which from and after the said day and thenceforward shall be imported into this Kingdome or any Ilands therto belonging in any ships or vessells that shall not truely and only belong to the Natives and inhabitants thairof (except in English or Irish vessells, Provyding alwayes that Scots vessells enjoy the lyke benefite of trade within the Kingdomes and dominions of England and Ireland and no otherwayes) Shall be lyable to double custome and pay accordinglie whither the saids goods perteane to natives or aliens. And further it is Statute and Ordained that from and after the said day and thenceforward all goods and commodities whatsoever belonging to aliens exported or imported in whatsoever ships or vessells whither forrane or Scotish shall be lyable to double custome and pay accordingly. And it is further Statute and ordained that from and after the said day and thence fordward, all goods or commodities whatsoever exported in any other ships or vessells then such as doe truely and only belong to the natives and inhabitants of this Kingdome shall be lyable to double custome and pay accordingly whither the saids goods apperteane to Natives or aliens. And it is further enacted and ordained by his Majestie with advice and consent forsaid That at and after the said day and thence fordward all ships and vessells belonging to this Kingdome

Shall be navigated only by Scotismen duelling in Scotland, at least the master and three fourt parts of the seamen being such, under the paine of being esteemed forraigne vessells and paying double custome for all the goods and commodities imported or exported within the same. . . . And it is further Statute and Ordained that no merchants belonging to this Kingdome shall imploy any alien or persone not borne within this Nation or naturalized or made a frie Denizen therof from and after the said day as factor in any place beyond seas for the use and accompt of the merchants of this Kingdome, under paine of a pecuniary mulct . . . It is always heirby provydit that this act nor any clause thairin contained extend not to or be meaned to restraine or prohibite the importation of any of the commodities of Asia, Africa or America, as also of the commodities of Musco and Italie from such ports and places and in such ships and vessells as may be gotten most conveniently untill such time as the merchants of this Kingdome have actuall trade to these respective places . . . It is heirby declared that it shall be lawfull to import any sort of cornes in tyme of dearth from any place or places in any ship or vessell whatsoever without being lyable to confiscation, double custome or any other penaltie contained in this present act ; the dearth and necessity of import being alwayes cognosced and declared by a publict act of the Privy Councill or Councill of Trade.

A.P.S., vii, 257, c. 277

In addition to the Navigation Act ' customs barriers ' were erected, and the protection of the cloth industry was particularly strengthened in 1663 by the imposition of heavy duties on English cloth. It is to be noted, too, in light of the ' Act discharging the exportation of skins and hides,' that duties were placed on English gloves as well as tobacco.

1663. *Act for ane new Imposition upon English Commodities*

The Estates of Parliament Considering how much it concernes the credite and wealth of the Kingdome that our oune native Commodities be manufactured amongst our selves, And that the endeavours of such persones as are setting up manufacturies and trades have been and are much retarded by the importation of such forraigne commodities as may be made within the Kingdome. Thairfor and for their due encouragement The Kings Majestie with advice and consent of the Estates of Parliament Statuts and Ordaines that from and after the first day of September next, tuelve pund scots upon ilk ell of broad english cloath sex punds upon ilk ell of yorkshire and all narrow cloath ; tuo pund eight shillings upon ilk ell of searge ; thirtie shillings upon ilk ell of castilians ; fourty eight punds upon ilk bevar hat ; tuenty four punds upon ilk demy beaver and vigon ; [1] and three punds upon the peice of ilk common hat ; thirtie sex punds upon the dozen of worsteid stockings ; tuenty four punds upon the dozen of stag gloves, and tuelffe punds upon the dozen of single stags, cordivans,[2] kid or shiverings ; [3] and tuenty four shillings upon ilk pund of tobacco imported either for sale or private use into this Kingdom from England, all scots money ; be exacted leveyed and collected ; and fourscore per cent upon all other sorts of commodities imported into this Kingdome from England and not particularly named in this act, and upon all the grouth and manufactury of that Kingdome though imported from any other place, And that over and above all other impositions put upon the samen already. And to the effect this present act may be the more exactly put to execution ; It is Statute and Ordained that all goods imported from England or of the grouth and manufactury of England, not above particularly exprest, shall be valued after sighting, by tuo skilfull honest men, upon oath, to be nominat by the Dean of Gild or his assessors or Magistrats of the burgh, or next adjacent Burgh to the Custome Office wher the saids goods are entered, or by the oath of the partie to whom the saids goods belongs and accordingly pay the said fourscore per cent . . . And if any of the forsaids goods or commodities shall be informed and made appear

[1] vicuña   [2] gloves of goat-skin   [3] split leather

to be brought in or shall be seized upon not being entered in the custome Office, or any other Office appointed for that effect, Then the same to be wholly confiscat, the one halff to his Majesties use, and the other halff to the first informer or seizer therof.

A.P.S., vii, 465, c. 23

Charles II's Dutch War, with its naval engagements in 1665, again interrupted Scotland's trade with the Low Countries, and now Scottish trade began to look westwards. Many of the old eastern ports which had for so long traded across the North Sea began to decline ; and this change led to the rise of Glasgow. The growth and development of Glasgow was at first mainly due to the post-1603 amicable relations with England which enabled the west-coast route to Europe to be used without running the hazard of English interception ; but then came a highly prosperous trade with America, authorised from 1654 to 1660, illicit from 1660 to the turn of the century, and permanent after 1707.

In both the following mid-century accounts Glasgow is spoken of as an already important mercantile port.

1655. *The Trade of Glasgow in the mid-seventeenth century*

The inhabitants [of Glasgow] are traders and dealers : some for Ireland with small smiddy coales, in open boates, from foure to ten tonnes, from whence they bring hoopes, ronges, barrell staves, meale, oates, and butter ; some from France with pladding, coales, and herring (of which there is a greate fishing yearly in the Westerne Sea,) for which they return salt, paper, rosin and prunes ; some to Norway for timber ; and every one with theyr neighbours the Highlanders, who come hither from the isles and westerne parts ; in summer by the Mul of Cantyre, and in winter by the Torban [Tarbert] to the head of the Loquh Fyn (which is a small neck of sandy land, over which they usually drawe theyr small boates into the Firth of Dunbarton) and soe passe up in the Cluyde with pladding, dry hides, goate, kid and deere skyns, which they sell, and purchase with theyr price such comodityes and provisions as they stand in neede of, from

327

time to time. Here hath likewise beene some who have adventured as farre as the Barbadoes ; but the losse they have sustayned by reason of theyr goeing out and comeing home late every yeare, have made them discontinue goeing thither any more. The scituation of this towne in a plentifull land, and the mercantile genius of the people, are strong signes of her increase and groweth, were she not checqued and kept under by the shallownesse of her river, every day more and more increasing and filling up, soe that noe vessells of any burden can come neerer up then within fourteene miles, where they must unlade.

Thomas Tucker, in Hume Brown, *Early Travellers In Scotland*, 177

1656.

We are to consider the merchants and traders in this eminent Glasgow, whose store-houses and ware-houses are stuft with merchandize, as their shops swell big with foreign commodities, and returns from France, and other remote parts, where they have agents and factors to correspond, and inrich their maritime ports, whose charter exceeds all the charters in Scotland ; which is a considerable advantage to the city-inhabitants, because blest with privileges as large, nay, larger than any other corporation. Moreover, they dwell in the face of France, and a free trade, as I formerly told you. Nor is this all, for the staple of their country consists of linens, friezes, furs, tartans, pelts, hides, tallow, skins, and various other small manufactures and commodities, not comprehended in this breviat. Besides, I should remind you, that they generall exceed in good French wines, as they naturally superabound with fish and fowl.

Richard Franck, ibid., 192

RECOVERY IN THE CLOSING DECADES OF THE CENTURY

In 1681 Parliament again turned its attention to the encouragement of trade and manufactures, and an act passed in that year,
virtually a repetition of the legislation of 1661, was a reaffirmation
of a full system of ' protection.'

1681. *Act for encouraging Trade and Manufacturies*

Our Soveraigne lord, from his princely cair for the wealth
and flourishing of this his ancient kingdom, considering that
the importation of forreign commodities (which are superfluous or may be made within the kingdom by encouragement given to the manufactures thereof) had exceidingly
exhausted the money of the kingdom and hightned the
exchange to forraign places so that in a short time the stock
of money behooved to be exhausted and the trade thereof
to fail. . . . Therefore His Majestie with advice and consent of the Estates of Parliament strictly prohibits and discharges all merchants and other persons whatsoever to
import into this kingdom any gold or silver threed, gold or
silver laces, fringes or traceings, all buttons of gold or silver
threed, all manner of stuffs or ribbands in which ther is any
gold or silver threed, all philagram of gold or silver to be
worne upon apparrell and all counterfeits of any of them,
all flour'd, strip'd, figur'd, chequer'd, painted or printed
silk stuffs or ribbands (noways comprehending changing
colloured or wattered stuffs or ribbands), all embroideries
of silk upon wearing cloathes, . . . any forraigne Holland
linnen, cambrick, lawn, dornick, damesk, tyking, bousten
or damety, tufted or stripped holland, calliqo, selesia or
East India linnen all other forraigne cloaths and stuffs made
of linnen or cottoun wooll or lint, . . . all foreign silk or
woolen stockings, all forraign laces made of silk, gimp or
threed, all forraign laces or point of any sort or colour, all
foreign-made gloves, schoes, boots, or slippers, all wearing
cloaths made abroad for men, women or children. . . .

Lykeas His Majestie ratifies and approves all acts alredy made for the encouragement of the manufactures of this kingdom and encouragement of strangers to come thereto and set up their several callings therin : and anent the weaving and bleatching of linnen cloath declaring that if any strangers shall come or be brought into this kingdom by natives to set up work and teach his art of making of cloaths, stuffs, stockings, soap or any kind of manufactory, that he shall enjoy the benefite of law and all other privileges that a native doeth enjoy : with power to set up manufacturies either in burgh or landward as they shall think fit and ther to dwell and exercise their trade without any stop or trouble ; and that they shall have libertie and freedome of trade, and to buy and purchas lands and immovable, and all other privileges, liberties and capacities that do belong to any native subject born within this kingdom.

And for the farther encouragement of manufacturies, all oyl, dying stuffs, forraigne wooll, lint and flax, pot-ashes or any other materials whatsoever usefull for manufactories that shall be imported, are hereby declared to be free of custome and excise, and all other publick dues in all tyme coming : and that all cloaths, stuffs, stockings or any other commodities to be made and exported by them shall be free of all custom and excise for the space of nynteen yeers after the date hereof. And it is farder declared that any stock imployed or to be imployed for erecting and entertaining any manufacturies, the same shall be free of all privat and publick taxes whatsoever, and all quartering and levyeing of soldiers ; and that all servants of the saids manufacturies shall be free of watching, warding, militia or levies during their actual service therin for the space of seven yeers after the date hereof.

A.P.S., viii, 348–9

By now the country had recovered from the exhaustion of the Civil War and the Cromwellian union ; and now arose a number of joint-stock companies of which the ' Cloth Manufactory at New Mills ' is a typical example, where it will be noticed that

' encouragement ' even extended to the remission of excise on liquor consumed locally by masters or servants. But other industries were also springing up. About fifty undertakings are known to have been ' erected ' under the act of 1681—most of them as joint-stock companies—including the Royal Fishing Company (capital, £25,000),[1] the Glasgow Soap Company (capital, £11,700), the Bank of Scotland (capital, £10,000), the Linen Company (capital, about £10,000),[2] and other ' privileged ' companies for sugar, silk, sail-cloth, rope and cordage, pottery, paper, gunpowder and iron.[3]

1693. *Act Erecting the Woollen Manufactory at Newmilnes in a free Incorporation*

Our Soveraigne Lord and Lady the King and Queens Majesties and the Estates of Parliament, Considering the great advantages that arise to other Nations, and particularly to our neighbour Nation of England, by the erecting and carrying on of Manufactories, especially these of Cloath, which do not only serve them at home, but vast Quantities thereof are to their great advantage exported, besides the imploying and plenteously intertaining a great number of poor people . . . And now seing that divers of their Majesties good subjects . . . have already entered into a Contract of Society and Copartnery for Erecting and Carrying on a Manufactory at Newmilnes, and advanced a considerable Stock for that effect, and have also agreed that the said Stock shall remain mortifyed for the ends forsaid,

[1] There had been previous attempts to cut out the prosperous Dutch fishing companies. In the reign of James VI a Scottish Whale Fishing Company was granted a patent, but the patent was recalled through opposition in England ; a new Fishing Company was set up in the reign of Charles I, but was a failure ; and this third attempt—the Royal Fishing Company—apparently lost the whole of its subscribed capital (*S.H.R.*, i, 174-5).

[2] See W. R. Scott (ed.), *Records of a Scottish Cloth Manufactory at New Mills* (Scot. Hist. Soc.), Intro., pp. xxxiv-xlvi.

[3] For details of a number of these industrial undertakings, see the articles by W. R. Scott in *S.H.R.*, i, 407-15 ; ii, 52-60, 287-97, 406-11 ; iii, 71-6.

331

And their Majesties and Estates forsaids being willing to give all due incouragement for advanceing so generous and profitable ane undertaking, Therefore their Majesties and Estates of Parliament not only declare the forsaid Society and Copartnery to be a Manufactory, but also erects The said Partners and Society into a free and lawful Incorporation, with all priviledges usuall . . . provyded in favoures of Manufactories by the former laws of this Kingdom. . . .

[*The principal Stock and all houses and buildings and warehouses to be used for carrying on the Manufactory. Arrangements for transfer of Stock. Books to be kept by the Society.*]

. . . And further their Majesties and Estates of Parliament Doe Statute and Ordaine That all Materialls, Instruments and others whatsoever needfull and usefull for the said Manufactory to be imported whether in forreigne vessells or these belonging to this kingdom, as likeways all Cloaths, Stuffs, Stockings or other work made by the Incorporation of the said Manufactorie and exported, shall be free of Custome, Excyse and all other publick dues for the space of twenty one yeares next after the date of this present act, And . . . that the Stock of the said Manufactory, advanced and to be advanced, and profites thereof, and all lands and others acquired for the use of the same, and houses built or to be built thereon shall be free of all Cesses, Supplyes, Taxations, Excyse, or other publick burthens imposed during the space forsaid. . . .

[*Liquor consumed by masters or servants within the town and lands of Newmilnes to be free of excise for the said space of twenty one years. The lands and houses, with their inhabitants, to be free of all quartering of soldiers. No military officer to enlist any of the servants of the Manufactory.*]

And that it shall not be lawfull to any person or persons whatsomever, or any other Incorporation or Manufactory, to entertain in their private service, or for the use of any other Manufactory, any of the servants belonging to the said Manufactory of Newmilns, untill they first serve out their time, conform to their severall agreements, and that the said Partners shall have power to call back and retain any

332

of their said Servants, wherever they can be found . . .
And further, it is hereby Statute and Ordained that all the
Regiments, Troops and soldiers of the Scots Establishment
shall be obliged to furnish themselves with Cloaths of the
product of this Kingdom, Discharging hereby any licence
or dispensation to the contrair. . . .

A.P.S., ix, 317, c. 53

1695. *Act in favours of Robert Douglas anent his Manufactories
of Soap, Sugar, and Starch at Leith*

Forasmuch as by the act of Parliament [1661] Intituled
Act for encourageing Soap works, all oyle potashes and other
materials of any kind to be imported for the use of Soap
works for making of Soap, and all Soap made within the
Countrey are Declared free of all Custom and excise and
all other publick and privat dues whatsoever And also that
all Soap so made and exported shall be free for the space of
nynteen years after the setting up of these works, Likas by
the Acts of Parliament [1661 and 1681] several Immunities,
Liberties and priviledges are granted to Manufactories for
the Encouragement therof, And his Majesty and the Estates
of Parliament Considering that Robert Douglas, Soapboyler
in Lieth, hath for these many years been a great promoter
of Manufactories and particularly hath much advanced the
Manufactory of Soap and for that end did much contribut
to the setting up of the Trade to Archangel in Russia and to
Greenland chiefly designed to be encouraged by these Acts,
As also hath laid out a great part of his stock in building
and preparing a Soap and Sugar work which he still intends
to prosecute with further improvements, And likewayes to
sett up two other Manufactories viz. one for making of white
and painted earthen veshels and pots commonly called leam
or purselein, and another for making of starch which may
tend to the great benefit and advantage of the Realm,
Therefore his Majesty with advice and consent of the forsaids Estates of Parliament Declares the said Robert
Douglas his Soap work already set up to be a Manufactory

And doth also revive his Sugar work, Declaring the same to be a Manufactory, And farder Doth hereby allow him to set up the forsaid Manufactory of making starch, white and painted earthen pots and veshels or scots purslein commonly called leam work And that the saids Manufactories shall have all the liberties priviledges and immunities granted by the forsaids acts And that the said Robert Douglas his Sugar work shall have all the priviledges and exemptions granted to the sugar works of Glasgow especially to make and vend Rhum to the quantity of eighteen tuns yearly free of all Custom and excise not to be made use of within the Kingdom, with Certification thir priviledges of the Manufactory shall be forfaulted, Therefore and for the greater Encouragement of the Manufactories forsaid and Trade to Archangel in Russia, Greenland and America It is Declared that this present Act as to the forsaid Manufactories and the liberties priviledges and immunities hereby granted to them shall Continow to the said Robert Douglas and also in favors of Robert Douglas his sone and their heirs, successors and partners for the space of nynteen years from and after Lambas One thousand Six hundred nynty five for the saids Manufactories.

A.P.S., ix, 491, c. 84

1695. *Act for Erecting a Publick Bank*

Our soveraign lord, considering how usefull a Publick Bank may be in this Kingdom . . . and that the same can only be best sett up and managed by persons in Company with a Joynt Stock sufficiently indowed. . . . Hath therefore allowed and with the advice and consent of the Estates of Parliament allowes a joynt stock amounting to the soume of twelve hundred thousand pounds money [1] to be raised by the Company hereby Established for the Carying on and manageing of a publick Bank. . . .

And all and every the persons Subscribing and paying in

---

[1] That is, £100,000 sterling, of which £10,000 sterling was paid up (see Charles A. Malcolm, *The Bank of Scotland*, App. A).

to the said stock . . . shall be and are hereby Declared
to be one Body Corporat and Politique by the name of
' The Governour and Company of the Bank of Scotland ' . . .

And it is farder hereby Statute and Ordained that it shall
be lawfull for the said Governour and Company to Lend
upon real or personal Security any summ or summs and to
receave annual rent for the same at Six per Cent as shall be
ordinary for the time . . .

It is hereby Statute that the joynt stock of the said Bank
continowing in money shall be free from all publick burdens
to be imposed upon money for the space of twenty one years
after the date hereof. . . .

And it is likewise hereby Provided that all Forraigners
who shall joyn as Partners of this Bank shall thereby be and
become naturalised Scotsmen to all intents and purposes
whatsoever.

A.P.S., ix, 494–7

As compared with cloth, however, the linen industry was now
proving more successful. The old act of 1661 ' discharging the
exportation of linen yarn ' was repeated in 1693 and 1695, the
import of linen yarn and the export of linen cloth were made
duty free, and in 1686, ' for the encouradgement of linen manufactories ' it had been laid down that burial was to be made in
' linen or cloath of hards [1] made and spunn within this kingdom.'

1686. *Act for burying in Scotts Linnen*

Our Soveraigne Lord, for the encouradgement of linen
manufactories within this Kingdome and prevention of the
exportation of the moneys therof, for the buying and importing of linen, Doeth, with advice and consent of his
Estates of Parliament, Statute and ordaine That hereafter
no Corps of any Person or Persons whatsoever shall be
buried in any shirt, sheet or any thing else except in plaine
linen or cloath of hards made and spunn within the Kingdom without lace or poynt, Dischargeing from hencefurth
the makeing use of Holland or uther linen cloath made in

[1] A coarser weave from flax

335

other Kingdomes all silke hair or woollen gold or silver or any other stuff whatsoever then what is made of flax or hards spunn and wrought within the Kingdome as said is, and that under the pain and penalty of thrie hundered punds scots toties quoties for a nobleman, and 200 lib. for each other Persone, wherof one halfe to the discoverer and the other halfe to the Poor of the paroch where the saids corps shall be so interred And for the better discovery of the contraveeners It is hereby further statute and ordained that every minister within the Kingdome shall keep a book containing ane exact accompt and register of all persons buried within ther said parish As also that some one or moe of the relations of the Person deceased or other Credible Person (tenents in the Countrey and Cottars being always excepted) shall within eight dayes after such interment bring a certificat upon oath in wryteing, witnessed by tuo famous persons, to the minister declareing that the said person was wind or wrapt in maner herein prescribed, which certificates are to be recorded by the minister or reader of the Parish gratis without exacting any money therfor, And if no relation of the Pairtie buried or other person shall bring such a certificat within the said tyme of eight dayes that then and in that caice the goods and gear of the Pairty deceased shall be and are hereby declared lyable to the forsaid forfaultur to be pursued at the instance of the minister of the said parish befor any Judge Competent. . . . And it is hereby statute and ordained that if the minister in whose parish any such Corps shall be so interred prove negligent in pursueing the Contraveeners within sex moneths after the said buriall he is hereby declared lyable for the said fyne the one halfe to the poor, and the other halfe to the discoverer to be divided in maner forsaid, As also his Majestie with advice forsaid, statuts and ordaines, that no wooden Coffin shall exceed ane hundered merks scots as the highest rate for Persones of the greatest quality and soe proportionaly for Persones of meaner qualitie under the paine of tuo hundered merks scots for each contravention.

A.P.S., viii, 598, c. 28

[This act was confirmed in 1695, with the additions : (1) 'That none presume to cause bury any in Scots Linen in value above twenty shilling Scots per ell under the same pains sett doun in the forsaid Act against burying in forraign Linen'; (2) 'That the nearest elder or Deacon of the paroch with one nieghbour or two be called by the persons concerned and present to the putting of the dead Corps in the Coffin, that they may see the same done, and that the forsaid Act with this present Addition is observed, and Subscribe the Certificat'; and (3) 'That it shall not be leisome to any person to make or sew any sort of dead Linen contrar to the forsaid Act and this present addition under the pain of fourty merks toties quoties, for the use of the poor as said is.'—*A.P.S.*, ix, 461, c. 66.]

1693.   *Prohibition of the Export of Lint and Linen Yarn*

[*On the narrative that the laws for the right making of linen cloth have been hitherto neglected, their majesties and the estates*] strictly prohibit and discharge all merchants or other persons natives or strangers to export from this kingdom any lint of the native growth thereof, or any linnen yarne whatsomever, under the penalty of confiscation [*and provide for uniform measurement of linen cloth and for the stamping of linen, before export, with a stamp of a royal burgh.*]

A.P.S., ix, 311

An Act of 1695 (*A.P.S.*, ix, 430) confirmed this statute and also ratified the privileges of the linen manufactory at Paul's Work, Edinburgh, and the Citadel of Leith, which had been incorporated in 1693 (*A.P.S.*, ix, 316).

THE DARIEN SCHEME

Tension between English and Scottish commercial interests had all along been inherent in the protectionist policy so vigorously pursued since the Restoration. If Scotland barred English cloth, England strove to bar Scottish linen ; Scotland wished to retain her wool for manufacture at home, and import English wool, whereas England would gladly have imported Scottish wool, retained her own, and exported her cloth. Other countries like-wise adopted a policy of protection, and Scotland, a late and poor competitor, found herself hampered by lack of markets. The effects of these developments were aggravated by the ex-clusive English colonial policy and by English foreign policy, for the wars with Holland and France had gone far to disrupt the traditional pattern of Scottish trade, and there was no com-pensation (despite a not inconsiderable illicit trade with the plantations) for the loss of old markets. In proportion as Scot-land's own policy of protection was successful in fostering her manufactures, the limitation of markets was increasingly felt, and the Darien Scheme was the outcome.

A ' Memorial concerning the Scottish plantation to be erected in some place of America ' was presented to the Privy Council's Committee of Trade in 1681,[1] and in succeeding years two attempts were made to form Scottish colonies—one in New Jersey (1682–1702) and another in South Carolina (1684–6).[2] In 1691 and 1693 colonial projects were again under consideration.[3]

In 1693 the Scottish parliament, in an Act for Encouraging of Foreign Trade, offered to companies formed to trade with the East and West Indies, Africa and the Mediterranean the privileges already enjoyed by companies for manufactures.[4] Two years later it passed the Act founding the Company of Scotland trading to Africa and the Indies. The Scottish desire to find new markets was only one element in the origin of this so-called ' Darien Company ' ; the scheme owed so much to *English* desires to find a legal means of competing with the existing East India Company that of the original capital of £600,000, half was for English subscription, the company's first headquarters were in London, and the directorate was half English. The act of incorporation did, however, authorise the planting of colonies.

William, who found himself king over two countries whose parliaments were supporting irreconcilable policies, dismissed the Commissioner who had given the royal assent to the act, on the ground that he had exceeded his instructions. In the English parliament, the East India Company and other trading interests were so effectively mobilised that they secured the withdrawal

[1] *R.P.C.*, 3rd ser., vii, 664–5
[2] See G. P. Insh, *Scottish Colonial Schemes*
[3] G. P. Insh, *The Company of Scotland*, 26   [4] *A.P.S.*, ix, 34

of English capital and the frustration of subsequent Scottish attempts to raise capital in Hamburg. The effect on the Scots was to reinforce commercial ambitions by patriotic resentment, and it was arranged that the whole of a reduced capital of £400,000 should be subscribed in Scotland.

The plan for the colony at Darien was a secondary development in the company's activities. Apart from the climatic disadvantages, Spanish hostility was certain ; and, in view of William's delicate negotiations on the subject of the Spanish Succession, English opposition was inevitable. The English colonies were forbidden to help the enterprise in any way ; this policy localised the breach with Spain, but ensured the failure of the colony.

Darien had brought to a head the long-standing tension between English and Scottish commercial interests, and the difficulties it raised for the king were a lesson in the weakness of the personal union. Above all, the scheme swallowed up so much of the available Scottish capital that the country was left without resources for new undertakings, and the need to share in English commercial and colonial enterprise was more urgent than ever.

1695. *Act for a Company trading to Africa and the Indies*

[*After reference to the act of* 1693, *which permitted the establishment of companies for foreign trade*] His majesty, understanding that several persons as well forreigners as natives of this kingdom are willing to engage themselves with great soumes of money in an American, Affrican and Indian trade, to be exercised in and from this kingdom, . . . therefore . . . doth . . . constitut John, Lord Belhaven [*and twenty other named persons*] . . . and all others whom the forsaids persons and these joyned with them, or major part of them being assembled, shall admitt and joyn into their joynt stock and trade . . . to be one body incorporat, and a free incorporation, with perpetual succession, by the name of the Company of Scotland tradeing to Affrica and the Indies, providing allwayes, likeas it is hereby in the first place provided, that of the fond or capital stock that shall be agreed to be advanced and imployed by the forsaid undertakers, and their copartners, the halfe at least shall be appoynted and allotted for Scottish men within this kingdom [*failing subscription by whom by* 1 *August* 1696, *Scotsmen residing abroad or foreigners may subscribe*] lik as the quota of every mans part of the said stock . . . shall be for the least one hundred pound sterlin, and for the highest or greatest, thre thousand pound sterlin ;

With power to the said company to have a common seal . . . as also to plead and sue, and be sued, and to purchase, acquire, possess and enjoy lordships, lands, tenements with other estate real or personal . . . and to dispose upon and alienat the same . . .

With power likwise to the forsaid company, by subscription or otherwise, . . . to raise a joynt stock or capital for.d of such a sum or sums of money and under and subject unto such rules, conditions and qualifications as by the forsaid company, or major part of them when assembled, shall be limited and appoynted to begin, carry on and support their intended trade of navigation and whatever may contribut to the advancement therof.

And the said company is hereby impowered to equip, fitt, sett out, fraught and navigat their own or hired ships in such manner as they shall think fitt [*with dispensation from the terms of the Navigation Act of* 1661] from any of the ports or places of this kingdom, or from any other ports or places in amity, or not in hostility with his majesty, in warlike or other manner to any lands, islands, countreyes or places in Asia, Affrica, or America, and there to plant collonies, build cityes, touns or forts, in or upon the places not inhabited, or in or upon any other place, by consent of the natives or inhabitants thereof and not possest by any European soveraign, potentate, prince or state . . . and by force of arms to defend their trade and navigation, colonies, cityes, tounes, forts and plantations . . . and to make and conclude treaties of peace and commerce with the soveraigns, princes, estates, rulers, governours or proprietors of the forsaids lands, islands, countries or places. . . .

None of the liedges of this kingdom shall or may trade or navigat to any lands, islands, countreyes or places in Asia, or

Affrica in any time hereafter, or in America for and during the space of thirty one years . . . without license and permission in writing from the said company. . . .

And it is further hereby enacted that the said company shall have the free and absolut right and property (only relieving and holding of his majesty . . . for the only acknowledgement of their alleagiance, and paying yearly a hogshead of tobacco, in the name of blensh duty, if required allennarly) in and to all such lands . . . that they shall come to . . . possess . . . as also to all manner of treasures, wealth, riches, profits, mines, minerals, fishings, with the whole product and benefit therof. . . .

And farder it is hereby statute that all ships, vessels, merchandise, goods, and other effects whatsoever belonging to the said company shall be free of all manner of restraints or prohibitions, and of all customs, taxes, cesses, supplies or other duties imposed, or to be imposed, by act of parliament or otherwise, for and during the space of twenty one years. . .

A.P.S., ix, 377–80

1698. *Sailing Orders for the first Expedition to Darien*

By the . . . Committee of the Court of Directors of the Indian and African Company of Scotland.

Gentlemen,—By virtue of the power and authority to us given by the Court of Directors of the Indian and African Company of Scotland, you are hereby ordered in pursuance of your voyage to make the Crab Island, and if you find it free to take possession thereof in name of the Company ; and from thence you are to proceed to the Bay of Darien and make the Isle called the Golden Island, which lies close by the shore some few leagues to the leeward of the mouth of the great River of Darien, in and about eight degrees of north latitude ; and there make a settlement on the mainland as well as the said island, if proper (as we believe) and unpossessed by an European nation or state in amity with his Majesty ; but if otherways, you are to bear to the leeward

. . . Given under our hands at Edinburgh the twelfth day of July 1698.

To the councellors for the time being appointed for the government of the Indian and African Company of Scotlands' intended Colony of Caledonia in America.

G. Pratt Insh, *Darien Papers* (Scot. Hist. Soc.), 64–5

The Expeditions to Darien

The first expedition reached Darien in November 1698 and abandoned the settlement in June 1699. When the ship *Caledonia* reached the Sound of Islay, Captains William Murray and Robert Drummond were sent to Edinburgh with a letter for the directors of the Company. At a meeting on 28 November these messengers were examined, and reported as follows :

That for near about two months before they came away, officers, seamen and planters were seized with a severe sickness of fever, ague and flux. That near about 200 persons died before they came away. That their sickness and mortality happened through want of fresh provisions and strong liquors, which they said was the occasion of their coming away. That the scarcity of fresh provisions and strong liquors was occasioned by the proclamations published against them in Jamaica and the other English plantations, which hindered several ships and brigantines that were desyned to come and others acoming to them till the proclamations stopped them. . . . That the men kept all their health very well as long as they had fresh provisions and strong liquors, for that climate was undoubtedly as wholesome as any in America and that water singularly good ; that the Indians were very angry at their coming away.

That they spent their time while there mostly in fortifying and building. That they had neither time nor hands enough to plant, but only some few things for experiment, such as yams, Indian corn and Jamaica pease, which they said came to perfection in five weeks time. . . .

That many of the landsmen seemed willing rather to stay than come away as dreading the danger and tediousness of a long voyage, but that the generality they believed were willing to come away by reason they had not heard one word from Scotland all the time they were there, and believed that by reason of the severity of the proclamations none would be allowed to be sent to them, which put them, they said, in a kind of despair that the Company was wholly crushed at home.

Darien Papers (Scot. Hist. Soc.), 109–10

A second, minor expedition reached Darien only to find the settlement abandoned, and a third sailed from Scotland in September 1699, before the news of the abandonment had been confirmed. The following letter was written by a member of the third expedition, from Jamaica, on 28 February 1700.

The people [in Montserrat] told us they were informed that ours had deserted the colony, which we took only for a made-story, but we found it but too true att our arrival there, which was on St. Andrew's day [in 1699]. You would best imagine how melancholy a disappointment it was to us, when we expected that all was in a flourishing condition, to find an entire desertion. . . . As to the transactions of those who had the first government, it's what I cannot give you an account, for we are still in the mist what game they played, there are shrewd suspicions that it has been all false. . . . There has certainly been a deal of villainy acted amongst them, but by whom is not yet found out. . . . I believe the company will never get a true account of their effects, for it's more than probable that some have made estates out of them. . . .

I hope the directors, by the sad experience they have had of the mismanagements of the former colony and the prejudice they have sustained by delays and misunderstandings, will fall upon methods to prevent the like for the future and to support this by sending speedy supplies, which is in a very tottering condition for want of provisions, particularly

343

liquor, which has caused a great mortality, for it is simply impossible that men can subsist on salt and water if they have not some strong drink to qualify it ; with which they cannot be so conveniently supplied from Scotland, because of the distance, as from this and the neighbouring islands, who would willingly not only trade but also come and live among us if the prohibition were taken off, without which I doubt much if ever we will maintain that colony.

I wish to God we may surmount the difficulties we are now in and fall into a right model of government and a good understanding that a regular way may be fallen upon for our subsistence till such time as we can do it of ourselves. If that be done, there's no doubt but that colony will prosper yet, and in time not only reimburse the vast charges the kingdom has been at, but also enrich us, so that we may be known in the world to be a nation. . . .

Henrietta Tayler, The Seven Sons of the Provost, 30–32

Chapter Nine

SOCIAL AND ECONOMIC CONDITIONS

Travellers' Accounts

1598. *Fynes Moryson*

. . . Touching their diet : They eate much red Colewort and Cabbage, but little fresh meate, using to salt their Mutton and Geese, which made me more wonder, that they used to eate Beefe without salting. The Gentlemen reckon their revenewes, not by rents of monie, but by chauldrons of victuals, and keepe many people in their Families, yet living most on Corne and Rootes, not spending any great quantity on fleshe. My selfe was at a Knights House, who had many servants to attend him, that brought in his meate with their heads covered with blew caps, the Table being more then halfe furnished with great platters of porredge,[1] each having a little peece of sodden meate : And when the Table was served, the servants did sit downe with us, but the upper messe in steede of porredge,[1] had a Pullet with some prunes in the broth. And I observed no Art of Cookery, or furniture of Houshold stuffe, but rather rude neglect of both . . . They vulgarly eate harth Cakes of Oates, but in Cities have also wheaten bread, which for the most part was bought by Courtiers, Gentlemen, and the best sort of Citizens. . . .

They drinke pure Wines, not with sugar as the English, yet at Feasts they put Comfits in the Wine. . . .

Their bedsteads were then like Cubbards in the wall, with doores to be opened and shut at pleasure, so as we climbed up to our beds. They used but one sheete, open at the sides and top, but close at the feete, and so doubled . . .

Hume Brown, Early Travellers in Scotland, 88–9

---

[1] That is, *pottage* or *broth*

1618. *John Taylor*

. . . For once in the yeere, which is the whole moneth
of August, and sometimes part of September, many of the
nobility and gentry of the kingdome (for their pleasure) doe
come into these high-land countries to hunt, where they
doe conforme themselves to the habite of the High-land-
men, who for the most part, speake nothing but Irish ; and
in former time were those people which were called the
Red-shankes. Their habite is shooes with but one sole
apiece ; stockings (which they call short hose) made of a
warm stuffe of divers colours, which they call Tartane :
as for breeches, many of them, nor their forefathers, never
wore any, but a jerkin of the same stuffe that their hose is of,
their garters being bands or wreathes of hay or straw, with
a plead about their shoulders, which is a mantle of divers
colours, much finer and lighter stuffe then their hose, with
blue flat caps on their heads, a handkerchiefe knit with two
knots about their necke. . . . Now their weapons are long
bowes and forked arrowes, swords and targets, harque-
busses, muskets, durks, and Loquhabor-axes. . . .

Ibid., 120–1

1633. *Sir William Brereton*

. . . About a mile from Dunbar, we observed this
husbandry ; the grass, weeds and wreck, brought by the
sea and with the tide, and left upon the sands, was carried
and laid thick upon the ground. This used for corn . . .
Hence [from Edinburgh Castle] you may take a full view
of the situation of the whole city, which is built upon a hill
nothing oversteep, but sufficiently sloping and ascending
to give a graceful ascent to the great street, which I do take
to be an English mile long, and is the best paved street with
bowther[1] stones (which are very great ones) that I have seen :
the channels are very conveniently contrived on both sides
the streets, so as there is none in the middle ; but it is the

[1] boulder

broadest, largest, and fairest pavement, and that entire, to go, ride, or drive upon.

. . . This street is the glory and beauty of this city . . . indeed the street, if the houses, which are very high, and substantially built of stone (some five, some six stories high), were not lined to the outside and faced with boards, it were the most stately and graceful street that ever I saw in my life ; but this face of boards, which is towards the street, doth much blemish it, and derogate from glory and beauty ; as also the want of fair glass windows, whereof few or none are to be discerned towards the street. . . . This lining with boards (wherein are round holes shaped to the proportion of men's heads), and this encroachment into the street about two yards, is a mighty disgrace unto it . . . if this outside facing of boards were removed, and the houses built uniform all of the same height, it were the most complete street in Christendom. . . .

Touching the fashion of the citizens, the women here wear and use upon festival days six or seven several habits and fashions ; some for distinction of widows, wives and maids, others apparelled according to their own humour and phantasy. Many wear (especially of the meaner sort) plaids, which is a garment of the same woollen stuff whereof saddle cloths in England are made, which is cast over their heads, and covers their faces on both sides, and would reach almost to the ground, but that they pluck them up, and wear them cast under their arms. Some ancient women and citizens wear satin straight-bodied gowns, short little cloaks with great capes, and a broad boun-grace [1] coming over their brows, and going out with a corner behind their heads ; and this boun-grace is, as it were, lined with a white stracht [2] cambric suitable unto it. Young maids not married all are bareheaded ; some with broad thin shag ruffs, which lie flat to their shoulders, and others with half bands with wide necks, either much stiffened or set in wire, which comes only behind . . .

Ibid., 135–41

[1] A shade or broad brim in front of the bonnet   [2] ? starcht, starched

1677. *Thomas Kirke*

The high-ways in Scotland are tolerably good, which is the
greatest comfort a traveller meets with amongst them ; they
have not inns, but change-houses (as they call them), poor
small cottages, where you must be content to take what you
find, perhaps eggs with chicks in them, and some lang cale ;
at the better sort of them, a dish of chap'd chickens, which
they esteem a dainty dish . . . your horses must be sent
to a stablers (for the change-houses have no lodging for
them) where they may feed voluptuously on straw only, for
grass is not to be had, and hay is so much a stranger to them,
that they are scarce familiar with the name of it.

The Scotch gentry commonly travel from one friend's
house to another, so seldom make use of a change-house ;
their way is to hire a horse and a man for two pence a mile ;
they ride on the horse thirty or forty miles a day, and the
man, who is his guide, foots it beside him, and carries his
luggage to boot . . .

Their money is commonly dollars, or mark-pieces,[1]
coined at Edenbrough, but the way of reckoning is sur-
prising to a stranger. To receive a bill of £100 in one of
their change-houses, when one wou'd not suppose they had
any of the value of a hundred pence ; they call a penny a
shilling, and every twenty shillings, *viz.*, twenty pence, a
pound ; so the proportion of their pound to ours is twelve
to one . . .

Ibid., 264–5

1689. *Thomas Morer*

The soil of the country seems to the eye very indifferent,
and tho' they have many fine valleys, which might be im-
proved into a competitorship with our English meadows,
yet for want of sufficient industry and care they become
almost useless, on the account of frequent bogs and waters

---

[1] That is, the fourteen shilling piece

348

in such places. Whence it is, that they have little hay in that kingdom. And tho' there is a competency of grass daily exposed to sale in their towns and villages, yet being cut out of the intervals or little spaces between the ridges of corn, sometimes very distant from one another, they think it more profitable to sell the grass, than to make it into hay for winter ; at which time their horses feed for the most part on straw and oats, which are sold in their markets at tolerable rates. And this is the reason likewise why their arable ground is very considerable ; and 'tis almost incredible how much of the mountains they plough, where the declensions, I had almost said the precipices, are such, that to our thinking, it puts 'em to greater difficulty and charge to carry on their work, than they need be at in draining the valleys.

Their harvest is very great of oats and barly, which is the more common grain of the country, the straw whereof is very serviceable to 'em for the support of the cattle. Not but they have beans, pease, and some wheat likewise, but the oats and barly are most in request, as on which they chiefly depend : on the first for bread, on the other for drink, which is sometimes strong enough to arm 'em against the coldness of the climate. And of their barly there are two sorts ; one of which has double ears, and they call it beer : This they make their malt of, and may be a reason for giving the drink that name. But that which employs great part of their land is hemp, of which they have mighty burdens, and on which they bestow much care and pains to dress and prepare it for making their linen, the most noted and beneficial manufacture of the kingdom.

We seldom meet with inclosures ; either because being a corn country, they would be [1] injured as little as may be by birds which harbour in the hedges ; or being without those long and kind leases the tenants of England have, they are not encouraged by their lords in that and some other improvements ; [2] or that there is want of industry in this,

---

[1] i.e. wish to be ; desire to avoid   [2] cf. vol. ii, 2nd edn., pp. 6–7

and the like cases : So it is, that their fields are open, and without fences, unless here and there they raise out of the road some little continued heaps of stone in the nature of a wall, to secure their crops from the incursions of travellers . . .

The High-landers are not without considerable quantities of corn, yet have not enough to satisfie their numbers, and therefore yearly come down with their cattle, of which they have greater plenty, and so traffick with the Low-landers for such proportions of oats and barly as their families or necessities call for.

They are in great subjection to their lords, who have almost an absolute power over 'em. So that whenever they summon'd 'em, they immediately got together, and attended them whithersoever they went, tho' to the loss of their lives and the little fortune they had. But of late years the scene is changed ; and tho' at this day there are divers instances to be seen of that power of their lords yet their present case is much better, and the yoke easier than it was before.

Nor are they more obedient to their lords than affectionate to their clans, and the heads of their tribes, or families whom they usually have so great a regard to, that they will not, as far as lies in them, suffer 'em to sink under any misfortune. But in case of a small estate, they make an honourable contribution on their behalf, as a common duty or concern to support the credit of their houses. . . .

[Of the Scotch in common] their bread, for the most part, is of oat-meal, which, if thin and well baked upon broad irons or stones for that purpose, is palatable enough, and often brought to gentlemen's tables. But the vulgar are not so curious, for they only water the meal into a convenient consistence, and then making 'em into thick cakes, called bannocks, they set 'em before the fire to be hardened or toasted for their use. These people prepare the oats after this manner—they take several sheaves, and setting fire to 'em consume the straw and chaff to ashes, which, after a convenient time, they blow away, then gathering up the grain sufficiently parched, they bruise it into meal . . .

The vulgar houses, and what are seen in the villages,

are low and feeble. Their walls are made of a few stones jumbled together without mortar to cement 'em : On which they set up pieces of wood meeting at the top, ridge-fashion, but so order'd that there is neither sightliness nor strength ; and it does not cost much more time to erect such a cottage than to pull it down. They cover these houses with turff of an inch thick, and in the shape of larger tiles, which they fasten with wooden pins, and renew as often as there is occasion ; and that is very frequently done. 'Tis rare to find chimneys in these places, a small vent in the roof sufficing to convey the smoak away . . .

They have excellent pit-coal, so bituminous and pitchy that it burns like a candle, and is both pleasant and useful. But this is chiefly for their gentry and boroughs ; the common people deal in peat and turff, cut and dried in the summer, and would be no bad fuel, but that at first kindling it makes a very thick and offensive smother.

They are fond of tobacco, but more from the snush-box than pipe. And they have made it so necessary, that I have heard some of 'em say, that should their bread come in competition with it, they would rather fast than their snush should be taken away. Yet mostly it consists of the coarsest tobacco, dried by the fire, and powdered in a little engine after the form of a tap, which they carry in their pockets, and is both a mill to grind and a box to keep it in. . . .

Stage coaches they have none,[1] yet there are a few hackneys at Edinburg,[2] which they may .hire into the country upon urgent occasions. The truth is, the roads will hardly allow 'em these conveniences, which is the reason that their gentry, men and women, chuse rather to use their horses. However, their great men often travel with coach and six, but with so much caution, that, besides their other attendance, they have a lusty running footman on each side the coach, to manage and keep it in rough places. . . .

They have no horse-posts besides those that ply 'twixt Berwick and Edinburg, and from thence to Port Patrick, for the sake of the Irish packets ; and if I forget not, every

[1] But see *infra*, pp. 354-5   [2] See *infra*, p. 353

town the post passes through contributes to the charges.
But from Edinburgh to Perth, and so to other places, they
use foot-posts [1] and carriers, which, tho' a slow way of
communicating our concerns to one another, yet is such as
they acquiesce in till they have a better . . .

[In Edinburgh] their new houses are made of stone, with
good windows modishly framed and glazed, and so lofty,
that five or six stories is an ordinary height, and one row
of buildings there is near the Parliament Close with no less
than fourteen. . . . Most of the houses, as they are parted
into divers tenements, so they have as many landlords as
stories. . . . Their stairs are unsightly and inconvenient :
for, being built out of the street for the service of every story,
they are sometimes so steepy, narrow, and fenceless, that
it requires care to go up and down for fear of falling. But
in their new houses the contrivance is better ; and the stair-
case, being made within the yard, or foundation of the
building, the ascent and descent is more decent and easie,
and rids the street of an incumbrance, which cannot be
avoided in the other houses. . . .

[In Glasgow] the two main streets are made cross-wise,
well paved and bounded with stately buildings, especially
about the centre, where they are mostly new, with piazzas
under 'em. . . .

Ibid., 266–88

COMMUNICATIONS

Although Kirke states that he found the roads ' tolerably good,'[2]
it is clear that he was referring to their use only for travellers
on horseback or on foot. Morer, writing in 1689, confirms this.[3]
Calderwood's ' Whilliwhaes ' may have been wheedling beggars,
but his wording rather suggests ' highwaymen.'

---

[1] Apparently until 1755 the mail between Inverness and Edinburgh
was still ' conveyed by men on foot ' (J. R. McCulloch, *Statistical
Account of the British Empire*, 1847, i, 299).
[2] *Supra*, p. 348   [3] *Supra*, p. 351

1615. *The Whilliwhaes*

About this tyme, certaine bair and idle gentlemen lay in wait upon passengers, by the ways about Edinburgh, and in other parts of Eist Lothian, and wold needs have money from them. The commone people called them Whilliwhaes.

Calderwood, vii, 201

Morer's reference to hackneys [1] is confirmed by the Edinburgh burgh records, which show that in 1673 there were twenty hackney coaches in operation,[2] and that regulations governing them were issued by the Town Council.

1673, August 20. *Regulations for hackney coaches in the City of Edinburgh*

All hackney coaches are to be numbered.
The coach hire from Edinburgh to Leith is to be 12s. for three persons, 16s. for four persons, 20s. for five persons, and the same for the return journey.
Coach hire from Edinburgh to the Abbey, 9s.
For waiting at Leith or the Abbey, over the time agreed upon, 6s. is to be paid.
A coachman who refuses a hire is to pay double the fare to the would-be hirers.
Coaches must neither trot nor gallop in the streets of the town and suburbs.
Masters and owners of coaches are responsible for their servants' misbehaviour.
Since masters of coaches are responsible for their servants, the latter are to find caution to obey orders.
Only burgesses and persons obtaining the Council's order may keep hackney coaches in or about Edinburgh.

Extracts from the Records of the Burgh of Edinburgh, 1665–80

[1] *Supra*, p. 351
[2] *Extracts from the Records of the Burgh of Edinburgh, 1665-80*, 29 Oct. 1673

In addition to these hackney coaches, the Edinburgh records also
show that there were several attempts to establish a regular coach
service between Edinburgh and Leith,[1] but even that short
journey was both ' difficult and dangerous.' There is thus little
likelihood of the fulfilment of more ambitious projects as, for
example, in 1658, when a stage coach was advertised to run from
London ' to Edinburgh in Scotland, once in three weeks ' at a
fare of £4 10s sterling,[2] or in 1678, when there was an ' intention '
to run a stage coach twice a week between Edinburgh and
Haddington.

1678.

*Supplication by William Lamb, bailie of Haddington, Mr. Robert
Swintoun, indweller there, and Mr. James Lauder, sheriff clerk of
the said burgh, as follows :   Whereas they* have intention to
erect two stage coaches to pass twyse a week throw the whole
year betuixt Edinburgh and Hadingtoun, which will be of
great conveniencie for travaillers of all sorts who may have
occasion to repair to Edinburgh from the eastward, to which
end the petitioners and some other partiners with them are
resolved to imploy a considerable stocke of money for
erecting the said stage coaches, buying of horses, and all
other furniture requisite, in expectatione of some small
profeit by progress of time from the hire of the saids coaches ;
and it being the custome of all princes and estates to encourage such new inventions as this is tending so much to
the good of the leidges, by granting the projectours the sole
benifite of such inventions for severall years *they hereby crave
this privilege for such a time as may be thought expedient. The
Lords grant sole liberty to them of keeping stage coaches between
Edinburgh and Haddington for the space of seven years.*

R.P.C., 3rd ser., v, 381

[1] In 1677 there was a project to set up a service by ' passage waggon,'
drawn by four horses, and to carry ten or more persons, at a fare of
two shillings in summer and three shillings in winter, and using the
coach-house of a former project of 1660 (*Extracts from the Records of the
Burgh of Edinburgh, 1665–80*, 20 April 1677).

[2] *Mercurius Politicus*, 20 May 1658, cited Chambers, *Domestic Annals
of Scotland*, ii, 247

In 1678 there was also a similar project for a stage coach to run between Edinburgh and Glasgow.

1678.

Supplication by William Home, merchant in Edinburgh, to set up with his co-partners stage coaches between Edinburgh and Glasgow, each coach containing with ease six persons, and travelling twice a week from March to September, and from September to March once weekly, or oftener as they shall have encouragement, Ilke persone for their passage shall pay noe more then four pound sextein shilling Scots money in summer, and five pound eight shilling in winter, being two shilling eight pennies Scots for each mile in summer, and three shillings for each mile in winter. *The petitioner will be at very great expense in providing coaches, coach-horses, furniture and servants* and will not be able for a longe tyme to be reimbursed of that charge far les to make any profeit, *so he craves the monopoly in accordance with custom, and that the horses belonging to the said ' post coaches ' shall not be pressed by any person upon any occasion.*

The Lords grant the desire of the petition for the space of seven years, provyding the petitioner keep up his stage coaches and serve sufficiently the leidges dureing that space at the rates mentioned in the petition.

R.P.C., 3rd ser., v, 483–4

And here we know that the venture cannot have succeeded, for the first regular stage-coach service between Edinburgh and Glasgow did not run until 1749, when it took twelve hours to cover the journey of forty-four miles.[1]

Some conception of the state of the roads, even at the end of the seventeenth century, may be gleaned from a supplication to the Privy Council in 1680 concerning the highway between Edinburgh and Musselburgh :

1680, 15 June.

Supplication by the noblemen, gentlemen and all others goeing to and frae the burgh of Edinburgh on the east and south

[1] *Glasgow Past and Present,* ii, 436

parts thereof, *as follows :—The public highway from the Clock-milne Bridge to the Magdalen Bridge* is become so ruinous that the petitioners, who are necessitat to passe that way tending to and from the city of Edinburgh as well by coatches, horse-back or on foot, and having use of carts and horse loads for transporting their goods, merchandize and other materialls and necessars that way to and from the said toune both by day and night, are in hazard in their passadge of their lives either by their coatches overturneing, their horse falling, their carts breaking, their loads casting, and horse stumbleing, the poor people with the burdens on their backs sorely grieved and discouradged ; and that the same highway being so publick ane entrance to the metropolitan citie of the kingdome, strangers passeing the same doe often exclaime thereat, so that not only the privat interest of all persones concerned but also even the honour of the king-dome doth call for a speedy reparation of the [same]. *It is therefore craved that a small custom be imposed to repair and uphold the same. The Lords grant warrant for exacting sixpence Scots of each loaded cart passing that way to and from Edinburgh, viz., from the Clockmilne to the Magdalen Bridge, and twopence for each horse passing that way with a load, commencing from the date hereof and continuing for three years ; and they appoint Sir William Sharp and Sir William Purves to oversee the repair and upkeep of the said highway, with power to them to appoint collectors of the said toll.*

R.P.C., 3rd Ser., vi, 466–7

If that was the state of a main thoroughfare leading into the capital, it may be imagined what was the state of the roads elsewhere.

Acts of 1617 and 1661 had put the maintenance of the highways under the charge and supervision of the justices of the peace [1] ; and in 1669 the duties of the justices in this connection were clarified, and an attempt was made to strengthen their hands.

[1] See *supra*, pp. 278 *et seq.*

1669. *Act for repairing High ways and Bridges*

Our Soverane Lord Considering how necesser it is for the good of the people that hie ways be made and mantained for readie and easie passage travell and traffick through the Kingdom ; And that the care therof which hath been layd upon the Justices of Peace hath yet for the most parte proven ineffectuall in regaird the saids Justices have not had speciall orders and warrands for that effect. For remeid whairof his Majestie with advice and consent of the Estates of Parliament, doth appoint and ordain the Shirreff of the shire and one of his deputies being always ane heretor therin and the Justices of Peace in each shyre to conveen at the heid burgh of the shire upon the first tuisday of May yeerly for ordering of highways bridges and ferries ; with power to them or major parte of them that shall happen to conveen To set doun a particular list of the hie ways bridges and ferries, within thair bounds, and to divyde the paroches of the saids bounds as they ly most euest [1] to the severall high ways to be repaired, and as they may have the most equall burden ; And to appoint such of their number or others oversiers of such parts & portions of the saids high ways as are most convenient & nearest to their ordinary residence ; And to nominat such of their number as they sie fit to survey and give an accompt of the hie ways bridges and ferries unto the rest ; with power to them to appoint meitings from tyme to tyme till the said survey list and division of the saids high ways be closed. Which persons . . . are heirby authorized and strictly required to call and conveen all tennents and coatters and their servants, within the bounds appointed for their parts of the high ways, by publict intimation at the paroch kirks upon Sabboth day immediatly after the first sermon, or any other way that they shall think fit, To have in readiness horses, carts, sleds, spades, shovells, picks, mattocks, and such other instruments as shall be required, for repairing of the saids high ways . . . With power to them also to designe such of the saids persons,

---

[1] nearest

24

as they find to be most skilfull, to attend and direct the rest
and to appoint them fit wages for their attendance. Provyding that the days they are required to work doe not exceid
the number of sex days for man and horse yeerlie for the
first three yeers and four days yeerlie therafter ; and that
they be only betuixt the bear seid yeerlie and hay time or
harvest therafter. With power to the saids Justices or Oversiers to poind the readiest goods of the absents for tuentie
shillings scots money for the absence of ilk man dayly and
threttie shillings for the man & horse, without farther
solemnity but appriseing the same upon the ground of the
land, and thairwith to hyre others in place of the absents . . .
Which high ways shall be tuenty foot of measure broad at
least, or broader if the same have been so of before, and
shall be so repaired that horses and carts may travell summer
and winter therupon . . . And because the work of the
inhabitants within the severall bounds will not be able
sufficiently to repair the high ways and others forsaid,
Thairfor his Majestie . . . doth heirby authorize and require the wholl freeholders and heretors of the severall shires
to conveen at the respective heid burghs the first tuisday of
June yeerly, and to call for ane account from the justices
of peace of what is neidfull for reparation of high ways and
others forsaid, and what charges and expences is requisite
. . . And accordingly to stent the heretors of the said shyre
. . . not exceiding ten shillings scots upon each hundreth
pund of valued rent in one yeer. . . .

A.P.S., vii, 574, c. 37

But despite some evidence of this act being put into operation,[1]
it was only casually observed, much depending upon the initiative
(and authority) of the local J.Ps. The very fact of its renewal
in 1686 (when the county commissioners of supply were also
brought in and conjoined with the justices),[2] and the drafting

---

[1] cf. Andrew Shearer (ed.), *Extracts from the Burgh Records of Dunfermline in 16th and 17th Centuries*, p. 301 (21 June 1673)—though even
there it is evident that the act had not been earlier observed.

[2] *A.P.S.*, viii, 590, c. 13

of similar acts in 1696 and 1698,[1] are all evidence of failure. A like act was again passed, after the Union, in 1719 ; but, as Graham observes, it too was ' quietly ignored, and in most places the utmost effort made was a few hours' grudging labour on what was called " Parish road day," when the male inhabitants turned out for their perfunctory and ineffectual task.' [2]

The first real roads, as compared with mere tracks for pack-horses, were not built until the roads of Wade and Caulfield opened up the Highlands. Later, from the middle of the eighteenth century, the Turnpike Trusts were busy constructing modern highways all over the country except in the Highland parts, and were quickly improving communications between all the main towns.

Until the work of the Turnpike Trusts the poor state of the roads kept people at home. People travelled only when they were compelled to do so. Thus the burghs and villages were largely isolated communities, self-interested and practically self-supporting, with wide differences in manners and customs. The new roads began to knit Scotland together as a whole.

PLENTY OR DEARTH

Scotland undoubtedly produced an ample supply of food for her population. Sir Thomas Craig, writing in the opening years of the seventeenth century, praised this ' rough plenty ' :

1603-1605. *Rough Plenty*

There is no country in which a man can live more pleasantly and delicately than Scotland. Nowhere else are fish so plentiful ; indeed unless they are freshly caught on the very day we refuse to eat them. We have meat of every kind. Nowhere else will you find more tender beef and mutton, or wildfowl more numerous and of greater variety, gratifying every whim of appetite and taste. We eat barley bread as pure and white as that of England and France. Our servants are content with oatmeal, which makes them hardy and

---

[1] *A.P.S.*, x, 12a, 133a ; App., 22a
[2] Henry Grey Graham, *Social Life of Scotland in the Eighteenth Century* (1909), p. 167

long-lived. The greater number of our farm hands eat bread made of peas and beans, and it is specially agreed in their articles of hire that they shall be required to eat no other ; for any other kind of bread they consider will weaken their strength and not yield them the nourishment necessary for the performance of their daily work. . . . Should there be a bad harvest the Highlanders are able to supply us with cheese, which is often used, and without any injury to health, when the supply of cereals is short. No-where will you find people of robuster physique, higher spirited, or longer lived, more active in their old age and later in reaching it, than among the Highlanders ; and that in spite of their entire dependence on cheese, flesh and milk, like the Scythians.

Sir Thomas Craig, *De Unione Regnorum Britanniae*
(Scot. Hist. Soc.), 417, 447

Nevertheless there were years of dearth (including the year 1600), due to bad harvests ; and then the lack of adequate inland communications bore heavily upon the towns, or upon particularly stricken areas :

1600, July.

About this tyme was a great dearth of bestiall, almost in all the parts of the countrie. A scheaffe of oat straw was sold for fourtie shillings in Edinburgh. There was also a great death of little childrein six or seven buried in one day.

Calderwood, vi, 27

1623, July.

The famine increased daylie, till at last manie both in burgh and land died of hunger. Manie poore came to Edinburgh for succour, of which number some died in the streets.

Calderwood, vii, 577

Sea communications helped to some extent in such difficult years, enabling victuals to be sent from the north to the south, or vice versa, and also enabling victuals received from France, Flanders and England to be more widely distributed ; and at such times acts were passed prohibiting the export of cattle and grain. In this respect it is pleasing to record an act of international relief in 1577, though one which also helped the Scottish grower to receive firmer prices for his produce.

1577, February.

Forsamekill as althocht it be statute and ordanit be Act of Parliament that nane of our Soverane Lordis lieges or strangearis sall cary ony victuallis furth of this realme to uther partis, except samekill as salbe thair necessar victualling for thair vayage . . . Yit the Regentis Grace and Lordis of Secreit Counsale, considering now that the occasioun of the making of the same Act hes bene derth and scarsnes of victuallis, quhairwith the realme at that tyme hes bene troublit, and that than and sindry yeris sensyne this cuntre being in the lyke necessitie, hes ressavit large help and support of victuallis out of the eistir seyis, France, Flanderis, and England, quhairby the liegis hes bene greitlie relevit ; the lyke favour and gude nychtbourheid, charitie and amytie cravis to be extendit towartis the people of the saidis cuntreis in this present yeir, quhen it hes plesit God to visie thame with the lyke derth and scarssitie, and this realme with sic incres and plenty of victuallis as sum part thairof may, without prejudice of the state, be sparit to the releif of our nychtbouris necessiteis. In respect alsua that the fermoraris and puyr labouraris of the ground, that hes na uther thing to leif on and to sustene all thair necessaris and chargeis bot thair cornis, sould be greitlie interessit gif thay were constranit to sell thair saidis cornis at the law pryces now currant . . . thairfore, and for certaine utheris gude caussis and considerationis, the saidis Lordis of Secreit Counsale hes thocht convenient—counsalit and advisit the Regentis Grace—to suffer and permit sum ressonabile quantitie of quheit and beir, at his gude discretioun, be transportit and careit furth of this realme for the releif and help of our nychtbouris, presentlie having neid thairof ; and that he may grant licencis to that effect, dispensand with the said Act of Parliament for this yeir onelie. . . .

R.P.C., ii, 588–9

The worst period of famine, and one long remembered, occurred at the end of the seventeenth century, when seven consecutive harvests failed. In 1698, in the midst of these seven 'ill years' (or 'King William's years,' as the Jacobites called them), Fletcher of Saltoun described the wanderings of two hundred thousand beggars (one-fifth of the population) of whom a half were 'families whom poverty and famine had driven to want, while thousands of our people are at this day dying for want of food,' and the kirk session records are evidence of the appalling increase in mortality. To some, these years of famine were the fulfilment of prophecies made by the persecuted Covenanters Cargill and Peden, and from Patrick Walker's account of the Life and Death of Mr Daniel Cargill we get one of our best descriptions of the horror of the time.

The ' Ill Years '

These unheard-of manifold Judgments continued seven Years, not always alike, but the Seasons, *Summer* and *Winter*, so cold and barren, and the wonted Heat of the Sun so much withholden, that it was discernible upon the Cattle, flying Fowls and Insects decaying, that seldom a Fly or Gleg was to be seen : Our Harvests not in the ordinary Months ; many shearing in *November* and *December*, yea, some in *January* and *February* ; The Names of the Places I can instruct : Many contracting their Deaths, and losing the Use of their Feet and Hands sharing and working amongst it in Frost and Snow ; and after all some of it standing still, and rotting upon the Ground, and much of it for little Use either to Man or Beast, and which had no Taste or Colour of Meal.

Meal became so scarce, that it was at Two Shillings a Peck, and many could not get it. It was not then with many, *Where will we get Silver ?* but, *Where will we get Meal for Silver ?* I have seen, when Meal was all sold in Markets, Women clapping their Hands, and tearing the Clothes off their

Heads, crying, *How shall we go home and see our Children die in Hunger ? They have got no Meat these two Days, and we have nothing to give them.*

Through the long Continuance of these manifold Judgments, Deaths and Burials were so many and common, that the Living were wearied in the Burying of the Dead. I have seen Corpses drawn in Sleds, many got neither Coffin nor Winding-sheet. . . .

Patrick Walker, *Biographia Presbyteriana*, ii, 25–6

The ' improvement ' of Scottish agriculture did not begin until after the Union of 1707. In the Restoration period acts were passed to facilitate the ' enclosing ' of land by the making of dykes and ditches and the straightening of marches, but they were in the main only confirmatory of earlier legislation and the object was chiefly the protection of plantations of young trees.

THE BURGHS

During the seventeenth century no changes of any importance took place in burgh administration. Each burgh had acquired a ' sett ' of its own ;[1] the participation of the craftsmen in burgh affairs, and the method of electing the magistrates and town council varied from burgh to burgh and were subject to occasional readjustments.[2] Vital changes were not to come until the Municipal Reform Acts of 1833.

Trade as a National Concern

The new developments in industry and trade, however, the introduction of patents of monopoly, the protectionist policy of the government and the conception of trade as a matter of national concern,[3] all naturally affected the old trading monopoly of the burghs and led to frequent protest. In 1623, for example, the Convention of Royal Burghs opened a whole series of ' grievances ' with :

[1] See vol. ii, 2nd edn., pp. 215–18
[2] See the ' Setts of the Royal Burghs of Scotland ' (1708), in *Miscellany of the Scottish Burgh Records Society.*   [3] *Supra*, pp. 316 *et seq.*

1623.

Quheras the monopolies and restraints of importation of forraine wair [1] ar prejudiciall to the subject and to the mercheand estait in speciall, in thair fre tred and negotiatioun, both in exportatioun of native commodities and importatioun of forrane [commodities], it is maist humblie craived that all monopolies and restraints may be recalled and publicatioun of the same maid at the mercat croces of the frie borrowis of this realme.

Records of the Convention of Royal Burghs, iii, 147

But such protests from the burghs fell on deaf ears. In 1663 a ' loyal act ' declared that ' the ordering and disposall of trade with forraigne cuntries, and the laying of restraints and impositions upon forraigne imported merchandices is . . . acknowledged to be propper to and inherent in the persones of all frie Princes as ane undoubted prerogative of the Croun,' [2] and an act of 1672 declared :

1672.

. . . that it shall be leisome to any of his Majesties good subjects, or any persone that shall buy from them, to export furth of this kingdome, by sea or land all maner of cornes that are of the grouth of the kingdome, all maner of cattell, nolt, sheip and horse, coall, salt and wooll, skins, hydes and all uther native commodities of the kingdome ; And that it shall be leisom to the burghs of regalitie and barronie, by any of their burgessis or members of society to export all their owne proper manufacture, or such goods as shall be bought by them in faires or markets. And that it shall be leisom to the saids burghs of regalitie or barrony or societies erected or to be erected for manufactories and all uthers exporting the native grouth of the kingdome as afoirsaid, to import in returne of the saids goods exported, or of the frawght & hire of the shipes, the goods & commodities following : viz.

[1] Foreign wares   [2] *A.P.S.*, vii, 503, c. 81

timber, iron, tar, soap, lint, lintseed, hemp, onions or uther necessars for tillage or building, or for the use of their forsaid manufactories ; and als to tope & retail all commodities whatsoevir. . . .

A.P.S., viii, 63, c. 5

Admittedly in 1690, after the royal burghs had reminded the king that they bore ' a sixth part of all publick impositions '[1] as well as other charges, a partial restatement of the burghs' monopoly of trade was made.

1690.

. . . Their Majesties and Estates of Parliament statute and ordaine that the importing of all forrain commodities and merchandise either by sea or land doth and shall belong to the freemen inhabitants of their Majesties royall burrowes allennerly excepting cattell, horses, sheep and other bestiall & likewise excepting such commodities as noblemen and barons shall import for their own use and whereof noe part shall be imported for sale ; And likewayes they statute and ordaine that the exporting by sea of all the native commodities of this kingdom doth and shall belong to the freemen inhabitants of the royall burrows, only excepting corns, cattell, horses, sheep, mettalls, mineralls, coals, salt, lime and stone, but prejudice to noblemen and barons to export as much of the other native product of the kingdome, whether staple commodities or others, as may answere to the value of the commodities which shall be imported by them for their own use as said is ; As alsoe but prejudice to all the leidges to transport by land out of this kingdom all the native commodities thereof . . .

A.P.S., ix, 152, c. 15

But this act was anachronistic and, in the prevailing economic conditions, incapable of enforcement. In 1693 and 1698, under what was known as ' Communication of Trade,' some of the

[1] *cf. supra*, p. 293

larger burghs of regality and barony were beginning to share the privileges of the royal burghs in return for contributing to the burghal proportion of national taxation (see William Mackay Mackenzie, *The Scottish Burghs*, p. 151). Even within the royal burghs themselves the new situation had been recognised.

1685.

Merchandise [is] an imployment whereby not onely Burghs, but Kingdoms and Commonwealths doeth mostly prosper and flowrish, if well and rightly improven ; therefore it not onely concerns the Merchants of the Burghs to endeavour the advancement and improvement of Trade . . . but the Powers and Rulers of the Kingdom . . . seeing it mostly advances the good of the whole nation, and the decay thereof tends so much to the Publick prejudice.

Alexander Skene,[1] *Memorialls for* . . . *the Royall Burghs*, 98–9

Markets

Already the erection of burghs of barony and burghs of regality, together with an increase in the number of royal burghs themselves, had broken the old ' trade precincts ' or market monopolies granted to the early royal burghs in the twelfth and thirteenth centuries. And now, with an increasing population, and with developing trade and industry, the old market monopolies were recognised to be out of date and vexatious. As early as 1571 Bowden, in Roxburghshire, had been granted a weekly market, for selling and buying, and two annual fairs,[2] although it had no status as a burgh of any kind ; and, particularly in the second half of the seventeenth century, the number of grants of extra-burghal markets and fairs increased enormously.

The position is well exemplified in a supplication to the Privy Council in 1628 by the inhabitants of the parish of Logie Durno, in Aberdeenshire, bearing that :

[1] Writing under the pseudonym *Philopoliteius*. Skene was a baillie of Aberdeen.
[2] *R.M.S.*, iv, No. 1988. Really a grant in favour of Walter Ker of Cessford.

1628.

. . . *Because they are sixteen miles distant from any burgh or public markets or fairs, they cannot provide themselves with fish, flesh and other necessaries, except at an extraordinary cost, which has so ruined many of them that they can no longer underlie the burden, and praying for the remedy of the same* . . . *the Lords*, knoweing perfytelie the great incommoditie and prejudice that the supplicants susteanes by thair removall and farre distance frome anie mercats, and being willing for thair greater ease and more seasounable furnishing with vivers to grant thame all the lawfull favour that in suche a caise can be allowed, *grant them power and warrant* to keepe and hold a publict mercat weekelie at the Chappell of the Garioch, as the most commodious and opportune plaice within the whole bounds of the parochin for suche a purpose untill the term of Martimes nixtocum allanerlie. Provyding alwayes . . . that if the burrowes or anie other persouns, finding thameselffes interessed [1] by keeping of the said mercat, sall compleane thairof to the Counsell, the saids Lords after consideratioun of thair greevance and reasouns of the same will take suche course for dischairging of this warrand or shortning of the tyme thairin conteanit as they sall find the merite of the caus to require.

R.P.C., 2nd ser., ii, 409

Thereafter new markets and fairs, wholly unconnected with burghs, were established here and there—at first gradually, then rapidly : many by act of parliament, on the ground that the people were ' at some distance from any royal burgh or market town,' and granting a market ' for buying and selling all goods, wares and merchandise ' and not merely a market for ' vivers.'

1681. *Warrand to William Blair of that Ilk for a weekly mercat at the village of Dalry*

Our Soveraigne Lord and Estates of Parliament taking into consideration that the Kirktoun or Villadge of Dalray

[1] affected

pertaining to William Blair of that Ilk doth lye at some
distance from any Royall Burrow or mercat Towne ; And
that it would be very convenient both for the incress of
policy at the said Villadge and for accommodating the
Leidges adjacent thereto if there were ane weekly mercat
thereat : Therefore his Majestie with advice and consent of
the Estates of Parliament doth hereby give and grant to the
said William Blair of that Ilk his airs and successors full
power priviledge and libertie to have a weekly mercat to
be holden within the said Village of Dalray ilk wednesday
yearlie for buying and selling all goods wair and merchandice
used to be sold and bought in any other mercat, with power
to the said Laird of Blair and his foresaids, or such as they
shall appoint, to uplift and exact all tolles customes casualities profites and dewties belonging to the said weekly
mercat, and to doe all other things requisit and necessar
thereanent. . . .

A.P.S., viii, 445, c. 183

In the parliament of 1669 twenty-eight such grants were made,
and in the parliament of 1681 twenty-nine. The voice of con-
servatism was not unheard,[1] but the grants continued ; it has
been calculated that at the time of the Union in 1707 one hundred and ten places had been granted the double privilege of
market and fair, five had been granted a market only, and one
hundred and thirty-one a fair.[2]

These market towns broke for ever the old trading monopoly
of the burghs. The burgh of Stirling which, in its earliest charters,
had a trading monopoly over the whole sheriffdom,[3] was granted
in a confirmation of its burghal rights and privileges, in 1678,
only Charles II's promise ' on the word of a prince ' that he
would ' never erect, nor suffer to be erected any town or village
within two miles of Stirling into a burgh of barony or regality, nor
shall we grant the privilege to have or hold weekly markets or
annual fairs ' within the same area.[4]

[1] cf. Sir George Mackenzie, *Memoirs of the Affairs of Scotland*, 177
[2] See, in general, William Mackay Mackenzie, *The Scottish Burghs*,
92–5, 143–53
[3] *Charters and Documents of Stirling*, Nos. VII, XIII ; confirmed as late
as 1641 (No. LV)   [4] Ibid., No. LVIII

Social Conditions

Although houses built of stone and roofed with slates were becoming more common, most of the houses in the burghs were still built of wood and roofed with thatch ; or, if the lower part were built of stone the upper part would still be built of wood or have a wooden front. Thus there was continual ' feir and dreddour ' of fire,[1] and the old regulations regarding the stacking and storage of ' combustable matter ' are constantly repeated in all burgh records. Even minuter regulations were from time to time laid down. Thus, in Edinburgh in 1676, chimneys were ordered to be swept twice a year ; in 1677 there was an attempt to secure that new buildings, and repairs or alterations to old buildings, were carried out in stone, and that new roofings were of ' sclaitt or tyll ' ; and in 1680, in one specific case, a ' laigh ' house was not to be used as a stable since that would involve the storage of straw and the use of candles. In the case of Edinburgh, moreover, because it was the capital, the Privy Council more than once interposed its authority to strengthen the hands of the Town Council :

1618.

Forsamekle as the Kingis Majestie and Lordis of his Prevey Counsaill considering the daingerous and feirfull abuse that hes bene of continewance thir mony yeiris bigane within the burgh of Edinburgh by the tollerance, connivence, and ovirsicht quhilk hes bene gevin to baxteris, brousteris, and otheris to big and keip stakkis of hedder, broome, quhynis, and other fewall in the hairt of the said burgh and [in] the vennellis and cloises of the same, quhair sindrie of his Majesteis guid subjectis inhabitantis of the said burgh hes with grite ch[airges] and expensis build mony guid housis and biggingis to the [credite of] the said burgh and for the policie and decoratioun of the same, [by] the quhilkis stakkis of hedder, broome, quhynnis, and uther

---

[1] In 1624, for example, the greater part of Dunfermline was burned down ; and in 1668 a great part of Kilmarnock.

369

fewall [big]git and keipit within the said burgh not onlie
are the nichtbou[ris] of the nixt adjacent pairtis thairunto
haldin in continewall fe[ir and] dreddoure, and are in
verie grite hasard and dainger gif outh[er be] negligence or
wilfull malice (as God forbid) fyre salbe set[tin to the] saidis
stakkis, as fell oute by the fyreing of some stakkis in P[*blank*]
Wynd in the 1584 yeir of God, bot a grite nomber of people,
who [ar] inclynit and disposit to bestow some pairt of thair
estaite upoun [the] bigging within the said burgh, are with-
haldin thairfra for feir [of] the saidis stakkis : And, besydis
this abuse, quhilk is both . . . dangerous and hes produceit
mony inconvenientis and grite skaith fra tyme to tyme to
the said burgh, thair is ane other schamefull abuse thairin,
whilk, althocht it be not so feirfull and daingerous as the
other, yit it is noysome to the haill civile and honnest
nichtbouris and to all the nobilitie and cuntrey people that
comes heir for thir privat adois, and with that it is detestable in the sight of strangeairis, corrupis the ayre, and
caryis mony disgracefull and schamefull imputationis aganis
the said burgh as being a puddle of filthe and filthynes,—to
witt, the ovirsicht that is gevin to candilmakeris to keip
thair choppis and housis quhair thay melt thair talloun and
craklingis within the hairt of the said burgh, and to fleschouris to keepe thair slauchter choppis within the toun and
to teime the filthe of the slauchtered goodis upoun the hie
streitis and in oppin vennellis and cloisis, quhairby it
oftymes fallis oute that in mony streitis and vennellis of the
said burgh the filthe of slauchtered goodis is in suche
aboundance exposed to the vew of the people and the
cloisis and streitis so filled thairwith as thair can no passage
be had through the same : For removeing of the quhilkis
tua abuseis so dangerous and disgracefull to the said burgh
the Kingis Majestie, with advise of the Lordis of his Secrite
Counsaill, hes resolvit, concludit, commandit, and ordanit
that fra the first day of Maij nixttocum thair salbe no
stakkis of heddir, broome, quhynnis, nor other fewall keepit
nor sufferit to be in ony of the vennellis, wyndis, or cloisis
of the said burgh nor within housis nor upoun the streitis

of the same, and that no flescheouris salbe sufferit, be thame selffis, thair servandis, or otheris in thair names, to keepe ony slauchter housis within this burgh, nor in na vennell, cloise, nor wynd of the same, nor to teime the blood and filth of thair slauchtered goodis upoun the streitis or in cloisis or vennellis, nor that na candilmakeris keepe thair melting housis within the said burgh, bot that the saidis stakkis of hedder, broome, quhynnis, or uther fewall salbe careyed and sett at some remote pairtis of the burgh besydis the portis, wallis, or North Loche syde, quhair thair is no housis ; and that the saidis flescheouris provide thame selffis of slauchter housis at the North Loche syde, quhair thay may haif the use of the watter for awaytaking of the filthe of thair slauchter[ed] goodis ; and that the candilmakeris provide thame selfis of housis for melting of thair talloun and craklingis at some remote pairt of the toun fra the commoun streitis, cloisis, and vennellis of the same . . .

R.P.C., xi, 310–11

The nuisance referred to in the second part of this act of the Privy Council was likewise common to all burghs. The disposal of domestic refuse and of the offal and trimmings of the fleshers and fish-sellers provided a perennial problem, and the tendency to throw everything on to the streets (in the absence of other facilities), and to leave the town council to make arrangements for the streets to be cleared, still persisted despite constant ' acts and statutes ' of the town.[1] Admittedly after the Reformation, the abandoned kirk-yards and other open places of the friaries and nunneries might be used as additional ' dumping grounds,' as the following extract from the Aberdeen records clearly shows :

[1] Town ' acts,' such as the following one in Glasgow (1574), are to be found in the records of every burgh and are often re-enacted annually : ' It is statut and ordanit that thair be na myddynnis laid upone the foirgaitt, nor yit in the greyn, and that na fleschouris teyme thair uschawis upone the foirgate, under the pane of viiijs. ilk falt unforgewin and that na stanes nor tymmer ly on the gate langir nor yeir and daye, under the pane of escheting of tham ' (*Burgh Records of Glasgow*, Maitland Club, 24). See also, in general, W. Croft Dickinson, ' Burgh Life from Burgh Records ' in *Aberdeen University Review*, 1946.

1606.

The samyn day, anent the bill gewin in be Alex^r Dauid-
soun, tymber man in Sanct Androis, mackand mentioun
that he hes agreit with the honest men that hes bocht the
Wod of Drum, for als mekill tymber as will big ane bark,
quhilk bark he intendis, God willing, to big within this
towne, and becaus the kirkyard of the Trinitie Freris,
quhilk is filthilie abusit be middingis, is the maist meit and
convenient place for bigging of the said bark, he humblie
desyred for sic service as he micht do to the towne, that
he may hawe licence and guidwill of that rowme for bigging
of the said bark . . . quhairanent the prouest, baillies, and
counsall advysing, they fund the desire thairof verie reasonable, and grantit and gawe licence to the said Alex^r Dauid-
soun to big his schip in the pairt forsaid, viz., in the said
Trinitie Freris kirkyaird . . . and for that effect ordanis
all these quho hes laid middingis in the said kirkyaird or
thairabout, to remowe and tak avay the same within aucht
dayes nixt efter the dait heirof . . .

*Extracts from the Council Register of the
Burgh of Aberdeen*, ii, 280–1

But that provided no solution to the problem ; nor, again in
Edinburgh, the capital, despite the orders of the Privy Council,
was it possible to keep the streets clean as (so it was said) ' is
done in other civil, handsome, and well governed cities.'

1619.

Forsamekle as the burgh of Edinburgh, quhilk is the cheif
and principall burgh of this kingdome, quhair the soverane
and heiche courtis of Parliament, his Majesteis Previe
Counsall and Colledge of Justeice, and the courtis of
Justiciarie and Admiralitie ar ordinarlie haldin and keipt,
and quhairunto in that respect the best pairt of the subjectis
of this kingdome, of all degreis, rankis, and qualliteis, hes
a commoun and frequent resorte and repair, is now become

so filthie and uncleine, and the streitis, vennallis, wyndis, and cloisis thairof so ouerlayde and coverit with middingis and with the filthe and excrementis of man and beast, as the nobilmen, counsalloris, senatoris, and utheris his Majesteis subjectis quho ar ludgeit within the said burgh can not have ane clene and frie passage and entrie to thair ludgingis, quhairthrow thair ludgeingis ar become so lothsum unto thame as thay are resolved rather to mak choise of ludgeingis in the Cannogate and Leyth or som utheris pairtis aboute the toun nor to abyde the sicht of this schamefull uncleannes and filthienes, quhilk is so universall and of suche aboundance through all the pairtis of this burgh as in the heitt of sommer it corruptis the air and gives greit occasioun of seiknes : And forder this schamefull and beistlie filthienes is most detaistabill and odious in the sicht of strangeris, quho, beholding the same, ar constrayned with reassoun to gif oute mony disgracefull speichis aganis this burgh, calling it a most filthie pudle of filth and uncleannes, the lyk quhairof is not to be seine in no pairt of the world : Quhilk being a great discredite to the haill kingdome, that the principall and heid burgh thairof sould be so voyde of pollicie, civilitie, ordour, and goode governement as the hie streittis of the same cannot be keipit cleine ; and the Lordis of Secreit Counsall under-standing perfytlie that the said burgh and all the streittis and vennallis thairof [may] verrie easelie and with litill ado be keipit and haldin cleane, gif the people thameselffis wer weill and civillie disposit, and gif the Magistratis [had a] cair to caus thame and everie ane of thame keipe the streittis . . . thair awin boundis clein, as is done in other civill, handsome, and w[eill] governit cityes : Thairfoir the Lordis of Secreit Counsall commandis and ordaines be thir presentes the Provest and Bailleis of Edinburgh to [mak] and sett doun some setled and solide ordour and course how the said burgh and the cloisis, wyndis, and streittis thairof may be haldin and keipit cl[ene], the middingis and all uther filthe and uncleannes removed and tane . . . ., and that na nychtbours lay thair middingis,

25

souppingis of thair housis, nor no uther filthe upoun his nichtbouris boundis and hie streitis, under some reassonable paines to be impoisit and exactit of the contravennaris. And that the saidis Provest and Bailleis appoynte a constabill for every close to sie thair ordinance put in executioun, and the contravennaris punist be exacting of the saidis paines frome thame : certifeing the saidis Provest and Bailleis, gif they be remisse or negligent heirin, the saidis Lordis will tak thame to thame selffis, and accordinglie will tak suche ordour heirin as they sall think expedient.   *R.P.C.*, xi, 530–1

Naturally, infectious diseases spread with appalling rapidity and the death-rate was high.   But it was not until the middle of the eighteenth century that the public attitude began to change, and not until the beginning of the nineteenth century did the Scottish burghs begin seriously to consider the provision of adequate sewers and other sanitary safeguards.[1]

THE POOR LAW

The problem of poverty has its place in legislation from the time that statutes were first recorded, and from the fifteenth century, when accounts of parliamentary proceedings become copious, each generation produces a crop of acts on the subject. The serious problem of the ' sorners ' or ' masterful beggars,' who ranged the countryside ' overlying ' the land and exacting maintenance as they went, had engaged the attention of James I in 1424.[2]   A statute of 1449 provided for the escheat of the possessions of sorners—their ' hors, hundis or uthir gudis '—and also imposed severe penalties on those ' that makis thaim fulis that ar nocht bardis or sic lik utheris rynnaris aboute.' [3]   In 1455 it was decreed that sorners should be treated as thieves or reivers.[4]

The problem of those who had no visible means of support was bound to continue even after the growth of law and order had in time removed the sorner.   Early legislation was purely negative and repressive.   In 1424 and 1457 it was laid down that no one

[1] See Thomas Ferguson, *The Dawn of Scottish Social Welfare*, 137–65.
[2] Vol. ii, 2nd edn., p. 12   [3] *A.P.S.*, ii, 36, c. 9   [4] Ibid., ii, 43, c. 8

between the ages of fourteen and seventy was to beg unless he could not otherwise gain a living, and that beggars must have tokens.[1] In 1425 sheriffs were instructed to inquire into the ' ydil men that has nocht of thare awin to leif apone,' and to arrest them, allowing them forty days to find masters or a lawful craft.[2] Only in 1493 was a constructive proposal made for dealing with the unemployed, when the government conceived the idea of fostering the fishing industry by employing the poor ' for the eschewing of vicis and idilnes and for the common proffeit and universall weill of the realme.' [3] The re-enactment of this measure in 1503 was accompanied by renewed prohibition of begging by others than ' crukit folk, blind folk, impotent folk and waik folk.' [4] An act of 1535 revived the legislation of the previous century, with an ' additioun ' confining beggars to their parish of origin.[5]

How far the monastic establishments, the hospitals and the almshouses of the Middle Ages had alleviated poverty, and whether the Reformation aggravated the problem, must remain uncertain. The reformed church had no sympathy with ' stout and strong beggars,' and it accepted the principle of the association of the pauper with his parish of origin, but its solicitude for the deserving poor emerges in the first Book of Discipline,[6] and in 1567 representations were made to parliament on their behalf.[7] In 1574 we have the first comprehensive post-Reformation statute for ' punishment of strang and ydle beggaris and provisioun for sustentatioun of the puyr and impotent,' and it permitted the levying of an assessment for the poor.[8] When its terms were repeated in 1579, provision was made for licensing beggars to beg their way back to their own parishes, and supervision of the poor was transferred from the elders and headsmen of parishes to provosts and bailies in burghs and ' justices,' to be appointed by the king, in landward parishes.[9] In 1592 it was further laid down that the ministers, elders and deacons of each parish should elect ' justices and commissioners ' for the execution of the poor law.[10] Although the parliament of 1600 repeated the familiar complaint that the acts were being neglected,[11] it appears from

[1] Ibid., ii, 8, c. 21 ; 49, c. 17   [2] *A.P.S.*, ii, 11, c. 20
[3] Vol. ii, 2nd cdn., pp. 230–31   [4] *A.P.S.*, ii, 251, c. 14
[5] *Infra*, p. 376   [6] Vol. ii, 2nd edn., p. 174
[7] *A.P.S.*, iii, 37, c. 9   [8] *Infra*, p. 377   [9] *A.P.S.*, iii, 139–42
[10] Ibid., iii, 576, c. 69   [11] Ibid., iv, 232

extracts printed below that in Aberdeen at least a conscientious effort was made to enforce their provisions.

Meantime, in 1581, attention had turned to one aspect of the problem of achieving ' full employment,' in that the importation of luxury articles, in both raiment and food, was condemned.[1]

Sixteenth century legislation had incorporated three principles which were to underlie the Scottish poor law until modern times —the association of the pauper with his parish of origin, permissive authority to impose a local assessment for poor relief, and the restriction of assistance to the impotent. After the Restoration the development of manufactures seemed to open the possibility of absorbing the unemployed, and an act of 1663 [2] permitted manufacturers to press vagabonds into their service. Another contemporary development which offered the prospect of disposing of vagabonds was Scottish trade with the American plantations, and we find merchants authorised to transport idle persons to Jamaica and Barbadoes. The great act of 1672, which remained the foundation of the poor law until 1845, proceeded mainly on traditional lines : assessment to supplement the church collections was permissive, beggars were confined to their parish of ' settlement,' and the fit were to be compelled to work, if only in workhouses.

1535. *Act restricting beggars to their own parishes*

For the restrenyng of the multitude of maisterfull and strang beggaris it is ordanit that the act maid thairupoun of befor be King James the first, apprevit and ratifiit be utheris oure soverane lordis predicessouris, be observit and kepit and put to scharp executioun in all punctis, with this additioun that na beggaris be tholit to beg in ane parochine that ar born in ane uther and that the hedismen of ilk parochine mak taikynnis and geve to the beggaris thairof and that thai be sustenit within the boundis of that parochine and that nane uther be servit with almous within that parochine bot thai that beris that takin alanerlie. . . .

A.P.S., ii, 347–8

[1] *Infra*, pp. 378-9   [2] *Infra*, p. 382

1574. *Act permitting assessment for the poor*

[*After reference to previous acts, which had not been put to due execution:*] It is thocht expedient and ordanit alsweill for the utter suppressing of the saidis strang and ydill beggaris, sa outragious ennemeis to the commoun weill, as for the cheritabill releving of the aigit and impotent puyr people, . . . that all personis . . . to be takin wandering and misordering thame selffis contrary to the effect and meaning of thir presentis salbe apprehendit . . . and . . . committit in ward in the commoun presoun, stokkis or irnis . . . quhill thay be put to the knawlege of ane assyise . . . and gif thay happin to be convicted to be adjugeit to be scurgeit and burnt throw the girssill of the rycht eare with ane het irne of the compasse of ane inche about . . . quhilk punisement anys ressavit he sall not suffer agane the lyke for the space of lx dayis thaireftir, bot gif at the end of the same lx dayis he be found to have fallin agane in his ydill and vagabound trade of lyff, than being apprehendit of new he salbe adjugeit and suffer the panis of death as a theif. . . .

All ydill personis gaying about in ony cuntre of this realme using subtile, crafty and unlauchfull playis, as juglerie, fast and lowis and sic utheris, the ydill people calling thame selffis egiptianis or ony uther that fenyeis thame to have knawlege in physnomie, palmestre or utheris abused sciencis quhairby thay perswade the people that they can tell thair weardis, deathis and fortunes and sic uther fantasticall ymaginationis, and all personis being haill and stark in body and abill to wirk allegeing to have bene hereit in the sowthland brint in the lait troubles about Edinburgh and Leith . . . and all menstrallis, sangstaris and taill tellaris not avowit in speciall service be sum of the lordis of parliament or greit barronis or be the heid burrowis and cities for thair commoun menstrallis . . . all vagaboundis scollaris of the universiteis of Sanctandrois, Glasgow and Abirdene not licencit be the rector and dene of faculte of the universitie to ask almous . . . salbe takin, adjugeit, demed and puneist as strang beggaris and vagaboundis. . . .

377

And sen cheritie wald that the puyr, aigit and impotent personis sould be als necessarlie providit for as the vagaboundis and strang beggaris ar repressit and that the aigit, impotent and puyr people sould have ludgeing and abyding places throuchout the realme to settill thame selffis intill, . . . the eldaris and deaconis in everie citie, burgh and gude toun and the heidismen of ilk parochyn to landwart sall . . . tak inquisitioun of all aigit, puyr, impotent and decayed personis borne within that parochyn or quhilkis wer dwelling and had thair maist commoun resort in the said paroche the last sevin yeris bipast quhilkis of necessitie mon leif be almous, and . . . mak a register buke . . . and . . . considdir quhat thair neidfull sustentatioun will extend to in the owlk and than be thair gude discretionis taxt and stent the haill inhabitantis within the parochyn according to the estimatioun of thair substance without exceptioun of personis to sic oulklie charge and contributioun as salbe thocht sufficient to sustene the saidis puyr people . . . and at the end of the yeir that alsua the taxatioun and stent roll be alwayis maid of new for the alteratioun that may be throw deith or the incres or diminutioun of mennis gudis and substance.

And that the eldaris in citeis, burrowis and gude townis and heidismen of the parochynnis to landwart sall gif a testimoniall to sic puyr folk as thay find not borne in thair awin parochyn sending or directing thame to the nixt parochyn and sa frome parochyn to parochyn quhill thay be at the place quhair thay were borne or had thair maist commoun resort and residence during the last sevin yeris.

A.P.S., iii, 86–8

1581. *Acts against luxury in clothing and food*

The kingis maiestie and estatis of this present parliament considering the greit abuse standing amang his subiectis of the meane estate presuming to conterfait his hines and his nobilitie in the use and wearing of coistlie cleithing of

silkis of all sortis, layne,[1] cameraige,[2] freinyeis [3] and pasmentis of gold, silver and silk and wollin claith maid and
brocht from uthir foryne cuntreis quhairthrow the pryces
of the same is groun to sic exorbitant derth as it is nocht
abill to be langer sustenit without greit skayth and inconvenient of the commone weill quhowbeit god hes grantit
to this realme sufficient commoditeis for cleithing of the
inhabitantis thairof within the self gif the pepill were
verteouslie employit in working of the same at hame,
quhairby greit numberis of pure folkis now wandering in
beging mycht be releissit alsweill to the honestie and welth
of the cuntrie, for remeid quhairof it is statute and ordanit
. . . that nane of his hines subiectis man nor woman being
under the degreis of duikis, erlis, lordis of parliament,
knichtis, or landed gentilmen, that hes or may spend of fre
yeirlie rent twa thowsand merkis or fiftie chalderis victuall
at leist or thair wyffis, sonnes, or dochteris sal eftir the
first day of Maii nixtocum use or weir in thair cleithing
or apparrell or lyning thairof onie clayth of gold or silver,
welvet, satyne, damas, taffateis or onie begaries,[4] freinyeis,
pasmentis or broderie of gold, silver or silk, nor yit layne,
cameraige or wollin clayth maid and brocht from onie
foryne cuntreis under the pane of ane hundreth pundis of
everie gentilman landit, ane hundreth merkis of everie
gentilman unlandit and fourtie pundis of everie yeman man
for everie day that his wyff, sone or dochter trangressis this
present act. . . . As alsua that the puir pepill may be the
bettir haldin in werk throw the laboring of the woll of the
cuntrie within the same, thairfoir it is statut and ordanit
. . . that na maner of woll be transportit furth of this
realme in tyme cuming under the pane of confiscation of the
same woll and of all the remanent guidis moveabill of the
personis awneris and transportaris thairof to oure soverane
lordis use. . . .

A.P.S., iii, 220, c. 18

---

[1] lawn [2] cambric [3] fringes
[4] piping, or ornamental strips of coloured cloth sewn on to the garment

Oure soverane lord and his thre estatis convenit in this present parliament understanding the greit exces and super-fluitie usit in brydellis and utheris banquettis amang the meane subiectis of this realme alsweill within burgh as to landwert to the inordinat consumptioun not onlie of sic stuff as growis within the realme bot alswa of droggis confectouris and spiceis brocht from the pairtes beyond sey and sauld at deir pryces to monie folk that are verie unabill to sustene thair coist, for stanching of the quhilk abuse and disorder it is statute and ordanit be our soverane with advise of his saidis thre estatis : That na maner of personis his subiectis being under the degree of prelatis, erlis, lordis, baronis, landit gentilmen or utheris that [ar] worth and may spend in yeirlie fre rent two thousand merkis money or fiftie chalderris victuale all chargeis deducit sall presume to have at thair brydellis or uther banquettis or at thair tabillis in daylie cheir onie droggis or confectouris brocht from the pairtis beyound sey. And that na ban-quettis salbe at onie upsittingis eftir babtizing of bairnis in time cuming. . . .

A.P.S., iii, 221, c. 19

1595. *Care of the poor in Aberdeen*

The said day, the haill toun, burgessis and craftismen, &c., the mater concerning the prouisioun for the pure being opinlie decleirit to thame be the bailleis and minister, and the act of parliament maid theiranent being publictlie red in all their audience, and the puir being devydit in four rankis, to wit, in babis, decayit persones houshalderis, leamit and impotent persones, and in sic as war decrepit and auld, borne and bred within this burght, at the leist that hes maid their commoun resort and residence within the same be the space of thir sevin yeris bypast, thay all in ane voce but any opposition or contradictioun, folowing first Goddis commandement, and nixt the directioun of the said act of parliament, grantit, agreit, and consentit, ilk man frielie and voluntarlie voting be himself, according to the ordour

of the suit roll, sum to receave in thair houssis ane baib,
and lykwayis to pay contributioun for help and support of
the remanent puir of the rankis forsaidis, borne and bred
within this toun, at the leist quha hes maid residence within
the same be the space forsaid, utheris to contribut, and ilk
man voting be himself, grantit to pay the contributioun
sett doun in the roll maid this day, for ane yeir, to be payit
quarterlie, with provisioune that the magistrattis tak sic
substantious ordour anent the expelling of extranear
beggaris, idill and vagabond persones, furth of this burght,
as the said act of parliament prescryvis, and that the purell
of this burght of the rankis forsaidis, be contenit within
houssis, helpit be the commoun contributioun, and not
sufferit to cum to the streittis, houssis, or yettis of this burgh
to seik almous, and according to the said voting, ilk man
speking be himself as said is, the roll was instantlie sett
down, and sic as everie man grantit be his awin mouth,
wreittin, and the babis delyverit to sic as war content to
receave tham, the receaveris name with the babis name,
wreittin lykwayes.

*Extracts from the Council Register of the
Burgh of Aberdeen*, ii, 124

The system of beggars' tokens, referred to in the act of 1535,
continued in use, as the two following extracts from the Register
of the Kirk Session of Aberdeen show :

1616, 10 March. The samen day, the magistrattis and
sessioun ordanit intimatioun to be maid out of pulpitt, that
na beggaris get any almes within this burgh, except sic as
bearis the townis taikine ; and intimatioun to be maid also
heirof be the drum, that the towne may be purgeit of
extranear beggeris and that the townis awin puir may be
the better helpit and susteanit.

Aberdeen Eccl. Records (Spalding Club), 83

1622, 11 August. The sessioun dischargis Williame Davidsone
of his office of expelling stranger beggaris and of all fie and

benefeit he had be the same, in respect he is fund giltie of tacking blak maill from the poore beggaris, to suffer thame beg throu the towne.

Ibid., 104

1663. *Act authorising Manufacturers to press Vagabonds into their Service*

[*After reference to acts of King James VI :*] Considering that the cheeff cause wherby the forsaids acts have proven ineffectuall and that vagabunds and idle persons doe yet so much abound, hath been that ther were few or no common works then erected . . ., and that now . . . common works for manufactures of diverse sorts are setting up in this kingdome ; thairfoir his majestie . . . ratifies and approves the forsaids acts of parliament, with this addition, that it shall be leisum to all persons or societies who have or shall set up any manufactures within this kingdom, to seize upon and apprehend the persons of any vagabonds who shall be fund begging . . . and to imploy them for their service as they shall see fit, the same being done with the advice of the respective magistrats of the place wher they shall be seized upon. . . .

Lykeas his majestie . . . ordaines the heritors of each paroche, or as many of them as shall happen to meit upon publict intimation made at the paroche kirk upon any sabboth at the dissolveing of the church from the first sermon, by any of the heritors of the paroche or by the imployers of the poore, to make up a stent roll for mantenance of the poore in their paroche who shall be imployed as said is, . . . the one halff therof to be payed by the heritors either conforme to the old extent of their lands within the paroche, or conforme to the valuation by which they last payed assessment or otherwayes, . . . and the other halff thairof to be layd upon the tennents and possessors according to their means and substance. . . .

And recommends to the lords of the privy councill to sie

this act and all former acts of parliament made against
sturdie beggars and vagabonds put to executioun. . . .

A.P.S., vii, 485-6

1665. *Supplications for authority to transport Beggars to the Plantations*

Supplication by George Hutcheson, merchant in Edinburgh, for himself and in name and behalf of his copartners, merchands of
the ship bounding for Gemaica and Barbadoes, *as follows :—
Out of a desire* to promote the Scottish and Inglish plantations in Gemaica and Barbadoes for the honour of their
countrey, *as well as* to frie the kingdom of the burden of
many strong and idle beggars, Egiptians, common and
notorious whores and theives and other disolute and louse
persons banished or stigmatized for grosse crymes, *they have
been by former acts of Council authorised to seize upon such persons
and transport them to the said plantations ; and though of late they
have by warrant from the sheriffs, justices of peace and magistrates
of burghs where the said persons haunt, apprehended some of them,
yet without authority of the Council they may meet with some
opposition in this good work. The Lords, having considered the
petition, grant warrant to the petitioner to transport all such persons
delivered to them by the magistrates*, provyding alwayes that ye
bring the saids persons before the Lord Justice Clerk, to
whom it is hereby recommendit to try and take notice of
the persons that they be justly convict for crymes or such
vagabonds as by the lawes of the countrey may be apprehendit to the effect the countrey may be disburthened of
them.

R.P.C., 3rd ser., ii, 101

1666.

Supplication by James Dumbar, merchant bounding for
Barbadoes, *as follows :—Out of his zeal for his country and promoting of trade and the credit of Scotsmen in the foreign plantations,
he has by warrant of the justices of peace seized several vagabonds
and idle persons to carry to the said plantations ; and*, seing there

are severall prisoners in Edinburgh, Cannongate, Leith and other places content to goe of their oune accord, *he therefore craves as follows. The Lords hereby authorise justices of peace to apprehend vagabonds and to deliver them to the petitioner for transport to the Barbadoes ; and ordain the magistrates of Edinburgh, Leith and Canongate to deliver to him such prisoners as are willing to go to Barbadoes, the Justice Clerk being first acquainted therewith and his consent procured.*

R.P.C., 3rd ser., ii, 128–9

1672. *Act establishing Workhouses*

[*After reference to previous statutes :*] And withall considering that the effect of all these good lawes hath bein frustrate because ther hath bein noe place provided wherin such poore people might be sett to worke, nor persones appointed to have the charge and oversight of them : For remeid wherof his majestie . . . ordaines that the magistrats of the burghs following betuixt and the terme of Whitsunday nixt 1673 provyde correction-houses for receaving and intertaining of the beggars, vagabonds and idle persones within their burghs, and such as shall be sent to them out of the shires and bounds aftirspecified, and that they appoint masters and overseers of the same, who may sett these poor persones to worke . . . [*burghs named as sites of correction-houses*], each of which houssis shall have a large closs, sufficientlie inclosed for keiping in the said poor people, that they be not necessitat to be allwayes within doors, to the hurt or hazard of their health. . . . And in the mean time, untill the saids houssis be provided, the magistrats of the saids burghs are required to dispose of these beggars and poor people who were either borne within their respective burghs or have haunted thairin the last thrie yeirs, in some convenient places. . . .

And for the bettir enabling of the saids burghs to beir the charges and expensis of the saids correction-houses, his majestie . . . ordaines that the contributions and allowances for maintaining of the poor, appointed by the

fifteinth act of the third session of his majesties first parliament [*i.e., the act previously quoted*] . . . be applyed for the
use of the saids correction houses . . . which contributions are to be payed by the paroches releived of the said
poor, in maner contained in the said act.

[*Ministers and elders are to compile lists of poor*], condiscend-
ing upon their age and condition, if they be able or unable
to worke, by reasoun of age, infirmity or disease, and where
they wer borne, and in what paroches they have most
haunted dureing the last thrie yeires preceiding the up-
takeing of these lists . . . and . . . . the heritors who, and
the possessors of their land, are to beir the burding of the
maintainance of the poor persones of each paroch, or any
of them who shall meit with the saids ministers and elders,
shall condiscend upon such as throwgh age and infirmity
are not able to work, and appoint them places wherin to
abide, that they may be supplied by the contributions at the
paroche-kirk : and if the same be not sufficient to entertaine
them, that they give them a badge or ticket to aske almes at
the dwelling houses of the inhabitants of their owne paroche
onlie, without the bounds quhairof they are not to beg. . . .

Such of the saids poor persones as are of age and capacity
to worke, be first offered to the heritors or inhabitants of
each paroche, that if they will accept any of them to become
their apprentices or servants they may receive them upon
their obleidgment to entertaine and sett to worke the saids
poor persones, and to releiff the paroch of them . . . and
that the rest of the saids poor persones be sent to the correction-houses : for whose entertainment the saids heritors
shall cause collect the saids contributions and appoint a
quarters allowance to be sent alongs with them, with cloathes
upon them to cover their nakedness and the said allowance
to be payed quarterlie theraftir, by way of advance.

With power also to the saids commissioners of excise in
each shire quarterlie to take ane account of the diligence of
these of each paroch for performeing of the premisses. . . .

And his majestie . . . doeth impower . . . the masters
of the correction-houses to put and hold the saids poor people

to worke as they shall see them most capable and fitt ; and incaice of their disobedience, to use all maner of severitie and correction, by wheeping or otherwise (excepting torture)....

It shall be lawfull to coallmasters, saltmasters and others who have manufactories in this kingdome to seize upon any vagabonds or beggars, wherevir they can find them, and to put them to worke in their coal-hewghs or other manufactories. . . .

A.P.S., viii, 89–91

THE 'SERVITUDE' OF COLLIERS AND SALTERS

By an act of 1606 colliers and salters were so straitly bound to their work that their conditions were little different from those of slavery.

1606.

Oure Soverane Lord and estaittis of this present parliament statutis and ordinis that na persone within this realme heireftir sall fie hyre or conduce ony saltaris coilyearis or coilberaris without ane sufficient testimoniall of thair maister quhome they last servit subscryvit with his hand or at leist sufficient attestatioun of ane ressonable cause of thair removeing maid in presens of ane baillie or magistrat of the pairt quhair they come fra. And incaise ony ressave fie hyre supplie or interteny ony of the saidis colyearis saltaris or coilberaris without ane sufficient testimonie as said is, the maisteris quhome fra they came challengeing thair servandis within yeir and day, that the pairtie quhome fra they ar challengeit sall delyver thame bak agane within tuentie four houris under the pane of ane hundreth pundis to be payit to the persones quhome fra they passit . . . And the saidis coilyearis coilberaris and saltaris to be estemit repute and haldin as theiffis and punischit in thair bodyes viz samony of thame as sall ressave foirwageis and feis. And the saidis Estaittis of this present parliament gevis power and commissioun to all maisteris and awneris of coilheuchis and [salt] pannis to apprehend all vagaboundis and sturdie beggeris to be put to labour.

A.P.S., iv, 286, c. 10

In 1641 this act was further extended to include 'watermen,' 'windsmen' and 'gatemen,' as well as colliers and coalbearers, and a six-day week was imposed.

1641.

. . . That becaus watermene who leves and drawes water in the coallheughe head in this kingdome and gaitesmen who worke the wayes and passages in the saidis heughes ar als necessar to the owneres and maisteres of the said coaleheuches as the coallhewers and beireres, It is therfore statute and ordeaned that no persone shall hyre ore seduce any watermen and windsmen and gaitsmen without a testimoniell of the maister whom they serve under the paines conteyned in the former actes in all poyntes ; And . . . that the saidis coallheweres and salteres and otheres workemen of coalheuches in this kingdome worke all the sex dayes of the weeke under the paines falloweing, that is to say that everie coallhewer or salter who lyes ydle shall pay tuentie shillingis for everie day by and attour the prejudice susteened by ther maister and other punishment of ther bodies.

A.P.S., v, 419, c. 124

Both Acts were ratified in 1661 (*A.P.S.*, vii, 304, c. 333),[1] and colliers and salters were excluded from the safeguards of the Act anent Wrongous Imprisonment (see page 502).

By interpretation these acts were held to mean that simply by accepting work in a colliery or salt-works the worker became 'astricted' to that work for the rest of his life ; and, if the colliery or salt-works were to be sold, the workmen passed therewith to the new owner. Colliers and salters were not released from this servitude until the belated acts of 1775 and 1799 (15 George III, c. 28 ; 39 George III, c. 39), when they were brought, like

[1] The act of 1641 being re-enacted because of the general Act Rescissory (*supra*, p. 153).

servants and other workmen, beneath the ' labour jurisdiction ' of the justices of the peace.[1]

Although no statute law astricted fishermen in a like way, it would appear from the two following extracts that ' seamen of fish boats in the North Country ' were ' by the constant custom of the place tied and obliged to the same servitude and service that coal hewers and salters were in the South.' (See *Introduction to Scottish Legal History*, Stair Soc., p. 137.)

1683.

Supplication by Sir William Keith of Ludqwharne, as follows :— Albeit the seamen of fish-boats in the North countrey are, by the constant custome of the ply, tyed and oblidged to the same servitude and service that coalyiers and salters are here in the South, and it is not lawfull for any man to resett, harbour and intertain the fishers and boatmen which belonged unto another ; *yet William Bruce, Gilbert Bruce, Andrew Ritchie, William Carle and   Carle, his son, James Hutcheon, Alexander Ritchie, Alexander Grant, and Robert Seller, who were seamen in the petitioner's service, have fled away from him and deserted his imployment,* to his exceeding great damnadge and prejudice except the Councill grant warrand for remanding and reclameing them and take such other course for preventing the like in time comeing. *The Lords finding it unjust and unwarrantable that any person should harbour or reset any of the petitioner's seamen who were actually in his service, they require all sheriffs, stewards, bailies of regality and bailiary, justices of peace, and magistrates of burghs, in whose bounds the said persons are, to cause their resetters deliver them back to the petitioner, and so to do in every such case in time coming.*

R.P.C., 3rd. ser., viii, 119

1684.

*Supplication by John, Earl of Erroll, as follows :—*Albeit the seamen of fish boats in the North Countrey are by the constant custom of the place tyed and obleidged to the same

---

[1] See the account in Cockburn's *Memorials* (1910), 70–2

servitud and service that coall hewars and salters are here in the South, and it is not lawfull for any man whatsomever to resett, harbour or intertain the fishers and boatmen which belong to another ; notwithstanding wherof true it is that Alexander Brodie and Andrew Buthlay, who wer seamen in the petitioners service, have fled away from him and deserted his implyoment to his damnadge and prejudice except the Councill grant warrand for remanding and reclaiming them and take such other course for preventing the lyke in tyme coming as the Councill shall think fitt. *He therefore craves order to be given to sheriffs, magistrates of burghs, and others, to cause restore the seamen to him, and to do so in time coming if any more run away from him. The Lords grant warrant to the sheriffs and magistrates foresaid to cause the resetters of the said fishers or seamen deliver them back to the petitioner.*

R.P.C., 3rd ser., viii, 495

BONDS OF MANRENT AND FRIENDSHIP

Owing to the many periods of weak government from the reign of Robert II onwards, and the inability of the central authority to maintain law and order, a widespread system of ' bonds of manrent ' grew up whereby the smaller man would commend himself for protection to the more powerful local lord—and also, thereby, the lord gained another ' follower.'

Under the bond of manrent the lord became the personal protector of the man who entered into his ' friendship,' and, if another lord injured the man, he had perforce to take up his cause with all the resources at his command ; otherwise his local status and authority was lost. Thus ' bonds of manrent ' might lead to an increase of local disorders rather than to the maintenance of ' peax and commone quietnes ' ; and there was the added danger that a powerful local lord might become too powerful in his own neighbourhood. Significantly, perhaps, whereas early bonds of manrent seem to stress that *A* has bound himself to protect *B* in return for *B's* adherence to *A*, the later bonds, such as that printed below, seem to stress that *B* will assist *A* with all his strength in any of *A's* actions and causes (usually with an added exception 'save only against the King's Majesty ').

In 1555 parliament declared all 'bonds of manrent and maintenance' to be null and void, 'except heretabill bandis gevin of befoir or gevin for asythment of slauchters '[1] but such an enactment, being incapable of enforcement, is merely evidence that parliament was alive to the dangers and undesirability of the practice.

Proscription was of no avail when the government was too weak to 'govern'; but the bond of manrent died a natural death as soon as the government began to make its authority felt even in the outlying parts—as it began to do in the reign of James VI.[2]

The 'band of friendship,' although often little different from a bond of manrent, may, as in the case of the one printed below, begin to represent an intermediate stage in which the parties pledge themselves to eschew quarrels and jointly to support the royal authority within their parts.

1592. *A Bond of Manrent*

Be it kend till all men be thir present lettres, me schir Umphrie Colquhoune of Luss, knycht, to becum man servand and dependar to ane nobill and potent lord George erlle of Huntlie, lord Gordoun and Baidyenocht, etc., that I, and all that I may mak, of kin, freindis, servandis, suirname, vassellis, and dependaris sall at all timis heireftir, witht our haill forces, serve, concur, and assist with the said nobill lorde, in all and quhatsumeuir his actionis and caussis, contra quhatsumeuir persoun or persones, clan or clannis, within this realm, for quhatsumeuir causs he hes to do, in deidlie feidis, by past, present, and to cum, and sall tak trew, plaine and eafald [3] pairt with, and sall entir in bluid witht his aduersar pairtie, and be reddy baith to perseu

---

[1] *A.P.S.*, ii, 495, c. 17. A bond of manrent entered into for ' asythment of slauchter ' was actually ratified by parliament in 1592 (*A.P.S.*, iii, 624, c. 157).

[2] *supra*, pp. 261, *et seq.*   [3] sincere, honest

and defend, and wair [1] our lyffis and heritages in his lord-
schipis adois, as we salbe employit, aganis quhatsumeuir
persones within this realme, the authorite only exceptit,
etc., in witnes quhairof, I have subscriuit this present band
of seruice, witht my awin hand, at Blacknes, the sextein day
of Marche, the yeir of God M.v^c four scoir alevin yeris, befor
thir witness, Aulay Makcaulay of Artingaipill, Gorg Gordoun
of Govlis, Thomas Gordoun of Drumbulg.

Wmphra Colquhone of Luss, knycht

Spalding Club Miscellany, iv, 247

1578. *The Band of Freindschip maid betuix the Erleis of Eglintoun, Glencarne, and Robert Lorde Boyd, Lairdes of Lowdoun and Craigie*

Be it kend till all men be thir present letres We Hew Erll of
Eglintoun Lord Montgomerie Williame Erll of Glencarne
Lord Killmawars Robert Lord Boid Sir Mathow Campbell
of Lowdoun knycht shereff of Air Johnne Wallace of Cragie
for him selff Hew Maister of Eglintoun James Maister of
Glencarne Thomas Maister of Boid Hew Campbell of
Tarringane our eldest sones and apparent airis and the said
Johnne Wallace of Cragie taking the burding apoun him
for Johne Wallace his sone and appering air quha salbe
comprehendit herin and subscrive thir presentis at his
majoritie Seing diverse querrelles and contraverseis arrysing
alsweill amangis our freindis as uthers our nychtbouris
tending to the truble and brek of the cuntre For repressing
quhairof and for the zeall and ernist affectioun we bear to
peax and commone quietnes and that we may be the mair
able frelie and without impediment to awaitt apoun the
Kingis Majesties service as it sall pleis his hienes to employe
us As alswa for confirming and gud interteinement of the
ald bandis amitie and kindnes amangis our houssis To be
bundin and oblist and be thir presentis apoun our fayth and
honouris the halie evangeill tuicheit solempnatlie bindis
and oblissis us to tak trew faythfull afald and plane partt all

[1] expend, bestow

togiddir and ilkane with utheris alsweill be way of law as
deid persutt as defence be our selffis our landis houssis guddis
freindis servandis dependaris and all that we may move in
all and quhatsumevir actionis causis querrellis contraverseis
and debettis movit or to be movit be or aganis us or ony
ane of us our servandis or freindis propirlie depending apoun
us aganis quhatsumevir persoun or personis (the Kingis
Majestie and his hienes auctoritie allanerlie except) and that
all actionis caussis and querrellis movit or to be movit be
or aganis us ony ane of us or our foirsaidis salbe ane and
comone as we and ilkane of us haid speciale and like
enteres thairintill That all our castellis houssis strenthis
pertening to us or ony ane of us salbe readie and patent to
us and ilkane of us as the cause and occasioun sall require
That we sall meit and convene als oft as salbe requisit sall
give uthir our trew faythfull best advise and counsall in all
effaris sall keip utheris counsallis and secreteis nocht reveill
nor bewray the samin and sall nocht wranguslie nor unkindlie
tak utheris guddis landis offices rowmes takkis steiddingis or
possessiones fee corrupt or accept utheris servandis feallaris
or dependaris procuir knaw or suffir the harme skayth or
dishonnour of ony of us bot sall resist and stop the samin
to our uttirmest and sall give als haistie knawlege thairof as
salbe possible to quhomesumevir of us it sall concerne and
sall speik nor do na thing directlie nor indirectlie that may
be prejudiciall dishonorabill or offensive to uthir in ony
soirt And give it salhappin as God forbid ony different
slauchtir blude or uther inconvenent to fall outt amangis
ony of us our freindis servandis or dependaris the samin of
quhatsumevir wecht or qualitie it be of salbe submittit to
the decisioun and jugement of the remanent of us subscriveris of this band quha salhave full powar and auctoritie
to juge decyde and decerne thairintill quhais sentence and
decreit bayth the pairteis sall byde att fullfill and observe
without reclamatioun or appelatioun and salbe als valide
and effectuall in all respectis and have als full executioun
as the samin haid bene gevin and pronuncit eftir cognitioun
in the cause be the Lords of Sessioun Justice Generale of

Scotland or ony uthir Juge ordiner within this realme And
will and grauntis that this band be als valide and sufficient
submissioun in all respectis as give the said different slauchtir
blude or inconvenient efter committing thairof war speacialie
submittit to the saidis persones subscriveris heirof be bayth
the pairteis be blank or uthirwayis quhilk also we promise
to do as we salbe requirit And in the meyntyme for the
bettir quietnes We and everie ane of us faythfullie and be
our aythis promisis bindis and oblissis us that quhasaevir
of us or our foirsaidis salhappin to be offendit be uthir of
us or thair foirsaidis we nor thay sall nawayis take revenge
thairof be way of deid quhill we have first desyrit the pairtie
offendent to repair and amend the samin give it be ane of
our selffis or cause the samin be repairit and amendit give
it be ane of our freindis servandis and dependaris and quhill
we have signifeit and gevin knawlege thairof to the remanent
subscriveris of this band that thai may cognosce and decerne
thairintill as said is And give it salhappin as God forbid ony
of us to be willfull obstinat or stubburne and haveing
offendit to refuise to repair and amend our offence at the
sycht of the remanent subscriveris heirof and to cause our
freindis servandis and dependaris do the lyk in thair estaitt
and degre Or being offendit to refuise mesour and reasoun
at the sycht of the remanent subscriveris heirof To be bundin
and oblist and be thir presentis letres bindis and oblissis us
to tak ane efald trew and plane pairtt with the ressonabill and
moderat pairtie aganis the willfull stubburne and obstinat
bayth be way of law and deid till he be constranit be law
force or freindlie dealling to cum to ressoun and conformitie, quhilk and all the premissis We and ilkane of us hes
be our aythis apoun our fayth and honnouris faythfully and
solempnantly promisit and sworne to observe and keip undir
the pane of perjurie infamie and perpetuall defamatioun In
witnes quhairof to thir presentis subscrivit with our handis
our seillis ar affixt At Striveling the xiij day of Junij The
yeir of God I^m v^c lx auchtene yeris Befoir thir witnes John
Conynghame sone to my Lord of Glencarne Johnne Coninghame of Corshill Johnne Baillie servand to my Lord of

Eglintoun Walter Colquhoun servand to my Lord Boyde
and Patrik Coninghame sone to the Laird of Aikett.

EGLYNTOUN.   WYLLYEM ERLL OF GLENCARN.
HEW MR OF EGLINTOUN.   JAMES MAISTIR GLENCAIRNE.
              R. BOYD.   MATHOW CAMPBELL OF LOWDON
                                   KNYCHT.
JOHN VALLACE OF CRAGGY. HEW CAMPBELL OF TERRINGYEN.

Abbotsford Club Miscellany, i, 44–7

FESTIVITY AND AUSTERITY

1593/4, 22 February. *Festivity*

The said day, the consall folowing the exampill of the
townis of Edinburght, Perth, Dundy, and Montroiss,
quhilkis laitlie within thir thrie or four dayis, for that it
hes plesit God to grant to his Majestie ane sone,[1] a prince
to this realme and cuntrie, had maid sum solemnitie according to the ancient custume maid at the birth of princes of this
realme, in signe and tokin of thair joyful hartis, be bigging
of fyris, praysing and thanking God for the benefitt, be singing of psalmes throu the haill rewis [2] and streittis of the
tounis, drinking of wyne at the croces thairoff, and uther
wayes liberally bestowing of the spyceries, ordanit the lyk
forme and ordour to be within this burght on Sunday nixt,
the xxiiij of this instant, immediatlie folowing the efter nune
sermone, and ane tabill to be coverit at the mercat croce of
the samen, for the magistrattis and bayth the consallis,[3] with
tua bunnis [4] of Inglis beir, to be placed and run at the said
mercat croce,[5] the wyne to be liberallie drunkin in sic a
ressonabill quantitie as the deane of gild sall devyse, four

---

[1] Henry Frederick, born in Stirling Castle 19 February 1593/4.
Died 6 November 1612.   [2] rows (cf. Fr. *rues*)

[3] That is, the council of the previous year and the council of the
present year (cf. Vol. ii, 199, 202–3).   [4] large casks

[5] In Edinburgh, to celebrate the birth of James VI in 1566, one
puncheon of wine, costing ten pounds, was run at the cross (*Edinburgh
Burgh Records*, iii, 219).

dussoun buistis of skorchettis,[1] confecttis, and confectionis, to be placed on the said tabill, and cassin amongis the pepill, with glassis to be brockin ; and ordanis Johnne Tilliedaffe, deane of gild, to provyd the samen and mak expenssis thairupoun, quhilk salbe allowit to him in his comptis.

Extracts from the Council Register of the Burgh of Aberdeen, ii, 90.

1641. *Austerity*

Friday the 25 of December, of old called Yool-day, and wheron preachings, and praises, and thanksgiveing was given to God in remembrance of the birth of our blessed Saviour, and therwith freinds and neighbours made mirrie with others, and had good cheir : now this day no such preachings nor such meittings with mirrieness, walking up and down ; but contrair, this day commanded to be keeped as ane work-day, ilk burgess to keep his buith, ilk craftsman his wark, feasting and idlesett forbidden out of pulpitts. Consistorie had no vaccance at this Yool, but had litle adoe. The people wes otherwayes inclyned, but durst not dissobey; yet litle merchandise wes sold, and alse litle work wrought on this day in either Aberdeins. The colliginers and other scholars keep the schools against their wills this day, but the colliginers gatt the play upon the 27th of December to the 3rd of January, and the gramariers to the 10th of Januar.

Spalding, *History of the Troubles*, i, 358

1642.

Pashe-day 10 Aprile, no fleshe durst be sold in Abirdene for making good cheir, as wes wont to be ; so ilk honest man did the best he culd for himselff. A mater never befoir hard of in this land, that Pashe-day sould be includit within Lentron tyme, becaus it wes now holding superstitious ; nor na communion givin on good-frydday nor this Pash-day

[1] Four dozen boxes of sweets.

as wes usit befoir. Mervallous in Abirdene to sie no Marcat, foule or flesche to be sold on Pash-evin.

Ibid., ii, 30

1575. *Sober Dress for Ministers*

Forsameikle as a comely and decent apparrell is requisite in all, namelie in the Ministers and sick as beares functioun in the kirk : First, we thinke all kynd of brodering [1] unseimlie, all bagaries [2] of velvett on gownes, hoses or coat, and all superfluous and vaine cutting out, steiking with silks ; [3] all kynd of costlie sewing on pasments, [4] or sumptuous or large steiking with silks, all kynd of costlie sewing or variant hews in sarks, all kynd of light and variant hewes in cloathing, as red, blew, yeallow, and sicklyke, quhilk declares the lightnes of the mynd ; all wearing of rings, bracelets, buttons of silver, gold or uther mettall ; all kynd of superfluitie of cloath in makeing of hose ; all using of plaids in the kirk be Reidars or Ministers, namely in tyme of thair ministrie and using thair office ; all kynd of gowning, coating, or doubliting, or breiches of velvett, satine, taffettie, or sicklyke ; all costlie gilting of whingers and knyves, [5] or sycklyke ; all silk hatts, or hatts of divers and light collours : Bot that thair haill habite be of grave collour, as black, russet, sad gray, sad browne, or searges, wirssett chamlet, [6] growgrame lytes wirsett, [7] or sicklyke : and to be short, that the good word of God be them and thair immoderatenes be not slanderit ; and thair wifes to be subject to the same ordour.

B.U.K., i, 335

[1] embroidery
[2] piping, or ornamental strips of coloured cloth sewn on to the garment
[3] with the addition of silk pieces
[4] additional decorative pieces of silk or lace
[5] but plain ' whingers and knyves ' are apparently allowed
[6] worsted camlet   [7] worsted of sober dye

THE COMMENCEMENT OF THE NEW YEAR

In early mediaeval times various dates were observed for the commencement of the new year : Christmas Day (25 December) ; Circumcision (1 January) ; Conception, or Annunciation (25 March) ; and Easter Day. And the practice varied not only in different countries but even within the same country. By the beginning of the thirteenth century, however, both Scotland and England were generally using 25 March as the commencement of the year.

Then, in 1582, Pope Gregory XIII issued a bull ordering the reform of the Calendar (which was increasingly divergent from the solar year), and at the same time decreeing that the new year was henceforth to begin on 1 January. This bull was not at once universally observed. Generally speaking the new Calendar and the new commencement of the year were quickly adopted by Roman Catholic countries, but some Protestant countries (including England) did not fall into line until the eighteenth century, and Russia, the Balkan countries and Greece not until the twentieth century.

Although James VI did not accept the Gregorian reform of the Calendar, nevertheless, being desirous that Scotland should not be behind ' other well governed commonwealths and countries' (and probably having in mind France and Holland), he issued an ordinance on 17 December 1599 decreeing that henceforth the first day of January should be the first day of the new year, and that the change should take effect on the 1 January following 31 December 1599.

Because of this, events in Scotland falling between 1 January and 24 March, inclusive, in any year prior to 1600 are usually given a double date in modern historical works—e.g. 17 March 1503/4 indicates that, at the time, the year was 1503 but, according to our modern reckoning from 1 January, it was 1504.

England maintained 25 March as the commencement of the year until the reform of the Calendar (for both England and Scotland) in 1751, when it was enacted that in England the new year was henceforth to begin on 1 January and so to begin on 1 January 1752.[1]

[1] See, in general, Harris Nicolas, *Chronology of History*, 37–45 ; *Handbook of Dates* (Roy. Hist. Soc.), 3–11.

1599, 17 December.

The Kingis Majestie and Lordis of his Secreit Counsall undirstanding that in all utheris weill governit commoun welthis and cuntreyis the first day of the yeir begynis yeirlie upoun the first day of Januare, commounlie callit new yeiris day, and that this realme onlie is different fra all utheris in the compt and reckning of the yeiris ; and his Majestie and Counsall willing that thair salbe na disconformitie betuix his Majestie, his realme and leigis, and utheris nichtbour cuntreyis in this particular, bot that thay sall conforme thameselffis to the ordour and custum observit be all utheris cuntreyis, especiallie seing the course and seasoun of the yeir is maist propir and ansuerabill thairto, and that the alteratioun thairof importis na hurte nor prejudice to ony pairtie : thairfoir his Majestie, with advise of the Lordis of his Secreit Counsall, statutis and ordanis that in all tyme cuming the first day of the yeir sal begin yeirlie upoun the first day of Januare, and thir presentis to tak executioun upoun the first day of Januare nix to cum, quhilk salbe the first day of the j^m and sex hundreth yeir of God ; and thairfoir ordanis and commandis the clerkis of his Hienes sessioun and signet, the directour and writtaris to the chancellarie and prevey seall, and all utheris jugeis, writtaris, notaris, and clerkis within this realme, that thay and everie ane of thame in all tyme heireftir date all thair decreittis, infeftmentis, charteris, seasingis, letteris, and writtis quhatsumevir, according to this present ordinance, compting the first day of the yeir fra the first day of Januare yeirlie and the first day of the j^m and vi^c yeir of God fra the first day of Januare nix to cum ; and ordanis publicatioun to be maid heirof at the mercat croceis of the heid burrowis of this realme, quhairthrow nane pretend ignorance of the same.

R.P.C., vi, 63

CHAPTER TEN

EDUCATION AND LEARNING

SCHOOLS

The Reformers in their two Books of Discipline had urged that the wealth of the old church should be devoted to the mainten- ance of the new ministry, to education and to the poor [1]; and although their proposals were rejected, the reformed church was consistently zealous in its efforts to improve, provide and maintain ' the schools.'

As early as 1562 the General Assembly moved to make supplica- tion to ' the higher power ' for the ' maintenance of schools for instruction of the youth in every parish,'[2] for, as it stated later, both kirk and school were ' requisite for erecting of a perfect reformed kirk '[3]; and the ' planting ' of schools was to go forward with the ' planting ' of kirks [4] so that the youth might be brought up to the service of God and the commonweal.

But because the schools were ' necessary instruments to come to the true meaning and sense of the will of God revealed in his Word,' [5] it was also vital to ensure that ' the instruction of youth be committit to none within this realme . . . but to them that professe Chrysts true religioun now publicklie preached,' [6] and in 1565 and 1567 the General Assembly laid down that teachers were to be ' tryed be the superintendents or visitors of the church ' to make certain that they were ' abill in doctrine.' [7] This was confirmed by parliament in December 1567.

1567. *Anent thame that salbe Teicheris of the Youth in Sculis*

Item Forsamekle, as be all Lawis and constitutiounis it is prouydit, that the youth be brocht up and instructit in

[1] See vol. ii, 2nd edn., pp. 176–8 and *supra*, p. 26.
[2] *B.U.K.*, i, 17   [3] *B.U.K.*, i, 311 (1574)
[4] In 1639 the commission appointed for the planting of kirks was also to consider the planting of schools (*A.P.S.*, v, 598a).
[5] *B.U.K.*, ii, 723 (1587)   [6] *B.U.K.*, i, 33 (1563)
[7] *B.U.K.*, i, 60, 108

the feir of God, and gude maneris : and gif it be utherwyse, it is tinsell [1] baith of thair bodyis and saulis, gif Goddis worde be not rutit in thame. Quhairfoir, our souerane Lord, with auise of my Lord Regent, and thre Estatis of this present Parliament, hes statute and ordanit, that all Sculis to Burgh and land, and all universiteis, and Collegis be reformit : And that nane be permittit nor admittit to have charge and cure thairof in tyme cuming, nor to instruct the youth priuatlie or oppinlie : bot sic as salbe tryit be the Superintendentis or visitouris of the Kirk.[2]

A.P.S., iii, 24, c. 11

One aim, from the Reformation onwards, was to ensure that the opinions of teachers did not deviate from those officially authorised at any particular time ; but ' visitations,' whether by super-intendents, bishops, presbyteries or commissioners, were also intended to ensure that the ' schooling ' was being carried out to the best of the limited resources available, and that scholars (and their parents) were not careless of the advantages provided for them. Thus presbytery and burgh records show that visita-tions of the schools, although not always faithfully carried out (and from time to time the General Assembly had to remind presbyteries of their duty in this matter), eventually became a regular routine in one form or another and continued until the passing of the Burgh and Parochial Schools (Scotland) Act of 1861.

On the question of faith, however, masters of schools were required in 1640 to subscribe the Confession of Faith and the Covenant,[3] and in 1690 they were required to subscribe the [Westminster] Confession and to take the oath of allegiance.[4] Particularly in the years immediately following 1690 many worthy and capable teachers were dismissed from their posts because of their refusal to subscribe the Confession and to take the oath.

In the early years of the reformed kirk, when there was a lack of schools and schoolmasters, many ministers filled the gap by

---

[1] loss
[2] This act was confirmed in 1581 (*A.P.S.*, iii, 210, c. 1)—possibly in view of the ' Popish scare ' at that time.
[3] *A.P.S.*, v, 272*a*   [4] *A.P.S.*, ix, 164*a*

acting as schoolmasters in their parishes. James Melville, who was singularly fortunate in this respect, has left an account of his schooling by the parish minister.

1563-1568.

When I was seavine . . . my father put my eldest and onlie brother, David, about a year and a halffe in age above me, and me togidder, to a kinsman and brother in the ministerie of his, to scholl, a guid, lerned, kynd man ; whome for thankfulnes I name, Mr Wilyam Gray, minister at Logie-Montrose [1] . . . Ther was a guid nomber of gentle and honest men's berns of the cowntrey about, weill treaned upe bathe in letters, godlines, and exerceise of honest geames.[2] Ther we lerned to reid the Catechisme, Prayers, and Scripture ; to rehers the Catechisme and Prayers *par ceur* ; also nottes of Scripture, efter the reiding thairof. . . . We lerned ther the Rudiments of the Latin Grammair, withe the vocables [3] in Latin and Frenche ; also dyverse speitches in Frenche, with the reiding and right pronunciation of that toung. We proceidit fordar to the Etymologie of Lilius and his Syntax, as also a lytle of the Syntax of Linacer ; therwith was joyned Hunter's Nomenclatura, the Minora Colloquia of Erasmus, and sum of the Eclogs of Virgill and Epistles of Horace ; also Cicero his Epistles *ad Terentiam.* He haid a verie guid and profitable form of resolving the authors ; he teatched grammaticallie, bathe according to the Etymologie and Syntax ; bot as for me, the trewthe was, my ingyne and memorie war guid aneuche, but my judgment and understanding war as yit smored [4] and dark, sa that the thing quhilk I gat war mair be rat ryme [5] nor knawlage. Ther also we . . . be our maister war teached to handle the bow for archerie, the glub for goff, the batons for fencing, also to rin, to loope, to swoom, to warsell,[6] to preve pratteiks,[7] everie ane haiffing

---

[1] See *Fasti Ecclesiæ Scoticanæ* (new ed.), v, 403   [2] games
[3] words ; vocabulary   [4] smothered   [5] rote
[6] wrestle   [7] to play

his matche and andagonist, bathe in our lessons and play.

Autobiography and Diary of Mr James Melvill
(Wodrow Soc.), 16–17

The concept of a separate school and schoolmaster for every parish, although hinted at in the Book of Discipline, and explicit in the Assembly act of 1562, was first clearly enunciated in an act of the Privy Council in 1616.

1616.

Forsamekle as, the kingis Majestie haveing a speciall care and regaird that the trew religioun be advanceit and establisheit in all the pairtis of this kingdome, and that all his Majesties subjectis, especiallie the youth, be exercised and traynned up in civilitie, godlines, knawledge and learning, that the vulgar Inglishe toung be universallie plantit, and the Irishe language,[1] whilk is one of the cheif and principall causis of the continewance of barbaritie and incivilitie amongis the inhabitantis of the Ilis and Heylandis, may be abolisheit and removit [2] ; and quhairas thair is no meane [3] more powerfull to further this his Majesties princelie regaird and purpois than the establisheing of scooles in the particular parrocheis of this kingdome whair the youthe may be taught at the least to write and reid, and be catechiesed and instructed in the groundis of religioun ; thairfore the kingis Majestie, with advise of the Lordis of his Secreit Counsall, hes thocht it necessar and expedient that in everie parroche of this kingdome whair convenient meanes may be had for interteyning a scoole, that a scoole salbe establisheit, and a fitt persone appointit to teache the same, upoun the expensis of the parrochinnaris according to the quantitie and qualitie of the parroche, at the sight and be the advise of the bischop of the diocie in his visitatioun. . . .

R.P.C., x, 671–2

[1] Gaelic   [2] See *supra*, pp. 261 *et seq.*   [3] no ways and means

This act of the Privy Council was ratified by Parliament in 1633 with an important ' addition·'

1633. *Ratificatioun of the act of counsall anent Plantatione of Schooles*

Our Soverane Lord with the advyse of the estates Ratifies the act of secreit counsall daited at Edinburgh the tent day of december ane thousand sax hundreth and saxteine yeirs maid anent the planting of schooles ; With this additione, that the Bischops in thair severall visitatiounes sall have power with consent of the heritors and most pairt of the parischioners and, if the heritor being lawfullie wairnit refuissis to appear, then with consent of the most pairt of the parischioners, to set downe and [1] stent upon everie plough [land] or husband land according to the worth for maintenance and establisching of the saids schooles. And if any persone sall find himselff greived it sall be lawfull to him to have recourse to the lords of secreit counsall for redres of any prejudice he may or doeth susteine ; And ordaines letters to be direct for chairging of the possessors for the tyme to answere and obey the schoolmaisters of the dewties that sall be appointed in maner forsaid.

A.P.S., v, 21, c. 5

The ' addition ' was the first attempt to lay the financial burden upon the heritors. Unfortunately the original phrase of 1616, ' where convenient means may be had,' provided a loophole for the heritors ; and although it would appear that a number of schools were established (particularly in more populous areas), the political and religious ferment of the immediately succeeding years was not conducive to so far-reaching a plan for the development of education. In September 1639, following the provisions of an act passed in August (*supra*, p. 118), the General Assembly petitioned Parliament for the erection of schools,[2] and the draft of a new act was apparently read before the Lords of the Articles in the October following.[3] In 1641 the General Assembly once more submitted a series of ' Overtours for Schooles,' praying that every

[1] *lege* ane   [2] *A.P.S.*, v, 594*a*   [3] *A.P.S.*, v, 610*b*

parish should have ' a reider and a schooll wherein childrene ar to be bred in reading wryting and grundis of religioun,' and stated that ' the meanes hitherto named or appointed for schooles of all sortis hath bene both litle and ill payed.' [1] The initiative was still coming from the Kirk, and its ' frequentlie reiterat desires . . . for founding and manteining schooles ' [2] were at length met by the act of 1646.

1646. *Act for founding of Schooles in everie paroche*

The Estates of parliament considdering how prejudiciall the want of schooles in manie congregations hathe bene and how beneficiall the founding therof in everie congregation wilbe to this kirk and kingdome Doe thairfore statute and ordane that there be a School founded and a Scholemaster appointed in everie paroche (not alreadie provyded) by advyse of the presbitrie. And to this purpose that the heritouris in everie congregation meet amongst themselfis and provyde a commodious hous for the schole and modifie a stipend to the schole master whiche sall not be under ane hundereth merkis nor above tua hundereth merkis to be payit yeirlie at tuo termes. And to this effect that they set doune a stent upon everie ones rent of stock and teind in the paroche proportionallie to the worth therof for mantenance of the schoole and payment of the scholemasteris stipend ; whiche stipend is declarit to be dew to the scholemasteris and clerkis of kirk sessionis.[3] And if the heritouris sall not conveene, or being conveened sall not aggrie amongst themselfis, than and in that case the presbitrie sall nominat tuell honest men within the boundis of the presbitrie who sall have power to establish a schoole, modifie a stipend for the schoolmaster with the latitude before exprest, and set doune a stent for payment therof upon the heritouris whilk salbe alse valide and effectuall as if the samen had bene done be the heritouris themselfis. . . .

A.P.S., vi, pt. i, 554, c. 171

---

[1] *A.P.S.*, v, 646*b*   [2] *A.P.S.*, vi, pt. i, 552*b*
[3] Both offices were normally held by the same man.

This act of 1646 was automatically rendered null and void in 1661 by the General Act Rescissory,[1] but the act of 1633 once more became operative. Schools and schoolmasters were multiplying, and in 1696 there was a further statute for ' settling of schools.'

1696. *Act for Settling of Schools*

Our Soveraign Lord considering how prejudiciall the want of schools in many places have been and how beneficiall the establishing and setleing therof in every paroch will be to this Church and Kingdom : Therfor His Majestie with the advice and consent of the Estates of Parliament statutes and ordains that there be a school settled and established & a schoolmaster appointed in every paroch, not already provided, by advice of the heritors and minister of the paroch ; And for that effect that the heritors in every paroch meet and provide a commodious house for a school and settle and modifie a sallary to a schoolmaster which shall not be under one hundred merks nor above two hundred merks, to be payed yearly at two terms, Whitsunday and Martinmass, by equall portions, and that they stent and lay on the said sallary conform to every heritors valued rent within the paroch, allowing each heritor relieff from his tennents of the half of his proportion for settling and maintaining of a school and payment of the schoolmasters sallary, which sallary is declared to be by and attour the casualities which formerly belonged to the readers and clerks of the kirk session. And if the heritors or major part of them shall not conveen, or being conveened shall not agree among themselves, then and in that case the presbitrie shall apply to the Commissioners of the Supply of the shire who, or any five of them, shall have power to establish a school and settle and modifie a sallary for a schoolmaster not being under one hundred merks nor above two hundred merks yearly as said is, and to stent and lay on the samen upon the heritors conform to their valued rent which shall be alse valid and effectuall as if it

[1] *Supra*, p. 153

had been done by the heritors themselves. . . . And lastly his Majestie with advice and consent forsaid ratifies and approves all former lawes customs and constitutions made for establishing and maintaining of schools within the Kingdom in so far as the same are not altered nor innovat by this present Act. *A.P.S.*, x, 63, c. 26

This act of 1696 virtually repeated the wording and provisions of the act of 1646 ; but the new power given to the presbyteries of calling in the county commissioners of supply [1] ensured that the act of 1696 could be rendered far more effective. The records show that in many cases a mere threat to bring a recalcitrant heritor before the commissioners was sufficient to bring in his part of the stent. Nevertheless the act took effect only very slowly. In 1758 there were still 175 parishes without schools— about a sixth of the total. Other agencies, however, supplemented the parochial schools. The Scottish Society for the Propagation of Christian Knowledge, founded in 1709, established its first three schools two years later—one of them in St Kilda— and the number of schools under its auspices increased to 150 in 1750 and 189 in 1809, while the number of their pupils rose from 2,757 in 1728 to 13,500 in 1808. The society declined to relieve heritors of their duty under the Act of 1696, and consequently refused to establish schools in parishes where there was *not* already a parochial school, but their work was a very valuable supplement to the statutory schools in the large and scattered Highland parishes. There were, in many parishes, ' adventure ' schools, privately conducted and maintaining their teachers, who were often of very low standard, by the pupils' fees, which were very meagre. At a later date there came Sunday Schools (initially for secular rather than religious education), and Gaelic Schools, which were established by societies formed for the purpose and which ultimately numbered 190.

In the burghs the ' grammar schools ' or ' burgh schools ' were under the patronage and management of the town councils, though there, too, much encouragement came from the church. The church, through the minister, exercised a large measure of control over the appointment of masters and their assistants, but the town council exercised an administrative control in such

[1] See *supra*, pp. 300-1

matters as school hours, vacations, the curriculum, repairs and equipment, and so forth.[1]

In general, the education offered in the parish schools was very elementary—the rudiments of reading and writing, the Catechism, the scriptures and a little simple arithmetic. In the burgh schools, however, and in some parish schools (depending largely upon the master) the course was more advanced, including Latin and sometimes Greek and sometimes French.

In the burgh schools, and in the larger parish schools, the scholars were all boys. Small children and girls were usually catered for in private schools, often run by ' dames,' where, in addition to reading and writing, the girls were taught how ' to sew a fine seam.' The town councils kept a close watch upon all private schools, however, and forbade them to take in boys above a certain age : partly in order to keep control in their own hands and partly to prevent the loss of school fees, small as those fees usually were.

By the end of the seventeenth century there were a few schools in Edinburgh for the daughters of lords and lairds, where, besides reading and writing, instruction was given in dancing, playing upon the virginals, sewing ' a white and coloured seam,' and the tasteful arrangement of wax fruits. Hugh Rose of Kilravock sent his daughter Margaret (then aged about 13) to one such school, and a statement of her school fees for one term has fortunately been preserved.

1700. *A Young Lady at School in Edinburgh*

Accompt the Laird of Kilraick for his daughter, Mrs. Margaret Rose, for her board and education, to Elisabeth Stratoun—

Imprimis, one quarter board, from the 2d
   September to the 2d of Decr., . . . £60 0 0
Item, Dancing, one quarter, ... 14 10 0
Item, One quarter singing and playing, and
   virginalls, ... 11 12 0

   Shee having two Masters for playing, I
   payed a dollar more to the second then
   to the first.

[1] See James Grant, *History of the Burgh Schools of Scotland.*

Item, One quarter at wryting, . . .	06	0	0
Item, For five writting books, ...	01	0	0
Item, For satine seame, and silk to her satine seame, ...	06	0	0
Item, One sett of wax-fruits, ...	06	0	0
Item, One looking glass that she broke, .	04	16	0
Item, A frame for a satine seam, . . .	01	10	0
Item, 12 dozen of linnen for smoaks to her, at 12 shilling per eln, ...	07	4	0
Item, One quarter at wryting, which I payed befor she entered a boarder, from the 2d December 1699 to 2d March 1700, . .	06	0	0
Item, A glass for her sattine seam, . . .	01	4	0

Summa £125 16 0

Discharged by ' Elizabeth Stratoun, indweller in Edinburgh.'

Family of Rose of Kilravock, 388–9

THE UNIVERSITIES

The reformed church concerned itself with the universities as well as with schools. The three existing universities—St Andrews, Glasgow and Aberdeen—were well-nigh moribund, and the [First] Book of Discipline had urged that they should be ' replenished with those that be apt to learning.' More than that, the Book of Discipline had presented a new curriculum of study which not only included Greek and Hebrew but also prescribed separate teachers for the more important subjects, or groups of subjects, together with a new concentration of work leading to degrees in Arts, Divinity, Medicine and Law. But again, the rejection of the Book led to the postponement of reform.

In the universities, as they then were, the course of study was still based upon Aristotle's Logic, Physics and Ethics (all read in Latin texts), with dictated notes, much memory work, and formal disputations in propugning or oppugning some thesis. Each master, or regent, took the same class of students the whole way through the four-year course,[1] and then took over a new class of first-year students to take them in turn through their four years' work. No regent professed one subject only, and specialised therein. There was little stimulation of the mind ; and the study was ' scholastic,' lacking in fervour and spirit.[2] James Melville, shortly after leaving the University of St Andrews, condemned the ignorance of its regents who had ' bot a few buikes of Aristotle, quhilk they lernit pertinatiuslie to bable and flyt [3] upon, without right understanding or use thairof,' [4] and, after his four years of study there, confessed that his uncle, Andrew Melville, found him to be ' bauche [5] in the Latin toung, a pratler upon precepts in Logik without anie profit for the right use, and haiffing sum termes of Art in Philosophie without light of solid knawlage.' [6]

Possibly the regents at St Andrews in James Melville's time suffered to some extent by comparison with Andrew Melville,[7] for, immediately upon his return to Scotland from Geneva in 1574, Andrew Melville stood out as the reformer and revolutioniser of Scottish higher education.

Appointed Principal of the University of Glasgow in the summer of 1574, Andrew Melville opened the new session in November of that year with a completely new curriculum and, with almost superhuman energy and ability, began to revivify university teaching.

1574.

. . . Mr Andro, entering principall maister . . . sett him haillelie to teatche things nocht hard in this countrey of befor, wherin he travelit exceeding diligentlie, as his

---

[1] strictly, three years and two terms

[2] It should be noted, however, that Archibald Hay's plan for the foundation of what later became St Mary's College in the University of St Andrews proposed the teaching of Greek and Hebrew, and, if possible, Arabic and Chaldaic. (See John Durkan, ' The Beginnings of Humanism in Scotland,' in *Innes Review*, iv, 5–24.)

[3] argue violently

[4] *Autobiography and Diary of Mr James Melvill* (Wodrow Soc.), 124.

[5] feeble ; of indifferent accomplishment   [6] Ibid., 46

[7] In one place in his *Diary* James Melville speaks affectionately of the ' loving care ' and kindness of his regent, Mr William Collace (ibid., 25).

delyt was thairin alleanerlie. Sa falling to wark with a few number of capable heirars, sic as might be instructars of uthers thairefter, he teatched tham the Greik grammer, the Dialectic of Ramus, the Rhetoric of Taleus, with the practise thairof in Greik and Latin authors, namlie, Homer, Hesiod, Phocilides, Theognides, Pythagoras, Isocrates, Pindarus, Virgill, Horace, Theocritus, &c. From that he enterit to the Mathematiks, and teatched the Elements of Euclid, the Arithmetic and Geometrie of Ramus, the Geographie of Dyonisius, the Tables of Hunter, the Astrologie of Aratus. From that to the Morall Philosophie ; he teatched the Ethiks of Aristotle, the Offices of Cicero, Aristotle de Virtutibus, Cicero's Paradoxes, and Tusculanes, Aristot. Polyb. and certean of Platoes Dialoges. From that to the Naturall Philosophie ; he teatched the buiks of the Physics, De Ortu, De Cœlo, &c., also of Plato and Fernelius. With this he joyned the Historie, with the twa lights thairof, Chronologie and Chirographie, out of Sleidan, Menarthes, and Melancthon. And all this, by and attoure his awin ordinar profession, the holie tonges and Theologie ; he teachit the Hebrew grammar, first schortlie, and syne mor accuratlie ; thairefter the Caldaic and Syriac dialects, with the practise thairof in the Psalmes and warks of Solomon, David, Ezra, and Epistle to the Galates. He past throw the haill comoun places of Theologie verie exactlie and accuratlie ; also throw all the Auld and New Testament. And all this in the space of sax yeirs ; during the quhilk he teatchit everie day, customablie, twyse, Sabothe and uther day ; with an ordinar conference with sic as war present efter denner and supper. His lerning and peanfulnes was mikle admired, sa that the nam of that Collage within twa yeirs was noble throwout all the land, and in uther countreys also. Sic as haid passed ther course in St Androis cam in nomber ther, and entered schollars again under ordour and discipline, sa that the Collage was sa frequent as the roumes war nocht able to receave tham. . . . Finalie, I dar say ther was na place in Europe comparable to Glasgw for guid letters, during

these yeirs, for a plentifull and guid chepe mercat of all
kynd of langages, artes, and sciences.

Autobiography and Diary of Mr James Melvill
(Wodrow Soc.), 48–50

But Andrew Melville was not merely concerned with teaching
new subjects, in a new way, and with the new ' humanism ' as
opposed to the old ' scholasticism,' he was also alive to the fact
that the old system of regents, under which each master ' professed
many subjects but was versed in few,' was out of date and in-
efficient, and needed to be replaced by a system under which
each master would profess only one subject, or one group of
related subjects, which would be ' his awin ordinar profession.'
His ' few number of capable heirars ' were instructed by him to
that end ; and by 1577 Blaise Laurie was established as permanent teacher of Greek and of Roman Eloquence, James
Melville as permanent teacher of mathematics, logic and moral
philosophy, Peter Blackburn of physics and astronomy, while
Melville himself taught divinity and oriental languages. A little
later a separate teacher was appointed for Hebrew.[1]

The new curriculum and the new methods of teaching were
defined in 1577 and formed an important part of what is usually
known as the *nova erectio* of the University of Glasgow.

1577. Nova Erectio *of the University of Glasgow*

. . . [*The Principal (Prepositus*)] in sacris literis probe institutus
ad aperienda fidei misteria et reconditos divini verbi the-
sauros explicandos idoneus linguarum etiam gnarus et
peritus sit oportet inprimis vero Hebraice et Syriace cujus
professorem esse instituimus linguam enim sanctam ut par
est promoveri inter subditos nostros cupimus ut scriptu-
rarum fontes et misteria rectius aperiantur. . . . Tres
insuper regentes putavimus e re et commodo Gymnasii fore
qui juventuti instituende presint et Preposito auxilientur.
Primus precepta Eloquentie ex probatissimis auctoribus, et
Grece lingue institutionem profitebitur Adolescentesque tum

---

[1] McCrie, *Life of Andrew Melville* (1819), i, 74–5

scribendo tum declamando exercebit ut in utriusque lingue facultate pares et ad philosophie precepta capescenda magis idonei evadere possint. Proximus Dialectice et Logice explicande operam dabit earumque precepta in usum et exercitationem proferet idque ex probatissimis auctoribus ut Cicerone Platone Aristotile de vita et moribus et policia administratione, que studia huic secundo regenti degustanda prebemus et pro adolescentulorum captu enarranda, Adjunget insuper elementa Arithmetice et Geometrie in quarum principiis non parum momenti ad eruditionem parandam situm est et ingenii acumen excitandum . . . Porro tertius regens Phisielogiam omnem eamque que de Natura est auscultationem utpote in primis necessariam quam diligentissime enarrabit, Geographiam etiam et Astrologiam profitebitur nec non generalem etiam Chrono-graphiam et temporum a condito mundo supputationem que res ad alias disciplinas et historiarum cognitionem non parum lucis adferet . . . Tres autem hos regentes nolumus prout in reliquis regni nostri Academiis consuetudo est novas professiones quotannis immutare quo fit ut dum multa profiteantur in paucis periti inveniantur verum in eadem professione se exerceant ut adolescentes qui gradatim ascendunt dignum suis studiis et ingeniis preceptorem reperire queant. . . .

Munimenta Alme Universitatis Glasguensis
(Maitland Club), ii, 106–9

Nor was Glasgow the only university to be reformed. In July 1579 the General Assembly petitioned the king and council for the reform of the Universtiy of St Andrews ; commissioners were appointed to visit and report ; and so speedily did the com-missioners work that their report was received and ratified by parliament in the November following.

1579. *The Reformatioun of the Universitie of Sanctandrois*

To the richt excellent richt heich and michty prince James the sext be the grace of God king of Scottis . . . your hienes commissioneris for reformatioun of the universitie of Sanct-

androis undersubscrivand . . . have . . . with commoun
consent divisit and drawin the forme and ordour following
As mair profitable to be observit in the said universitie in
tyme cuming to the glorie of god, honnour of your majestie,
proffite of this commoun welth, and gude upbringing of the
youth in sciences neidfull for continewing of the trew
religioun to all posterities.

First we ordane the new college [1] for the studee of theologie allanerlie : In the quhilk five maisteris daylie teacheing sall in four yeiris compleit the haill cours of the new and
auld testament and the commoun places in this ordour viz.,
The first lectour in the first sex monethis sall teiche the
preceptis of the Ebrew grammer and practize thairof in
David, Salamon, Job ; in the uther sex monethis the preceptis
of Caldaicque syraicque and use of the samin in Daniell
Esera the paraphrasis and syriacque new testament. The
secund lectoure in the secund yeir and ane half sall interpreit
out of the ebrew, and sensiblie oppin up the law of Moses
and the historie of the auld testament, Conferring with the
paraphrasis Septuagintis and uther lernit versionis quhar
neid beis. The thrid lectour in the last yeir and ane half
sall with the like diligence expone the prophettis greit and
small. The fourt lectour sall teiche the new testament out
of the greik toung during the haill course conferring with
the syriacque. The fyft lectour sall reid the commoun
places during the haill cours Swa that the studentis of
theologie heiring daylie thrie lessonis the space of foure
yeiris sall with meane diligence becum perfite theologians.
To this end thair salbe daylie repititionis, Anys in the oulk
publict disputationis, Everie moneth declamationis, Thrie
solemne examinationis in the cours—The first in the end
of the first yeir in the toungis And sa fer as they have hard
of the commoun places and new testament ; The secund
examinatioun efter the secund yeir and ane half in the law
historie and samekle as salbe red of the commoun places and
new testament ; And the thrid examinatioun in the end of
the cours in all the toungis the haill bible and commoun

[1] St Mary's

places. Thir thrie solemne examinationis salbegyne the tent day of september quharin everie learnit man salbe frie to dispute. And becaus thair is greit raritie at this present of men learnit in the knawlege of the toungis and uther thingis neidfull for sic professouris we have thairfoir electit certane of the maist qualifiit personis knawin to us as the saidis five maisteris for teacheing of the course of theologie in the order befoir writtin in the said new college, To begyne howsoune possibillie they may be transportit thairto ; Of the quhilkis thrie to entir this present yeir. . . .

Item that the youth may atteane unto perfite knawlege of humanitie and trew philosophie we ordane that in aither of the uther tua collegis viz Sanctleonardis and Sanct-salvatouris Thair salbe, besydis the principall, foure ordiner professouris or regentis everie ane continewing in his awin professioun. The first regent in the first yeir of the course Sall teache the preceptis of the greik toung and use thairof in the best and maist easie authouris with exerceis in com-positioun the first sex monethis in latine the rest in greik. The secund Regent sall teiche the preceptis of inventioun dispositioun and elocutioun the secund yeir schortest easiest and maist accurat with practize thairof in the best authouris of bayth the toungis. The thrid Regent sall teitche the maist proffitable and neidfull pairtis of the logikis of Aristotle with the ethikis and politikis all in greik and the offices of Cicero in latine. The fourt Regent sall teiche in greik samekle of the phisikis as is neidfull with the spheir.

Item that the buikis maist neidfull and proffitable salbe appointit for everie classe be the rectour deanis of facultie & thair assessouris.

Item that everie Authour be red in that toung quhilk they write into.

Item that the tua classis of humanitie sall spend at the leist ane hour daylie in compositioun.

Item that in the last sex monethis of the secund yeir they salbegyne to declame anys in the moneth in greik and latyne alternatim, besydis thair daylie compositionis quhilk declamatioun sall continew the tua last yeiris. . . .

Item becaus the youth tynis mekle tyme yeirlie be lang vaicance we ordane that the vaicance sall induir the onlie moneth of September. And befoir the first day of october everie ane sall returne, At the quhilk day the examinatioun of the scollaris of humanitie and philosophie salbegyne Amangis quhome the worthie to be promovit and the negligent to be haldin back. . . .

That the principall of Sanctsalvatouris College salbe professour in medicine and the principall of sanctleonardis in the philosophie of Plato Quhilkis sall reid ordinarlie foure tymes in the oulk monunday tuysday wednisday and fryday at the houris to be appointit be the electouris and maisteris of the universitie. . . . That the lawer now appointit to remane and be in sanctsalvatouris college sall reid within the same foure lessonis of the law ouklie viz on monunday tuysday wednisday and fryday To the quhilkis lessonis in the law salbe ordiner auditouris all the advocattis and scribis in the consistorie and sic utheris as ar desirous to proceid in the facultie of the law And that nane be admittit befoir the lordis or uther jugeis to ordiner procuratioun Except they sall gif first specimen doctrine in the universitie of sanctandrois and report a testimoniall of the said universitie witnessing thair qualificatioun And howfar they have proceidit in the studie of the law. . . . That the mathematiciane now in sanctsalvatouris college sall reid within the same foure lessonis ouklie in the mathematik sciences in sic dayis and houris as salbe appointit to the saidis lawer and mathematiciane be the rectour and maisteris of the universitie quhilkis alsua sall appoint the ordiner auditouris for the mathematiciane. . . .

A.P.S., iii, 178, c. 62

Although Melville's name does not occur among those of the commissioners, the recommendations made in their report are so closely allied to the *nova erectio* of Glasgow that it is difficult to believe he had no hand in the drafting. Moreover, in December 1580 he accepted the office of Principal of St Mary's College, and was then able to exercise in St Andrews the same remarkable zeal and energy which had characterised his work in Glasgow. Writing under the year 1581, his nephew, James Melville, reports that ' within a yeir or twa, Mr Andro, be his delling in publict and privat with everie an of tham [the regents and scholars], prevalit sa, that they fell to the Langages, studeit thair Artes for the right use, and perusit Aristotle in his awin langage ; sa that, *certatim et serio,* they becam bathe philosophers and theologes, and acknawlagit a wounderfull transportation out of darknes unto light.' [1]

It is also beyond doubt that Melville tried to secure reform in Scotland's remaining university—King's College, Aberdeen. In 1575 he is reported to have conversed with Alexander Arbuthnot, the Principal, to have explained to him his new ' order ' in Glasgow, and to have agreed with him a scheme for ' the new reformation of the said Colleges of Glasgow and Aberdeen.' [2] But what, if anything, was done at this time we do not know. In the parliament of 1581 a large number of articles, including three anent ' Reformatioun of the college of Abirdene ; for erectioun of ane college in Orknay ; [and] for consideratioun and Reformatioun of the state of the universiteis and collegis in generall ' were held over for consideration by certain of the Lords of the Articles who were to prepare statutes thereupon which were to have full effect until the end of the next parliament and to be fully effective thereafter if the next parliament did not abrogate them [3] ; but no statutes upon these three particular articles appear to have been drawn up. In 1583 the General Assembly noted that a visitation had taken labour with the University of Aberdeen and that an ' order ' had been ' set doune which is in the Principalls hands ' [4] ; and Calderwood reports a ' new erectioun made by the Erle Marshall, the Commendatar of Deny,[5] and certan brethrein, who had charge by the king's commissioun and the Assemblie to visite the said colledge.' [6] It may be that some changes were, in fact, introduced in King's College, Aberdeen, but possibly they were introduced only half-heartedly, or there was too much opposition and too long delay ; certainly in 1593 George, fifth Earl Marischal, founded Marischal College as a separate university, only about

[1] *op. cit.,* 124
[2] *Autobiography and Diary of Mr James Melville,* ut cit., 53
[3] *A.P.S.,* iii, 214, c. 9   [4] *B.U.K.,* ii, 614   [5] Deer
[6] Calderwood, iii, 707

a mile from King's College, and a university in which the ' order ' was to be closely parallel to that of the Melvillian conception, with an insistence upon Greek and Hebrew and stress upon masters who ' shall work in the same professorship.' Moreover, Peter Blackburn and David Cunningham, both of whom had been with Melville at Glasgow, were both closely associated with the new Marischal foundation at Aberdeen.[1]

The following extracts translated from the foundation charter [2] indicate the scope and method of the instruction to be given.

1593. *Foundation Charter of Marischal College, Aberdeen*

. . . THE PRINCIPAL, it is especially requisite, must be an upright and godly man, who shall look after the whole Academia and each of its members, and to whom we entrust the ordinary jurisdiction over each individual of our ' College '. He must be well versed in the Scriptures, able to unfold the mysteries of faith and the hidden treasures of the Word of God. He must also be skilled and learned in languages, and especially in Hebrew and in Syriac, which we wish to be spread abroad. Every week upon Monday he shall teach in the Scriptures one hour. He shall also (after the eight acroamatic books which the third Regent will explain) set forth all the rest of Physiology from the Greek text of Aristotle, to which he shall add a short explanation of Anatomy. He shall also expound Geography, History and the outlines of Astronomy. Moreover, he shall also add Hebrew Grammar, together with some practice in the rules. After the course of studies has been completed, he shall invest those that are qualified with the Master's cap. . . .

THE REGENT next after the Principal shall expound the elements of Arithmetic and Geometry, selections from Aristotle's books of Ethics and Politics from the Greek text, to which he shall add Cicero's books *De Officiis*, to mould the character and extend acquaintance with the Latin

---

[1] See G. D. Henderson, *The Founding of Marischal College, Aberdeen*, especially pp. 12–18. [2] Ratified by Parliament (*A.P.S.*, iv, 35, c. 48)

tongue, and towards the end of the third year he shall interpret the acroamatic books of Aristotle's *Organum Physicum*. The third in order shall teach the *Organum Logicum* and a system of rules of invention [1] and judgment from the best authors of both languages, and shall exercise the youths both in writing and in public speaking, that they may make equal progress in mastering both languages. The fourth, and lowest, shall profess instruction in Greek, explaining also the easiest authors of both languages, and shall accustom the students, by frequent written exercises, for the first six months to compose in Latin, and during the rest that follow to write Greek, to which he shall add a short compendium of logical invention and judgment. . . .

IT IS OUR DESIRE that the teachers of our Academia shall not shift about to new professorships, but shall work in the same professorship, that the youths who ascend step by step may have a teacher worthy of their studies and talents. . . . But, that the teachers may preside over the youths with advantage, and that the youths may make excellent progress in their studies, it shall be the duty of the Principal, Rector, Chancellor and Dean of Faculty to prescribe the authors that are to be laid before the youths, provided, however, that all the authors be explained to the students in those languages in which they originally wrote. It is also our desire that our foresaid Regents shall accustom those committed to their care to prove, write, declaim, dispute, with the utmost diligence in the literary arena, but especially the students of the two lowest classes, to compose daily ; and shall devote one hour at least to this every day. Likewise, after the first eighteen months, all the students are to be exercised every month in public declamation in Greek and in Latin alternately. . . .

(Translation in) *Fasti Academiæ Mariscallanæ Aberdonensis*
(New Spalding Club), i, pp. 63–5

[1] The finding or selection of topics or arguments for discussion, and the devising of the method of treatment.

But this period also saw the foundation of a fourth university [1] in Scotland—the University of Edinburgh, which sprang from the concept in the [First] Book of Discipline that there should be a ' college ' in every ' notable town.'

The idea of a ' college ' in Edinburgh had earlier exercised the mind of Robert Reid, Bishop of Orkney and, at the time of his death in 1558, President of the College of Justice. Reid, who was an enlightened prelate and a munificent patron of learning, devised a sum of 8,000 merks to found a college in Edinburgh in which, after a general course in Arts, the students could proceed to the study of canon and civil law. But immediately thereafter the Reformation struggle broke out, and, after that, the succeeding six years of Mary's personal rule were not favourable to the furtherance of either Reid's project or that laid down in the Book of Discipline. Not until 1579 did the Town Council and ministers of Edinburgh seriously apply themselves to the idea of a ' town's college ' and, when they did, their intentions followed the concept of the Book of Discipline rather than Reid's concept of a college for law. But part of Reid's bequest was still available ; and in 1582, when James VI granted a charter to the burgh of Edinburgh giving it leave to erect a college, he added to Reid's bequest by making available the lands and buildings of the collegiate church of St Mary in the Fields (the Kirk o' Field of Darnley's murder) and also allowing the Town Council to use for the needs of the college certain funds previously disponed by Queen Mary for the use of the ministry, the schools, the sick and the poor.

1582. *Charter by James VI to the Town Council of Edinburgh*

[*After reciting Queen Mary's charter granting to the burgh of Edinburgh the lands, buildings and revenues pertaining to chaplainries, altarages, prebends etc. within the liberty of the burgh, the grounds and rents of the Friars, and any mortifications devoted to the saying of the Mass—to be held for the use of the ministry, the schools, the sick and the poor, and now to be held for the use*

[1] With the foundation of Marischal College in 1593 the Scottish universities numbered five, while for a short period Fraserburgh raised the number to six (see R. G. Cant, ' Scottish " Paper Universities " ' in *The Scots Magazine*, October 1945).

of the college—and after confirming the resignation and gift of the collegiate church of St. Mary in the Fields, with all its lands, buildings and revenues] maxime apta et commoda pro constructione domorum et edificiorum ubi professores bonarum scientiarum et literarum ac studentes earundem remanere et suam diuturnam exercitationem habere poterint ultra et preter alia loca convenientia pro hospitalitate [*the charter proceeds*] ideo nos enixe cupientes ut in honorem dei et commune bonum nostri regni literatura indies augeatur volumus et concedimus quod licebit prefatis preposito consulibus et eorum successoribus [burgi nostri de Edinburgh] edificare et reparare sufficientes domos et loca pro receptione habitatione et tractatione professorum scolarum grammaticalium humanitatis et linguarum philosophie theologie medicine et jurium aut quarumcunque aliarum liberalium scientiarum quo declaramus nullam fore rapturam predicte mortificationis ; ac etiam prefati prepositus ballivi et consules ac eorum successores cum avisamento tamen eorum ministrorum pro perpetuo in posterum plenam habebunt libertatem personas ad dictas professiones edocendas maxime idoneas uti magis convenienter poterint elegendi cum potestate imponendi et removendi ipsos sicuti expediverit. . . .

Charters, Statutes, etc. of the University of Edinburgh
(ed. Morgan and Hannay), No. II

In October 1583 the college began its first session, and its right to grant degrees, assumed from the beginning, was confirmed by parliament in 1621.[1]

The University of Edinburgh was thus entirely different in its foundation from St Andrews,[2] Glasgow[3] and Aberdeen.[4] In particular, the right of ' inputting and outputting ' the teachers pertained to the Town Council ; and the Provost of the burgh became the Rector of the university, not, as in the older univer-

[1] By an act which gave to the college of Edinburgh all the liberties, privileges and immunities enjoyed by any other college in the realm (*A.P.S.*, iv, 670, c. 79)   [2] Vol. i, 2nd edn., pp. 212–16
[3] Vol. ii, 2nd edn., pp. 117–20   [4] Vol. ii, 2nd edn., p. 120

sities, to protect the liberties of the students and teachers, but to act as the ' eye of the town council ' to see that all went well in the ' town's college.'

In Edinburgh the system of ' regenting,' whereby each regent took his class the whole way through the four-year course, prevailed from the beginning ; in St Andrews the act of 1579 had ceased to be observed at least as early as 1588 ; and Glasgow and Aberdeen had reverted to the regenting system certainly by the middle of the seventeenth century. Despite the efforts of Andrew Melville, the old tradition had proved too strong. A system of university professors, each a specialist in his own subject and teaching his own subject, was only finally and definitely attained in the eighteenth century—Edinburgh in 1708 ; Glasgow in 1727 ; St Andrews in 1747 ; Aberdeen (Marischal College) in 1753, and Aberdeen (King's College) in 1798.[1]

A brief description of university life in Glasgow in 1672 is contained in the note-book of Josiah Chorley, an English student who, unable to continue his studies at Trinity College, Cambridge, because of his non-conformity, was encouraged to proceed to Glasgow.

The University of Glasgow in 1672

I was admitted in the Batchelor year, having studied Logic and Philosophy so long in England, and came under the presidency and tuition of that celebrated philosopher Mr. John Tran. . . . I soon found my great account in it, to sit constantly at his feet, for as keen as my appetite was to learning, here was rich provision enough to satisfy it, in daily dictates, disputations, etc. . . .

The good orders of the College were very agreeable to mine inclination. At five o'clock in the morning the bell rings, and every scholar is to answer to his name, which is then called over. The day is spent in private studies and public exercises in the classes ; at nine at night every

---

[1] See, in general, W. Croft Dickinson, *Two Students at St Andrews, 1711–1716*, xxii–xxvi.

28

chamber is visited by the respective regents.[1] The Lord's days strictly observed, all the scholars called to the several classes, where, after religious exercises, all attend the Primar and Regents to church, forenoon and afternoon, and in the same order from church. Then, in the evening, called again to the classes, and then come under examination concerning the sermons heard, and give account of what was appointed the foregoing Sabbath in some theological treatise, viz., Wollebius, or Ursin's Catechism, etc., and other religious exercises ; and then to supper and chambers ; so that there is no room for vain ramblings and wicked prophanations of the day, if we were so disposed. . . .

Cosmo Innes, *Sketches of Early Scotch History*, 232-3

The University of Edinburgh remained under the control of the Town Council until the Universities (Scotland) Act of 1858, by which those chairs to which the Town Council had previously made appointments were henceforth to be filled by seven ' Curators of Patronage,' four appointed by the Town Council and three by the University. The Act also united King's College and Marischal College to form the one University of Aberdeen (1860). But the Universities (Scotland) Act of 1858 is probably of greater importance in its provisions governing all four universities. In addition to drawing up new degree regulations, including regulations for Honours degrees, now instituted for the first time, the Act also introduced important changes giving all four universities a parallel constitution and administrative structure. Henceforth the Rector was to be chosen by the undergraduates, and the Chancellor by the graduates (henceforth incorporated as the General Council). The Senatus Academicus was to superintend teaching and discipline and to administer the property and revenue, subject to the control and review of a new body—the University Court.

Later, by the Universities (Scotland) Act of 1889, the powers of the Senatus Academicus and of the University Court were more clearly defined, the Court becoming the supreme governing body, but the Senatus Academicus remaining the supreme

[1] In St Andrews the regents took this ' perlustration ' of the chambers in turn for a week at a time ; and the regent on duty each week was known as the ' hebdomadar.'

authority in all teaching matters. By this same Act, and its sub-sequent ordinances, the teaching session was extended to include a summer term ; women were for the first time admitted to degrees ; and the Students' Representative Council was officially recognised. Less fortunate, perhaps, were the minute details giving to each university an identical organisation and identical degree curricula, and prescribing that any change or development desired by one university should be by ordinance, submitted to the other three universities for approval, and then, finally, for the approval of a central committee to be established as the Scottish Universities Committee of the Privy Council. Any one university wishing to establish a new degree, or a new chair, or to venture in any other way into new fields of study and research may thus find its proposals subject to long (but at present un-avoidable) delay.

Later changes in the position of the teaching staff, including readers, lecturers and assistants, were made by the Act of 1922 ; many changes in degree regulations, in the arrangements for teaching, in the establishment of chairs and so forth have been, and constantly are being, made by ordinance.

THE BOOK TRADE

1590.

Anent the complaint maid to the Lordis of Secreit Counsaill be Andro Hairt, burges of Edinburgh, and Johnne Nortoun, Englishman, makand mentioun that quhair, thay considder-ing quhat hurte the legis of this realme sustenit throw the scairsitie of buikis and volumes of all sortis, and to quhat exorbitant priceis the buikis and small volumis ar rissin to, quhilkis wer brocht hame frome Lundone and uthiris pairtis of England, and sauld in this realme at the thrid advantage, thay, upoun a eirnist zeale to the propagation and increse of vertew and letters within this realme, interprisit twa yeiris syne or thairby the hamebringing of volumis and buikis furth of Almanie and Germanie, fra the quhilkis pairtis the maist parte of the best volumis in England ar brocht, and in this tread have sa behavit thameselffis that this toun is furneist with bettir buikis and volumis nor it wes at ony

423

tyme heirtofoir, and the same volumis sauld be thame in
this cuntrey to the haill legis als gude-chaip as thay ar to
be sauld in Lundone or ony uther part of England, to the
grite ease and commoditie of all esteatis of personis within
this realme ; in consideratioun of the quhilk commoun
benefite thay luiked to haif enjoyit the libertie and previlegeis grantit in all esteatis and kingdomes to personis
usaris of this trade,—to witt, that thair haill buikis and
volumis suld be custum free : nevirtheles, thay ar dalie
troublit be the custumaris for payment of grite custumes
for thair saidis buikis and volumis, quhilk is ane new impost
and exactioun, at na tyme heirtofoir cravit within this
realme, and nawise permittit or sufferrit in ony uther
cuntrey ; and thay doubt nocht bot the saidis Lordis will
disallow of sic preparatives and novalteis to be usit aganis
thame. And, upoun the like complaint be Thomas Vaut-
rallier, imprentair, he obtenit ane decrete, dischargeing the
provest and baillies of this burgh and thair custumair, for
thameselffis and remanent commissionaris of burrowis, fra
all seiking, asking or craving of ony custumes fra the said
Thomas for ony buikis sauld or to be sauld be him, alsweill
within this burgh as outwith the same, as the said decrete
beiris, like as at mair lenth is contenit in the said complaint.
Quhairunto David Seytoun of Parbroth, comptrollair to our
Soverane Lord, and Johnne Gourlaw, custumair of Edinburgh, being warnit to answer, and thay compeirand baith
persounallie, and the said Andro Hairt compeirand alswa
personallie, for himselff and in name of the said Johnne
Nortoun, the ressonis and allegationis of baith the saidis
pairteis being hard and considderit be the saidis Lordis and
thay ryplie advisit thairwith, the Lordis of Secreit Counsaill
ordanis the said Johnne Gourlaw, custumair of Edinburgh,
and all uthiris custumaris of quhatsumevir uther burrowis
and portis of this realme, to desist and ceis fra all asking,
craveing or suteing of ony custum fra the saidis complenairis
for any buikis or volumis brocht or to be brocht and sauld
be thame within this realme in tyme cuming, dischargeing
the saidis custumaris thairof and of thair offices in that

parte ; providing alwayes that the saidis Andro Hairt and Johnne Nortoun present all pakkis, punsionis and barrellis, quhairin the saidis buikis and volumis salbe brocht hame heireftir, to the custumair of that burgh quhair thay sall arryve, befoir the samin be lowsit, brokin up, sauld or disponit upoun, quhairthrow the samin may be sene gif thair be ony uther wairis or mercheandice thairin nor the saidis buikis and volumis, that the custum of the same wairis, gif ony be, may be pait to the saidis custumaris as effeiris,—utherwise thir presentis to be null and of nane avail, force nor effect.

R.P.C., iv, 459–60

THE ADVANCEMENT OF LEARNING

The preceding sections on the schools and the universities would be incomplete without a brief note on some of the many notable advances in learning in the second half of the seventeenth century. In 1681 Lord Stair published his *Institutions of the Law of Scotland*, an orderly and scientific statement of Scots Law which has 'furnished the model and basis for all subsequent treatises of its kind,'[1] and in 1682 the Advocates' Library, which has now become the National Library of Scotland, had been definitely established through the initiative of Sir George Mackenzie. This period also saw the earlier work of Timothy Pont continued by such cartographers as Robert Gordon of Straloch, his son James Gordon of Rothiemay, and John Adair ; it was the period of James Gregory of the reflecting telescope, and of his nephew David Gregory the mathematician. Finally at this time the Botanic Garden in Edinburgh was established, the Royal College of Physicians was founded, and the Edinburgh Medical School was beginning to acquire its fame.[2]

[1] Lord Cooper, ' Some Classics of Scottish Legal Literature ' in *The Scottish Bankers' Magazine*, January 1950.
[2] An admirable brief survey of these and other advances in learning is given in Henry W. Meikle, *Some Aspects of Later Seventeenth Century Scotland* (Glasgow, 1947).

Chapter Eleven

POLITICAL RELATIONS BETWEEN SCOTLAND AND ENGLAND

From the Abdication of Mary (1567) to the Death of Elizabeth (1603)

Relations with England following the accession of James VI were determined by (i) the problems arising out of Mary's arrival in England as a fugitive, and her subsequent long captivity ; (ii) the English interest to prevent Scottish foreign policy from damaging England and, in particular, to prevent Scotland from being used as a northern base by France or Spain ; and (iii) in their later stages, James's endeavours to secure his succession to Elizabeth— the ' great prize ' which might, after all, elude him.

The frequent instability of Scottish politics during these years of a delicately balanced European situation was a perpetual stimulus to intrigue in which English and Scottish agents, Elizabeth, James, the continental powers, Protestant and Roman Catholic partisans, and disaffected or self-seeking Scottish politicians all played a part.

Anglo-Scottish relations until 1603 are therefore complicated by an atmosphere of intrigue and plot which pervades the diplomatic correspondence, and is to be read in the contemporary private memoirs and diaries. The extracts which follow can give only an indication of the main trends.

The York-Westminster Conference, 1568

Elizabeth's first reaction to the proceedings of the Confederate Lords against Mary was one of undisguised disapproval. Rebellion against a lawful reigning sovereign was a dangerous precedent ; successful rebellion more dangerous still. Mary's flight into England and her personal appeal for help, however, created a new situation ; thenceforward Mary's presence in England created a constant conflict between principles and expediency. In the end, Fotheringhay was to be the only solution.

It was to Elizabeth's interest that Scotland should be Protestant ;
the Earl of Moray, who had accepted the regency in 1567, was
a strong Protestant and a firm believer in an 'understanding'
with England ; Mary, on the other hand, was a Roman Catholic
and a claimant to the English throne. What was to be done
when Mary, the deposed sovereign of a neighbouring kingdom,
appealed for aid ? Undoubtedly the regency of Moray would
be more acceptable than the rule of Mary ; and if, indeed, Mary
could be shown to have had guilty knowledge of Darnley's murder,
that would be sufficient justification for any refusal of help,
perhaps for any future treatment which might be accorded to her.
Possibly such considerations lay in the background of the
suggested arbitration at York. Only if Elizabeth understood the
reasons for the rebellion against Mary, it was argued, would
Elizabeth be able to answer Mary's appeal. Both sides could
rest some hopes upon an inquiry, and the English arbitration was
accordingly accepted. The resulting conference, meeting first
at York and then at Westminster, was inconclusive. After the
production of the Casket Letters Mary's commissioners pressed
for the dissolution of a conference so derogatory to the honour
of their Queen, or at least that Mary should be allowed to answer
personally before Elizabeth as another sovereign and her peer.
But the production of the Letters gave Elizabeth an excuse for
refusing to allow Mary an audience—she could not receive her
'without manifest blemish' to her own honour ; and on 10 January 1569 Cecil is reported to have pronounced a decision which
was no decision at all. Moreover, the production of the Casket
Letters had hopelessly besmirched Mary's name and reputation,
and had made it virtually impossible for her to regain her former
honour and estate. In addition, James, her infant son, was now
the crowned King of Scots, and the lords who were in opposition
to Mary, and willing to work in co-operation with England, held
the 'authority.'

1568. 15 December

. . . And that where the Quene of Scottes commissioners
being made privee of this the accusation of the sayd quene,
have forborn to answer to the same, refusyng also to have
any furder conference in this matter, pressyng only to have

the Quene thyr maistres permitted to come to the presence
of the Quenes majesty to make hir answer—and otherwise
to make no answer at all—it hath bene considered by hir
majesty, and thought not unmete in this sort followyng to
answer the said commissioners, if they shall persist in ther
said request—That hir majesty will be very willing and
desirous that some good answer may be made by the said
Quene either by hir commissioners and delegates or by hir
owne self, before such sufficient persons as hir majesty wold
send to hir. But considering hir majesty had at hir first
comming into the realme, found it not mete for hir owne
honour to have hir (being so commenly defamed of so
horrible crimes) to comme to hir presence, before she might
be therof some wise purged—so also now the crimes (wherwith she hath ben by commen fame burdened) being by
many vehement allegations and presumptions, upon
thynges now producid, made more apparant : she cannot
without manifest blemish of hir owne honour in the sight
of the world, agree to have the same Quene to come into
hir presence, untill the said horrible crimes may be by some
just and reasonable answer avoyded and removed from hir
—which her majesty wold wish might also be. . . .

Calendar of Scottish Papers, ii, No. 921

1569.

The Bishop of Rosse,[1] in his memorialls, reporteth that
the regent and the rest of his collegues, commissioners, came
before the queen's Majestie's counsell of England, where
Sir William Cicill, secretar, at the queen's Majestie's
command, and her Highnesse' counsell, gave them suche
answere in effect as followeth, upon the 10th of Januare :

' Whereas, the Erle of Murrey and his adherents come
in this realme at the desire of the queen's Majestie of
England, to answere to suche things as the queene, their
soveran, objected against them and their alledgances [2] :

---

[1] John Lesley, one of Mary's commissioners at the arbitration
[2] allegations

for so muche as nothing hath beene deduced against them as yitt, that may impaire their honour or alledgances, and on the other part, there had nothing beene sufficientlie produced nor showne by them against the queen, their soverane, whereby the Queene of England sould conceave or tak anie evill opinioun against the queene, her good sister, for anie thing yitt seene and alledged by the Erle of Murrey, yitt, in respect of the unquiett estat and disorder of the realme of Scotland now in his absence, her Majestie thinketh meete not to restraine anie farther the said erle and his adherents' libertie ; but suffer him and them at their pleasure to depart ; relinquishing them in the same estate in the which they were of before their comming within this realme, till she heare farther of the Queen of Scotland's answeres to suche things as have been alledged against her.'

Calderwood, ii, 471-2

Elizabeth and Morton

The break-up of the Westminster proceedings left Moray in control in Scotland, but in England the danger of Mary's position as the Roman Catholic heiress to the throne (if not indeed, despite the Treaty of Edinburgh,[1] the rightful queen), and hence the focus of Catholic aspirations and plots, was brought home to Elizabeth by the Northern Rebellion of 1569. In its course it found aid, encouragement and finally refuge from Mary's supporters in the south of Scotland. Moray's assassination in 1570, followed by civil war between the ' King's men ' and the ' Queen's men,' meant a renewed danger to England from the north and, coinciding with the papal bull excommunicating Elizabeth, forced the English queen to give material help to the Protestant party.

The situation was similar to that of 1559–60 when decisive measures were necessary to prevent a political development in Scotland which might threaten English security. At first, the pretext for English military intervention in 1570 was action against the harbourers of refugees from the 1569 rebellion as well as retaliation for a raid by Fernieherst and Buccleuch who,

[1] cf. vol. ii, 2nd edn., pp. 180–1

in company with the exiled Earl of Westmorland, had harried the lands of those who were loyal to Elizabeth in the northern parts. But the English force did little save waste the lands of Fernieherst and Buccleuch and destroy the seat of the Hamiltons.

1570.

. . . The Erle of Sussex, Lieutenant of the North, Lord Hounsdane, Wardane of the East Marche, and Sir Johne Foster of the Middle Marche, wasted the lands and razed the castells belonging to Balcleuche, Phairnihirst, and their assisters . . . the castell of Hume was randered and spoiled. . . . The Lord Scroope spoiled the Laird of John-stoun's lands in the west. . . . It was concluded that the obstinate Hammiltons sould be punished in their substance, and by demolishing of their castells and houses. . . . The castell [of Hamilton] was spoiled, and therafter blowne up with powder. The palace and toun were burnt by the furious multitude. . . . The English departed the 1st of June.

Calderwood, ii, 562-4

Elizabeth now toyed with the idea of restoring Mary, upon conditions,[1] but the negotiations proved abortive. After all, Mary could be restored only if James were deposed. So the civil war grew more bitter. In November 1571 the regent Mar appealed for English help for the ' mantenance and protection of the trew religion ' and for ' pacifying of the troublit estait of our realme ' [2] ; but Elizabeth was reluctant to intervene. After the death of Mar, James Douglas, 4th Earl of Morton, was elected Regent and accepted the office in parliament on 24 November 1572. He at once (1 December 1572) wrote to Burghley and to the Earl of Huntingdon, President of the North, announcing his intention of continuing ' the good intelligence with England ' and craving Elizabeth's ' favourable protection and maintenance.'

[1] See also the ' Articles presented to the Queen of Scotland by Sir William Cecil,' 2 October 1570, in *Warrender Papers* (Scot. Hist. Soc.), i, No. LXVII.   [2] *Warrender Papers*, i, No. LXX

1572   1 December.

Morton to Lord Burghley

 . . . The knowledge of her Majesty's meaning has chiefly moved me to accept the charge [the regency], resting in assured hope of her favourable protection and main-tenance. . . . Praying your lordship, therefore, effectuously, as I have heretofore felt your favourable good will and friendship before I accepted this charge, and as you have been a special instrument for the continuance of the amity and for the common commodity of both the countries, so to continue in the same disposition . . . and I shall always be ready to ' pleasure ' your lordship to my power in any-thing that shall lie in me to do.

Calendar of Scottish Papers, iv, No. 488

Morton to the Earl of Huntingdon

Announces his election as regent by the choice of the nobility and estates of Scotland, and promises that there shall be no lack in him in that which may continue the good intelligence with England.

Foreign Calendar, Elizabeth, 1572–4, No. 655

Following the Pacification of Perth, in February 1572/3,[1] and seeing increasing danger from the Catholic powers in Europe, Elizabeth at length decided to send a small English force to help Morton in the reduction of Edinburgh Castle (May 1573), held by Kirkcaldy of Grange in the name of Mary, and Mary's last stronghold in Scotland.

1573.   *The Siege of Edinburgh Castle*

Within tua dayes efter [8 April] came a hundreth pioners out of Ingland, to brek and prepayre the grund for placing of cannons . . . Sum cannons war also broght be water from the castell of Sterling to Leyth. . . . Efter this entrit

[1] *R.P.C.*, ii, 193 *et seq.*

the Marshall of Berwick [1] in Scotland, with the rest of his armie be land ; and thair provisioun of gunnis, bullats, and poulder be sea. In his armie be land, he had fyve hundreth hagbutters and sevin score pickmen. The Regent before hand had directit young Douglas of Kilspyndie, Johne Cunynghame, sone to the Erle of Glencarne, the Master of Ruthven, and Johne Sempill sone to my Lord Sempill, to enter in England as pledges for the army and gunnis, unto the tyme of thair returne. . . .

The Inglish armie began thair batterie on Trinitie Sonday, at tua houres efternone, whilk was the 17 day of Maij, 1573, and shot perpetuallie at all the circuit thareof, and thus continewit till eight houres in the nycht. In the meyne tyme, sum hagbuts war shot furth of the castell, that hurt and slew dyvers Inglishmen ; and the batterie indurit to the 22 day of the said moneth, that thre quarters of the great towre callit King Davids towre fell doun, and the haill towre of the portculeis, with sum portions of the forewall, and a great quantitie of the bak wall that lyis to the south and south west, for scailling with ledders for thare easie entrie ; and on the 26 day thay assailyeit the castell on the east syd, whilk was easilie win ; bot thais that scaillit on the wast syde thay war repulsit fra sevin howres in the mornyng till ten houris. Mr. Drurie the Marshall then tuik trewis, and the Capten [2] consentit, and the Regent was dissassented. . . . During the whilk tyme thay consultit within the castell what was best to be done. Bot thay war devydit in tua myndis and drew to factions: The a partie desyrit to hald, and the uther partie desyrit to geve over ; and the Capten indeid was the cheif of thais that wald have haldin, bot the nomber of thayme that war of his opinion was sa small and waik, that he thoght himself in an evill cace. . . . The Capten finding himself thus destitute, was resolvit to rander himself to the Queyne of Inglands mercie, and to the will of hir Lieutenent, bot na way to the Regent : and so upon the 29 day of Maij, the Capten came over the fallin wark, and randrit himself to

[1] Sir William Drury   [2] Sir William Kirkcaldy of Grange

the Marshall of Berwick. . . . The adverteisment of this randring was quicklie sent to the Queyne of Ingland ; bot she sent worde back, and commandit all the preasoners to be restorit to the Regent, to do with thayme as he sould think maist expedient . . . the capten, Sir James Kirkaldie his brother, James Mosman, and James Cockie, goldsmythis of Edinburgh, war hangit upon the 3 day of August, and thair heiddis placit upon the maist eminent places of the castell wall.

Historie of King James the Sext
(Bannatyne Club), 141–5

A strong Protestant and pro-English government now seemed to be assured in Scotland ; and throughout his regency Morton consistently pursued an anglophile policy.

The Fall of Morton

Esmé Stuart, Lord D'Aubigny,[1] was regarded with suspicion both by the Kirk and by Elizabeth. But an English plot to assassinate D'Aubigny and kidnap James with the help of Morton was discovered[2] ; and when, through the instigation of D'Aubigny, Morton was imprisoned,[3] Elizabeth viewed the situation with alarm, but typically failed to take sufficiently strong measures to save the man who had consistently advocated and pursued a pro-English policy in Scotland, and who could ensure the continuance of that policy. Randolph was sent to Scotland with a threat of English invasion, but it was known to be a threat and nothing more.

After Morton's execution, D'Aubigny (now Duke of Lennox) and his ally James Stewart (now Earl of Arran) were, for the time, supreme.

---

[1] *Supra*, p. 31

[2] See *Correspondence of Sir Robert Bowes* (Surtees Soc.), 22 *et seq*. There was also a counterplot by D'Aubigny, Argyll, Beaton and Lesley to kidnap James and carry him off to France to be brought up as a good Catholic. But to what extent the various plots of this time were realistic is another matter.   [3] See *supra*, p. 32

1581 **6 January.** *Instructions by Elizabeth for Thomas Randolph*

. . . You shall declare to him [1] that we cannot sufficiently marvail how it could be wrought in the heart of so young a Prince to put on so hard a mind against a personage of such quality and of so great desert as the said Earl of Morton is, being not only a subject and nobleman born, but also the person in whose hands the managing of that whole realm has for the greatest part of his minority lain, and not without honour to him and profit to his State, and all this to be wrought by one so suddenly come thither, being a stranger by birth, and also by marriage, how near soever he be [by] nature or blood, no less behind the other in good parts me[et] for government than he is in years. But the matter we principally weigh in this case, and whereof we think meet to advertise the King, is to let him understand that the end and chief cause of D'Aubigny's repair into the realm is but to breed some alteration in the State, howsoever it be dissembled in the meantime, and to turn him away from the true service of God, and to re-establish in that realm the Romish religion. For truth and good proof whereof you shall lay before the King the copies of such advertisement—which shall be delivered to you—as we have received from foreign parts, most plainly discovering the secret of this practised overthrow of that State. Which thing, if he rightly considers, he cannot but see of what evil consequence it will be to him, for that it cannot be compassed without the bloodshed of infinite numbers, the overthrow of the Gospel, and an unrecoverable dishonour to his name and the provoking of God's wrathful indignation against him and his posterity. And for that no trouble can happen in that realm especially tending to the alteration of religion, but that it is meant also should reach to us, we cannot—besides the care we have of his well doing—but for our own surety seek by all the means we may to prevent the same ; and hereupon, if you shall be so advised by those that you know [to be]

[1] i.e., King James VI

434

well affected towards us, you may use some threats.   For
the second point :—if you shall not find him inclining to
restore the Earl to his favour, then you shall seek to enter
into conference with the party which you shall find and
know to wish well to the King, and have a desire to have the
practices of D'Aubigny encountered, and to know of them
what they can be resolved to do, and what party they are
able to make in case ' her majesty ' sends a power into that
realm to preserve both the King and that realm from the
mischief of these foreign practices ; whom you may likewise
assure that we have already given order to the Earl of
Huntingdon and Lord Hunsdon to put a power in readiness
to be forthwith sent into that realm in case a milder course
will not be taken by the King in discerning his friends from
his enemies by good effects.   And in case it shall be objected
—as a pretended reason for the committing of the said Earl
—that he had over secret dealing, and more than became a
subject, with such our ministers as from time to time we sent
thither, you shall declare to him that we cannot but find
it strange that he should be charged with his conferences
with our ministers as with a fault, considering we have been
during the whole time of his minority, and since, so far from
being enemy to him, as that he must needs confess, as a thing
known to all the world, that he has received at our hands
only, and by no means else, both the quieting of his troubled
State and the continual preservation of the same from daily
troubles and invasion most dangerously practised by those
that through these beginnings will let him see to his utter
ruin and destruction in the end what they have of long time
intended, but have been kept from putting it in execution
through God's goodness, and the watchful care we have had
of him and his State ; and for so good offices to be recom-
pensed with that dishonour that the conference of a subject
of that realm with a minister of ours having nothing committed to his charge nor intending anything but conservation of the mutual peace betwixt the realms, should be
thought a cause sufficient for his imprisonment, as we
think it very strange so he may be well assured we will not

435

'put it up' if we be not otherwise and more honourably satisfied.

And for that it is to be doubted that those who have entered this violent course against the Earl of Morton mean with no less extremity to prosecute the matter against all those who are either affected to him or have showed themselves to embrace the cause of religion and to be devoted to us, we have thought meet, for the prevention of the inconvenience that might ensue thereby, to give order and full authority to our President of York to send into that realm such forces, and at such time, as by you shall be thought [meet], without attending any direction from hence to that purpose, lest that by the delay that might be used therein the opportunity of using timely assistance might be taken away. . . .

Calendar of Scottish Papers, v, No. 651

1581   8 January.   *Huntingdon, President of the North, to Walsingham*

. . . But, for the saving of Morton, he thinks that will be past help before she can send any thither. Yet, if it be so, he could wish that she were pleased to show herself now to be as willing and as able to strike the stroke in the government of that State as heretofore she has been. Has no doubt she can do it if she pleases. Though Morton be gone, as he fears he will be, yet her majesty may in nowise suffer D'Aubigny to have the rule. Is bold to write to him what he thinks, and although he cannot think that all Scotland can yield her majesty such an instrument as Morton was in many respects, yet some may be found fit enough to serve that turn and, perhaps, in some respects better than Morton, if he may be better backed than of late Morton has been. But, howsoever that be, D'Aubigny must not have the chief rule. . . . Is of opinion that if he holds the course he begins, the King and State shall be utterly alienated from her majesty, to their ruin and the great trouble of England. . . .

Calendar of Scottish Papers, v, No. 658

The Anglo-Scottish League, 1586

Under the influence of Lennox there was a danger that Scotland would enter upon a policy of French alignment and Roman Catholic sympathy, which caused alarm in England—as seen in Elizabeth's instructions to Errington. The success of the Raid of Ruthven, however, finally freed James from Lennox's influence,[1] but, on James's escape from the raiders, Arran became as supreme as Lennox had been before him, and Arran was equally unacceptable to Elizabeth's advisers. Walsingham's mission to try to 'woo' James to England was unsuccessful ; but the formation of the 'Catholic League' in 1585 led to more determined and hopeful efforts and, by taking advantage of a Border 'incident,' Elizabeth was able to secure the overthrow of Arran and the return of the Protestant lords who had been banished for an earlier attempt (in the spring of 1584) to free James from Arran.[2] A 'Protestant League,' offensive and defensive, was finally concluded between Scotland and England in July 1586.

1581   26 October.   *Instructions to Nicholas Errington*

' Private instructions given by the whole of her majesties Privye Counsell, to Nicolas Eringeton, esquier, sent unto the Kinge of Scottes.'

The Queen of England finding by such advertisements as she receives daily out of Scotland, that the whole scope of the Duke of Lennox's actions tend to no other end but to the overthrow of religion and the dissolving of the amity with England, has thought it most necessary, for avoiding of dangers, that somewhat should be done to prevent the same. And therefore she conceives that he, being sent into Scotland about her other affairs, may, under colour of charge committed to him in his general instructions, by such well affected instruments as he shall find, there in most secret sort devise some good way to disappoint these intents. And forasmuch as it is thought here—not without good ground—that nothing will more further her intent

[1] *Supra*, p. 39   [2] See *S.H.R.*, xx, 181-6.

than, by some secret practice, a division between the Duke of Lennox and the Earl of Arran ; which carries the more likelihood to be performed with less difficulty, if it be true, as it is reported, that there is already a secret drift between them, which being ' pusshed over ' by such as may secretly procure to be workers therein, it will be the more easy to bring the same to pass ; in the compassing whereof he is to have especial regard that he does not attempt it unless he shall perceive either by speech with Arran or by other such assured means as he may use therein, that he has of himself a disposition that way. . . . Wherefore it is to be showed to him that it will be as well for the King of Scots' security as for his own safety . . . to consider that there can be no more dangerous course held for the King than to alienate himself from her majesty and the good liking of England ; which seems to be Lennox's principal intent, and therefore if he or any other looked uprightly into the cause of her dealings from time to time, he shall find that the whole scope of her doings tends to no other end but the preservation of his person and the maintenance of his country in peace, which kind of proceedings she means to continue if he shall not give just cause to the contrary. Lest Arran may either dissemble in showing him a disposition to oppose himself against Lennox, or hereafter may change his mind, and so impart this advice to Lennox, he may do well to tell Arran that the Queen of England has not any particular misliking of Lennox for his own person or for his greatness of credit, but only for respect of the weal of the King and for continuance of concord between the two realms ; wherein, if she might be assured that Lennox's actions would concur with her good meaning, she would not mislike of Lennox or of his greatness of credit.

As for such devices and allurements as are proposed by Lennox, tending to work the alienation from her majesty by bearing of him [the King] in hand that he shall have the Pope, Spain, and France to assist him in such attempts as, by his persuasion, he may be drawn to enter into against her . . . if he seek any alteration of religion, it will be found dangerous counsel to carry a very young Prince into so perilous a cumber upon such vain grounds and persuasions ; and therefore if the displeasure of God, the weakness of his supporters, the division of his own realm, the loss of the favour of England, and her majesty's forces by sea and land be duly weighed, all such as are well affected in Scotland cannot but seek to stop the course of these violent causes and advise the King of Scots to seek effectually her majesty's goodwill and devotion to him.

It is thought meet also that he acquaint such as he finds to be well affected to the amity of this crown with the overture, contained in his general instructions, propounded by the Scottish Queen for the resignation of her title to the crown of Scotland to her son, as a thing by him desired ; letting them understand that if his title be called in question by yielding to any such request, it cannot but prove very dangerous to such as give their voice and consent, by Parliament, to the removing of the Queen of Scots. A copy of the project is now sent to him. Besides the confusion it may breed in Scotland, it cannot but work a breach of the good amity between the two crowns ; therefore it will behove them, if any such thing be attempted, providently to foresee and provide for the inconveniences that may ensue thereby. And in case the resignation shall tend only to the fortifying of the King's title, without calling the validity of the Parliament, by which the regal authority was cast on him, in question, then were it not convenient that any opposition should be used.

Lastly, he shall make known to the well affected in Scotland how careful the Queen of England is for the welfare of that realm and the maintenance of the religion there professed ; assuring them that she will not fail, upon any opportunity that shall be offered, to do anything that shall lie in her power for the preservation and continuance of the same. And if he shall find a disposition in those who are of quality to enter into any part, by promise, to such effect, to remove all scruples that may, perhaps, be conceived by some of them that the same may be dangerous to the King and themselves, it is to be shown to them that she desires no promise or party in Scotland, but with these conditions : (1) That the religion may be maintained ; (2) The King's person preserved ; (3) The quiet of Scotland continued ; (4) Foreign servitude avoided ; (5) The well affected noblemen in disgrace with the King restored to his favour ; (6) Reciprocal justice to be used against offenders as well as by sea as land ; (7) The amity between the two countries continued.

Forasmuch as in the broken State, so full of factions, the King being carried away with the passion of such of the nobility there as possess him, it may be that many points contained as well in these as in his general instructions were better forborne than uttered, it is, therefore, thought meet to leave it to his discretion to use them as he shall find convenient and agreeable with the circumstances of the time and persons he shall have to deal withal.

Calendar of Scottish Papers vi, No. 72

Although Walsingham's mission of 1583 had been a failure,[1] the more responsible statesmen in Scotland and England realised that the Protestant religion was the ' fondamentall suirtye ' whereupon both crowns were settled, and, in pursuance of former policies strove that ' this ile naturallie joyned bye situation, language, and most happelie be religion, may be by the indissolubill amitye of the two princes fullie united.' [2] The threat from the continental Catholic powers finally influenced James to agree to a Protestant league with England, but it is to be noted that therein he saw himself one step nearer to the English throne and that the strong English desire for the league and Elizabeth's serious view of the European situation are shown in her willingness to secure James's ' support ' by a pension of £4,000 a year.[3]

[1] *Calendar of Scottish Papers*, vi, No. 639
[2] Maitland to Leicester, August 1585 (*Warrender Papers*, i, No. cxix).
[3] *Calendar of Scottish Papers*, viii, Nos. 302, 467

1586. *Protestant League between James VI and Elizabeth*

The treaty was made on the following articles :

1. That both their majesties, finding by the course of the present proceedings in foreign parts, that divers princes, terming themselves catholics and acknowledging the pope's authority were joined in confederacy for extirpating true religion, not only within their own states and dominions but also in other kingdoms, lest they should seem to be less solicitous for the defence thereof than were their enemies who thought to overthrow the same, have thought it necessary as well for the preservation of their own persons on whose safety doth the weal of their subjects depend, as for the better maintenance of the true ancient Christian religion which they now profess, to join and unite themselves in a more strict league than hath been between any princes their progenitors.

2. That they should labour and procure by their best endeavours to draw the princes professing the same religion to join and concur with them in like defence thereof.

3. That this league should be offensive and defensive against all that should attempt to disturb the exercise of true religion within their kingdoms, notwithstanding of any former leagues of friendship or amity contracted with the said attempters.

4. That if any prince or state whatsoever should invade the realms and dominions of either of their majesties or attempt any injury against their persons or subjects, upon notice thereof given or received, neither of them should yield aid, counsel, advice or support, directly or indirectly to the said invader, notwithstanding any consanguinity, affinity, league or treaty made or to be made.

5. That in case of invasion they should aid and assist each other in matter and form following. That is to say, if the realm of England be invaded by any foreign forces in parts remote from the realm of Scotland, the king, upon signification by the queen of England, should furnish two thousand horsemen, and five thousand footmen, or a lesser number

as it shall please the said queen to require, and should cause them to be conducted from the borders of Scotland into any part of the realm of England upon the charges of the said queen. And in case the said realm of Scotland be invaded in any part remote from England by any foreign force, the queen of England, upon requisition made to her by the king, should furnish three thousand horsemen and six thousand footmen, or a lesser number at the option of the said king, and shall cause them to be conducted to any part of the realm of Scotland upon the king's charges.

6. That in case the invasion should be upon the north parts of the realm of England within sixty miles of the borders of Scotland, the king, being required by the queen, should gather all the forces he could make and join with the English power for pursuing the said invaders, and keep them together for thirty days, or so much longer (if required), as the subjects of Scotland are usually accustomed to stay in the fields for the defence of their own kingdom.

7. That upon any invasion or trouble arising in the realm of Ireland the king, upon notice given to him thereof, should not only inhibit the repair thither of any of the inhabitants of Argyle, isles and places adjacent, or any other parts of his dominions ; but also, if it shall happen [blank] or any number of them to go into Ireland with a number extraordinary, and in hostile mannner, the king, upon signification of the same, should denounce them his rebels and pursue them as traitors.

8. That neither of their majesties should hereafter aid, supply, assist or entertain the rebels or adversaries of the other, nor permit them to reside either privately or publicly in any part of their dominions ; but upon the first requisition of the prince to whom they are rebels they should undelayedly be delivered according to the old leagues and treaties, or then expulsed forth of their dominions, and redress made for any injuries they should happen to commit during their abode in the same.

9. That all controversies about matters of borders or wrongs committed in the marches since the time of the king's

accepting the government in his own person, and by the space of four years preceding, should be friendly determined and satisfied at the sight of commissioners to be appointed on both sides, who should meet at the confines within six months after the date of the presents, and decide thereupon.
10. That neither of the majesties should enter into any league or treaty (without the consent of the other, by letters signed with their own hands under their privy signet) with any other prince or state whatsoever, to the prejudice of the present treaty. . . .
13. Lastly that the king at his coming to the perfect age of twenty-five years, should cause the present league to be ratified by the States of the kingdom ; likeas the queen at the same time should cause it to be confirmed in her parliament of England.

Rymer, Foedera, xv, 803

James VI and the English Succession

From now onwards James's political energies were concentrated on ensuring his succession to Elizabeth's throne. During the negotiations for the ' Protestant League ' Maitland of Thirlstane apparently advised James to press for a recognition of his ' right and title ' by the additional articles :

For the better setlyng of the quyet of the hole Iland and that no controversye aryse at any time heirefter for the title or succession to the crowne of England and Ireland, wherebye there majesties good intention may be frustrat and this halye ligue rendred ineffectuall, her majestie shall sa sone as convenientlye she may assemble the estates and Parliament of England and in the same declare the sayd king heyr apparent and immediat lawfull successour of the crown of England and Ireland yf her majestie shall happen to depart without heyres of her owne bodye, and shall no wayes directlye or indirectlye prejuge or empaire his right and titill nor publictlye or privatlye declaire any uther to succede her in her crowne, realmes or dominions.

That for the better increase of the amitye betwene the

two realms and subjects therof all of the Scottis nation be naturalized English and as frie danizens in all the sayd quenes dominions, and all of the English nation in lyke maner naturalized Scottis as frie danizens in all the sayd kingis dominions.

Warrender Papers, i, No. cxxii

But no such articles were added to the League, and although Elizabeth refused to make any formal declaration relating to the succession she did inform James that she would not prejudge whatever ' right, title or interest ' he might have or claim to have. But there was still the critical problem of Mary. It is significant that almost immediately upon the conclusion of the League the English Council felt strong enough to proceed against Mary, and that her execution took place six months later. James was well aware that Mary's ' right, title and interest ' could be placed before his own ; and although he made a strong plea for his mother's life, ' as the dictates of honour and shame and of filial piety demanded ', he realised that it was impossible to save his mother and also secure the English succession. The English agents in Scotland reported that James would not break the League, and therewith his hopes, even if his mother were to be put to death. And the English agents reported aright. James pled and protested, but he did no more ; and, after a year of chilly relations, James acknowledged himself to be content with Elizabeth's explanations.[1]

1586 15 December. *James VI to the Earl of Leicester*

. . . But to my first purpos, this farre shortlie may I say, I am honest, no changear of course, altogether in all thingis as I professe to be, and quhosomevir will affirme that I had ever intelligence with my mother sen the Master of Grayis being in England, or ever thocht to preferre her to my selff in the title or ever delt in any uther foreyne course, they lie falselie and unhonestlie of me. But speciallie how fonde and

[1] See Robert S. Rait and Annie I. Cameron, *King James's Secret* ; and *Warrender Papers* (Scot. Hist. Soc.), i, pp. 220 *et seq.*

inconstant I were if I shulde preferre my mother to the title [1]
let all men judge.   My religioun ever moved me to haite her
course althogh my honour constraynis me to insist for her
lyffe. . . .

King James's Secret, 101–2

1586/7   26 January.[2]   *James VI to Elizabeth*

Madame and dearest sister, if ye coulde have knouin quhat
divers thochtis have agitat my mynde since my directing of
Williame Keith unto you for the sollisting of this matter
quhairto nature and honoure so greatly and unfeynedly
bindis and obleissis me, if I say ye kneu quhat dyveris
thochtis I have bene in and quhat just greif I hadd veying
the thing itself if so it shoulde proceide, as Godd forbidd,
quhat eventis micht follou thairupon, quhat number of
straitis I volde be drevin unto and amongst the rest hou
it micht perrell my reputation amongst my subjectis if
thaise thingis I yett say againe vayre knouin unto you, then I
vot but ye wold so farr pittie my cace as it volde easely mak
you at the first to solve youre ouin best intoit.   I doubt
greatlie in quhat facon to vritt in this purpois for ye have
allreaddie takin sa evill with my playnness as I feare if I shall
persist in that course ye shall rather be exasperattit to pas-
sions in reading the vordis then by the plainness thairof be

---

[1] ' It is only fair to James to point out that the words " prefer my
mother to the title " may not have been intended to convey anything
more than the expression which immediately precedes, viz. " prefer
her to myself in the title," i.e., that he could not have been conspiring
with Mary because such conspiracy would imply that his mother and
not himself was Elizabeth's natural successor.   But even if this is so,
the words " prefer my mother to the title " constituted an ingenuous
revelation of the motives which actuated the writer.   James knew that
Douglas [the Scots ambassador at London] had told Leicester that a
report that he would break the League if his mother's life was taken
was unfounded, and in this letter he gave him clearly to understand
that he cared more about the succession than about Mary, and that
his appeal for her life was made merely because he could not honourably assent to her execution ' (*King James's Secret*, 102*n*).

[2] Mary was executed on 8 February 1586/7.

persuadit to consider richtlie the simpill treuth. Yett justlie prefferring the deutie of ane honest freind to the suddaine passionis of one quho hou soone thay be past can vyslier vey the reasons then I cann sett thaime doune, I have resolvid in feu vordis and plaine, to gif you my freindly and best advyce, appealing to youre rypest judgement to discerne thairupon. Quhat thing, madame, can greatlier touche me in honoure, that both is a King and a sonne, then that my nearest neihboure being in straittest freindshippe with me shall rigouruslie putt to death a free soveraigne prince and my naturall mother, alyke in estaite and sex to hir that so uses her, albeit subject I grant to a harder fortoune, and touching hir nearlie in proximitie of bloode ? Quhat lau of Godd can permitt that justice shall strikke upon thaime quhom he hes appointed supreame dispensatouris of the same, under Him, quhom He hath callid Goddis, and thairfore subjectid to the censoure of none in earth, quhose anointing by Godd can not be defylid be man unrevenged by the authoure thairof, quho being supreme and immediatt lieutenant of Godd in heaven cannot thairfore be judgit by thair equallis in earth ?

Quhat monstruouse thinge is it that souveraigne princes thaime selfis shoulde be the exemple giveris of thaire ouen sacred diademes' prophaining ? Then quhat shoulde move you to this forme of proceiding—supponin the vorst quhiche in goode faith I looke not for at youre handis—honoure or profeitt ? Honoure vaire it to you to spaire quhen it is least lookid for honoure vaire it to you—quhiche is not onlie my freindlie advyce but my earnist suite—to take me and all other princes in Europe eternally beholdin unto you in granting this my so reasonable request, and not—appardon I pray you my free speaking—to putt princes to straittis of honoure quhair throuch youre generall reputatione and the universall—allmost—mislyking of you may daingerouslie perrell both in honour and utillitie youre persoune and estate.

Ye knou, madame, vell aneuch hou small difference Cicero concludis to be betuixt *utile* and *honestum,* in his discourse thairof, and quhiche of thaime oucht to be framed to the other, and nou, madame, to concluide, I pray you so to vey thir feu argumentis that as I ever presumed of youre nature, so the quhole vorlde may praise youre subjectis for thaire deutifull caire for youre preservation and youre self for youre princelie pittie, tho doing quhairof onlie belangis unto you, the performing quhairof onlie apparteynis unto you, and the praise thairof onlie will ever be youris. Respect then, my goode sister this my first so long contineuid and so earnist request, dispatching my ambassadouris vith suche a confortable ansoure as may become youre persone to give, and as my loving and honest hairt unto you meritis to resave. But in caice any do vaunt thaime selfis to know further of my mynde in this matter then my ambassadouris do, quho indeid are fullie aquented thairvith, I pray you not to takk me to be a cameleon, but by the contraire, thaime to be maliciouse impostouris as suirlie thay are. And thus praying you hairtlie to excuse my to ruide and longsum lettir, I comitt you, madame, and dearest sister to the blessid protection of the most Hie, quho mott give you grace so to resolve in this maitter as may be most honorabill for you, and most acceptable to Him. From my palless of Holyrudhouse. [*Signed :*] Youre most living and affectionat brother and cousin, James R.

Calendar of Scottish Papers, ix, No. 245

1588   6 August.   *William Asheby to Walsingham*

. . . First, concerning her majesty's innocency touching the death of the late Queen his mother, he [the King of Scots] is thoroughly satisfied with her majesty's letter : yet in respect of the world it is desired that some public note of the judgment given in the Star Chamber touching that matter should be made, and sent hither, signed with the hand of the officer of that Court.

Secondly, a public instrument, signed by all the judges of the realm, that such right as the King may any way pretend hath not or cannot in any sort be weakened, impuned, or prejudiced by the said sentence. . . .

Calendar of Scottish Papers, ix, No. 486

From this time forward James entered into innumerable negotiations, many of them secret, with various European princes, and even the Catholic powers and the Pope, in his endeavours to secure his accession to the English throne.

It should be noted, however, that despite the wording of some of the documents, James was always chary of agreeing to direct help from the Catholic powers who might help only to hold. Nevertheless he still strove for support from Protestants and Catholics alike, for he could never be sure what the religion of England would be upon the death of the ' Protestant Queen.'

In addition to the diplomatic correspondence printed in the volumes of State Papers and in the Reports of the Historical Manuscripts Commission, further information is to be found in such collections as the *Correspondence of James VI with Sir Robert Cecil and others* (Camden Soc., 1861), *Letters of Queen Elizabeth and King James VI* (Camden Soc., 1849), *Warrender Papers* (Scot. Hist. Soc., 1931, 1932), and *Negotiations between King James VI and Ferdinand I* (ed. J. D. Mackie, 1927). These represent only a small proportion of the available material. In addition, many papers, based on various sources, have been contributed to learned journals (see, in particular, *Scottish Historical Review*, vols. ix, xii, xxi ; *Scottish History Society Miscellany*, vol. i ; *Collected Essays and Reviews of Thomas Graves Law*).

In the following extracts the first shows James debating the possibility (and deciding against the desirability) of help from Spain ; the others show the extent of his diplomatic contacts with the minor princes of Europe.

1592. *A memorial drawn up by James VI weighing the advantages and disadvantages of a Spanish invasion of England*

After recounting ' The Reasons Why ' and ' The Reasons to be objected to the contrary. Antithesis '—this latter part containing the conclusion, ' Wherefore I think it easier and more honourable to do it only by myself, with some small help of men and money only from foreign parts '—the Memorial ends :

448

Upon all this then that I have submitted, I conclude that this enterprise cannot be well executed this summer for my unreadiness, for the Queen of England's suspecting of it, and for over many strange princes dealing into it. Wherefore my opinion is, that it die down, as I said before. In the meantime, I will deal with the Queen of England fair and pleasantly for my title to the crown of England after her decease, which thing if she grant to (as it is not impossible howbeit unlikely) we have then attained our design without stroke of sword. If by the contrary, then delay makes me to settle in [1] my country in the meantime; and when I like hereafter, I may in a month or two (forewarning of the King of Spain) attain to our purpose, she not suspecting such thing, as now she does. Which if it were so done, it would be a far greater honour to him and me both.

[*Endorsed*] Copy of the Scotch King's instructions to Spain which should have been sent by Powry Oge [John Ogilvie of Powrie], but thereafter were concredit to Mr. George Kerr, and withdrawn at his taking for safety of his Majesty's honour,[2] 1592.

Historical Manuscripts Commission, *MSS of the Marquis of Salisbury*, iv, 214

1598. *Mandate of James VI for his ambassadors, and delivered by them to the King of Denmark [Christian IV] at Copenhagen in August* 1598

The King our sovereign lord wishes us . . . to instruct you more clearly and fully as to his right to the English

---

[1] Probably meaning to ' settle ' in the sense of securing law and order and crushing all opposition.

[2] Calderwood records that, according to Mr John Davidson's Diary, when the so-called Spanish Blanks were found on George Ker (brother of Lord Newbattle) in December 1592, among them was ' found one to the Prince of Parma, which tuiched the king with knowledge and approbatioun of the traffiquing, and promise of assistance, &c., but that it was not thought expedient to publish it ' (*History of the Kirk of Scotland*, v, 251). But see *Innes Review*, iii, 81–103, and *S. H. R.*, xxxii, 195–6.

throne upon the death of Queen Elizabeth . . . [He] begs you to make an immediate and affectionate declaration of the help which he may expect from you, if he should have to vindicate his claim by force of arms on the death of the Queen . . . But his Majesty has considered that it would not be ungrateful for the Queen of England . . . to declare him and his children to be by indubitable right the nearest heirs and successors to the crown. Although he does not despair that she will some time do the right thing, neverthe-less he wishes that his kinsmen and especially the Princes of the Holy Roman Empire would importune her to make this declaration. He asks lovingly in this case that your Highness, being forewarned by letters about the business and the time, will in brotherly fashion join your ambassadors with his and those of other kings and princes. In the mean-time, he requests that you will be diligent in commending the matter to all your neighbours and confederate princes, to enlist their support in so just a cause.

Warrender Papers, i, No. cxviii

1598. *Frederick William, Duke of Saxony, to James VI*

. . . You have committed to our faith and friendship this cause anent the English succession, explained your rights and refuted the counter-claims of your adversaries, and (if the fates so will it) ask our advice and help in securing what you believe to belong to you . . .

As the ambassadors and your Majesty may easily under-stand, it is necessary for us to deliberate with the other Electors and Princes of the Holy Roman Empire con-cerning your Majesty's desires. We beg you to consider that we are not at liberty to make any definite promise in the matters proposed by your Majesty. Nevertheless, we will gladly undertake to do what we can to promote your cause, by letters or embassies, among our kinsmen and confederate princes. . . .

Warrender Papers, ii, No. cxxx

[In the same collection there are similar replies to like embassies
sent to the Duke of Mecklenburg, the Elector of Brandenburg,
the Duke of Saxony, the Landgrave of Hesse, the Duke of Bruns-
wick, and the Duke of Schleswig. Ibid., ii, Nos. cxxvii, cxxix,
cxxxi, cxxxiii, cxxxv, cxxxvii.]

1599. *Reply of Ferdinand I, Grand Duke of Tuscany, to
James VI.*[1]

1. We doo acknowlege the Kings title and rycht to be most
just and nerest to the crowne of England.

2. Itt is most necessary and convenient that the King sowld
with all princes his freindes, alliances and confederats,
renew and establiche his freindschip. Bot itt is to be
observed that he trait with thaim bothe warlie & secretlie,
and especiallie in his dealing with the King of Hispanie.
That the Quene of Ingland may nocht be inducett to have
ony suspition, or that scho may nocht heirby be moved
to think that he sowld in anywayes practis the schortning
off hir lyff.

3. The King sall doo most wyslie to dissimulat with Irland
and nocht to mak schew off ony freindschip that he hathe
with thaime induring the Quenes lyff.

4. Itt is most necessary that the King sowld mak ane freind-
scip with the Pape, by[2] quhome goodlie I do nocht sie
quhow he can be assisted be princes catholikes. It is to be
observett that this freindschip can nocht be nather weill
nor secretlie done be ony off his awin. For the knawlege
off the mater, & the devulgating off the dealing, may spill
and hinder all good success, without finisching off ony
good effect. (Nota de Crichtonio[3]). . . .

5. Itt is requesett to renew the awld leige with France,

---

[1] It is, of course, not easy to say how much of this was Ferdinand I
and how much Sir Michael Balfour, James's envoy.   [2] *without*

[3] A reference to Father Crichton, whose attempts to bring James
into touch with the Pope produced the famous ' Elphinstone Letter '
of 1599. (A brief analysis is given in *Scots Peerage*, i, 557–60 ; a full
analysis will be found in A. O. Meyer, *Clemens VIII und Jakob I von
England*.)

and mak greit freindship with the King, for putting fuirthe off his head ony eylest [1] that he may have off your greitnes, and in giffin him assurance that ye will nocht, nor myndes nocht ever to persew ony tit[le] that the kings of England hathe to France. Nota Constab[le] [2]. . . .

6. Itt is most requesett & most necessary that quhen God callethe the Quene of England that the king sowld immediatelie enter in that contrie having ane oppin and ready way, so stronglie, that no enemie may resist him, & for this effect latt the King daylie & howrlie furniche him selff of all things necessary to double fuirthe suche ane interpryse. Nota also that the king be war to put in hasart of a battle his good title & rycht to the crowne, and that he sowld nocht be inducett heirto, lat him forsie weall, to be furniched of vivers, off all munition of wares, of armes etc.[3] also that he have ane number of capitanes & experimented suldates, that he may finiche and achive so worthie ane exploit as becomethe so noble ane wearior.

7. Itt pleses us the faction that the king hathe in Ingland bot that they have owther spreites or force to doo the king's towrne we doo nocht sie itt, alvayes latt thaim be interteneet, & dealt with prevelie, to sie giff they can bring in discredit & to confusion his onfreindes.

8. So greitt is the good will that the Earl of Essex hathe conqueset of the suldats & bravest spreits of Ingland, and so liberall & beneficiall hathe he bene and is he towards thaim that his force and powar is mor to be thocht of nor onyes in theis partes bot that in ony wayes goodlie he may pretend ony title or rycht to the crowne, except he

[1] *jealousy*

[2] The reference is to Henry Constable, an ardent Catholic, who represented the ' French ' as opposed to the ' Spanish ' Catholics.

[3] As early as February 1598 the Privy Council had ordered a general arming of the lieges, ratified by an Act of Convention in June. In November 1599 the lieges entered into a general band to secure the king's title to the thrones of England and Ireland, and Conventions in March and June 1600 voted £40,000 (upon conditions), for the purchase of arms. (See *A.P.S.*, iv, 168-9, 190, 191 ; *R.P.C.*, v, 446 ; vi, 18, 62-3, 121*n*.)

com to mare Ar[a]bella[1] we doo nocht sie itt. Alvayes
he may advance or hinder ony man that invite the heirto
moir nor ony man els. Quhairfor itt [is] most necessary
that he be dealt with & large offers maid to him, etc.
9. Gif the king can nocht assuredlie be him selff be me
he may, etc. Nota the good opinion that the Catholikes
hathe of the earl.
It is requesett to use diligence in this becaus the gretest
compeditor[2] mynds be this way to mak him selff ane
easier access to that crowne.

Negotiations between King James VI and Ferdinand I, No. vi

The most fruitful of James's policies, however, was the fostering,
during the last years of Elizabeth's reign, of a close connection
with Sir Robert Cecil, the English Secretary, who, not without
an eye to his own future position, was working for James's succes-
tion to the English throne. The correspondence between them
conveys an atmosphere of intrigue, the persons referred to being
designated by numbers and the question of James's succession as
' the subject.' Cecil kept James informed of events and political
proposals at the English court and advised his course of action.
The nature of the relationship is illustrated by the following two
extracts from their correspondence : the second extract clearly
indicating Cecil's acceptance of James as Elizabeth's successor.

1601. *James VI to Cecil*

I ame most hairtelie glaid that 10 [Sec. Cecil] hath noıı
at last maid choice of tuo so fitt and confident ministeris[3]

---

[1] Arabella Stewart, daughter of Charles, Earl of Lennox, the brother
of Darnley. She was so near to the throne as to be the centre of intrigues
in the closing years of the reign of Elizabeth and the opening years
of the reign of James VI and I. Her marriage in 1610 to William
Seymour, grandson of Edward Seymour, first Earl of Hertford, and
a possible heir to the English throne, so frightened James that he caused
her to be imprisoned. She died in the Tower, 1615.
[2] The king of Spain
[3] John, seventh Earl of Mar, and Mr Edward Bruce, afterwards Lord
Kinloss, sent by King James as ambassadors to Queen Elizabeth in
February 1601.

quhom with he hath bene so honorablie plaine in the
affaires of 30 [K. James], assuring 10 [Sec. Cecil] that 30
[K. James] puttis more confidence in thaime, according
to the large and long proofe that he hath had of thaime,
then in any other that followis him, lyke as 10 [Sec. Cecil]
is most beholden unto thaime for the honorable reporte
that thay haue maid of him to 30 [K. James], quhomto
thay haue, upon the perrel of thaire credit, geuin full
assurance of the sinceritie of 10 [Sec. Cecil] ; and because
30 [K. James] can not haue the occasion to speake face
to face with 10 [Sec. Cecil], that, out of his owin mouthe,
he may giue him full assurance of his thankefull acceptance
of his plaine and honorable dealing, he thairfore prayes
10 [Sec. Cecil], to accepte of his long aproued and trustie 3
[Lord Henry Howard],[1] both as a suretie of his thanke-
fulnes and his constant loue to him in all tymes hearafter,
as also to be a sure and secreate interpretoure betwixt 30
[K. James] and 10 [Sec. Cecil], in the opening up of euerie
one of thaire myndis to another. . . . This farre hath 30
[K. James] thocht goode to comitte to paper, to be a uit-
nesse to 10 [Sec. Cecil] of his inuarde disposition touardis
him, assuring him that he takes in uerrie goode pairt his
warenes in dealing, lyke as he doth promeise, upon his
honoure, that in all tymes heareafter, the suspition or
disgraceing of 10 [Sec. Cecil] shall touche 30 [K. James]
as neare as 10 [Sec. Cecil], and quhen it shall please god
that 30 [K. James] shall succeide to his richt, he shall no
surelier succeide to the place then he shall succeide in
bestowing as greate and greater fauoure upon 10 [Sec.
Cecil] as his predecessoure doth bestow upon him, and in
the meane tyme ye maye rest assured of the constant loue
and secreatie of

Youre most louing and assurid freinde,

30 [KING JAMES].

[1] Second son of Surrey the poet. King James, shortly after his
accession to the throne of England, advanced Lord Henry to the Earldom
of Northampton.

454

[Indorsed by Sec. Cecil],

' 1600. 30, first letter to 10.' He has subsequently added in explanation of 30 and 10, ' The K.' ; ' Secretary.'

Correspondence of King James VI of Scotland with Sir Robert Cecil and others (Camden Soc.), No. i

Cecil to James VI

. . . Thus have I now (*ex mero officio*) to my souverayne, and out of affectionate care to your Majesties future happines, whom God hath instituted to sitt (in his dew tyme) in the chayre of state, at the feet whereof I dayly kneele exposed my self to more inconvenience than ether your Majesties former indisposition or my own caution (in a jealous fortune) should adventure seeing (by it) I doe reape noe other purchase then what I know your justice would yield to all, which is to be secured thus farr (in my owne honest and paynfull labours) that I shalbe censured by cleare and upright proofes, and not by borrowed lightes of envy and revenge. . . .

Ibid., No. iv

In these closing years the position was wholly in James's favour. Scotsmen, Catholic and Protestant alike, wanted James, a Scot, to succeed to the English throne ; in England, Protestants looked for the maintenance of the ' true religion,' and Catholics looked for, at least, toleration ; the only possible Roman Catholic competitor was Isabella, daughter of the dead Philip II, and, after the glory of English arms against Spain, even Catholic Englishmen were not favourable to her cause ; above all, the navy and the army of England were in the control of Cecil's party, and Cecil and his party were in favour of James.

When Robert Carey galloped north to tell James of the death of Elizabeth, it was beyond question that his message was, in effect, an announcement of James's succession to the English throne.

From the Union of the Crowns (1603) to the Revolution (1689)

The union of the crowns effected a diplomatic union between England and Scotland, and from 1603 to the Revolution of 1689 relations between the two countries were of a purely domestic nature. The foreign policy of England was that of Scotland—though often, as in the case of the two Dutch wars, that foreign policy was detrimental to Scottish interests. Here it should be noted, moreover, that the crown was more than an effective integrating force. In Scotland the king, through the Lords of the Articles, the Privy Council, and the Court of Session had control of the legislature, the executive and the judiciary. The king sat in London and governed Scotland ' by his pen,' and the ' government ' of Scotland was apt to be in accord with the needs and wishes of England.

Closer Union

The union of 1603 was a purely personal one ; and James VI, who regarded the union of the crowns as ' nothing comparable to the union of two ancient and famous kingdoms,' at once strove for something much closer. The legislation of 1607 of the amenable Scottish parliament represents the king's wishes but, apart from an act abrogating hostile laws against Scotland, the English parliament, which was wholly opposed to any closer union, made no parallel move.

The decision in Colville's case (1608), however, did secure that *post-nati* (that is, those born in Scotland after James's accession to the English throne) were *ipso facto* naturalised subjects of England.

1607. *Act Anent the Union of Scotland and England*

Where as the Estaitis of this kingdome . . wes movit in the parliament haldin at Perth . . . 1604 to direct a number of commissioneris of all Estaittis to treat with the commissioneris of the parliament and Estait of England for the union of the twa antient and famous kingdomes Scotland and England . . . The saidis Commissioneris haveing exhibitit to the Estaittis of this Realme presentlie conveynit in this parliament the haill Treatie and all that wes condiscendit on betuix thame and the commissionaris for the Parliament of England . . . to be proponit to the nixt sessioun of parliament of baith the Realmes to be considerit and to ressave sic strenth and approbatioun as to thair great wisdome suld appeir convenient, As the said Treatie presented sealled and subscryved be all the commissionaris of baith the kingdomes present for the tyme off the date at Westminster the sext day of december in the yeir of God J^m vj^c and four yeiris at mair lenth proportis ; The saidis Estaittis of this kingdome presentlie convenit . . . in full resolutioun . . . to advance sua far as possiblie they may this happie unioun alreadie begun in his sacred majesties royall persone. . . .

[*Abrogate and utterly extinguish the particular hostile laws hereafter enumerated . . . certain laws cited, including ' Buying and selling of English goodis forbiddin undir payne of escheatt'.*

All laws, customs and treaties of the Borders to be abrogated and abolished. The name of Borders to be extinguished. Offences committed by Scotsmen in England to be tried in future by the Justice General and his deputes in the Justice-ayres of Berwick, Roxburgh, Selkirk, Peebles and Dumfries. No Scotsman to be sent out of Scotland into England to be tried for any treason or any other crime whatsoever. . . . [1]]

And forther the Estaittis of Scotland answerand to that article of the foirsaid treatie tuicheing the communioun and participatioun of mutuall commoditeis and commerce : First concerning the importatioun of merchandice in Scotland frome forene pairtis, That where as certane commoditeis are wholie prohibitit by the lawes of Scotland to be brocht in the samyn kingdome frome ony forane pairtis by the native subjectis of Scotland thame selffis or be ony

[1] For the parallel English statute abrogating hostile laws, etc., see Prothero, *Select Statutes and other Constitutional Documents of the reigns of Elizabeth and James I* (4th ed., 1913), 268–70.

uther, The saidis Estaittis stattutis and ordanis that na Englishman may bring into Scotland ony of the saidis prohibitit waris or commoditeis ; And yit nevirtheless gif the saidis commoditeis be maid in England it sall be lauchfull to Englishmen to bring thame furth of England into Scotland as na forane commoditeis. And as for the commoditeis and merchandice nocht prohibitit by law to be brocht into Scotland, And specialie concernyng the trade of wynes or uther commoditeis frome Burdeaulx, The saidis Estaittis of Scotland findis and declairis that the Englishmen sall be frie for transportatioun of wyne and utheris commoditeis frome Burdeaulx into Scotland according to the determinatioun of the Commissionaris of both kingdomes contenit in the said treatie Payand the samyn customes and dueteis that the Scottismen payis in Scotland. . . .

Nixt concernyng the Article of Exportatioun, the Estaittis of Scotland statutis and ordanis that all suche gudis or commoditeis as ar prohibitit and forbiddin to Scottishmen thame selffis to transporte furth of Scotland to ony foirane pairt The samin sall be unlauchfull for any Englishman or ony uther to transporte to ony forane natioun over sea, And that under the samyn penaltie and foirfaltouris that Scottishmen are subject unto, Bot nevirtheless findis and declairis that suche goodis and merchandice as ar licencit and ar lauchfull to Scottishmen (not specialie Privilegeit [1]) to transporte out of Scotland to ony forane pairt the samin may be lykwayes transportit be Englishmen thither . . . bund onlie to pay the ordinarie custome that Scottishmen thame selffis do pay at the exporting of suche waris. And as for these native commoditeis quhilkis aither of the countreyis do yeld [2] and may serve for the use and benefite of the uther, The saidis Estaittis of Scotland statutis and declairis that thair may be transportit furth of Scotland into England all suche waris as ar of the grouth or handy wark of Scotland without payment of ony custome impost or exactioun and als frelie in all respectis as ony wairis may be transportit in Scotland frome porte to porte excepting . . . for the propir

[1] e.g. by a grant of monopoly   [2] *yield*

and inward use of Scotland . . . woll, scheip skynnes and fellis, cattell, leather, hydis and lynnen yairne . . . Exceptand also and reserveand to Scottishmen thair trade of fisheing within thair loches firthis and bayis within land and in the seas within fourtene mylis of the costis . . . The Estaittis declaris also that Englishmen sall nocht be debarrit frome being associat in ony Scottish companie of merchandis adventuraris or ony utheris upoun suche conditionis as ony native Scottishman may be admittit; It is nevertheles statute and ordinit be the foirsaidis Estaittis of Scotland that the libertie foirsaid of exportatioun and trade frome Scotland to England sall serve for the inward use onlie of England and nawayes for transportatioun of the saidis commoditeis into forane pairtis [*penalties of escheat and forfeiture laid down for offenders ; a bond and obligation to be entered into at the time of lading of the ship ; a like bond and obligation to be entered into by Scotsmen lading their ships in England*] And fordermoir tuicheing the indifferent schipping of commoditeis ather be Scottishmen or Englishmen in Scottish bottomes The saidis Estaittis statutis and declairis that Englishmen may fraucht and laid thair goodis in Scottish schippis and bottomes paying onlie Scottish customes within the Realme of Scotland nochtwithstanding of ony contrarie lawes or prohibitionis. . .

And becaus the foirsaidis Estaittis of this Realme estemis it requisit that the mutuall communicatioun afoirsaid shall nocht onlie be extendit to materis of commerce bot also to utheris benefittis and privileges of naturall borne subjectis, Thairfoir findis and declairis that all the subjectis of the Realme of England borne since the deceis of Elizabeth the lait Quene of England And all that sall be borne heireftir undir the obedience of his majestie and his royall progenie, Ar, by the commoun lawes of Scotland, and shall be for evir enhabillit to obtene succede inhered and possess all landis goodis and chattellis honouris digniteis offices liberteis privileges and benefices ecclesiasticall or civill in parliament and in all utheris places of the said kingdome of Scotland in all respectis and without ony exceptioun whatsumevir als

459

fullelie and amplie as the borne subjectis of Scotland mycht have done or may do in ony sorte . . . and findis and declaris all the subjectis of the kingdome of England borne [eftir] the deceis of the lait Quene of England to be enhablit and maid capable to acquire purches and inhered succede use and dispose of all landis inheretances goodis offices honouris digniteis liberteis privileges immuniteis beneficis and prefermentis quhatsumevir within the kingdome of Scotland with the samin fredome and als lauchfullie and peciablie as the verie native and naturall borne subjectis of this realme [1] . . . other than to acquire possess succede or inhereitt ony office of the Crowne, office of judicatorie, or ony voit, place or office in parliament All whiche to remane still frie frome being clamede held or injoyit be the subjectis of England within the realme of Scotland . . . And nocht-withstanding of this abonewrittin exceptioun The foirsaidis Estaittis exprestlie reserves his majesties prerogative royall to devysat inhable and prefer to suche offices honouris digniteis and benefices quhatsumevir in the said kingdome of Scotland as ar heirtofoir exceptit in the preceding reserva-tioun all English subjectis borne befoir the deceis of the said laitt Quene als frelie als sovereignlie and absolutelie as ony his majesties royall progenitouris or predecessouris kings of Scotland micht have done. . . .

And forsamekle as the foirsaidis Estaittis of this kingdome of Scotland hes maid grantit and consentit to all the actis and statutis befoir specefeit and to all the speciall liberteis and privileges thairin contenit upoun provisioun and con-ditioun onlie that the foirsaid unioun shall procede work and tak the lyk finall end and effect upoun the pairt of the estaitis of England in favouris of Scotland eftir the forme and tennour of the foirsaid treatie of unioun . . . and na uther-wayes, Thairfoir the saidis Estaittis of Scotland statutis determinis and declaris that all the abonewrittin actis liberteis privileges and ilkane of thame and everie heid article and member thairof shall ceis, abyd suspendit and

[1] Thus Scotland anticipated the English decision in ' Colville's Case ' (*infra*, p. 461).

be of na strenth force nor effect heireftir ay and quhill and
unto the speciall tyme that the Estaittis of England be thair
actis and statutis in parliament decerne grant and allow the
samin and als mony actis privileges liberteis fredomes and
immuniteis to the subjectis of the kingdome of Scotland to
be injoyit and bruikit be thame within the realme of England
conforme to the foirsaid treatie in all pointis.

A.P.S., iv, 366, c. 1

1608. *The Judgment of the Lord Chancellor in Colville's Case*

Although the English parliament had refused to accept the
opinion of the legal advisers to the crown that all persons born
in Scotland after James's accession to the English throne were,
by the common law, naturalised English subjects, the decision in
the case of Robert Colville, an infant born in Edinburgh and
seeking to hold lands in England, secured the legal status of the
post-nati. The action brought before the courts, to decide whether
or not Colville was an alien in England, was a collusive one, but
Coke prophetically recognised it as ' the weightiest for the consequent, both for the present and for all posterity.'

. . . Thus I have here delivered my concurrence in opinion
with my lords the judges, and the reasons that induce and
satisfy my conscience that Ro. Calvine,[1] and all the post-
nati in Scotland, are in reason and by the common law of
England natural-born subjects within the allegiance of the
King of England, and enabled to purchase and have freehold
and inheritance of lands in England and to bring real
actions for the same in England.

State Trials, xi, 106

Scotland and the Civil War

The Scottish opposition to Charles I, expressed in the National
Covenant,[2] anticipated the English rebellion. Indeed, in the
' Bishops' Wars ' the Scots had twice assembled in arms to defend

---

[1] *rectius*, Robert Colville, Master of Colville, son of James, first Lord
Colville (see *Scots Peerage*, ii, 557–8).   [2] *Supra*, p. 95

their kirk before the English rose in arms to defend their parliament. The king's difficulties in Scotland, however, and the rise of an active opposition to him there, played an important part in the English outbreak.[1]

But, just as Charles had aimed at conformity between the two realms on an Anglican and Episcopalian foundation, so now his enemies aimed at conformity on a Presbyterian and Puritan foundation. The united activity of the two parliamentary oppositions was effected by the Solemn League and Covenant,[2] and the Scots contributed largely to the parliamentary victory at Marston Moor.

But, at root, the English were fighting for civil liberty, the Scots for a Presbyterian Church; and, with the emergence of the Independents, and their ultimate control in England, the alliance of 1643 quickly fell apart. Nevertheless it is to be noted that the Scottish ' Engagers,' who designed to implement the Solemn League and Covenant on a royalist basis, required the king not only to confirm ' Presbyterial Government ' in England for an initial period of three years, but also to ' endeavour a complete union of the kingdoms, and, if that could not be speedily effected, the mutual communication of economic privileges '.[3]

The various aspects of this period of Anglo-Scottish relations are fully covered on pp. 114 *et seq.*; though it is also interesting to observe that in 1644 the use of committees and commissioners for joint action shows the English parliament adopting a traditional Scottish parliamentary device.[4]

Cromwellian Union

The divisions of Scottish parties, their religious extremism, and the willingness of a strong group to support Charles II (who accepted both Covenants as the price of a Scottish coronation in 1651) brought defeat and conquest at Cromwell's hands.[5] The Protectorate and its constitutional reorganisation brought complete legislative, executive and economic union.

After its victory at Worcester the English parliament seemed likely to treat Scotland as a conquered country and to annex it

[1] *Supra*, p. 114   [2] *Supra*, p. 122   [3] See *supra*, p. 138
[4] See Gardiner, *Constitutional Documents of the Puritan Revolution* (3rd ed.), 271–4   [5] See *supra*, p. 144

to England.   On 9 September 1651 a committee was appointed
' to bring in an Act for asserting the right of this Commonwealth
to so much of Scotland as is now under the forces of this Commonwealth,' and three weeks later an act ' asserting the title of England to Scotland ' was read for the first time.[1]   But wiser counsels
prevailed.   Eight commissioners were appointed to proceed to
Scotland to prepare the way for a union of the two countries ;
the burghs and shires were ordered to elect representatives with
powers to submit to the Commonwealth and to agree to the
union which was ' tendered ' ; and, that done, the burghs and
shires were again called upon to elect representatives to choose
twenty-one deputies to proceed to London to place before the
committee appointed by the English parliament any views they
might wish to put forward with regard to Scotland's place in
the new union.   All these proceedings, beginning in January
1652, culminated in an ' Act of the Parliament of the Commonwealth of England for the Uniting and Incorporating of Scotland
into one free State and Commonwealth with England ' which
was brought in on 4 October 1653 but, although read a second
time, was automatically dropped when the ' Nominated Parliament ' (or ' Barebones Parliament ') voted its own abdication
of power.

Cromwell now began his rule as Protector, and the Instrument
of Government which laid down the constitutional form of the
Protectorate was drawn up on the assumption of union between
England, Scotland and Ireland into one Commonwealth, with
one common parliament.

1653.   16 December   *The Instrument of Government*

The Government of the Commonwealth of England,
Scotland, and Ireland, and the dominions thereunto
belonging.

I. That the supreme legislative authority of the Commonwealth of England, Scotland, and Ireland, and the dominions
thereunto belonging, shall be and reside in one person, and
the people assembled in Parliament : the style of which
person shall be the Lord Protector of the Commonwealth
of England, Scotland, and Ireland.

[1] *Scotland and the Commonwealth* (Scot. Hist. Soc.), p. xxiii

II. That the exercise of the chief magistracy and the administration of the government over the said countries and dominions, and the people thereof, shall be in the Lord Protector, assisted with a council, the number whereof shall not exceed twenty-one, nor be less than thirteen. . . .

VII. That there shall be a Parliament summoned to meet at Westminster upon the third day of September, 1654, and that successively a Parliament shall be summoned once in every third year, to be accounted from the dissolution of the present Parliament. . . .

IX. That as well the next as all other successive Parliaments shall be summoned and elected in manner hereafter expressed ; that is to say, the persons to be chosen within England, Wales, the Isles of Jersey, Guernsey, and the town of Berwick-upon-Tweed, to sit and serve in Parliament, shall be, and not exceed, the number of four hundred. The persons to be chosen within Scotland, to sit and serve in Parliament, shall be, and not exceed, the number of thirty ; and the persons to be chosen to sit in Parliament for Ireland shall be, and not exceed, the number of thirty.

X. . . . The distribution of the persons to be chosen for Scotland and Ireland, and the several counties, cities, and places therein, shall be according to such proportions and number as shall be agreed upon and declared by the Lord Protector and the major part of the council, before the sending forth writs of summons for the next Parliament. . . .

XXII. That the persons so chosen and assembled in manner aforesaid, or any sixty of them, shall be, and be deemed the Parliament of England, Scotland, and Ireland ; and the supreme legislative power to be and reside in the Lord Protector and such Parliament, in manner herein expressed. . . .

Gardiner, *Constitutional Documents of the Puritan Revolution*
(3rd ed.), 405–17

The Ordinance of Union

One of the first tasks of Cromwell and the council appointed under the Instrument of Government was not only to determine the distribution of the Scottish seats in the new united parliament but also to determine all aspects of the new union between Scotland and England. This was done in the Ordinance of Union which was approved by the Protector and council on 12 April 1654.[1] Monck, who had successfully completed Lilburne's work in crushing Glencairn's rising, published the Ordinance in Edinburgh on 4 May 1654, and on the same day Cromwell was proclaimed there as Protector.

The Ordinance was confirmed and converted into an Act by Cromwell's second parliament in November 1656.

A second ordinance of 27 June 1654 settled the electoral districts for the Scottish members, but most of the members chosen were either officers or government officials (see *supra*, pp. 250-1).

Nevertheless, although Scotland had been united into 'one Commonwealth' with England, the union was maintained only by force and military occupation. In 1653, at the time of Glencairn's rising, Lilburne had in Scotland a force of about twelve thousand foot and two thousand horse, and although the building of forts at Inverlochy, Inverness, Ayr, Perth and Leith, and the adaptation of castles and houses to form some twenty subsidiary forts and garrisons, enabled gradual reductions in strength to be made, the number of occupation troops was still considerable. With the completion of the citadel at Leith, and of a fort at the head of Loch Ness, Monck estimated, in 1657, that thereafter six regiments and five companies of foot, three regiments of horse, and two troops of dragoons would be sufficient, distributed as follows :

1657. General Monck's Proposals

A List of the horse and foote which are to be left in Scotland, and the places of their quartring, in case your Highnes shall draw away the rest if there bee occation.

[1] See *supra*, p. 248

	Foote.	Horse.
Invernes, whereof 30 foote in the Castle, .	490	100
Ruthven Castle, ...	070	015
Sinclaire Castle, ...	070	015
Scalloway Castle in Zetland, . . .	070	
Kirkwall in Orkney, ...	140	
Head of Loughnes, ...	140	050
Boggygeith,[1]	070	030
Inverloughee, ...	210	
Dunstaffnage Castle, ...	035	
Dowart Castle, ...	070	
Aberdeene, ...	070	
Dunnotter, ...	070	012
Braymarre, ...	035	006
S. Johnstone, ...	420	100
Blaire Castle, ...	070	020
Finlarick, ...	070	015
Sterling, ...	910	300
Cardrosse and 20 horse of those in Sterling,	035	
Downe, Buchannon, and 12 horse each of those in Sterling, ...	035	
Dunbarton Castle, ...	070	020
Linlithgow, ...	070	030
Ayre, ...	490	100
Leith, ...	490	100
Edinburgh Castle, ...	140	
Tymtallon and the Basse, ...	035	
Douglas Castle, ...	035	030
Anderwick [2] and Dunce, ...	070	040
	4680 [3]	983

Scotland and the Protectorate (Scot. Hist. Soc.), 370

Naturally the cost was enormous ; and although the pay of the forces in Scotland, which had amounted to nearly £36,000 a month in June 1654, had been reduced to slightly less than

[1] Bog o' Gight [2] Innerwick [3] *rectius*, 4480

£21,000 a month in December 1657,[1] and although more than
half the cost was met by England, Scotland had still to find a
' cess ' which, amounting at first to the nominal figure of £10,000
a month, was later, in 1657, fixed, levied and raised at £6,000
a month.[2]

The Restoration in 1660 was hailed as the restoration of national
independence, the end of a hated union, and relief from intolerable
exactions which had well-nigh reduced the country to bankruptcy.

The Restoration

With the Restoration the Cromwellian union came to an end ;
Scotland and England returned to the status of two separate
countries and governments under one king. In this second half
of the seventeenth century, however, a hardening of English
commercial policy and the exclusion of Scottish merchants from
English colonial markets [3] brought about a growing appreciation
in Scotland of those commercial benefits of union which had been
tasted for a while and in a small way under the Cromwellian
administration. Charles II's attempts to arrange a closer union
were therefore greeted in Scotland with more enthusiasm than
James VI's had been, and particularly by the commercial and
industrial ' undertakers,' though hostility to the general idea of
union still remained, and Lauderdale could write, ' You cannot
imagine what aversion is generally in this kingdom to union.
The endeavour to have made us slaves by garrisons and the ruin
of our trade by severe laws in England frights all ranks of men
from having to do with England.' [4]

Commissioners of both parliaments duly met at Westminster
in the autumn of 1670, adjourned after two months, and never
reassembled. Scottish representations for a favourable interpretation of the English Navigation Acts (and, as a natural corollary,
Scottish inclusion in the English colonial trade) were wholly unacceptable to England ; in addition, the Scottish demand that
in the united parliament their country should have as many
representatives as it then had in the Scottish parliament betrayed
a complete lack of realism.

[1] *Scotland and the Protectorate* (Scot. Hist. Soc.), liii, 217, 381
[2] See *supra*, pp. 147, 297   [3] See *supra*, pp. 322-3
[4] *Lauderdale Papers* (Camden Soc.), ii, 154

England and Scotland, separated in 1660, were to remain separate for more than a further generation. Again each endeavoured to safeguard its trade and commerce to its own advantage and at the expense of the other. But one result of Scotland's exclusion from England's overseas markets was the ill-fated Darien Scheme,[1] and that, in turn, lay in the background of the Treaty of Union in 1707.

[1] See *supra*, pp. 337 *et seq.*

CHAPTER TWELVE

THE UNION WITH ENGLAND [1]

The independence from monarchical control which the Scottish parliament secured in 1690 [2] made the crown no longer adequate, or even relevant, as an instrument of union, for the means of ensuring Scottish acquiescence in policies made in England had been removed. The resultant strain on the personal union was aggravated by the special problems of William's reign. His ecclesiastical policy [3] was such as to antagonise almost all shades of opinion ; his own lack of understanding of Scottish affairs combined with faction and jealousy among Scottish politicians to bring about the resentment which followed the Massacre of Glencoe [4] ; and the conflict between the economic policies of Scotland and England came to a head in the Darien episode.[5] King William himself drew the correct lesson from Darien— ' that difficulties may too often arise with respect to the different interests of trade between the two kingdomes unless some way be found to unite them more neatly and completely,' and at the beginning of 1700 he recommended as a solution ' some happy expedient for making England and Scotland one people.' [6] The English House of Lords did pass a bill for the appointment of commissioners to discuss the question of union, but it was rejected by the Commons. Two years later, just before his death, William again commended union ; Queen Anne introduced the subject to her first English parliament, and a joint commission did meet to consider terms of union, but failed to overcome the stumbling-blocks of commercial privileges and taxation.

The matter had now become more urgent, because to the long-standing question of commercial relations there were added the question of the succession to the throne and the international situation arising from England's entry into the War of the Spanish

---

[1] Only a brief editorial comment is given here, since the whole subject has been dealt with at greater length by G. S. Pryde in *The Union of Scotland and England* (1950).   [2] *Supra*, pp. 209-10, 240
[3] *Supra*, pp. 211 *et seq.*   [4] *Supra*, pp. 219-23   [5] *Supra*, pp. 337 *et seq.*
[6] *Lords' Journals*, xvi, 497, 511

Succession. In 1689 both England and Scotland had settled the succession on the issue of William and Mary, whom failing the issue of Mary, whom failing Anne and her heirs, whom failing the issue of William. But after Anne's surviving son, the Duke of Gloucester, died in 1700, and the English Parliament, by its Act of Settlement, adopted the Hanoverian line as successors after Anne, no such provision was made by the Scottish parliament. Meantime, James VII had died and the French King had recognised his son as King James III and VIII ; moreover, Scotland and France were traditional allies. English statesmen were thus faced with the possibility that Scotland, by choosing a different successor from England, might open England's ' back door ' to Jacobite and French influence.

The Scottish parliament, by three measures passed in 1703, brought home to England the potential danger of the situation. The Wine Act was an assertion of commercial independence and an attempt to maintain the old French connection, and the Act Anent Peace and War provided for an independent Scottish foreign policy after Anne's death, even if the personal union continued. The Act of Security contained a threat to dissolve the personal union on Anne's death unless the sovereignty of Scotland, the power of its parliament and the freedom of its religion and commerce were secured from English interference. This measure was originally passed through the estates in 1703, but the Commissioner refused to give the royal assent and remitted it to London for the queen's consideration. This action aroused great resentment, and the estates retaliated by withholding supply. In the next year the bill was again presented, along with the grant of the Land Tax for six months, and Anne had to choose between giving her assent or disbanding Scottish troops. Marlborough had won his great victory at Blenheim on 13 August 1704, but it had not been reported when the queen gave her assent (15 August).

England retaliated by the Alien Act, which imposed serious disabilities on Scots until their parliament had settled the crown on the Hanoverian line ; but it also authorised the appointment of commissioners to treat for union as soon as the appointment of similar commissioners was authorised in Scotland. The Scots were not likely to accept the Hanoverian succession and thereby throw away their chief bargaining weapon, but they agreed to the appointment of commissioners. The queen named the commissioners on 21 September, and the Alien Act was repealed on 27 November. The commissioners sat from 16 April to 22 July 1706, when the Articles of Union were signed.

On the Scottish side the keen desire for inclusion in English colonial trade was combined with a wish to maintain national institutions. The English demanded the sacrifice by the Scots of one national institution—their parliament—in order to bring about an incorporating union, and the Scots agreed to this on condition that they received equality of commercial rights. Scottish proposals for a federal union were thus dropped, but the Scottish bargaining position was sufficiently strong to obtain the preservation of Scots Law and the Scottish legal system, to secure the Church of Scotland as established, and to exact several fiscal concessions.

The real debates took place not among the commissioners but in the Scottish parliament, between 3 October 1706 and 16 January 1707, on which date the Articles of Union, with only minor changes, were ratified by statute.[1] After the English parliament had likewise adopted the treaty, it received the royal assent on 6 March 1707 and came into effect on 1 May following. Three statutes, in addition to the Articles, form part of the Act of Union : Scottish statutes securing the presbyterian establishment and defining the method of electing the sixteen peers and forty-five members of the House of Commons who were to sit at Westminster, and an English statute for the security of the Church of England.

Judgment on the union in the light of the conditions of the time must be that it was a statesmanlike bargain. Each country made concessions as part of the price of a union which England desired in order to ensure a common front against France and which Scotland desired in order to gain opportunities to develop her overseas trade. It may be argued, further, that the sovereignty with which Scotland parted was somewhat shadowy, and that through the union she received the tangible benefit that her economy was completely transformed in less than a century. On the other hand, from 1689 to 1707 the Scottish Parliament and General Assembly were both finding a new force and a new vitality, and opinions may differ as to the hypothetical consequences had the union not come about. In any event, judgment

---

[1] *A.P.S.*, xi, 406

on the union of 1707 in 1707 must not be influenced by the view
taken of the union in the twentieth century, when the wide
extension of governmental activity at the expense of the liberty
of the subject, of private enterprise and of the powers of local
authorities, has produced a situation in which the framers of the
union never conceived that it would operate.

1703. ACT ANENT PEACE AND WAR·

OUR Sovereign Lady, with advice and consent of the Estates
of Parliament, statutes, enacts, and declares, That after her
Majesty's decease, and failyieing heirs of her body, no person
being King or Queen of Scotland and England, shall have
the sole power of making War with any Prince, Potentate
or State whatsomever without consent of Parliament ; and
that no Declaration of War without consent foresaid, shall
be binding on the subjects of this Kingdom, Declaring
alwayes, that this shall no ways be understood to impede
the Soveraign of this Kingdom to call furth, command, and
imploy the subjects thereof to suppress any insurrection
within the Kingdom, or repell any invasion from abroad,
according to former Laws ; and also Declaring, that everything which relates to Treaties of Peace, Alliance and Commerce, is left to the wisdom of the Soveraign, with consent of
the Estates of Parliament who shall declare the War : And
her Majesty with consent foresaid, repells, casses, and annulls
all former Acts of Parliament, in so far as they are contrair
hereunto or inconsistent herewith.   *A.P.S.*, xi, 107, c. 6

THE 'WINE ACT'

1703. *Act allowing the Importation of Wines and other forreign
        Liquors*

   Our Sovereign Lady with advice and consent of the
Estates of Parliament Statutes and Declares that it shall
be lawfull from and after the date hereof to import into
this Kingdom all sorts of Wines and other Forreign Liquors,
any former Act or Statute in the contrary notwithstanding,
which her Majesty with advice and consent foresaid

Rescinds and Declares void and null in so far as they are inconsistent with or contrare to this present Act. The said Wines or other liquors which shall be imported paying allwayes the former customes, excise and other duties, reserveing to the Peers and Barons of the Kingdom the same immunities and freedoms from customes for wines which they had by the two hundreth fifty first Act fifteenth Parliament King James the Sixth.   *A.P.S.*, xi, 112, c. 13

THE ACT OF SECURITY

1703. *Withholding of the Royal Assent to the Act of Security*

[*On* 10 *September*, 1703] her Majesties high Commissioner made a speech to the Parliament in manner following.

My Lords and Gentlemen

It was with great uneasiness to me that I was forced to be silent yesterday when so many did appear earnest that I should speak. I have all the inclination in the world to give yow full satisfaction but I thought that I ought not to be pressed to give the royal assent or to declare my instructions in Parliament which I had made known to many noble and worthy members besides the Queen's Servants.

Now that these instances are let fall and that yow have proceeded to other business, to testifie how willing I am to give yow contentment in any thing that's in my power I tell yow freely that I have received her Majesties pleasure and am fully impowered to give the royal assent to all the acts voted in this session excepting only that act intituled Act for Security of the Kingdom ; Yow may easily believe that requires her Majesties further consideration. At the same time her Majestie expects that yow will mind your own safety in makeing necessary provisions for the troops upon the present establishment and that you will put the trade and customes on that foot that the Civil list may be supported, and I intreat your lordships to finish these as quickly as possible that this session may be put to a speedy and happy conclusion.

It was thereupon moved that there may be an address

473

of Parliament to her Majestie humbly intreating that her Majestie may be pleased to give the royal assent to the said act, and after some debate upon that motion the vote was stated—Address or proceed to other business, and carried —proceed to other business.

A.P.S., xi, 101–2

[*On* 16 *September* 1703 *the Commissioner made the following speech.*]

My Lords and Gentlemen

We have now past several good Acts for our Religion Liberty and Trade which I hope will be acceptable to all her Majesties good subjects. I wish you had also given the Supplies necessary for the maintaining of her Majesties forces and preserveing the peace and safety of the Kingdom : But since I hope this may yet be done in due time, and that besides some Questions and difficulties are fallen that in all probability yow have no time to determine ; And that withall it is fit Her Majestie should have time to consider upon some things that have been laid before her, And that we may know her mind therein more perfectly a short recess seems at present to be necessary, and that this Parliament be adjourned for some time ; And therefore I have ordered my Lord Chancellour to adjourn this Parliament till the twelvth day of October next.

A.P.S., xi, 112

1704. *Act of Security*

OUR Soveraign Lady, the Queen's Majesty, with advice and consent of the Estates of Parliament, doth hereby statute and ordain, That in the event of her Majesties death, or of the death of any of her Majesties heirs or successors, Kings or Queens of this Realm, this present Parliament or any other parliament that shall be then in being, shall not be dissolved by the said death. . . . And if the said Parliament be under adjournment the time of the said death, it shall notwithstanding meet precisely at Edinburgh the twentieth day after the said death, excluding the day thereof, whether the day of the said adjournment be sooner or later. And it is further statute and ordained, that in case there shall be no Parliament in being at the time of the death foresaid, then the Estates or members of the last preceding Parliament, without regard to any Parliament that may be indicted, but never met nor constituted, shall meet at Edinburgh on the twentieth day after the said death, the day thereof excluded. . . . And the said Estates of Parliament, appointed in case of the death foresaid, to continue or meet as above, are hereby authorised and impowered to act and administrate the government in manner after-mentioned ; that is, that upon the death of her Majesty, leaving heirs of her own body, or failing thereof lawful successors designed or appointed by her Majesty and the Estates of Parliament, or upon the death of any succeeding King or Queen, leaving lawful heirs and successors, as said is, the said Estates of Parliament are authorised and impowered, after having read to the said heir or successor the Claim of Right, and desired them to accept the government in the terms thereof, to require of, and administrate to the said heir or lawful successors, by themselves, or such as they shall commissionat, the Coronation Oath, and that with all convenient speed, not exceeding thirty days after the meeting of the said Estates, if the said heir or successor be within the Isle of Britain, or if without the same not exceeding three months after the said meeting, in order to their exercising the regal power, conform to the Declaration of the Estates containing the Claim of Right. . . . And further, upon the said death of her Majesty, without heirs of her body, or a successor lawfully designed and appointed as above, or in the case of any other King or Queen thereafter succeeding and deceasing without lawful heir or successor, the foresaid Estates of Parliament conveened or meeting are hereby authorised and impowered to nominat and declare the successor to the Imperial Crown of this Realm, and to settle the succession thereof upon the heirs of the said successor's body, the

475

said successor, and the heirs of the successor's body, being always of the Royal Line of Scotland and of the true Protestant Religion. Providing always, That the same be not successor to the Crown of England, unless that in this present session of Parliament, or any other session of this or any ensuing Parliament during her Majesties reign there be such condicions of government settled and enacted, as may secure the honour and soveraignty of this Crown and Kingdom, the freedom, frequency and power of Parliaments, the religion, liberty and trade of the nation from English, or any foreign, influence, with power to the said meeting of Estates to add such further conditions of government as they shall think necessary, the same being consistent with, and no way derogatory from those which shall be enacted in this and any other session of Parliament during her Majesties reign. And it is hereby declared, that the said meeting of Estates shall not have power to nominat the said Successor to the Crown of this Kingdom in the event above exprest during the first twenty days after their meeting; which twenty days being elapsed, they shall proceed to make the said nomination with all convenient diligence. And it is hereby expressly provided and declared, That it shall be High Treason for any person or persons to administer the Coronation Oath, or be witnesses to the administration thereof, but by the appointment of the Estates of Parliament in manner above-mentioned, or to owne or acknowledge any person as King or Queen of this realm in the event of her Majesties decease, leaving heirs of her own body, until they have sworn the Coronation Oath, and accepted the Crown in the terms of the Claim of Right : And in the event of her Majesties decease, without heirs of her body, until they swear the Coronation Oath, and accept on the terms of the Claim of Right, and of such other condicions of government as shall be settled in this or any ensuing Parliament, or added in the said meeting of Estates, and be thereupon declared and admitted as above, which crime shall be irremissible without consent of Parliament. . . .

[*It is further enacted*] that the whole protestant heretors

and all the burghs within the same [kingdom] shall furth-
with provide themselves with fire arms for all the fencible
men who are Protestants within their respective bounds . . .
and the said heretors and burghs are hereby impowered and
ordained to discipline and exercise their said fencible men
once in the moneth at least. . . .   *A.P.S.*, xi, 136, c. 3

THE 'ALIEN ACT'

1705.   *The (English) Alien Act*

An Act for the effectual securing the kingdom of England
from the apparent dangers that may arise from several
acts lately passed by the parliament of Scotland.

For preventing the many inconveniences which may speedily
happen to the two Kingdoms of England and Scotland, if a
nearer and more compleat union be not made between the
said Kingdoms ; Be it enacted by the Queen's most excellent
Majesty, by and with the advice and consent of the Lords
Spiritual and Temporal, and Commons, in this present
Parliament assembled, and by the authority of the same,
That such persons as shall be nominated by her Majesty,
under her Great Seal of England, or such and so many of
them as shall in that behalf be appointed by her Majesty
to be of the quorum, shall, by force of this Act, have full
power, commission and authority, at such time and times,
and in such place or places, as her Majesty shall be pleased
to appoint, to assemble and meet, and thereupon to treat
and consult, according to the tenor and purport of their
authority or commission in that behalf, with certain Commissioners as shall be authorised by authority of the Parliament of Scotland, of and concerning such an union of the
said Kingdoms of England and Scotland, and of and concerning such other matters, clauses and things, as upon
mature deliberation the greatest part of the said Commissioners, assembled as aforesaid, and the Commissioners to
be authorised by the Parliament of Scotland, according to
the tenor or purport of their commissions in that behalf,
shall in their wisdoms think convenient and necessary for

the honour of her Majesty, and the common good of both the said Kingdoms for ever. . . .

Provided always, and be it enacted and declared, That no such Commission or Authority as aforesaid shall be granted, until an Act of Parliament shall be made in the Kingdom of Scotland, impowering her Majesty to grant a Commission under the Great Seal of that Kingdom, nominating Commissioners to treat concerning the union of the two Kingdoms. . . .

And be it further enacted by the authority aforesaid that from and after the five and twentieth day of December [1705] no person or persons being a native or natives of the Kingdom of Scotland (except such as are now setled inhabitants within the Kingdom of England or the Dominions thereunto belonging and shall continue inhabitants thereof and such as are now in service in her Majesties fleet or army) shall be capable to inherit any lands, tenements or hereditaments within this Kingdom of England or the Dominions thereunto belonging or to enjoy any benefit or advantage of a natural born subject of England, but every such person shall be from thenceforth adjudged and taken as an alien born out of the allegiance of the Queen of England, until such time as the succession to the Crown of Scotland be declared and settled by an Act of Parliament in Scotland in the same manner [as] the succession to the Crown of England is now settled by Act of Parliament in England. . . .

From and after the said [25 December 1705] until such time as the succession to the Crown of Scotland be declared . . . as aforesaid, no great cattle or sheep shall be brought out of or from the Kingdom of Scotland into the Kingdom of England or Ireland, Dominion of Wales or town of Berwick upon Tweed, under the penalty of forfeiting all such great cattle or sheep to him or them who will seize or sue for the same and also the full value of such great cattle or sheep . . . ; no Scotch coals shall be imported out of the Kingdom of Scotland ; . . . no Scotch linnen shall be imported or brought out of Scotland. . . .

Statutes of the Realm, viii, 349–50

APPOINTMENT OF COMMISSIONERS TO TREAT FOR UNION

1705. *Act for a Treaty with England*

The Estates of Parliament considering with what earnestness the Queen's Majesty has recommended to them the settling of the Succession to the Imperial Crown of this her ancient Kingdom in the Protestant Line, failyieing heirs of her own body : And also to enter into a treaty with her Kingdom of England, as the most effectual way for extinguishing the heats and differences that are unhappily raised betwixt the two nations : and in prosecution of her Majesty's royal and just purpose, of having a treaty set on foot betwixt her two independent Kingdoms of Scotland and England, without which these things of great consequence betwixt them cannot be accommodat : Therefore her Majesty, with advice and consent of the Estates of Parliament, doth enact, statute, and ordain, That such persons, and quorum thereof, as shall be nominat and appointed by her Majesty under the Great Seal of this Kingdom shall have full power and commission . . . to treat and consult with such commissioners as shall be authorised by authority of the Parliament of England, of and concerning an union of the Kingdoms of Scotland and England, and of and concerning such other matters, clauses and things as, upon maturer deliberation of the greatest part of the said commissioners assembled as aforesaid, and the commissioners to be authorised by authority of the Parliament of England, according to the tenor of their commissions in that behalf, shall think necessary and convenient. . . . ; And it is further provided, that no matter or thing to be treated of, proposed, or agreed by the said commissioners, by virtue of this Act, shall be of any strength or effect whatsoever, until it be first confirmed and established by Authority, and an Act of the Parliament of Scotland ; Providing also, That the said commissioners shall not treat of or concerning any alteration of the Worship, Discipline and Government of the Church of this Kingdom, as now by Law established.

A.P.S., xi, 295, c. 50

1706. *Repeal of the Alien Act by the English Parliament*

An Act to repeal several Clauses in the Statute made in the Third and Fourth years of her present Majesty's Reign, for securing the Kingdom of England from several Acts lately passed in the Parliament of Scotland.

[Extract]

Whereas, since the making of the said Act, an Act hath been made and passed in the Parliament of Scotland for enabling her Majesty to appoint Commissioners to treat with Commissioners for the Kingdom of Scotland, of and concerning an Union of the said Kingdoms of England and Scotland : Now to the end that the good and friendly disposition of this Kingdom towards the Kingdom of Scotland may appear ; Be it enacted by the Queen's most excellent Majesty, by and with the advice and consent of the Lords Spiritual and Temporal, and Commons, in Parliament assembled, and by the authority of the same, That the said Clauses be from henceforth absolutely repealed and vacated to all intents and purposes whatsoever.

Statutes of the Realm, viii, 486

1706-7. *The Articles of Union* [1]

I. That the Two Kingdoms of England and Scotland shall upon the First day of May which shall be in the year One thousand seven hundred and seven, and for ever after, be united into one Kingdom by the name of Great Britain ; and that the Ensigns Armorial of the said United Kingdom be such as Her Majesty shall appoint, and the Crosses of St. George and St. Andrew be conjoined in such manner as Her Majesty shall think fit, and used in all Flags, Banners, Standards and Ensigns, both at Sea and Land.

II. That the Succession of the Monarchy to the United Kingdom of Great Britain, and of the Dominions thereunto belonging, after Her most Sacred Majesty, and in default

---

[1] The full text is given in G. S. Pryde, *op. cit.*

of Issue of her Majesty, be, remain, and continue to the most excellent Princess Sophia, Electoress and Duchess Dowager of Hanover, and the Heirs of her Body being Protestants, upon whom the Crown of England is settled by an Act of Parliament made in England in the Twelfth year of the Reign of his late Majesty King William the Third, intituled, An Act for the further Limitation of the Crown, and better securing the Rights and Liberties of the Subject : [1] And that all Papists, and persons marrying Papists, shall be excluded from, and for ever incapable to inherit, possess, or enjoy the Imperial Crown of Great Britain, and the Dominions thereunto belonging, or any part thereof ; and in every such case the Crown and Government shall from time to time descend to, and be enjoyed by such Person, being a Protestant, as should have inherited and enjoyed the same in case such Papist, or Person marrying a Papist, was naturally dead, according to a Provision for the Descent of the Crown of England made by another Act of Parliament in England in the First year of the Reign of their late Majesties King William and Queen Mary, intituled, An Act declaring the Rights and Liberties of the Subject, and Settling the Succession of the Crown.[2]

III. That the United Kingdom of Great Britain be represented by One and the same Parliament, to be stiled, the Parliament of Great Britain.

IV. That all the Subjects of the United Kingdom of Great Britain shall, from and after the Union, have full Freedom and Intercourse of Trade and Navigation to and from any Port or Place within the said United Kingdom, and the Dominions and Plantations thereunto belonging ; and that there be a communication of all other Rights, Privileges, and Advantages, which do or may belong to the Subjects of either Kingdom ; except where it is otherwise expressly agreed in these Articles.

V. That all ships or vessels belonging to Her Majesty's Subjects of Scotland, at the time of ratifying the Treaty of Union of the two Kingdoms in the Parliament of Scotland,

[1] Act of Settlement   [2] The Bill of Rights

though foreign built, be deemed, and pass as ships of the build of Great Britain. . . .

VI. That all parts of the United Kingdom for ever from and after the Union shall have the same allowances, encouragements and drawbacks, and be under the same prohibitions, restrictions and regulations of trade, and lyable to the same customs and duties on import and export . . . ; and that from and after the Union no Scots cattle carried into England shall be lyable to any other duties . . . than these duties to which the cattle of England are or shall be lyable. . . .

VII. That all parts of the United Kingdom be for ever from and after the Union lyable to the same excises upon all exciseable liquors. . . .

VIII. . . . Scotland shall for the space of seven years from the said Union be exempted from paying in Scotland for salt made there the dutie or excise now payable for salt made in England. . . .

IX. That whenever the sum of [£1,997,763, 8s. 4½d.] shall be enacted . . . to be raised in that part of the United Kingdom now called England, on land and other things usually charged in Acts of Parliament there for granting an aid to the Crown by a land tax, that part of the United Kingdom now called Scotland shall be charged by the same Act with a further sum of [£48,000] free of all charges, as the quota of Scotland to such tax, and so proportionably. . . .

X–XIII. [*Scotland exempted from existing English duties on stamped paper, vellum and parchment, windows and lights, coal, culm and cinders, and malt.*]

XIV. . . . That any malt to be made and consumed in that part of the United Kingdom now called Scotland shall not be charged with any imposition upon malt during this present war. . . .

XV. [*Whereas Scotland will become liable to customs and excise duties which will be applicable to the payment of England's existing National Debt, and whereas the yield of these duties will increase and a portion of the increase will be applied to the same end, Scotland is to receive as an ' Equivalent': (1) a lump sum of*]

£398,085, 10s., ' *due and payable from the time of the Union* ' *and* (2) *the increase in Scotland's customs and excise revenue for the first seven years after the Union, and thereafter such part of the increase as would be required for the debt. This ' Equivalent ' is to be devoted to,* (a) *recompensing those who lost through the standardising of the coinage,* (b) *payment of the capital* (*with interest*) *advanced for the Darien Company* (*which is to be dissolved*), (c) *the payment for the public debts of the Scottish Crown, and* (d) *payment of £2000 yearly for seven years to encourage the wool manufacture and thereafter to promote fisheries and other ' manufactures and improvements'*.]

XVI. That from and after the Union, the Coin shall be of the same standard and value throughout the United Kingdom, as now in England, and a Mint shall be continued in Scotland, under the same Rules as the Mint in England, and the present Officers of the Mint continued, subject to such Regulations and Alterations as Her Majesty, Her Heirs or Successors, or the Parliament of Great Britain shall think fit.

XVII. That from and after the Union, the same Weights and Measures shall be used throughout the United Kingdom, as are established in England, and Standards of Weights and Measures shall be kept by those Burghs in Scotland, to whom the keeping the Standards of Weights and Measures, now in use there, does of special right belong : All which Standards shall be sent down to such respective Burghs, from the Standards kept in the Exchequers at Westminster, subject nevertheless to such Regulations as the Parliament of Great Britain shall think fit.

XVIII. That the Laws concerning Regulation of Trade, Customs, and such Excises to which Scotland is, by virtue of this Treaty, to be liable, be the same in Scotland from and after the Union as in England ; and that all other Laws in use within the Kingdom of Scotland, do after the Union, and notwithstanding thereof, remain in the same force as before, (except such as are contrary to, or inconsistent with this Treaty) but alterable by the Parliament of Great Britain ; with this difference betwixt the Laws concerning Public Right, Policy and Civil Government, and those which concern Private Right, that the Laws which concern Public Right, Policy, and Civil Government, may be made the same throughout the whole United Kingdom ; But that no alteration be made in Laws which concern private Right, except for evident utility of the Subjects within Scotland.

XIX. That the Court of Session, or College of Justice, do after the Union, and notwithstanding thereof, remain in all time coming within Scotland, as it is now constituted by the Laws of that Kingdom, and with the same Authority and Privileges as before the Union, subject nevertheless to such Regulations for the better Administration of Justice as shall be made by the Parliament of Great Britain ; and that hereafter none shall be named by her Majesty or her Royal Successors, to be Ordinary Lords of Session, but such who have served in the College of Justice as Advocates or Principal Clerks of Session for the space of Five years ; or as Writers to the Signet for the space of Ten years ; with this provision that no Writer to the Signet be capable to be admitted a Lord of the Session unless he undergo a private and public Trial on the Civil Law before the Faculty of Advocates, and be found by them qualified for the said Office two years before he be named to be a Lord of the Session ; yet so as the Qualifications made, or to be made, for capacitating Persons to be named Ordinary Lords of Sessions, may be altered by the Parliament of Great Britain. And that the Court of Justiciary do also after the Union, and notwithstanding thereof, remain in all time coming within Scotland, as it is now constituted by the Laws of that Kingdom, and with the same Authority and Privileges as before the Union, subject nevertheless to such Regulations as shall be made by the Parliament of Great Britain, and without prejudice of other Rights of Justiciary. And that all Admiralty Jurisdictions be under the Lord High Admiral or Commissioners for the Admiralty of Great Britain for the time being ; and that the Court of Admiralty now established in Scotland be continued, and all Reviews, Reductions, or Suspensions of the Sentences in maritime Cases competent to the Jurisdiction of that Court remain in the same manner after the Union as now in Scotland, until the Parliament of Great Britain shall make such Regulations and Alterations as shall be judged expedient for the whole United Kingdom, so as there be always continued in Scotland a Court of Admiralty, such as in England, for determination of all Maritime Cases relating to private rights in Scotland, competent to the Jurisdiction of the Admiralty Court, subject nevertheless to such Regulations and Alterations as shall be thought proper to be made by the Parliament of Great Britain ; And that the Heretable Rights of Admiralty and Vice-Admiralties in Scotland be reserved to the respective Proprietors as Rights of Property, subject nevertheless, as to the manner of exercising such Heretable Rights, to such Regulations and Alterations as shall be thought proper to be made by the Parliament of Great Britain. And that all other Courts now being within the Kingdom of Scotland do remain, but subject to alterations by the Parliament of Great Britain ; And that all Inferior Courts within the said limits do remain subordinate, as they now are, to the Supreme Courts of Justice within the same in all time coming ; And that no Causes in Scotland be Cognisable by the Courts of Chancery, Queen's Bench, Common Pleas, or any other Court in Westminster Hall ; and that the said Courts, or any other of the like nature, after the Union, shall have no power to cognosce, review, or alter the Acts or Sentences of the Judicatures within Scotland or to stop the execution of the same ; And that there be a Court of Exchequer in Scotland after the Union, for deciding questions concerning the Revenues of Customs and Excises there, having the same power and authority in such cases, as the Court of Exchequer has in England ; and that the said Court of Exchequer in Scotland have power of passing Signatures, Gifts, Tutories, and in other things as the Court of Exchequer at present in Scotland hath ; and that the Court of Exchequer that now is in Scotland do remain, until a new Court of Exchequer be settled by the Parliament of Great Britain in Scotland after the Union ; and that after the Union, the Queen's Majesty, and her Royal Successors, may continue a Privy Council in Scotland, for preserving of public Peace and Order, until the Parliament of Great Britain shall think fit to alter it, or establish any other effectual method for that end.

XX. That all Heretable Offices, Superiorities, Heretable Jurisdictions, Offices for Life, and Jurisdictions for Life, be reserved to the Owners thereof, as Rights of Property in the same manner as they are now enjoyed by the Laws of Scotland, notwithstanding this Treaty.

XXI. That the Rights and Privileges of the Royal Burghs in Scotland, as they now are, do remain entire after the Union, and notwithstanding thereof.

XXII. That by virtue of this Treaty, of the Peers of Scotland at the time of the Union, Sixteen shall be the number to sit and vote in the House of Lords, and Forty-five the Number of the Representatives of Scotland in the House of Commons of the Parliament of Great Britain ; and that when Her Majesty, her heirs or Successors, shall declare her or their Pleasure for holding the First or any subsequent Parliament of Great Britain, until the Parliament of Great Britain shall make further provision therein, a Writ do issue under the Great Seal of the United Kingdom, directed to the Privy Council of Scotland, commanding them to cause Sixteen Peers, who are to sit in the House of Lords, to be summoned to Parliament, and Forty-five Members to be elected to sit in the House of Commons of the Parliament of Great Britain, according to the Agreement in this Treaty, in such manner as by an Act of this present Session of the Parliament of Scotland is or shall be settled ; which Act is hereby declared to be as valid as if it were a part of, and ingrossed in this Treaty. And that the names of the persons so summoned and elected shall be returned by the Privy Council of Scotland into the Court from whence the said Writ did issue. And that if her Majesty, on or before the First day of May next, on which day the Union is to take place, shall declare under

the Great Seal of England, that it is expedient that the
Lords of Parliament of England, and Commons of the
present Parliament of England, should be the Members of
the respective Houses of the First Parliament of Great
Britain, for and on the part of England, then the said Lords
of Parliament of England, and Commons of the present
Parliament of England shall be the Members of the respective Houses of the First Parliament of Great Britain for
and on the part of England ; And Her Majesty may by
her Royal Proclamation under the Great Seal of Great
Britain appoint the said First Parliament of Great Britain
to meet at such Time and Place as Her Majesty shall think
fit ; Which time shall not be less than Fifty days after such
Proclamation ; and the time and place of the meeting of
such Parliament being so appointed, a Writ shall be
immediately issued under the Great Seal of Great Britain
directed to the Privy Council of Scotland for the Summoning of the Sixteen Peers, and for electing Forty-five Members
by whom Scotland is to be represented in the Parliament
of Great Britain ; and the Lords of Parliament of England
and the Sixteen Peers of Scotland, such Sixteen Peers being
summoned and returned in the manner agreed in this
Treaty, and the Members of the House of Commons of the
said Parliament of England, and the Forty-five Members
for Scotland, such Forty-five Members being elected and
returned in the manner agreed in this Treaty, shall assemble
and meet respectively, in the respective Houses of the Parliament of Great Britain, at such time and place as shall be so
appointed by Her Majesty, and shall be the two Houses of
the First Parliament of Great Britain ; and that Parliament
may continue for such time only, as the present Parliament
of England might have continued if the Union of the Two
Kingdoms had not been made, unless sooner dissolved by
Her Majesty. . . .

XXIII. That the aforesaid Sixteen Peers mentioned in
the last preceding Article, to sit in the House of Lords of the
Parliament of Great Britain, shall have all Privileges of
Parliament which the Peers of England now have, and which

they or any Peers of Great Britain shall have after the Union, and particularly the Right of Sitting upon the Trials of Peers : And in case of the Trial of any Peer in time of adjournment, or prorogation of Parliament, the said Sixteen Peers shall be summoned in the same manner, and have the same powers and privileges at such Trial, as any other Peers of Great Britain. And that in case any Trials of Peers shall hereafter happen when there is no Parliament in being, the Sixteen Peers of Scotland who sat at the last preceding Parliament shall be summoned in the same manner, and have the same powers and privileges at such Trials, as any other Peers of Great Britain ; and that all Peers of Scotland, and their Successors in their Honours and Dignities, shall from and after the Union be Peers of Great Britain, and have Rank and Precedency next and immediately after the Peers of the like Orders and Degrees in England at the time of the Union, and before all Peers of Great Britain of the like Orders and Degrees who may be created after the Union, and shall be tried as Peers of Great Britain, and shall enjoy all privileges of Peers as fully as the Peers of England do now, or as they, or any other Peers of Great Britain may hereafter enjoy the same, except the Right and Privilege of sitting in the House of Lords, and the Privileges depending thereon, and particularly the right of sitting upon the Trials of Peers.

XXIV. That from and after the Union there be one Great Seal for the United Kingdom of Great Britain, which shall be different from the Great Seal now used in either Kingdom ; And that the Quartering the Arms, and the Rank and Precedency of the Lyon King of Arms of the Kingdom of Scotland, as may best suit the Union, be left to Her Majesty ; and that in the meantime the Great Seal of England be used as the Great Seal of the United Kingdom, and that the Great Seal of the United Kingdom be used for sealing Writs to elect and summon the Parliament of Great Britain, and for sealing all Treaties with Foreign Princes and States, and all public Acts, Instruments, and Orders of State which concern the whole United Kingdom, and in all other matters relating to England as the Great Seal of England is now used. And that a Seal in Scotland after the Union be always kept and made use of in all things relating to private Rights or Grants, which have usually passed the Great Seal of Scotland, and which only concern Offices, Grants, Commissions and private Rights within that Kingdom ; and that until such Seal shall be appointed by her Majesty, the present Great Seal of Scotland shall be used for such purposes : And that the privy Seal, Signet, Casset, Signet of the Justiciary Court, Quarter Seal, and Seals of Court now used in Scotland be continued ; but that the said Seals be altered and adapted to the State of the Union, as her Majesty shall think fit ; and the said Seals, and all of them, and the Keepers of them, shall be subject to such Regulations as the Parliament of Great Britain shall hereafter make. And that the Crown, Sceptre, and Sword of State, the Records of Parliament, and all other Records, Rolls, and Registers whatsoever, both Public and Private, General and Particular, and Warrants thereof, continue to be kept as they are within that part of the United Kingdom now called Scotland ; and that they shall so remain in all time coming notwithstanding the Union.

XXV. That all Laws and Statutes in either Kingdom, so far as they are contrary to, or inconsistent with, the Terms of these Articles, or any of them, shall from and after the Union, cease and become void, and shall be so declared to be, by the respective Parliaments of the said Kingdoms.

A.P.S., xi, 406–13

SECURITY OF THE CHURCH

1707. *Act for securing the Protestant Religion and Presbyterian Church Government*

Our Soveraign Lady and the Estates of Parliament considering That by the late Act of Parliament for a Treaty with England for an Union of both Kingdoms It is provided That the Commissioners for that Treaty should not Treat of or concerning any alteration of the Worship Discipline and Government of the Church of this Kingdom as now by

Law established, Which Treaty being now reported to the Parliament, and it being reasonable and necessary that the True Protestant Religion, as presently professed within this Kingdom with the Worship Discipline and Government of this Church should be effectually and unalterably secured ; Therefore Her Majesty with advice and consent of the said Estates of Parliament Doth hereby Establish and Confirm the said True Protestant Religion and the Worship Discipline and Government of this Church to continue without any alteration to the people of this Land in all succeeding generations. And more especially Her Majesty with advice and consent foresaid Ratifies Approves and for ever Confirms the fifth Act of the first Parliament of King William and Queen Mary Entituled Act Ratifying the Confession of Faith and settling Presbyterian Church Government, with the haill other Acts of Parliament relating thereto in prosecution of the Declaration of the Estates of this Kingdom containing the Claim of Right bearing date the eleventh of Aprile One thousand six hundred and eighty nine And Her Majesty with advice and consent foresaid expressly Provides and Declares That the foresaid True Protestant Religion contained in the abovementioned Confession of Faith with the form and purity of Worship presently in use within this Church and its Presbyterian Church Government and Discipline, that is to say, the Government of the Church by Kirk Sessions, Presbytries, Provincial Synods and Generall Assemblies, all established by the forsaid Acts of Parliament pursuant to the Claim of Right shall Remain and Continue unalterable, and that the said Presbyterian Government shall be the only Government of the Church within the Kingdom of Scotland.

And further for the greater security of the foresaid Protestant Religion and of the Worship Discipline and Government of this Church as above established Her Majesty with advice and consent foresaid Statutes and Ordains That the Universities and Colledges of Saint Andrews Glasgow Aberdeen and Edinburgh as now Established by Law shall Continue within this Kingdom for ever. And that in all time comeing no Professors, Principalls, Regents, Masters or others bearing office in any University Colledge or School within this Kingdom be capable or be admitted or allowed to continue in the Exercise of their said functions but such as shall own and acknowledge the Civill Government in manner prescribed or to be prescribed by the Acts of Parliament. As also that before or at their Admissions they do and shall acknowledge and profess and shall subscribe to the foresaid Confession of Faith as the Confession of their faith, and that they will practise and conform themselves to the Worship presently in use in this Church and submit themselves to the Government and Discipline thereof and never endeavour directly or indirectly the prejudice or subversion of the same, and that before the respective Presbytries of their bounds by whatsoever gift presentation or provision they may be thereto provided.

And further Her Majesty with advice foresaid expressly Declares and Statutes that none of the Subjects of this Kingdom shall be lyable to, but all and every one of them for ever free of any Oath Test or Subscription within this Kingdom contrary to or inconsistent with the foresaid True Protestant Religion and Presbyterian Church Government Worship and Discipline as above established : And that the same within the bounds of this Church and Kingdom shall never be imposed upon or required of them in any sort. And Lastly that after the Decease of Her present Majesty (whom God long preserve) the Soveraign succeeding to her in the Royal Government of the Kingdom of Great Britain shall in all time comeing at his or her accession to the Crown Swear and Subscribe That they shall inviolably maintain and preserve the foresaid settlement of the True Protestant Religion with the Government Worship Discipline Right and Priviledges of this Church as above established by the Laws of this Kingdom in prosecution of the Claim of Right.

And it is hereby Statute and Ordained That this Act of Parliament with the Establishment therein contained shall be held and observed in all time coming as a fundamentall and essentiall Condition of any Treaty or Union to be Concluded betwixt the Two Kingdoms without any Alteration thereof or Derogation thereto in any sort for ever. As also that this Act of Parliament and Settlement therein contained shall be Insert and Repeated in any Act of Parliament that shall pass for agreeing and concluding the foresaid Treaty or Union betwixt the Two Kingdoms. And that the same shall be therein expressly Declared to be a fundamentall and essentiall Condition of the said Treaty or Union in all time coming. *A.P.S.*, xi, 402, c.6

ELECTIONS TO THE PARLIAMENT OF GREAT BRITAIN

1707. *Act Settling the manner of Electing the Sixteen Peers and Forty Five Commoners to represent Scotland in the Parliament of Great Britain*

Our Sovereign Lady, Considering, That by the Twenty Second Article of the Treaty of Union, as the same is ratified by an Act past in this Session of Parliament upon the sixteenth of January last, it is provided, that by virtue of the said Treaty, of the Peers of Scotland at the time of the Union, sixteen shall be the number to sit and vote in the House of Lords, and fourty five the number of the representatives of Scotland in the House of Commons of the Parliament of Great Britain ; and that the said sixteen Peers, and fourty five Members of the House of Commons be named and chosen in such manner as by a subsequent Act in this present Session of Parliament in Scotland shall be settled ; Which Act is thereby declared to be as valid as if it were a part of, and ingrossed in the said Treaty. Therefore Her Majesty, with advice and consent of the Estates of Parliament, statutes, enacts, and ordains, That the said sixteen Peers who shall have right to sit in the House of Peers in the Parliament of Great-Britain on the part of Scotland, by virtue of this Treaty, shall be named by the said Peers of Scotland whom they represent, their heirs or successors to their dignities and honours, out of their own number, and that by open election and plurality of voices of the Peers present, and of the proxies for such as shall be absent, the said proxies being Peers, and producing a mandat in writing duly signed before witnesses, and both the constituent and proxy being qualified according to law ; Declaring also that such Peers as are absent, being qualified as aforesaid, may send to all such meetings, lists of the Peers whom they judge fittest, validly signed by the said absent Peers, which shall be reckoned in the same manner as if the parties had been present, and given in the said list : And in case of the death or legal incapacity of any of the said sixteen Peers, that the foresaid Peers of Scotland shall nominat another of their own number in place of the said Peer or Peers in manner before and after mentioned. And that of the said fourty five representatives of Scotland in the House of Commons in the Parliament of Great-Britain, thirty shall be chosen by the Shires or Stewartries, and fifteen by the Royal Burrows, as follows :. . . One for every shire or stewartry excepting the shires of Bute and Caithness, which shall choise one by turns, Bute having the first election, the shires of Nairn and Cromarty, which shall also choise by turns, Nairn having the first election, and in like manner the shires of Clackmannan and Kinross shall choise by turns, Clackmannan having the first election. And in case of the death or legall incapacity of any of the said members from the respective shires or steuartries above-mentioned to sit in the House of Commons, it is enacted and ordained that the shire or steuartry who elected the said member shall elect another member in his place.

And that the said fifteen representatives for the royall burrows be chosen as follows, viz., That the town of Edinburgh shall have right to elect and send one member to the parliament of Great Britain, and that each of the other burghs shall elect a commissioner in the same manner as they are now in use to elect commissioners to the Parliament of Scotland ; which commissioners and burghs (Edinburgh excepted) being divided in fourteen classes or districts shall meet at such time and burghs within their respective districts as her Majestie, her heirs or successors, shall appoint, and elect one for each district, viz. [*Kirkwall, Wick, Dornoch, Dingwall and Tain ; Fortrose, Inverness, Nairn and Forres ; Elgin, Cullen, Banff, Inverurie and Kintore ; Aberdeen, Inverbervie, Montrose, Arbroath and Brechin ; Forfar, Perth, Dundee, Cupar and St. Andrews ; Crail, Kilrenny, Anstruther Easter, Anstruther Wester and Pittenweem ; Dysart, Kirkcaldy, Kinghorn and Burntisland ; Inverkeithing, Dunfermline, Queensferry, Culross and Stirling ; Glasgow, Renfrew, Rutherglen and Dumbarton ; Haddington, Dunbar, North Berwick, Lauder and Jedburgh ; Selkirk, Peebles, Linlithgow and Lanark ; Dumfries, Sanquhar, Annan, Lochmaben and Kirkcudbright ; Wigtown, New Galloway, Stranraer and Whithorn ; Ayr, Irvine, Rothesay, Campbeltown and Inveraray*]. And it is hereby declared and ordained that where the votes of the commissioners for the said burghs met to choise representatives from their severall districts to the Parliament of Great Britain shall be equal, in that case the president of the meeting shall have a casting or decisive vote and that by and attour his vote as a commissioner from the burgh from which he is sent. . . . And in case that any of the said fifteen commissioners from burghs shall decease or become legally incapable to sit in the House of Commons, then the town of Edinburgh or the district which choised the said member shall elect a member in his or their place. . . .

[*In the event that the existing members of the Parliament of England continue as the English members of the first British Parliament, then the Scottish representatives to the first British Parliament are to be chosen* ' in this present session of Parliament and out of the members thereof in the same manner as committees of Parliament are usually now chosen.']

A.P.S., xi, 425–6

[For the changes made in Scottish representation in the House of Commons by the Reform Acts of 1832 and later years, see Rait and Pryde, *Scotland,* 159–63.]

The English Act of Union

The Act of Union, as passed by the English Parliament, incorporated, in addition to the Articles of Union, the statutes for the security of the two national churches (declaring them to be ' fundamental and essential conditions of the said union ' and ' essential and fundamental parts of the said Articles and union ') and also the Scottish Act defining the method of election of the Scottish members of the British Parliament (*Statutes of the Realm*, viii, 566 *et seq.*).

1708. *Abolition of the Scottish Privy Council*

An Act for rendring the Union of the Two Kingdoms more Entire and Complete

Whereas by her Majesty's great wisdom and goodness the Union of the two Kingdoms hath been happily effected, and the whole Island is thereby subject to one Sovereignty, and represented by one Parliament. To the end, therefore, that the said Union may be rendered more complete and entire, Be it enacted by the Queen's most excellent Majesty, by and with the advice and consent of the Lords Spiritual and Temporal, and Commons, in this present Parliament assembled, and by the authority of the same, that from and after the First day of May, in the year of our Lord One thousand seven hundred and eight, the Queen's Majesty, her Heirs and Successors, shall have but one Privy Council in and for the Kingdom of Great Britain, to be sworn to her Majesty, her Heirs and Successors, as Sovereigns of Great Britain ; and such Privy Council shall have the same powers and authorities as the Privy Council of England lawfully had, used, and exercised at the time of the Union, and none other.

Statutes of the Realm, viii, 736

ADDITIONAL DOCUMENTS

THE RESTORATION SETTLEMENT

10 August 1660. *Letter of Charles II to the Presbytery of Edinburgh* (see *supra*, p. 153)

By the letter you sent to us with this bearer, Mr. James Sharp, and by the account he gave of the state of our church there, we have received full information of your sense of our sufferings, and of your constant affection and loyalty to our person and authority : and therefore we will detain him here no longer (of whose good services we are very sensible), nor will we delay to let you know by him our gracious acceptance of your address, and how well we are satisfied with your carriages, and with the generality of the ministers of Scotland, in this time of trial, whilst some, under specious pretences, swerved from that duty and allegiance they owed to us. And because such, who by the countenance of usurpers, have disturbed the peace of that our church, may also labour to create jealousies in the minds of well meaning people, we have thought fit by this to assure you that, by the grace of God, we resolve to discountenance profanity and all contemners and opposers of the ordinances of the Gospel. We do also resolve to protect and preserve the government of the Church of Scotland, as it is settled by law, without violation, and to countenance, in the due exercise of their functions, all such ministers who shall behave themselves dutifully and peaceably, as becomes men of their calling. We will also take care that the authority and acts of the General Assembly at St. Andrews and Dundee, 1651, be owned and stand in force until we shall call another General Assembly (which we purpose to do, as soon as our affairs will permit) and we do intend to send for Mr. Robert Douglas and some other ministers, that we may speak with them in what may

499

further concern the affairs of that church. And as we are very well satisfied with your resolution not to meddle without your sphere, so we do expect that church-judicatories in Scotland, and ministers there, will keep within the compass of their station, meddling only with matters ecclesiastic and promoting our authority and interest with our subjects against all opposers : and that they will take special notice of such who, by preaching, or private conventicles, or any other way, transgress the limits of their calling by endeavouring to corrupt the people or sow seeds of disaffection to us or our government. This you shall make known to the several presbyteries within that our kingdom. . . .

Wodrow, i, 13

GROWTH OF PARLIAMENTARIANISM
(see *supra*, p. 252)

6 July 1672.

The parliament satt yeasterday in the afternoone till neir
nyn aclock at night and after greatt reasoning and debate
be severallis of everie estaitt of Parliament (except be the
Bishopes or Clergie) ther past ane act of Parliament quiche
will prove verie heavie and grivous to the haill land *viz.* 12
monethes cess to be collected of the land rent payable
within 2 yearis space at four severall termes, the first terme
designed to be at this present Lambas ensewing. . . .
Mr William Monroe [Moir] advocatt for some rash
unadvysed wordes past be him in reasoning for ane delay
in the forsaid particular wes ordoured yeasternight to
prisone in the Tolbuithe and it is expected that he wilbe
liberat therfra once this day.

Aberdeen Council Letters, v, 154

No. 3

Act anent Wrongous Imprisonment

One of the grievances listed in the Claim of Right was that of ' imprisoning persons without expressing the reason, and delaying to put them to tryal ' (*supra*, p. 202). The Crown, in fact, was governed by no rules requiring prosecution within a reasonable time of arrest (as was the case in private prosecutions) ; and the drafters of the Claim of Right undoubtedly had in mind the long periods of imprisonment without trial recently suffered by religious and political opponents of the government. Not until 1701, however, did Parliament pass the ' Act for preventing wrongous Imprisonment and against undue delayes in Tryals ' which gave to Scotland something similar to the protection afforded in England by the procedure of Habeas Corpus. Yet it is to be noted that the act of 1701 applied only to imprisonment for crime, that colliers and salters were excluded from the benefit of its provisions (*supra*, p. 387), and that special arrangements were still retained for the Highlands and the Borders (cf. *supra*, p. 261).

1701.

Our Soveraign Lord Considering it is the interest of all his good Subjects that the liberty of their persons be duely secured ; And that it is declared by the claim of right that the imprisonment of persons without expressing the reasons thereof and delaying to put them to tryal is contrare to Law, Therefore His Majestie with advice and consent of the Estates of Parliament Statutes Enacts and Ordains that all Informers shall signe their Informations and no person shall hereafter be imprisoned for custody in order to tryal for any crime or offence without a warrand in writ expressing the particular cause for which he is imprisoned, and of which warrand the messenger or executor thereof before imprisonment, or the keeper of the prison receiveing the same, is hereby ordained to give a just double immediatly under his hand to the prisoner himselfe for the end after specified Declareing that all warrands for imprisonment . . . either proceeding upon informations not subscribed or not expressing the particular cause shall be void and null, and the Judge or Officiar of the Law and all others whatsomever subscribeing the same, and the Executor or keeper of the prison who shall receive and detain the person so wrongously ordered to be imprisoned, or refuseing a double as said is, shall be lyable in the punishment of wrongous imprisonment hereafter exprest. And to the effect that persons who are or shall be imprisoned for custody in order to tryal may not be wrongously delayed and detained . . . all Crimes not inferring capital punishment shall be bailable : And . . . it shall be lawfull to the prisoner or person ordered to be imprisoned to . . . offer to find sufficient Caution that he . . . shall appear and answer to any lybell that shall be offered against him for the crime or offence wherewith he is charged at any time within the space of six moneths. [*Here follow details of the bail to be found, fixed according to rank*] . . . And upon the parties finding sufficient baill [*the amount to be fixed within twenty-four hours of the application*] . . . the Judge or Magistrate shall be oblidged and is hereby appointed and ordained to accept of the forsaid baill and set the prisoner at liberty . . . And upon application of any prisoner for Custody in order to tryal, whither for capital or bailable Crimes, to any of the Lords of Justiciary or other Judge or Judicatory competent for judgeing the crime or offence for which he is imprisoned . . . the said Judge or Judicatory . . . are hereby Ordained within twenty four hours after the said application . . . to give out letters or precepts direct to messengers for intimating to his Majesties Advocat or Procurator fiscall . . . to fix a dyet for the tryal within sixty dayes after the intimation Certifieing his Majesties Advocat or Procurator fiscall . . . that if they failyie the prisoner shall be discharged and sct at liberty without delay . . . And the dyet of tryal being prefixt . . . his Majesties Advocat or Procurator fiscall shall insist in the lybell and the Judge put the same to a tryal and the same shall be determined by a final sentence within fourty dayes if before the Lords of Justiciary and thirty dayes if before any other Judge. And if his Majesties Advocat or Procurator fiscall do not insist in the tryal at the day appointed and prosecute the same to the conclusion . . . the dyet shall then be simpliciter deserted and the prisoner immediately liberat from his imprisonment for that crime or offence . . . *[But if new criminal letters are raised against him it shall be lawful]* to imprison him of new tho the said Letters be raised for the same Crime for which he was formerly incarcerat *[but if for a second time the Crown fails to pursue then he is]* to be for ever free from all question or process for the forsaid crime or offence . . . Declareing that the liberation provided by this present Act is . . . without prejudice of all personal diligence or imprisonments for payments of debts . . . And sicklike it is hereby provided and declared that this present Act is no wayes to be extended to Coalliers or Salters and the same is without prejudice or derogation from former Laws requiring baill to be given by Chiftains Landlords or others in the Highlands ; Reserveing likewayes Committments Imprisonments and the prosecution of thefts robberies and depredations in the borders and highlands according to the former laws and customes any thing in this Act notwithstanding . . . *[Pains and penalties laid down for failure to observe the provisions of the act]* . . . Also that no person be transported furth of this Kingdom except with his own Consent given before a Judge or by legal sentence. . . .

A.P.S., x, 272, c. 6

No. 4

The Public Register of Sasines

From the earliest times of which we have evidence, any transfer of lands, or the entry of an heir to the lands of his inheritance, was done openly and publicly. Witnesses, often of a stated number, were required ; and certain formal and symbolic acts were performed—such as handing over ' earth and stone ' of the lands to the new possessor. In the absence of written record the presence of witnesses and the performance of symbolic acts helped to secure ' memory ' of the ownership of the land.

With the growth of written records sasine (or the giving of real, corporal and actual possession) of land began to be certified in the records of local courts—notably those of barons and burghs—and soon, in all the more important courts of justice, contracts, deeds, sasines and so forth could be registered in the court books for permanent record, security and due observance.

At the same time, and in full practice in the latter half of the fifteenth century, copies of agreements, contracts, sasines and so forth could be entered in the protocol books of notaries for permanent record and security.

But the protocol books of notaries were many in number and might be lost or destroyed, particularly upon the death of a notary. Thus in those cases where there was no record in the books of a court or the registers of a burgh, ownership might be questioned or fraudulent transference might take place.

In 1504, in the case of crown lands, sheriffs, stewards and bailies were to enter the dates of sasines in their court books and to bring their books to exchequer ; and in 1540 this act was renewed in words which suggest that the sheriffs were to keep separate books for registering sasines—and the re-enactment tells us that such registration was intended to enable the king, and ' all others having interest, ' to know who were the actual possessors of the lands (*A.P.S.*, ii, 253, c. 35 ; 360, c. 14). In 1555, in a further attempt to secure uniformity and certainty, sasines of lands not held direct of the crown were to be registered in the court books of the sheriff of the shire in which the lands lay, and the entry in the court books was to give the names of the lands, the notary and the witnesses (*A.P.S.*, ii, 497, c. 21). In 1567 it was enacted that the protocol books of deceased notaries were to be handed in to the sheriff of the shire (or, within burghs, to the provost and bailies of the burgh) ; and, in 1587 (and again in the act of 1617), they were to be handed in to the Clerk Register.

Then in 1599, because, it was said, there was much forgery and no certainty in titles to land, the Secretary was to keep a register, as from 11 November 1599, in which all sasines which were not registered in the books of Council and Session (the Register of Deeds of the Court of Session), and except sasines of burgage lands within the royal burghs, were to be recorded within forty days under pain of nullity. Scotland was divided into seventeen districts in each of which the Secretary was to appoint a responsible officer to keep the register for his district (*A.P.S.*, iv, 184 ; 237, c. 36). This register, known as ' The Secretary's Register, ' was kept until 1609 when, strangely, it was abolished on the argument that it was unnecessary and served ' for little or no other use than to acquire gain and commodity to the clerks, keepers thereof ' (*A.P.S.*, iv, 449, c. 40).

Nevertheless a system of uniform registration of land-transfers administered under government control was too valuable to be allowed to lapse ; and in 1617, in order to avoid ' the great hurt sustained by His Majesty's lieges ' and to overcome ' many inconveniences ' a new Public Register of Sasines was established which, with certain minor changes, is still in operation today.

By the act of 1617 all sasines of lands, and all writs relating to land-ownership and to burdens and charges upon lands, were to be registered within sixty days. The country was again divided into seventeen districts, for each of which there was to be a ' particular ' register, and a ' general ' register was to be kept in Edinburgh. Sasines and writs could be entered either in the ' particular register ' appropriate to the district in which the lands lay or in the ' general register ' in Edinburgh. Burgage lands in the royal burghs were still excluded ; but in many burghs the protocol books of the notaries who acted as town clerks had long formed, in effect, burgh registers of sasines. In 1681, however, the provisions of the act of 1617 were extended to the burghs, and town clerks were required to keep official burgh registers of sasines (*A.P.S.*, viii, 248, c. 13).

In 1868 the Land Registers Act prescribed that registration

should be made in registers according to a simple county division, and that all registers of all counties were to be maintained in the General Register House, Edinburgh.

It has been well said that ' by the Land Registers of Scotland owners of property enjoy a certainty of title which many generations of learned lawyers have failed to evolve south of the Tweed. '[1]

1617. *Anent the Registratione of Reversiones Seasingis and utheris writis*

Oure Soverane Lord Considdering the gryit hurt sustened by his Majesties Liegis by the fraudulent dealing of pairties who haveing annaliet [2] thair Landis and ressavit gryit soumes of money thairfore, Yit be thair unjust concealing of sum privat Right formarlie made by thame rendereth subsequent alienatioun done for gryit soumes of money altogidder unproffitable whiche can not be avoyded unles the saidis privat rightis be maid publict and patent to his hienes liegis ; For remedie whereoff and of the manye inconvenientis whiche may ensew thairupoun, His Majestie with advyis and consent of the estaittis of Parliament statutes and ordanis That thair salbe ane publick Register in the whiche all reversiounes regressis [3] bandis [4] and writtis for making of reversiounes or regressis assignatiounes thairto, dischargis of the same, renunciatiounes of wodsettis [5] and grantis off redemptioun and siclyik all instrumentis of seasing salbe registrat within thriescore dayes efter the date of the same : It is alwayis declared that it sall not be necessar to registrat anye bandis and wreatis for making of reversiounes or regressis unles seasing pas in favoures off the pairties makeris of the saidis bandis or writtis, In the whiche cace it is ordaned that the samen salbe registrat within thriescore dayes efter the date of the seasing. The extract off the whiche Register sall mak faith in all caces except where the writtis so registrated ar offered to be improvin.[6] And gif it salhappin any of the saidis writtis

---

[1] J. Maitland Thomson, *The Public Records of Scotland*, 86
[2] alienated, or sold   [3] legal rights   [4] bonds
[5] wadsets, or mortgages   [6] disproved

whiche ar appoynted to be registrat as said is not to be
dewlie registrat within the said space of thriescore dayes,
Then and in that cace his majestie with advyse and consent
foirsaid Decernis the same to mak no faithe in judgment
by way off actioun or exceptioun in prejudice of a third
pairtie who hathe acquyred ane perfyit and lauchfull right
to the saidis landis and heretages, but prejudice alwayis to
thame to use the saidis writtis aganis the pairtye maker
thairof, his heiris and successoures. It is alwayes declared
that this present Act sall nowayis be extendit to instrumentis of seasing and reversiounes thairin contened gevin
be provest and bailyeis of frie burghis royall of landis lyand
within thair libertyes and friedomes haldin be the saidis
burghis in frie burgage of his majestie nor to na uther
heretable writtis thairoff nor yit to reversiounes incorporat
in the bodye of the infeftmentis maid to the persounes
aganis quhome the saidis reversiounes ar useit . . . And
to the effect the said register may presentlie and in all
tyme cuming be the moir faithfullie keipit, Thairfore our
said soverane Lord with advyis and consent foirsaid statutes
and ordanis the same registeris and registratiounes foirsaidis to be insert thairin to appertene and belang to the
present Clerk of Register and his deputtis to be appoynted
be him to that effect and decernis and ordanis the same
Registeris to be annexed and incorporated with the said
office. [*The Clerk Register to appoint deputes to*] receave fra
the pairties thair evidentis and to registrat the same within
the space of fourtie aucht houres nixt efter the recept
thairoff and to engrose the haill bodie of the write in the
register . . . and within the same space sall delyver to the
presentar of the samen the evidentis markit be him with
the day moneth and yeir of the registratioun and in what
leaff of the booke the same is registrat, and sall tak allanerlie
for his paynis tuentie sex schillingis aucht pennyes money
of this realme as for the price of ilk leafe of his register . . .
And the saidis Registeris efter the filling of the same to be
repoirted [1] to the said Clerk of Register to remayne with

---

[1] brought in

him and his deputtis and be patent to all oure soverane
Lordis liegis and extractis thairoff to be gevin be him and
his deputtis . . . to all salhave adoe with the same whiche
sall mak als gryit faithe as the principallis except incace of
improbatioun.[1] [*Registers to be kept in seventeen particular
places for seventeen districts*] And the saidis evidentis to be
registrat in the particular bookes appoynted for the landis
within the boundis [*of the particular district*] or, in the optioun
of the pairtie in the bookes of Register or sessioun keiped
be the said Clerk of Register him selff or his deputtis . . .
in Edinburgh. . . .

A.P.S., iv, 545, c. 16

[1] an action brought to prove the writ to be false or forged

INDEX OF SUBJECTS

(See also Table of Contents pages vii to x)

Printed in Great Britain by
Thomas Nelson and Sons Ltd, Edinburgh